LAND, CUSTOM AND PRACTICE
IN THE SOUTH PACIFIC

CAMBRIDGE ASIA-PACIFIC STUDIES

Cambridge Asia-Pacific Studies aims to provide a focus and forum for scholarly work on the Asia-Pacific region as a whole, and its component sub-regions, namely Northeast Asia, Southeast Asia and the Pacific Islands.

Editor: John Ravenhill

Editorial Board: James Cotton, Donald Denoon, Mark Elvin, David Goodman, Stephen Henningham, Hal Hill, David Lim, Ron May, Anthony Milner, Tessa Morris-Suzuki

LAND, CUSTOM AND PRACTICE IN THE SOUTH PACIFIC

EDITED BY

R. GERARD WARD and ELIZABETH KINGDON

Research School of Pacific and Asian Studies
Australian National University

CAMBRIDGE UNIVERSITY PRESS
Cambridge, New York, Melbourne, Madrid, Cape Town, Singapore, São Paulo

Cambridge University Press
The Edinburgh Building, Cambridge CB2 2RU, UK

Published in the United States of America by Cambridge University Press, New York

www.cambridge.org
Information on this title: www.cambridge.org/9780521472890

© Cambridge University Press 1995

This publication is in copyright. Subject to statutory exception
and to the provisions of relevant collective licensing agreements,
no reproduction of any part may take place without
the written permission of Cambridge University Press.

First published 1995
Hardback version transferred to digital printing 2006
Digitally printed first paperback version 2006

A catalogue record for this publication is available from the British Library

National Library of Australia Cataloguing-in-Publication data

Land, custom and practice in the South Pacific
Bibliography.
Includes index.
1. Land tenure – Oceania. I. Ward, R. Gerard (Ralph
Gerard), 1933– . II. Kingdon, Elizabeth, 1949– . (Series:
Cambridge Asia-Pacific studies).
333.32099

ISBN-13 978-0-521-47289-0 hardback
ISBN-10 0-521-47289-X hardback

ISBN-13 978-0-521-03071-7 paperback
ISBN-10 0-521-03071-4 paperback

Contents

List of Figures	vi
List of Tables	vii
Contributors	ix
Acknowledgements	xi

	Introduction	1
1	Land Use and Tenure: Some Comparisons	6
	R. Gerard Ward and Elizabeth Kingdon	
2	Land Tenure in the Pacific Islands	36
	R. Gerard Ward and Elizabeth Kingdon	
3	Breathing Spaces: Customary Land Tenure in Vanuatu	65
	Margaret Rodman	
4	From Corporate to Individual Land Tenure in Western Samoa	109
	J. Tim O'Meara	
5	Right and Privilege in Tongan Land Tenure	157
	Kerry James	
6	Land, Law and Custom: Diverging Realities in Fiji	198
	R. Gerard Ward	
7	Beyond the Breathing Space	250
	Antony Hooper and R. Gerard Ward	

Bibliography	265
Index	280

Figures

	The Pacific Islands	xiv
2.1	Land divisions and soils on Atiu, Cook Islands	41
2.2	Cattle-farm leases, Sote-Naitutu beef scheme, Fiji	60
3.1	Vanuatu	70
3.2	Longana land holdings, 1978	94
3.3	Waileni, 1978	98
3.4	Waileni, 1993	99
3.5	The hamlet of Lovatuweliweli, north Waileni, 1982	100
3.6	The hamlet of Lovatuweliweli, north Waileni, 1993	101
4.1	Western Samoa	116
4.2	Type of tenure within Vaega village, 1993	125
4.3	Type of tenure of agricultural plots, Vaega village, 1983	126
4.4	Type of tenure of agricultural plots, Vaega village, 1993	127
4.5	Sub-types of 'Old tenure', Vaega village, 1993	136
4.6	Sub-types of 'New tenure', Vaega village, 1993	137
4.7	Sub-types of 'Changed to new tenure', Vaega village, 1993	139
5.1	Tonga	158
5.2	'Falahola' Island	170
5.3	Transmission of land and people on 'Falahola': case I	175
5.4	Transmission of land and people on 'Falahola': case II	176
5.5	Expansion of the urban area of Nuku'alofa	194
6.1	Fiji	201
6.2	Viti Levu	202
6.3	Former settlement sites of Sote village *mataqali*	205
6.4	Conflicting land claims, Dreketi River area	214
6.5	Garden and land ownership, Saliadrau village, 1958	228
6.6	Garden and land ownership, Saliadrau village, 1983	229
6.7	Registered and hypothetical land ownership, Sote village	231
6.8	Garden and land ownership, Sote village, 1959	234
6.9	Garden and land ownership, Sote village, 1983	235

Tables

3.1	Registered land in the New Hebrides, 1976	76
3.2	Frequency of siblings as land holders	96
3.3	Mode of land acquisition	96
5.1	Land holding in Tonga, 1989	184
6.1	Distribution of land by class of tenure	199
6.2	Relationship between garden and land ownership	227

*To our Pacific Island
hosts and friends*

Contributors

KERRY JAMES has worked at the Universities of Canterbury, New England and the South Pacific, as well as the Australian National University and the East-West Center, Honolulu. She is the author of many articles on Tonga and editor of *Women in Rural Australia* (1989), *Religious Cooperation in the Pacific Islands* (1989) and *Pacific Village Economies*, a special issue of *Pacific Viewpoint* (1993).

ANTONY HOOPER is Professor Emeritus, University of Auckland and Fellow, East-West Center, Honolulu. His field research in the Pacific Islands has focused in particular on French Polynesia and Tokelau and in addition to many articles he is an author or editor of *Why Tikopia has Four Clans* (1981), *Transformations.of Polynesian Culture* (1985), *Class and Culture in the South Pacific* (1985), *Matagi Tokelau: History and Traditions of Tokelau* (1991) and *Tokelau: Migration and Health in a Small Polynesian Society* (1992).

ELIZABETH KINGDON is Research Assistant in the Research School of Pacific and Asian Studies, Australian National University. She was formerly Editorial Assistant with the Asian Studies Association of Australia's *ASAA Review* and Assistant Editor of the *Australian Journal of Chinese Affairs* and has worked on Pacific Island research for some years.

J. TIM O'MEARA is Senior Lecturer in Anthropology, University of Melbourne. He is the author of *Samoan Planters: Tradition and Economic Development in Polynesia* (1990) and articles on Western Samoa and Pacific Island anthropology.

MARGARET RODMAN is Professor of Anthropology, York University, Toronto. She is the author of *Masters of Tradition: Consequences of Customary Land Tenure in Longana, Vanuatu* (1987) and *Deep Water: Development and Change in Pacific Village Fisheries* (1989) as well as many articles on Vanuatu and other areas.

x   CONTRIBUTORS

R. GERARD WARD is Professor of Human Geography, Research School of Pacific and Asian Studies, Australian National University. Books of which he is an author or editor include *Land Use and Population in Fiji* (1965), *American Activities in the Central Pacific, 1790–1870* (8 vols. 1966–69), *Man in the Pacific Islands* (1972), *The Settlement of Polynesia: a Computer Simulation* (1973), *South Pacific Agriculture: Choices and Constraints* (1980), and *New Directions in the South Pacific* (1988). His field experience includes Fiji, Western Samoa, Vanuatu and Papua New Guinea.

Acknowledgements

We would like to express our thanks to the governments and people of Fiji, Tonga, Vanuatu and Western Samoa for accepting us as guests in their countries on many occasions. We have also benefited from opportunities to undertake research in other Pacific Island countries and in the course of preparing this volume such visits have been important for the comparative perspectives they have provided. We are most grateful to all the island people who have made this possible.

With our field experience in the Pacific Islands spanning several decades, we have received support from many 'home institutions' and research grant bodies. We acknowledge these in general, but must also mention some specifically.

Antony Hooper is grateful to Sitiveni Halapua, Director of the Pacific Islands Development Program at the East-West Center, Honolulu, for allowing him to take up the opportunity to participate in this project.

Kerry James would like to acknowledge the support of the Australian Research Grants Committee for funding her field work in Tonga from 1982 to 1984. She thanks the people of Tonga, and in particular those of 'Falahola', for their friendship and assistance.

Tim O'Meara's research in Malie and Neiafu in 1984 was supported by the University of the South Pacific and the Food and Agriculture Organisation of the United Nations. Research in Satupaitea from 1981 to 1983 was supported by a grant from the U.S. National Science Foundation. Tupuola Tavita and Tuisugaletaua Sofara provided oversight as successive Directors of the Department of Agriculture, Forests and Fisheries. Tapusatele Keli Tuatagaloa and Galumalemana Netina Schmidt greatly facilitated the research as successive Registrars of the Land and Titles Court, as did members of their staff in Mulinu'u and Tuasivi. The Chiefs and Orators of Malie, Neiafu, and Vaega supported the research in their villages. Nu'u Vili and Faleilemilo Fa'alaga were primarily responsible for guiding the field mapping of plots in Vaega.

ACKNOWLEDGEMENTS

Margaret Rodman acknowledges the funding of her research in and on Vanuatu by the Social Sciences and Humanities Research Council of Canada in 1978–9, 1982 and 1985; the Wenner–Gren Foundation for Anthropological Research in 1993; and York University in 1993. Over the years the people of the Longana District have helped her understanding of matters of land and custom and she expresses her gratitude to them.

Gerard Ward's work in Fiji was funded initially by the New Zealand University Carnegie Social Science Research Committee, and later by the Colonial Social Science Research Council, London, the Central Research Fund of the University of London, and the Australian National University. He is indebted to many people in Fiji for help since first working there in the 1950s but in connection with this study he is particularly grateful to the people of Nabudrau, Saliadrau, and Sote villages who gave hospitality and assistance in 1958, 1959 and 1983.

In 1993 the authors of the four country studies were all able to make brief visits to those countries to renew contacts and re-check or extend field data. These visits were all made possible by fieldwork grants from the Australian National University and we are grateful to the University for this assistance. The whole group also benefited from the Visiting Fellowships which the University awarded to Antony Hooper, Kerry James, Tim O'Meara and Margaret Rodman to enable them to assemble in Canberra on two occasions to work together on their chapters.

We are all grateful to Keith Mitchell, Cartography Unit, Research School of Pacific and Asian Studies, Australian National University, for his skilful preparation of the maps and diagrams.

In the course of preparing this volume we all benefited from discussions with many colleagues in the Pacific Islands, in our home universities, and in other places. We all asked colleagues to read and comment on all or parts of our chapters and their advice helped us a great deal. The list of such people is very long and we hope that they will accept our thanks and appreciation in a general acknowledgement which is no less warm for its anonymity.

Our prime thanks, however must go to our many Pacific Island hosts and guides who over many years have helped us in our research and become good friends and colleagues. It is to them this book is dedicated.

Antony Hooper
Kerry James
Tim O'Meara
Margaret Rodman
Elizabeth Kingdon
Gerard Ward

Lilli Pilli, NSW
Australia

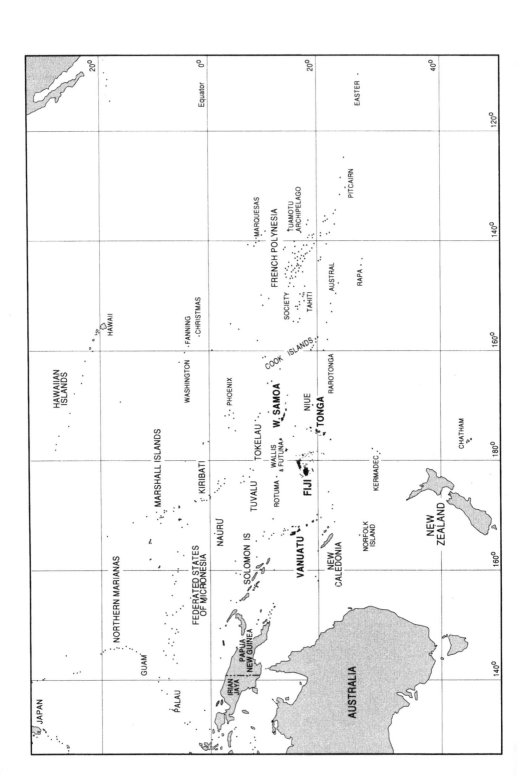

Introduction

Life in the Pacific Islands has been transformed over the last century and a half, economically, geographically, politically and socially. Nevertheless, for the majority of islanders land is still central to their life and the land tenure arrangements which people use help shape their settlement patterns and agricultural systems, and are important components of socio-economic and political structures. The majority of land in all South Pacific Island countries remains under what are commonly described as 'traditional', 'customary' or 'native' land tenure systems. This book argues that in many parts of the region the ways in which the 'customary' land is now held by owners or users have changed to a much greater degree than is commonly acknowledged. The changes are intimately linked to concurrent changes in the socio-economic and political organisation of Pacific Island communities, but they are not unique to the region. They are specific cases which have, or have had, parallels in other parts of the world. The details are not identical, but the general processes of transformation have led to a widening range of situations in which land formerly held in common, or used through various communal arrangements, is now controlled and used exclusively by individuals or small family groups. In a broad sense much customary land is being privatised. Historical parallels can be found in Japan and China over the last millennium or more, in the mediaeval and later enclosure movements in Europe, and in Africa and insular Southeast Asia in the present century.

A central component of the socio-economic transformations, of which the tenure changes are part, is the change from subsistence to market economies. Cooperative or communal modes of life, with both labour mobilisation and the exchange of goods and services based on reciprocal obligations, have been, or are being replaced by wage labour and money.

2 LAND, CUSTOM AND PRACTICE IN THE SOUTH PACIFIC

The nuclear family is often emerging as the main socio-economic unit at household level. As group interests weaken and individual interests strengthen in the economic and social realms, attitudes towards land have changed. Land has become a commodity rather than simply a stage on which activities take place. In several Pacific Island countries, individuals and small groups use customary practices to acquire usufruct and then longer term and more exclusive rights to land for non-customary purposes. Informal and formal privatisation has occurred and inequality in land holding is increasing. In some cases landlessness has emerged or is in prospect. Rural settlement patterns have changed in concert with the changing balance between community and individual interest, and the increase in the relative importance of the commercial component of agriculture.

Changes in land tenure practices have not proceeded at the same pace or in the same way in all countries. Neither are they inevitable. Nevertheless, to retain older styles of life and socio-economic organisation in the face of the incorporation of the region into global commercial and political systems would require extraordinarily strong commitments to customary practices, and a degree of community solidarity which the people of few other regions have achieved in the face of comparable forces. One country, Vanuatu, has taken constitutional steps towards such a goal. More commonly, leaders declare that the country's system of 'customary land tenure' is a basic component of the national way of life. But what is set out as that system is usually a standard description of practices followed in some earlier, and often unspecified, period in some part of the country. The divergences between this officially accepted 'custom' and the practice of agricultural villagers, or even urban dwellers, tends to be ignored by national leaders and development planners.

In countries where customary land tenure systems have been codified, as in Fiji, key aspects of former land tenure arrangements, such as redistribution mechanisms, including the possibility of alienating land, were lost. Regional variations in practice were overridden by written and uniform laws covering the whole country. Fiji's new colonial and Tonga's constitutional land tenure systems came to attain the status of 'tradition' in the eyes of some. In Fiji the colonial orthodox model 'has been adopted as a protective device into the Fijian ethos. It has come to be regarded as immemorial tradition. For the strength of tradition depends less on its historical accuracy than on its social significance' (France, 1969:174).

Despite the absorption of new conventions into tradition, many features of pre-codification land tenure remain in use. For example, mechanisms for land transfer which are now extra-legal, but which

INTRODUCTION 3

accord with older customary principles, have continued to be used in some areas with the result that significant areas of land are now used by people who have no legal rights to that land. Some of the constraints of codified systems are being ignored, as for example in Fiji or Tonga, where forms of renting of land which are technically illegal or extra-legal are common. The divergences between de facto, de jure and customary land tenure arrangements, and the changes within the realm of customary land, are beginning to be recognised publicly in some countries. In others they are not. Politicians and government agencies find it extremely difficult to deal with these problems through reform of the tenure systems, not least because the rhetoric of cultural preservation, and the fostering of national or ethnic identity for new states, often depend on the maintenance of the image of an idealised social system founded on 'traditional' land tenure conventions. The old systems often formed the bases of elite power and status and it is to the advantage of many who hold leadership positions in the new democracies to call on tradition as well as the ballot box to bolster their position and their influence over followers. Yet at the same time governments and aid agencies foster development programs the social results of which undercut the customary foundations of leadership.

Each author of the four studies of this book had undertaken research in one or more Pacific Island countries which revealed marked divergences between current practices and either proclaimed 'custom' or codified land law, or both. Each had come to similar conclusions about the effects on land tenure of broad tendencies such as the individualisation of economic and social life, commercialisation of agriculture and other activities formerly covered within the subsistence arena, and the widening of the role of the state in all spheres of island life. Each had become aware of the socio-political role given to land tenure by island leaders in the rhetoric of national identity, but also of the discrepancies between this rhetoric and the practices they observed in villages and towns where communal land was being privatised, the rhetorical ideal of access to land for all was not being met, and illegal or extra-legal practices were commonplace. Thus the present collaboration arose.

The four studies are anchored in the authors' fieldwork but also examine the historical changes which have occurred over the last century or more. The detail of the story is different for each country but there are striking parallels as well as contrasts. The parallels stem from the common exogenous economic, social, geographic and political forces which have affected the region, as well as a certain uniformity in the pre-colonial economic and technical systems which people used.

4 LAND, CUSTOM AND PRACTICE IN THE SOUTH PACIFIC

The contrasts arise from differences in the forms of the old indigenous social and political organisation, different colonial policies and histories, and different degrees of involvement (over both time and space) in the worlds of commerce and post-colonial independence.

The order of the country chapters emphasises some of these contrasts. Vanuatu, the most recently independent of the four countries, proclaimed in its constitution that all land belongs to the customary owners. This includes land which had become freehold under the colonial regimes but which was now returned to the customary owners. But the customary ways of the 1990s are not those of the pre-colonial era. The ending of internal warfare and the opportunities offered by commercial agriculture encouraged some leaders to use the latter as a new route to prestige, influence and money. To this end they established large personal land holdings under the guise of custom. Thus there is now an open question as to what is the customary tenure which should be recognised by government.

In Western Samoa customary tenure has not been codified but the Land and Titles Court does have exclusive power to rule on disputes. Its rulings and most accounts of the Samoan 'system' of land tenure tend to present a picture of relatively unchanging adherence to old and uniform ways of land management under the guidance of the *matai* (chief) of the *'aiga* (extended family). But in Old Samoa there was some variation in practice from village to village, and from family to family. In recent decades there has been an increasing transfer of ownership of land from the *'aiga* under authority of its chief to the heads of nuclear families. Until recently the change towards greater individualism in the control of land has received very little public recognition.

In the other two countries studied land tenure has been codified. In Tonga, customary tenure was replaced by an entirely new land law based on quite different principles. In Fiji, a simplified, standard version of customary tenure was established. In both countries many people ignored the codified land tenure laws for decades and continued to follow former practices. But when new needs emerged and commercialism penetrated the countryside more thoroughly, some began to exploit and conform to the codified system if it suited their personal circumstances. Others continued to ignore it, or found extra-legal ways to circumvent it that best served their personal ends.

For as much as a century, pragmatism and the pursuit of self-interest in this region, as elsewhere in the world, has meant that practices in matters of land use and tenure have often been at odds with both 'custom' and the law. With people keen for 'development', and this being fostered throughout the region by governments, international aid agencies and donor countries, it is doubtful whether the discordance between

INTRODUCTION

practice and the customary or codified law can continue to be masked indefinitely. Pressure for both 'customary' systems and codified systems to match current needs will increase. At present this pressure for change is not widely accepted at policy-making levels of government. If it is accepted and acted upon, dramatic modifications of the social, economic and geographic character of Pacific Island countries could result.

CHAPTER 1

Land Use and Tenure: Some Comparisons

R. Gerard Ward and Elizabeth Kingdon

Land tenure in the Pacific Islands has always been subject to change. Even in pre-colonial times, which are sometimes portrayed as a time of stability and little change, land tenure practices were modified pragmatically to meet changing conditions, and control of land frequently passed from one group to another as a result of warfare, changing demographic pressures, or migration. Indeed, all tenure systems change over time, conditioned by broader socio-political shifts, demographic trends, technological and economic innovations, and alterations in the extent to which land is a scarce good. The current complexity and state of flux in the tenure arrangements for what is usually defined in the Pacific Islands either as 'native land' or 'customary land' is not unique. Comparable situations can be found in many other places and at many other times. One of the themes of this book is the occurrence in the Pacific Islands of particular cases of what is arguably a world-wide trend for communalistic forms of land tenure to be replaced by forms in which individual ownership plays a much greater role.

What makes the South Pacific Islands unusual is, first, the relatively recent occurrences of major changes in land tenure. Second, many of the changes have been unusually rapid. Third, national leaders in the region often refer to traditional land tenure as one of the important markers of national or cultural distinctiveness. At the same time a reluctance to acknowledge the extent to which the customary practices of today differ from those of a supposedly immemorial tradition is coupled with a willingness to ignore the divergence between current practices and the law where the conventions of land tenure have been codified. Keesing has pointed out that 'across the Pacific, from Hawai'i to New Zealand, in New Caledonia, Aboriginal Australia, Vanuatu, the Solomon Islands and Papua New Guinea, Pacific peoples are creating pasts, myths of ancestral ways of life that serve as powerful symbols' (1989:19). The process is a common one world-wide, and in the political sphere some of the most important of these 'myths' relate to land.

The economic, geographic, political and social transformations taking place in the Pacific Islands gained force in the colonial period and there has been a tendency to regard them all, including the changes in land tenure, as a consequence of colonialism. As is shown later in this chapter, the comparable changes which occurred in other parts of the world were not necessarily associated with colonialism. They often stemmed from the pressures of commercialism, population growth or decline, or the introduction of new technologies in agriculture. These and other changes frequently provided new opportunities for individuals to further their own ambitions in ways not available within the older socio-economic systems in which social position was often ascribed and economic structures favoured communalism. In many parts of the world these forces were internally generated. They sometimes followed the integration of formerly isolated and self-sustaining communities into wider political units and more complex societies and states. Furthermore, the comparable changes in other parts of the world often took place centuries ago, with the result that the evidence is now fragmentary and spread over a long time span. It usually lacks the detail of variations which must have occurred from place to place and from time to time in the acceptance of, or resistance to change. Thus, when studying the changes in such regions, there is a tendency to see the very broad trends as having uniformity and inevitability.

Colonialism and commercialism came to the Pacific Islands relatively recently and the creation of independent nation states is very recent. Some states still lack internal coherence and a widely accepted sense of national identity. While these new nation states provide the opportunity for more detailed examination of comparable changes, the mass of detail available can give rise to an opposite tendency wherein the variety of local conditions may obscure the presence of broader trends. The outlines given later in this chapter of some comparative cases from other parts of the world serve to counter the assumption of too great an element of specificity for the Pacific Islands.

What is Required from Land Tenure

Land is one of the essential resources for most societies, and one which is often in short supply. Thus ownership of land, and control of access to its use, can be a primary basis for power and authority, and a source of status for those who wield that authority. People's use of land is always mediated through some set of conventions which the majority accept,

8   LAND, CUSTOM AND PRACTICE IN THE SOUTH PACIFIC

either willingly, out of necessity, or under some degree of duress. For effective functioning of agricultural systems and other forms of land use, the conventions of land tenure must be reasonably consistent with the requirements of the particular economic, agricultural, and socio-political systems in operation. However, as all these contextural systems are constantly changing in themselves and in their interrelations, the level of consistency inevitably varies from place to place and time to time, and from the needs of one land user to those of another. Furthermore, a particular set of land tenure conventions or laws may match the needs of an elite group, or a particular ideology, extremely well but be economically inefficient or socially inequitable for others in the community. Those whose needs are not well met may follow practices which do not accord with the law, or general custom, but are condoned by their community because they meet local needs. As societies become increasingly complex the likelihood of such divergent practice increases until land tenure laws are reformed or the new practices are absorbed into the conventions of custom to become part of a new orthodoxy. In the rapidly changing conditions of the Pacific Islands it is not surprising to find considerable variation and lack of fit between practice, custom and law in land tenure. These will be examined in later chapters.

The variety of land tenure

A great variety of land tenure arrangements can be found around the world. At one extreme might be versions of freehold or fee-simple tenure wherein an individual holds permanent, inheritable, but alienable rights giving exclusive and unconstrained ownership and use of specified pieces of land. At the other would be state ownership of all land, with all use being at the discretion of the state. These are extremes and the reality in most places lies somewhere between. In the absence of a state as a supra-local organisation, the ultimate level of land ownership often rested with the communal group which functioned as the unit within which most people's work and social life revolved on a daily basis. In such cases individuals might have no rights to outright ownership of land, but a great variety of rights to the use of the communal or common land and its products which gave them basic security. Elsewhere a great variety of more or less individual rights over land may be found.

In practice no ownership or usufruct of land is absolute. In strict terms, 'human beings do not own land: what they own is rights to land, that is, rights vis-à-vis other human beings' (Crocombe, 1972:220). Even where freehold tenure is the norm, it is never totally unconstrained. Individuals and groups other than the owner will have interests in a parcel of land and these interests might include rights to hunt or gather, of easement or

SOME COMPARISONS

as a mortgagor, or the right of a neighbour to prevent an owner using land in a manner detrimental to that neighbour's interest. Local authorities, whether in the form of village or town meetings, chiefs, or local government bodies may impose constraints on the use and tenure of land in the interests of a wider community. Thus the 'tenure' of any parcel of land is likely to involve a combination of overlapping interests of a number of individuals or entities. This has always been as true in the Pacific Islands as anywhere else (Crocombe, 1972:220–8).

In common usage, however, we can accept that the term 'ownership' encompasses the situation in which the 'owner' or 'owning' group has the prime right of property over the land entailing a relatively high degree of exclusivity in its use, the right to sell or otherwise alienate, and the discretion to pass it on to heirs. Where such a degree of ownership is not found or lay with a broad community group, as was the case in many Pacific Islands two centuries ago, the rights of individuals or families over land tended to be those of usufruct, with use sanctioned for particular purposes and for limited periods.

Tenure and the rural economy

The Pacific Islands have had rural economies based primarily on root crop and tree crop agriculture for the last few millennia.[1] In a few cases fishing, hunting and gathering have remained the main sources of sustenance, but in most communities these activities have been secondary. As elsewhere in comparable economies, the nature and technical requirements of gathering or farming have shaped features of land tenure. For hunters and gatherers it may not be necessary for each small group, family or individual to hold exclusive rights of ownership over specific plots of land, provided they have the right to travel and hunt over a territory and to gather produce when they require. In such circumstances it is common for control over extensive areas to rest with the community in general, with its members having common access in order to fulfil their hunting and gathering needs. Boundaries with the territories of neighbouring groups may be ill-defined and only delimited by agreement or force when conflict or other need arises. In some instances, however, particular trees and their produce, or specific sites for the extraction of workable stone, ochre or other high value resources may be controlled by smaller groups.

The tenure arrangements found in many communities using shifting or swidden cultivation may be seen as a partial modification of those used by hunters and gatherers. Such arrangements and the specific lines of authority through which they are controlled vary considerably although certain characteristics are widespread. A group may claim a territory, the

10   LAND, CUSTOM AND PRACTICE IN THE SOUTH PACIFIC

boundaries of which may not be precisely defined, but within which those group members who clear and plant an area may claim usufruct for as long as their crop remains in production and perhaps while any explicit intent to re-use the plot remains. But as the land lapses into fallow and reverts towards forest, its tenure also reverts towards that of the pool of common land. Eventually it may be re-allocated, or taken by others for cultivation. In such a system an individual or family has clear rights to use part of the land of their group, but the particular part or parts may not be precisely or permanently defined. Clearly, concepts of outright ownership in the sense of exclusive and perpetual control of a defined plot of ground, such as are embodied in the ideas of freehold or fee simple, are scarcely applicable in such systems. Bohannan, referring to the Tiv of Nigeria, describes such a system with considerable insight, noting that the Tiv 'see geography in the same image as they see social organization' (1963:105).

> The 'map' in terms of which the Tiv see their land is a genealogical map, and its association with specific pieces of ground is of only brief duration – a man or a woman has precise rights to a farm during the time it is in cultivation, but once the farm returns to fallow, the rights lapse. However a man always has rights in the 'genealogical map' of his agnatic lineage, wherever that lineage may happen to be in space. These rights, which are part of his birthright, can never lapse. A mathematician . . . suggested that whereas the Western map, based on surveys, resembled geometry, the Tiv notions resembled topology, which has been called 'geometry on a rubber sheet'. Whereas the Western map is rigid and precise, the Tiv map is constantly changing both in reference to itself and in its correlation with the earth. . . . Every Tiv has a right to an adequate farm on the earth which holds his *tar* [the people, the compounds and the farms]. This is a right to a *farm*, not a specific piece of land. A farm lasts only for two or three years, then reverts to fallow and the specific right lapses. However, the right to *some* farm in the *tar* never lapses. . . . [So] Tiv might be said to have 'farm-tenure', but they do not have 'land tenure'. (Bohannan, 1963:105–6)

Such arrangements can be satisfactory indefinitely under swidden cultivation, provided the area available to the population involved is large enough for soil fertility to be maintained through long fallow periods. But once fixed field cultivation or long-term tree cropping are introduced, changes are necessary.

Where an agricultural system is able to maintain fertility and productivity over a long period through the use of techniques such as crop rotation, composting, irrigation with nutrient rich water, use of fertilisers, or the alternation of cropping with intensive grazing, farmers need longer-term rights and the inbuilt re-allocation mechanisms of swidden cultivation systems may not be appropriate. The same is true when farmers depend primarily on long-term tree crops. Such rights can be maintained under many forms of tenure, ranging from outright ownership to

SOME COMPARISONS

long-term tenancies, leases or share farming arrangements. The longer and larger investment made in particular plots and the absence of the lengthy fallows and related reversion to a condition of communal tenure of swidden systems means that different measures for transferring land between potential owners are usually needed.

In many parts of the world the shift from swidden cultivation to fixed field farming has been accompanied by a change from forms of communalistic 'farm tenure' to long-term or permanent land tenure of specific plots held by individual land holders. The move from predominantly subsistence to predominantly commercial farming has often had a similar effect. Both transitions have frequently been dependent on the adoption of new crops and technologies, but the move to commercial farming may also carry with it a much wider set of new conditions for farmers to meet, and to which their land tenure may have to adjust. These include requirements imposed by the market for regularity of supply and quality maintenance; ready means of access and transport to markets; and access to capital for investment and to labour at times when the market or agricultural cycle determines. Such requirements alter the relative value of different plots of land on the basis of new location factors in addition to the value stemming from its quality for agricultural use. New components of land valuation reinforce the need for some form of market in land or other means of transferring land rights, be they formal and legal, informal or extra-legal.

The transition to commercial farming may also lead to a change from mobilising labour through communal reciprocity to the use of wage labour and thus alter socio-economic linkages within communities. The commitment of land to individuals for long periods and the use of money as the basis for labour mobilisation may also remove some of the key roles of traditional leaders and undercut older power structures. Thus land tenure changes are integral parts of much wider socio-economic and political transformations. The brief outlines given later in this chapter of such transformations in other parts of the world show that parallels to the transitions the Pacific Islands are now making can be found in many other places or other times.

Land tenure and ideology

Changes in land tenure stemming from the influences noted above can take a variety of courses. Ideology can play an important role, as under communist regimes in eastern Europe and Asia when land, and much other property, was nationalised and allocated to communes or collectives for management and use. Within feudal systems of earlier centuries the idea of outright ownership of land, and in some cases the virtual ownership of people, by the nobility was an integral part of

12   LAND, CUSTOM AND PRACTICE IN THE SOUTH PACIFIC

contemporary concepts of the proper form of society. Equally, societies which believed in a greater degree of egalitarianism, or communality, might well eschew ideas of freehold and outright ownership in favour of the commons and the limitation of individual rights to those of temporary or lifetime usufruct without inheritable interests.

In the context of the Pacific Islands there is little need to pursue the matter of the impact of different ideologies on land tenure at any length. Prior to the arrival of Europeans, the concept that the normal order of things should include individual, alienable and exclusive ownership of specific pieces of land was generally lacking. So were ideologies of socialist collectivism. Thus the extreme ideologies of state ownership and of individual rights and ownership were both absent. Subsequently, ideas for nationalisation of land, or land reform to divide large estates and distribute the land to peasant smallholders have not taken root, with the possible exceptions of the application of an approximation to the last of these strategies in nineteenth-century Tonga (see Chapter 5) and the return of freehold land in Vanuatu to customary tenure following independence (see Chapter 3). In Melanesia the traditional ideology favoured a communal egalitarianism within which all should have access to land for their own sustenance. Status was not ascribed, and leaders emerged on the basis of their own efforts and capabilities. Such an ideology had two somewhat contrary effects in relation to land tenure. First it tended to impose a degree of uniformity in the area of garden land relative to the size of families and limit the extent to which land holdings were directly inherited. It thus limited land accumulation beyond one generation. Obviously this characteristic was related to the subsistence nature of the economy and to the mechanisms, outlined above, which periodically redistributed land in areas practising swidden cultivation. Secondly, it allowed individuals who were sufficiently politically skilled or proficient in farming to establish larger than normal holdings and thus build up their status as 'big men' through the accumulation of valuables, such as pigs, or reciprocal obligations from their fellow villagers, to justify their actions on the basis of custom. Later, this argument could be turned to new purposes, still under the guise of 'custom'.

Another feature of Pacific Island systems was their essential pragmatism. As in pre-colonial Africa, 'custom was loosely defined and infinitely flexible. Custom helped to maintain a sense of identity but it also allowed for an adaptation so spontaneous and natural that it was often unperceived' (Ranger, 1983:247). Communities could choose to do what suited them, and to allow what variation they wished, usually within the sanction of community-endorsed 'custom'.

In Polynesia, while some of the above ideals were current, in the more strongly stratified societies of Tonga, Tahiti or Hawaii, land tenure was

SOME COMPARISONS

much more intricately linked with the relationship between chiefs and their people. Hierarchies of rights over people and land tended to match the political hierarchies of lesser chiefs owing allegiance to higher chiefs up to the highest levels of society where semi-divine status gave spiritual backing to power over both people and land. It is not surprising that some early European visitors from strongly hierarchical societies found, or thought they had found, societies with structures not unlike their own. The extension of this idea to the assumption that Pacific Island chiefs had similar powers over land to those of their supposed counterparts in Europe may be understandable, but was rarely accurate. Whereas in England, for example, the power of a noble over his estates might be constrained by the overriding power of the Crown, with its overtones of divine right, in the Pacific Islands, with the exception of some parts of Polynesia, the chief's power over land was ultimately constrained by the overriding custom of access to land for all members of the community.

Tradition, Custom and Practice

The terms 'tradition' or 'traditional' and 'custom' or 'customary' have a variety of meanings. When used in the Pacific Islands, they can have nuances which may not be common elsewhere. In this volume we use the term 'traditional' with some of the connotations which Weber gave in his discussion of justifications for the legitimation of authority. People call on tradition as 'the authority of the "eternal yesterday," i.e. of the mores sanctified through the unimaginably ancient recognition and habitual orientation to conform' (Weber, 1947a:78–9). Weber recognised that the past to which tradition appealed for legitimation of an action or convention need not be historically accurate when he spoke of the authority or 'domination that rests upon . . . piety for what actually, allegedly or presumably has always existed' (1947b:296). This recognition is at the core of the idea of 'invented tradition' as 'a set of practices, normally governed by overtly or tacitly accepted rules and of a ritual or symbolic nature, which seek to inculcate certain values and norms of behaviour by repetition which automatically implies continuity with the past . . . [and preferably] a suitable historic past' (Hobsbawm, 1983:1). The continuity implied may be 'largely factitious'. The new, or so-called 'invented' traditions are 'responses to novel situations which take the form of reference to old situations, or which establish their own past by quasi-obligatory repetition'. In the post-colonial world of the Pacific Islands such traditions are useful and powerful because they suggest a less uncertain and socially more secure life which is 'unchanging and invariant' in contrast to 'the constant change and innovation of the modern world' (Hobsbawm, 1983:2).

14   LAND, CUSTOM AND PRACTICE IN THE SOUTH PACIFIC

Invented traditions are common in the Pacific, and they have often been used as a key element in the establishment of government or other authority (e.g. see France, 1969; Keesing and Tonkinson, 1982; Keesing, 1989; Lawson, 1993). A number of the invented traditions deal with land, and some subsequent chapters provide examples of how what is now said to be 'traditional' in respect to land tenure may not be 'unimaginably ancient' and of how the power of the assertion of tradition depends on implied, but not necessarily actual, continuity with the past. Invented traditions about land are also found in other parts of the world and in Africa cases have been recorded of 'traditional' rules being 'invented on the spot to legitimate a course of action desired by the very realistic manipulators of the local scene' (Colson, 1974:76). It is commonly such people of influence who have the necessary power to express an idea as an invented tradition, and have it accepted broadly as 'real' tradition. At one level, as Keesing points out, 'perhaps it does not matter whether the pasts being recreated and invoked are mythical or "real," in the sense of representing closely what actual people did in actual times and places' (1989:19). Factually correct or not, they are political symbols of great potency, and much of their power stems from conveying the idea of what Hobsbawm calls 'invariance' (1983:2). It is also important to stress that 'invented traditions' have been created by Westerners in the Pacific Islands as often as by islanders. Perhaps the most widespread of such 'traditions' would be the myth of the Pacific Islands as 'paradise' which is acted out in tourist sites all over the region and beyond. But they also include what is now the orthodox version of 'traditional' Fijian land tenure which was in large measure a colonial invention (France, 1969).

Within the Pacific Islands 'tradition' is 'often taken to imply the precolonial or at least precontact past ... [and] the prevailing notion among both Pacific islanders and outside commentators is that the genuinely (or authentically) traditional or customary is that which is unpolluted by Western influences' (Lawson, 1993:11). 'Tradition' is understood in opposition to 'Western', 'modern', and 'colonial' and is often appealed to explicitly in the creation of ideas of independence and national identity. Amongst the strongest elements of tradition when used in this way in the region are the distinctive forms of tenure of customary land vis-à-vis that held by non-indigenous people, and the emotional ties people claim to have with their customary land. In this context, the assumption of invariance in 'traditional' land tenure can have a variety of benefits, political and personal, for those who seek to legitimate by claiming tradition.

'Custom' is not identical with tradition as it allows much more variation and 'cannot afford to be invariant, because even in "traditional" societies life is not so' (Hobsbawm, 1983:2). Custom embraces what people do within a band of acceptable divergence from the community's

SOME COMPARISONS

norms. In one sense it includes the allowable, or locally accepted variations of what people might claim to be traditional. In the Pacific many phrases are used to encapsulate 'custom' and to give justification to patterns of behaviour on the basis that it is 'what we do'. At a regional level the phrases 'the Pacific Way', 'the Melanesian Way', and 'the Polynesian Way' are commonly used in an ideological sense (Lawson, 1993:2). Phrases such as *fa'aSamoa*, *vakavanua* or *vaka Viti*, 'the way of Samoa', 'the way of the land and people' of Fiji, and 'the way of Fijians' respectively, are the national equivalents and in their use carry some of the legitimating intent of 'tradition', especially when applied to the validation of differences from others. In Vanuatu, the term '*kastom*' in the lingua franca, Bislama, is more explicitly parallel to 'tradition', as it is used consciously as a term to describe some unspecified ideal of pre-colonial ways in opposition to things Western and colonial (see Chapter 3).

The claim that some action is 'customary' is a claim for general legitimacy, allowing for variation to meet local or temporal conditions. But many actions or activities, including many to do with land, are ones for which no further legitimacy is required or claimed beyond the fact that they occur. In this volume we use the term 'practice' for such cases, with no necessary implication of either customary, traditional or legal sanction. It is one of our central themes that much of what is currently done in relation to native (or 'customary') land tenure in the Pacific Islands is neither traditional, nor customary, nor legal, but is practice which has evolved to meet conditions neither foreseen in the pre-commercial era nor allowed for in codified laws. This leaves open the question of when, and under what circumstances, does a community accept that divergent practice can be given the status of custom, or even be regarded as traditional. In the case of land tenure, the answer will be affected by whether or not customary tenure has been codified by the state.

Transformations of Land Tenure: Some Examples

Conservatism and lack of change are often stated to be features of the 'traditional' or 'customary' societies with which Europeans came in contact through the centuries of European expansion and colonialism. Many Europeans, confident in their belief in the superiority of their own technological capacities and social and economic systems, saw other peoples and cultures as inferior, and ascribed that inferiority to conservatism and an inability to adjust to innovation and change. This was seen to be in contrast to their own success in innovation and 'progress'. Paradoxically, they also 'believed themselves to have a respect for the customary . . . [and] liked the idea of age-old prescriptive rights', feeling that traditions, albeit invented, 'gave reassurance because they represented what was

16   LAND, CUSTOM AND PRACTICE IN THE SOUTH PACIFIC

unchanging in a period of flux' (Ranger, 1983:247). It is not surprising, therefore, that when describing the land tenure arrangements they observed in other regions, they often supposed that these too were relatively unchanging. It was a natural mistake given their limited knowledge of the history of these regions, their own world view and current ideas about the evolution of human societies, and the snap-shot like evidence, devoid of temporal depth, which they were able to obtain. Once it is possible to take a longer view, it is the fact of change in land tenure arrangements as new conditions emerge which becomes most striking. This becomes clear from even a brief comparative examination of modifications in land tenure which took place in diverse parts of the world as people adjusted to new social, political, economic and technical conditions. The time scales involved and level of detail available vary greatly from place to place but informative parallels can be drawn between these different cases and changes in the Pacific Islands over the last hundred or more years. One may agree with the missionary Turner when he exclaimed, 'What a surprising unity of thought and feeling is discoverable among the various races of mankind from a comparison of such customs as these!' (Turner, 1884:134) while still being cautious about the partial nature of much of the evidence.

There are obvious risks in seeking similarities in the modifications in land tenure which have occurred in parts of the world as diverse as East Asia, Western Europe, Africa and the Pacific Islands. The time scales over which what appear to be similar trends have occurred and for which data are available were very different. The political and cultural contexts were also different. Yet comparable trends have occurred, starting from somewhat similar bases, and moving at various speeds and along a variety of paths towards somewhat similar destinations. The starting points were often a form of community-based tenure in which members had rights to use common and community-owned land, while the later phases saw land owned and used by individuals. The underlying forces which brought these trends into being, and in the process changed the tenure requirements of land users and gradually or speedily changed land tenure, may be summarised as follows.

First, societies changed from situations in which nobles, landlords or chiefs were bound in unequal, but nevertheless mutually dependent and often ascribed relationships with followers, commoners, tenants or villeins to one in which landlords, tenants and independent freeholder farmers were associated through monetary relationships. Second, subsistence orientation of rural economies changed to commercial orientation, in which production of crops, animals, or animal products for sale directed the decisions of farmers and land owners. Third, changing demographic conditions influenced the course of events. Declining

SOME COMPARISONS 17

populations in both Europe and in the Pacific Islands have, at very different times, resulted in land going out of cultivation as the supply of labour shrank, and demand or prices fell. At other times rising populations have put added pressure on limited land and resulted in changed tenure arrangements. Fourth, new technologies reduced or altered the labour requirements of farming, allowing farmers to operate without the help of their fellow villagers. Thus many were progressively freed from the need to participate in community-centred and reciprocity-based systems of mobilising labour for specific time-constrained or equipment-dependent tasks. Fifth, acceptance of new cropping and animal husbandry systems altered the balance between types of farming and changed the land and tenure requirements of farmers. Sixth, the increased commercialisation of rural life gave the opportunity for some to accumulate and multiply monetary wealth in ways which were not practical within subsistence and communalistic communities. This possibility led to growing inequalities and, in association with the greater use of wage labour on farms, to the emergence of increased numbers of landless people in rural areas. Finally, people found new opportunities in non-agricultural occupations and ceased to be bound to manor, noble, or kin group. It became common for lords, land owners, or chiefs whose power to mobilise the labour of those resident on the land they controlled was declining to become lessors of land as an alternative to direct involvement in farming, or to turn to the towns and the realms of commerce or politics to pursue their goals of influence or wealth. On the land a peasantry of individual tenant farmers or freeholders often emerged with different social relations with their fellows, living in settlements of different form, and answering to the imperatives of a commercial rather than a subsistence economy. Although the detailed sequencing and speed of events and the relative importance of the above forces varied from place to place, examples from different continents and countries demonstrate some of the commonalities in trends.

Japan

In Japan major changes occurred in land tenure systems over more than a millennium as the goals of communities, and the interests of different groups and individuals within them, were modified in the face of changing economic or political conditions. Prior to the mid-seventh century, land had been held by clan chiefs as 'private preserve' but then, in the Taika Reform, the central government claimed ownership and decreed that land would be allocated to farming families for their use with the area granted being related to family size and age structure (Dore, 1984:8). Land was taxed but could not be alienated, so the rights of the

18 LAND, CUSTOM AND PRACTICE IN THE SOUTH PACIFIC

occupiers did not extend to those of a full freehold or fee simple system. Regular redistribution was to take place through some bureaucratic process to reflect demographic change, although this flexible arrangement was not sustained. Dore states that it is not clear how thoroughly these reforms were applied and certainly other arrangements continued or emerged. One change occurred when some land was given by the central power to nobles and tax-free status was allowed. These holdings, combined with tax-free land reclaimed for cultivation from marsh or forest by those with the resources to do so, led to considerable areas passing from the status of public land into private control. Eventually this private land became one of the bases for the establishment of the power of a new group of estate owners and the emergence of *shoen* estates, a type of feudal manor (Dore, 1984:9).

Within the *shoen* estates, a close web of reciprocal obligations linked landlord and tenant. In some cases landlord, tenants, serfs or wage employees formed a group akin to an extended household or village community. Tenants or land holders paid rent or taxes in kind to the landlord and their entitlements to land were legally protected. The landlord in turn was expected to provide employment in off-farm occupations, assist in obtaining inputs such as seed or fertiliser from town merchants, help with provision of education services, help tenants through periods of poor harvest by reducing rents, and generally provide leadership for the village community (Waswo, 1977:31–4). Some land holders also had obligations to fight for 'the land owning warrior class' when called upon (Furushima, 1991:479).

As conditions changed, this system gradually broke down to produce, in the sixteenth and seventeenth centuries, a pattern of predominantly smallholdings out of which a new form of landlordism emerged in the Tokugawa and Meiji periods. The process of change was given more formal impetus when, in an attempt 'to achieve national hegemony', the Taiko cadastral survey of agricultural land was begun 'which permanently altered the nature of rural land tenure in the final decades of the sixteenth century' (Furushima, 1991:479). The aim was to bring stability to rural areas and:

> establish a system of agriculture based on the small independent farmer (*shono*). Discrete social units consisting of members of the immediate family were to become the principal source of the annual land revenues, and the act of cultivation was now deemed as the most important criterion for determining who possessed the land and who paid the annual rent. (Furushima, 1991:482)

In the seventeenth century the sale of peasants' land was again prohibited but, as farmers were often faced with debt, this prohibition was

SOME COMPARISONS   19

avoided by mortgaging of land which led to an emerging class of merchants or wealthier peasants (Dore, 1984:12). The law did not keep up with the changing needs of the people. Peasants began to grow new crops for the market and found they had to meet new conditions for quality maintenance and delivery schedules. Individual interests began to clash with cooperative community interests, and 'as cooperation languished and social groups lost their cohesiveness, individual interests came out of hiding, and the market defined them more clearly by pitting one against another' (Smith, 1959:157). Concomitantly a new attitude to land emerged. Smith notes that 'so long as land was thought of primarily as a means of subsistence rather than a source of profit, the urge to acquire it was relatively weak; or at least there was no strong motive to acquire more than was needed for subsistence since land generally produced no considerable surplus and any surplus it might produce was difficult to sell'. However, with the prospect of accumulating wealth through sale of crops, and the ability to cultivate more land with wage labour than would be possible with family labour alone, the social checks on the growth of individual holdings were progressively removed (Smith, 1959:157).

The eighteenth century saw further improvements in agricultural techniques, the introduction of new crops with new labour or input requirements, and a further concentration of land ownership (Smith, 1959:158–9). In particular the relative importance of the subsistence component of the rural economy declined as the commercial component increased and 'the money economy, through commercial transactions and the lending of capital, penetrated directly into the agricultural communities' (Sheldon, 1958:169). Increasingly villagers were employed for wages on the farms of fellow villagers while others left home to work for wages in towns or other villages for varying periods (Hanley and Yamamura, 1977:254–6).

The Meiji Restoration of 1868 marked the start of even more rapid economic change. An early step was to bring in land reforms to meet the changing needs of the increasingly commercial rural economy and a deliberate policy of modernisation. Land was declared to be the property of the peasants and a few years later land surveys were begun and registers established. The ban on alienation was removed and 'peasants formerly bound to the land by feudal ties became independent proprietors free to use and dispose of the land as they wished' (Dore, 1984:14). But some also lost certain land use rights as areas of communal village land from which firewood or fodder had been gathered were declared to be state land or became the private property of those with influence (Dore, 1984:16).

Over time the interests of landlord and fellow villagers increasingly diverged and by the early decades of the present century the functional links were weak. The peasants had gained access to different sources of

20 LAND, CUSTOM AND PRACTICE IN THE SOUTH PACIFIC

information and farm inputs; the rice which had to be provided as tax was now delivered to the warehouses of government agencies rather than to the landlord; many landlords had taken employment in the bureaucracy or in service industries; and roles such as settling intra-village disputes or assisting in times of hardship had passed from landlord to government or other agencies. The older community obligations which previously implied security could now become hindrances to a successful commercial enterprise. After enumerating such changes, Waswo concludes that 'even if not absentees in a physical sense, many landlords became absentee owners in a functional sense' and 'only when both parties made a special effort to maintain personal contact, or in remote villages relatively untouched by change, did traditional ties remain fully in force' (1977:93). The process described by Waswo through which the functional link between village organisation and the allocation and management of land was broken took place at different rates and to differing degrees in different areas. When and where it did occur, the norm became individual land ownership oriented towards commercial farming rather than a feudal or community-based system more suited to risk-avoiding subsistence production.

China

Many of the changes in land tenure and related land management systems which occurred in China over the thousand years prior to 1949 show similarities with those in Japan. Early in the first millennium AD, land was held in forms of communal tenure by 'relatively autonomous peasant communities' (Elvin, 1970:100). In contrast, in the mid-1930s, Buck (1964:192) reported that 'farm land in China is owned in fee simple, 93 per cent being thus privately owned, chiefly in small holdings', and this had been true at least from the mid-nineteenth century (ibid.:193). The transition between these two states had been complex and had occurred at a different pace in different parts of the country.

Prior to 1000 AD, an increasing and significant percentage of land came under a form of manorial control on private estates. It was a system, like that in Japan, in which there was reciprocity between landlord and tenants although the latter were bound to the land in practice if not de jure. These communities, whose members were often bound together across the lines of status, wealth and authority by lineage organisations (Spence, 1990:13), had a largely subsistence economy in which most nutritional and material needs were provided from their own land while labour requirements were met from within the community. For tasks which required completion within a short period or were beyond the capacity of a single household, labour was mobilised under the author-

SOME COMPARISONS 21

ity of the landlord and used equipment and draught animals which were the property of the manor. The estate owners were the active leaders of the manor's agricultural activities (Elvin, 1970:103).

By 1000 AD commercial activity outside the towns was extensive and expanding. As in much of western Europe at an equivalent period, and parts of West Africa today, a large proportion was handled by pedlars within a system of periodic markets held in small centres which formed the lowest rung of the urban hierarchy (Spence, 1990:12; Shiba, 1970:140–64). In the following centuries growing numbers of landlords found commercial ventures, the bureaucracy, or money lending to be more profitable than land owning. For those who were free to move, life in towns was more attractive than direct involvement in agriculture (Elvin, 1970:105–7). With many absentee landlords and, in southern China at least, a system under which the subsoil might belong to an original proprietor 'while the permanent tenant had the rights to the surface, both of which could be sold separately', many tenants had long-term occupation rights which were inheritable. The result was the emergence of forms of individual ownership, at least over the rights to crop, which bore out a Chinese proverb: 'long tenancy becomes property' (Elvin, 1970:107). Thus, as in Japan, commercialisation, a breakdown in the reciprocal relationships between leaders or landlords and their farmer tenants, and the move of many landlords away from their old manorial estates or other types of holdings, led to a system of de facto tenure in which, after 'cultivation for many years in succession' land would 'simply be occupied by the . . . [so-called tenants] as their hereditary property' (Fu I-ling, 1961, quoted in Elvin, 1970:108). The process of fragmentation of the former larger holdings and individualisation of small holdings continued, albeit at varying rates and to varying degrees in different parts of the country, through to the nineteenth and twentieth centuries. By the 1930s it had reached the situation described by Buck wherein, for example, over 80 per cent of the cultivated land of the winter wheat-kaoliang area of the north China plain was owned by those who farmed it (1964:196). Communalism had been almost entirely replaced by individual holdings, under the influence of the same forces which had very similar effects in Japan.

European cases

On the other side of the world, quite independently, similar processes were taking place in the face of comparable changes in social, political, economic and technical conditions. In the eleventh century, England and Scotland had predominantly rural economies with large subsistence components. Although local details of rural settlement, land use and

22 LAND, CUSTOM AND PRACTICE IN THE SOUTH PACIFIC

customary land practices varied, long-term changes occurred in land use and land tenure arrangements over the following centuries, generally in a direction away from communal orientation and towards more individualistic forms.

Much of rural England was settled in a pattern of manors held by lords as estates under grants from or recognised by the Crown. Few of the residents were freeholders; most were serfs or villeins, born into that status and bound to the land and the manor. For the majority of people the village, hamlet or local district in which they were born was where they would spend most of their lives, in a community often made up of a small number of related families. Unable to migrate, required to perform service for the lord of the manor and to work on his estate for set periods of the year, the villein was locked into an unequal relationship, but one in which there were reciprocal obligations for both lord and villein. 'The lord and his villeins shared the manor and its produce between them' (Trevelyan, 1959:131). Although required to work on the lord's farm, a villein did hold 'lands of his own which he tilled on those days of the year when his lord had no claim upon him or his oxen. And he had his share in the use and the profit of the village meadow, the village pasture, and the village woodland and waste, where the swine and geese were turned loose' and 'the custom of the manor' gave him protection, even from a rapacious lord (ibid.:131).

In eastern and midland England the normal manorial farming settlement was one in which the houses of freemen and villeins clustered near the church and the manor house, and this nucleated village was surrounded by two or three broad 'open fields'. Each open field was divided into strips approximately one furlong (220 yards/201 metres) in length and up to one acre (0.4 ha.) in area. Although the lord might have a single block of land as a home farm, each other land holder, and sometimes the lord as well, would hold several strips scattered in each of the open fields (Trevelyan, 1959:134–5). In an idealised system each open field was cultivated as a whole in the one crop, commonly wheat, barley or oats. Much of the work, especially that requiring the pooling of equipment such as ploughs and bullock teams, was done communally. After the harvest the people would graze their cattle on the stubble across all the strips as if on common land. Thus there were overlapping rights to the open field land. After a second crop in the next season, the field would be fallowed for a year before being ploughed and planted once more. This form of simple rotation, with the dung of the livestock providing some manure, was the means of ensuring the relatively reliable, if not high, yields essential for subsistence security.

The system had advantages. Each man had rights to land for family subsistence. Nobody had a monopoly over all the best land, and all had

SOME COMPARISONS 23

access to the various parts and products of the village land. Each family could supplement the produce of its open field strips by grazing livestock on the commons or the meadows and by collecting firewood or other needs from the common 'waste' land. Ownership of strips could be transferred to accommodate the changing needs of families. Such a system could serve community interests well, giving a place and security in the society for the members, even though this was a lowly place for most. For the lord of the manor there were clear advantages in the presence of a labour force bound to the manor.

There were also disadvantages. Mantoux noted for a later period that:

> each farmer was tied down to the common rules. The system of crop rotation adopted for the whole parish was only suitable for some of the lands, and the other lands suffered thereby. The cattle and sheep fed on weeds, and their promiscuous mixing together was the cause of murrains. As for improvements, any man who attempted them would have ruined himself. He could not drain his fields without the consent and concurrence of his many neighbours. Each plot was contained within fixed limits and was too narrow to admit of cross-harrowing, as recommended by Jethro Tull. Before a farmer could choose his own time for sowing, the custom of allowing the open field to be used as a common grazing ground for several months in every year had first to be abolished. No such thing could be contemplated as growing an unwonted crop, or sowing clover where there had been rye or barley. . . . In the olden days, when farming had been a traditional calling, an accepted inheritance that supported a man year in and out, such a state of things could be put up with. But to the modern farmer, who looks upon agriculture as a business undertaking and reckons up exactly his expense and profits, the compulsory waste on the one hand, and, on the other, the sheer impossibility of doing anything whatever to increase the produce, are simply intolerable. (1928:168–9)

No such system remains unchanged, and in the mid-fourteenth century bubonic plague, the Black Death, 'decimated an already vulnerable and unstable population' which had previously suffered from harvest failures, epidemics and a period of rising wages and falling food prices (Baker, 1973:187). Declining returns from grain encouraged some land holders to lease more of their holdings, to put arable land into pasture enclosed by fences, walls or hedges, or to leave some of their open field strips in grass. Some open field land was taken out of the communal system and service was replaced by leasing as the basis of the relationship between the lord and villagers. When wool prices rose and grain prices declined in the mid-fifteenth century, even more land owners turned arable land into pasture to gain a better personal income. Even where full-scale enclosure of the open fields did not take place, some individuals began to farm their strips separately from the rest of the open field. They left strips in grass rather than plant the regular grain crop; erected light fences to control their own grazing animals; or planted new crops.

24   LAND, CUSTOM AND PRACTICE IN THE SOUTH PACIFIC

Some people, with the power or influence to ignore the interests of others, sought to increase their holdings by fencing in – 'enclosing' – sections of the common land and thereby appropriating it for their personal use.

In the sixteenth century the piecemeal enclosure of open fields continued. In upland parts of the country, where tenants were few and did not have the power to resist the loss of their access to the common land, considerable areas of common were enclosed by wealthier farmers wishing to increase their sheep flocks to take advantage of higher prices for animal products (Baker, 1973:210–11). By about 1600, over 50 per cent of the land of western England, Kent, Suffolk and Essex and the lower land of the northeast had been enclosed. 'Lowland England included a variety of irregular open fields, and also areas where enclosures and open fields existed side by side' (Emery, 1973:255–6).

In the seventeenth century the agricultural revolution gained strength with the introduction of new crops, new implements, new systems of cultivation and crop and pasture rotation, the breeding of better animals, and an increased orientation towards the market. Turnips became a major field crop, grown in rotation with grain and a ley of cultivated, and hence higher quality pasture. Clover, with its beneficial nitrogen-fixing properties, was introduced. Carrots, peas, and lentils were added to the rotation by some farmers and such people found it advantageous to take their land out of the open field system. New techniques for soil improvement were discovered, including the use of waste products from industry, the application of lime to heavy soils or clay marls to light soils. Improving the quality of one's livestock, and keeping them on one's own land to retain the advantages of their manure, was easier if they were segregated from the neighbours' stock within enclosed fields. New types of plough, which did not require the use of such large, and formerly shared, draught teams were introduced in the later eighteenth century and other improved implements were invented and increasingly adopted in the following century (Darby, 1973:313–21).

Such innovations influenced the shape of fields as the advantage of the furlong strip, always ploughed in the same pattern with the heavy oxen-drawn mouldboard plough, no longer applied. Just as there was advantage in an enclosed field for livestock control, so a rectangular field which could be cross-cultivated was now preferred. To create such fields out of the open field required re-allocation of holdings and major changes in tenure. A new wave of enclosures followed and reached a peak in the first fifteen years of the nineteenth century when 1,427 enclosure acts went through Parliament (Turner, 1980:68).

In such 'parliamentary enclosures' commissioners had the task of re-allocating the land. The advantages of enclosing land into individual

SOME COMPARISONS

farms were often greatest for the lords of manors, the farmers with the larger holdings within the open fields, and those who saw personal advantage in adopting the new agriculture. Others could suffer disadvantage. They might be allocated a poor section of the open fields by the commissioners. Some could not legally prove the rights to the use of the common which they had formerly exercised and thus lost both access to firewood and grazing on part of the newly enclosed common lands, and the opportunity to use the meadow land (Trevelyan, 1959:457). Although each yeoman who could demonstrate his rights would be allocated a piece of the common to be held as freehold, the size of the portion was 'in proportion to the number of animals he used to graze on the lord's waste' and was therefore often small. Following the decisions on the enclosure allocations, the yeomen had to fence or otherwise enclose his new farm and fields with hedges or walls and the cost could severely stretch a poor man's resources (Mantoux, 1928:174–5). Soon after a manor had been enclosed some fields, or even whole farms, would be sold or leased as those in debt sought a solution to their financial problems. The number of landless labourers increased. Land ownership became concentrated in fewer hands, and the average size of farms increased.

The pattern of settlement also changed. Farmers who now had a consolidated holding at some distance from the village, and were no longer bound to work on the lord's land or to participate in communal work on the open fields, built new houses on their own land. The farmer saved time as he no longer had to walk between scattered plots in different parts of the village lands. As farmers began to specialise in particular crops for sale, rather than growing a range of products for home consumption, they did not need to have scattered plots of land to give personal access to different ecological sites for security of food or other supplies. They could sell part of their produce from their consolidated holding and buy the hay, the firewood or fruit they needed from those who specialised in these products. The nucleated village declined in relative importance as a dispersed pattern of rural settlement emerged. The English village, the rural landscape and the systems of land allocation, management and tenure had all been transformed and communal obligations had given way to individualism and wages as the basic principles and cement of rural life.

Scotland and some other parts of upland Britain had long had a different system for communal allocation and use of the land:

> . . . characterised by the infield-outfield system under which the arable land of a township was divided into two unequal parts. That nearest the cultivators' houses was called the infield. It received all the manure of the settlement and was cropped continuously year after year. Beyond, lay a large outfield comprising some five to ten enclosures from the waste. Each enclosure was

26   LAND, CUSTOM AND PRACTICE IN THE SOUTH PACIFIC

> cropped for a few seasons and then allowed to revert to its former condition until its turn to be ploughed came round again. The arable land was disposed in ridges; the holdings of tenants were intermixed, and in some places there was an annual re-allotment of strips. The main crops were oats or barley or a mixture of both. (Darby, 1964:213)

In the eighteenth century this system also began to change under the influence and attractions of the new agriculture, but in Scotland there was no common land and it was simpler for land owners and tenants to reorganise the system than in England. Nevertheless it was usually the land owner's wishes which were paramount. The tenants did not have the common rights of the English yeomen to give them protection, but there was a tendency for tenants to obtain longer leaseholds in the process of consolidation of holdings and the permanent enclosure of the outfields. As in England, it was new agricultural techniques and the new emphasis on the market which allowed the poorer land of the outfield to be incorporated into more permanent arable farming. It was no longer necessary to follow a system akin to shifting cultivation in the outfield as 'a robber economy when dung was insufficient and the ground too rough for the infield' where 'the same plot of land [was used] continuously by the regular application of dung, as in a garden' (Fairhurst, 1967:205). The breeding of better cattle and the growing markets of the urbanising lowlands made new forms of individual arable farming on the better soils and cattle grazing on the former outfields and wastes more attractive. The infield-outfield system with its nucleated hamlets, communal use of equipment, relatively regular re-allocation of the infield lands and shifting use of the outfield gave way to a settlement pattern of dispersed, individually operated and consolidated farms. In parts of Wales, Ireland and the southwest of England where systems similar to the infield-outfield of Scotland were found, the same process of individualisation of tenure and farming took place. By the middle of the nineteenth century 'subsistence farming was giving way to commercial agriculture. New crops, new ideas, and hedged fields were producing a new countryside' (Darby, 1964:214).

Processes similar to those in England and Scotland also occurred in northwest Europe where the twelfth and thirteenth centuries saw a 'fairly general decay of the manorial system of farming' and the release of 'many peasants from labour services on their lord's demesne, which they had performed with increasing reluctance; the services were commuted to rents' (Huggett, 1975:11). With commutation, and often with considerable struggle and at very different rates in different places, the powers of lords declined and the opportunities for tenant farmers and small land holders increased. As peasant freeholders grew in number, common rights gave way to individual rights by 'a slow and gradual

SOME COMPARISONS 27

process, involving as it did not only a change in agricultural technology, but a much more profound transposition from an ancient way of life based on the sharing of scarce resources to individual enterprise of the modern profit-seeking kind' (Huggett, 1975:26).

While the process took centuries in some places, the transition was rapid in others. Within 40 years of 1788 when the serfs were decreed to be free citizens, 'over half of Denmark's farmers had become freehold-ers', the strips in the open fields had been consolidated 'into compact farms' and people had been 'encouraged to move out of the old nucle-ated villages into their own homes on enclosed farms by government loans at low rates of interest' (Huggett, 1975:98).

Africa

Whereas in Japan, China and Europe the process of change from some form of community-related tenure to something akin to individual free-hold tenure usually took a number of centuries, in some parts of the world such processes have occurred much more swiftly. While the detail of what occurred in east Asia and Europe centuries ago has mostly been lost, this is not the case in other regions where comparable forces have become important much more recently. Nevertheless it is easy to misin-terpret the changes even where detailed records are available. This is particularly true where a colonial power brought its own ideas of social and economic structures and interpreted and recorded indigenous structures in terms of foreign concepts. The incorporation of the economies of colonies into an imperial or world economy often occurred quickly and with state encouragement. At the same time, some colonial powers sought to work through existing power structures under indirect rule, and to this end bolstered what they saw as traditional struc-tures. But while seeking to preserve, they often changed these struc-tures. Such cases are common in parts of Africa where clusters of dispersed tribal groups have been exposed in telescopic fashion to Western political and economic influence.

The impact of European contact on traditional African land tenure has been greatly influenced by the variety of meanings that Africans attached to land and its ownership, and the differences between these and Western viewpoints (Bohannan, 1963). Lord Hailey described how within community-based groups which led a pastoral or semi-nomadic existence it was families or kin groups rather than individuals that held land and tended the herds. Adopting an evolutionary interpretation, he argued that as the family or community incorporated cultivation into their activities, patterns of land holding emerged which were based on similar community and family concepts. Notions of ownership were

28 LAND, CUSTOM AND PRACTICE IN THE SOUTH PACIFIC

functional and confined only to a sense of the practical use of the land (Hailey, 1957:802). Similarly Meek explained that there was 'traditionally no conception of "ownership" of land in the Western sense. Land belongs to God. Its use belongs to the people who occupy the land. And so we may find members of unrelated groups farming together, without any feeling of appropriation of the land' (Meek, 1957:113).

Meek also referred to the sacred nature of land and the significance of first clearance of the land for cultivation and the establishment and exercise of the range of rights that this act secures for the individual or the group (Meek, 1949:23–4). In some circumstances different individuals or groups may have an interest and rights in the same piece of land. These can include cultivating rights, grazing rights, and rights to trees, each of which might be held by different people (Mifsud, 1967:42). This complex of rights and the accompanying duties and obligations implicit in group membership, combined with the variability of land, environment and society, help to create more diversity in African land tenure systems than European administrators recognised.

Despite this diversity, which is still a feature of African land tenure, several more or less common features are identifiable in many traditional tribal societies. These generally derive from the right of all members of the community (clan, tribe or village) to use part of the community's land. While vested in the group, the community's land is entrusted to the group's chief or headman for allocation to its members through the head of each family unit (Caroe, 1954:153). Each family has a continuing right to the use of the land allocated to it, provided its members conform to the tribal laws or customs associated with its use. Should the land be abandoned, or laws or customs breached, the plot reverts to the broader group for re-allocation by the tribal authority (Ault and Rutman, 1979:171–2). The reversion of land to the wider group when it is no longer used provides a means for adjustment to the changing size and needs of the families. Thus the head of the tribe is the custodian of land for the community, although he acquires no advantage in relation to the land other than the right to claim a share of the produce as tribute, and the prestige and respect that custodianship and chieftainship entail (Hellen, 1969:324). Usufruct rights over more land may accrue to the family through inheritance but since the family does not own the land itself, they cannot buy or sell it.

In such systems, access to land is assured to all, and the individual and the community are bound together and to their land in a network of rights and obligations. These communal forms of tenure, in which links to land reflected the community structure, usually evolved in an environment where land was plentiful and where the agricultural systems based on shifting cultivation were geared to the subsistence needs of the

SOME COMPARISONS

community. In tribal Africa it ensured that no-one was without access to land and at the same time customary constraints on use practices helped maintain the quality of the land (Ghai and Radwan, 1983a:18).

Over time, African communities have modified their tenure systems to accommodate changes in economic, political and social needs. Changes resulting from migrations, contacts with other peoples, the spread of religious ideas, technological developments and ecological variations have been absorbed by different societies and in the process they have reshaped the details of existing tenure systems (Biebuyck, 1963:56). Where subsistence-based systems have been modified by the introduction of commercial production, customary land tenure has come under pressure from new land practices, which usually generate tendencies towards individualisation of tenure.

Some modifications in tenure systems resulted from conditions imposed by European colonialism in the nineteenth century. Regions were influenced differently, depending upon the dominant policy or ideology of the particular European administration and upon the particular circumstances of the region. Although it was not always the policy of the particular government to interfere with customary law, and in some cases the policy of indirect rule deliberately sought to maintain customary practices, colonial administration still affected the communities concerned. Settlement patterns changed under administrative fiat or as new agricultural techniques were adopted. Tribal group arrangements and established land tenure patterns were disturbed. While older arrangements were rarely totally replaced, there was a 'tendency towards *de facto* land ownership on a personal or family basis and a growing market for land transactions' (Ghai and Radwan, 1983a:19).

The colonial presence left a variety of impressions on tenure arrangements throughout Africa. Large tracts of land were alienated for use by European settlers and plantations in areas such as Kenya, Malawi and Mozambique and, along with commercialisation of indigenous agriculture, this limited the area remaining for customary use and transformed many aspects of indigenous African land use and tenure. In Ghana the emphasis was on acquiring land for cash crop production, originally using family labour, and later by migrants from neighbouring countries. Migrant African farmers started to acquire land for cocoa farming towards the end of the nineteenth century and from that time family production for the individual household's subsistence was weakened. Rural entrepreneurs expanded cocoa production by 'reinvest[ing] their surplus . . . into new land and labour and continued to expand into areas where suitable land could be purchased or leased' (Bequele, 1983:227). Resulting holdings ranged from small family enterprises to plantations, incorporating hired labour, share cropping and tenancy arrangements

30   LAND, CUSTOM AND PRACTICE IN THE SOUTH PACIFIC

where rents varied from small tributes to a percentage of the commercial crop (Ghai and Radwan, 1983a:19). Food crops could also be grown but usually without the necessity to share with the landowner. Thus, with the introduction of commercial agriculture, a new pattern of land holding emerged which reflected new social organisation arrangements and greater individualisation of farm operations.

In Malawi, economic activity had been based on hunting, grazing and cultivation by family units using shifting cultivation (Ghai and Radwan, 1983b:72). European settlers had begun to acquire land in southern Malawi in pre-colonial times when plantations geared to the cash crop production of coffee were established. Whereas the Europeans often considered that they were being granted permanent title to land, the chiefs understood they were giving permission for the use of the land and they did this freely. Extensive areas were turned over to European use, but the different perceptions of the transactions led to cases in which the same land was 'given' to more than one European. Conflicting claims arose amongst Europeans (Kandawire, 1980:135). Meanwhile, pressures caused by population growth and relative land shortage resulted in social differentiation within the indigenous population and in southern Malawi land disputes increased at the village level (ibid.:125).

After the establishment of British colonial rule in Malawi in 1891, a clash of land claims led the administration to classify land into either freehold or Crown land. This reduced the status of Africans residing on what became freehold land to that of tenants, providing service to the landlord rather than working in a kin-based community using community-held land. Those remaining on what had been customary land, but was now Crown (and later Trust) land, were left to customary arrangements but were called on to perform services for the administration. Many Africans were forced off the land by pressure from European planters who considered African methods of subsistence agriculture to be inefficient. Some found wage labour in mines and on farms of neighbouring countries (ibid.:135–43). For others, where the lighter agricultural activities could be left to women,' seasonal male migration provided a means to supplement family incomes. By 1966 these trends saw 35 per cent of the male labour force in wage employment with women taking a significant role in subsistence production on family holdings (Ghai and Radwan, 1983b:72–7).

Variations in ecology and population densities in different parts of Kenya created particular problems for land use and tenure. For example, in the Kipsigis district, common land had become overgrazed because some of those with grazing rights put more cattle onto the land for their personal advantage. This was a classic case of the 'tragedy of the

SOME COMPARISONS   31

commons' (Hardin, 1968) in which the individual pursues a course favourable to himself or herself to the detriment of the land or the community as a whole. As in parts of England in the Middle Ages, and for the same reasons, the counter in the Kipsigis district was to enclose the unfenced common land by creating privately-owned, fenced fields. Tribal chiefs supported this strategy of the colonial administration on the grounds that a stockholder who limits his stock must protect himself against other users of the common who do not adopt similar practices (Ault and Rutman, 1979:174–5).

In the Kikuyu districts in the same period, land previously worked by traditional family groups was passing into a tenuous system of private ownership. Land shortage and congestion, or efforts to build up larger holdings, led the Kikuyu to acquire land by 'tenancy', 'payment of goats or cash', or by 'jumping the boundary' (Hennings, 1952:123, 128). Since none of these methods guaranteed their rights to the land, methods such as adding improvements or long-standing residency were exercised to tighten hold over the land and avoid eviction. However, tenure continued to be in doubt since the original owner was still able to reclaim the land in exchange for the cost of improvements, if these were within his ability to pay, or he could demand a 'refresher' payment from the tenant as a further instalment for the original purchase (similar to the original payment made in goats). Even if the court dismissed the 'refresher' claim, the tenancy remained uncertain as it was not strictly in accord with 'traditional land law and custom' and nor was it based on 'legal title' (Hennings, 1952:129). Such uncertainties were not uncommon. In a broader discussion of land tenure in the late colonial period, Simpson remarked that where tenure resembles a 'freehold' form, 'some central governments and civil courts will not recognise it because it is inconsistent with "native custom"' (Simpson, 1954:51–2). Although new practices may develop and be accepted within the relevant indigenous communities, when formal adjudication is sought from a government court or tribunal, a frequent result is a finding that current practice is outside native customary law. This happens even though that native customary law is no longer practised or relevant to the contemporary conditions.

Recognition of the disjunction between law, custom and practice led to a program of systematic consolidation of land and registration of title in Kenya in the mid-1950s. The government's intent had been to encourage African farmers to consolidate holdings under individual ownership. Legal titles were granted to individual household heads who were then encouraged to produce cash crops for export. The selling of titles was permitted and a new market in land was created resulting in widening disparities in land ownership as wealthier farmers bought out poorer

32 LAND, CUSTOM AND PRACTICE IN THE SOUTH PACIFIC

farmers. In some districts, consolidation resulted in landlessness and unemployment as the cultivation rights of tenants who farmed more remote plots of larger land holders were extinguished (House and Killick, 1983:52–3).

Dissatisfaction with emerging systems of individualisation of land ownership and disparities in wealth accumulation and agricultural production have seen some post-colonial governments attempt to return to 'traditional' land tenure systems of the type which they assumed had existed prior to European contact. This has not always been an easy conversion. The systems existing immediately prior to independence had already changed to meet the contemporary economic situation, while the 'custom' on which the revived forms of 'customary land tenure' were based was no longer appropriate to the context in which it was now applied. A detailed study by Feldman of the maize farming area of Ismani in Tanzania illustrates some of the consequences of the attempt to reintroduce a 'customary' tenure system.

Under customary law the village headman had given generous allotments of land to immigrants in the 1940s. The intent of the migrants was not to participate in subsistence agriculture but to grow cash crops. Commercial production expanded. New economic factors came into play. Both altered the farmers' perceptions of their rights and obligations to the political unit, and led to new values being attached to the land. A land market emerged using sales and lease arrangements (Feldman, 1974:311–2). In effect, a traditional system of land allocation had resulted in de facto individual rights to land being acquired (ibid.:315).

After independence the socialist government sought to reestablish the traditional communal land tenure system and a Village District Council (VDC) was founded to replace the headman's land allocation role which had been formally abolished at independence. As individual ownership of land had effectively been established in Ismani, the main role of the headman in guarding group interests had in fact already disappeared (Feldman, 1974:316), leaving only the allocation of bushland to be transferred to the VDC. Little bushland remained. All other land transfers had come to be negotiated by individuals who wished to lease or purchase rights from existing land holders. However, under both the old and the reimposed customary law, transfers of land were only recognised by repayment of the cost of clearing the land and then only to the original owner, who might not be traceable. Thus, reimposition of 'custom' meant that land transfers which had been common for several decades became effectively illegal (Ault and Rutman, 1979:180). Similarly, rent for land was not recognised under the 'new' customary law which added to the tendency to bypass the VDC in order to conduct private land deals. This in itself was an acknowledgement that the transactions were

SOME COMPARISONS

illegal leaving 'the way . . . open for abuse by at least one of the parties' (Feldman, 1974:317). The ineffectiveness of the VDC thus can be attributed to the fact that 'the tenure system it is supposed to control does not exist' (ibid.:316).

Increasingly, the courts in Ismani are being called upon to settle disputes and in fact represent the only guaranteed method of 'establishing rights to land which has been acquired through private agreements', and since 'court hearings are expensive, and . . .,genuine cases may be lost . . . many tenure disputes are resolved simply in favour of the stronger party' (ibid.:317–18). The problems in Ismani provide a warning that the consequence of a policy of returning to, or artificially maintaining customary mechanisms may be the imposition of a system of tenure for which the present social and economic conditions are not appropriate and to which 'custom' no longer relates.

Some Pacific Parallels

Evidence is presented in Chapters 3 to 6 of changes in Pacific Island land tenure for which parallels can be found in the trends sketched above in cases from Asia, Europe and Africa. These parallels are not surprising given the tendency for humans to react in rather similar ways to similar opportunities or pressures, despite variability in the detail of behaviour arising from different cultural mores and circumstances. However, with the important exception of the work of Crocombe (e.g. 1971; 1972; and (ed.) 1971 and 1987a), much that has been written about land tenure in Pacific Island countries deals with particular communities, islands or countries with little comparative analysis. Studies of the Pacific Islands are often insular in more ways than one.

Amongst the trends which have emerged in the Pacific Islands, as in many parts of the world, is a reduction in communal forms of organising land tenure and a corresponding increase in individual forms. Common or community-controlled land has increasingly come under the control of individuals, through processes of formal or informal enclosure. As described above, similar processes occurred elsewhere in earlier times. The reduction of the large land holdings of nobles and the establishment of smaller independent farms in sixteenth-century Japan following the Taiko cadastral survey was analagous in some respects to the division of Tongan chiefly estates begun under Tupou I in the latter part of the nineteenth century. In Britain in the seventeenth and eighteenth centuries, the agricultural revolution and growing commercialism in agriculture helped speed up the enclosure movement. The consequent emergence of individual consolidated farm holdings and new dispersed settlement patterns were results which have parallels in parts of modern

34   LAND, CUSTOM AND PRACTICE IN THE SOUTH PACIFIC

Africa, and to which recent events in Fiji, Western Samoa, Vanuatu, Papua New Guinea and other Pacific Island countries bear some similarity as individuals establish large consolidated holdings on customary land, or take up farms in development projects excised as leaseholds from such land.

As commercialism penetrated parts of China, Japan and Western Europe, the commodification of land increased. Despite the ban on the sale of land in seventeenth-century Japan, peasants in financial difficulties used alternative ways to sell usage or other rights over land. In England, the enclosures were also followed by land sales when poorer farmers could find no other way to solve financial problems. These developments and the emergence of legal land markets in Kenya, or extra-legal land dealing in Tanzania, were similar responses to similar needs and opportunities. Tonga and Fiji now have comparable extra-legal land markets or alternative and non-customary means of transferring land use rights. As in Europe and Africa the results in the Pacific Islands include the emergence of landless groups.

As early as the mid-seventh century, the central government began to take a role in land tenure matters in Japan, and in all the countries discussed above, state law rather than local community practice has tended to become the primary legal basis for managing the distribution of rights to land amongst people. Governments or government instrumentalities rather than local communities now tend to be the arbiters, and this is also true in a number of the Pacific Island states. The Pacific Islands' cases in which customary land was brought under the control of government instrumentalities also find precedents in Africa. Vanuatu is an exception, but even this case, in which the independent government declared constitutionally that land would remain in the hands of the customary owners, has its parallels in Tanzania.

In China, Europe and Japan, a concomitant of commercialisation in the countryside and the weakening of the functional links between lords or landlords and their subjects or tenants was a tendency for the former to opt out of agricultural leadership in favour of commercial and governmental activities in towns. The changing role of Pacific Island chiefs is not dissimilar, and the opportunities and motivations for personal rather than communal advancement are much the same.

The rates of changes such as the above have varied, from a time span of over 1,000 years in parts of China or Japan, to a few decades in parts of Africa and the Pacific Islands. The relative importance of the different elements of change have also varied both temporally and spatially. But there has been a degree of commonality in the forces driving the changes with commercialism, technological change, and the widening range of opportunities for people to choose different social and economic ways of

SOME COMPARISONS 35

life being major factors in all areas. Whereas in parts of Asia and Europe these forces were often internally generated, in Africa and the Pacific Islands they often came as part of the incorporation of these regions into imperial or global political and economic systems. The short time span of this incorporation has meant that tenurial changes have been particularly rapid in these regions and, because they tended to be generated as part of the colonial experience, people's reactions to, and interpretation and valuation of them may well be very different to those of people who experienced the slower and more endogenous changes described in some of the northern hemisphere examples.

Notes

1. The period of recorded human occupation ranges from over 40,000 years in Papua New Guinea, to 3,200 in Vanuatu, 3,000 in Fiji, and less than 2,000 years in the more remote islands of French Polynesia (Groube et al., 1986; Spriggs, 1990; Spriggs and Anderson, 1993). Although the presence of grains of taro starch on tools from Buka, dated at 28,000 years BP (Loy, Spriggs and Wickler, 1992), indicates the early use of plants which were later amongst the main domestic cultivars in the region, the oldest evidence of complex agricultural systems comes from the highlands of Papua New Guinea where swamp drainage systems associated with root crop cultivation have been dated at 9,000 BP (Golson, 1989).
2. For a description of the impact of land tenure changes on women in Africa, see Davison, 1988.

CHAPTER 2

Land Tenure in the Pacific Islands

R. Gerard Ward and Elizabeth Kingdon

Most Pacific Islanders living in rural areas use land tenure arrangements which are commonly described by islanders and outsiders alike as 'traditional' or 'customary'. Yet current tenure practices on 'customary' or 'native' land often differ considerably from the 'customary' practices described by early observers, land commissions or in recorded oral history. What are now described as 'traditional' or 'customary' tenure arrangements are often greatly simplified or modified models of what was 'customary' in the mid-nineteenth century or earlier. Fiji and Tonga provide examples. In the former, 'the land tenure system which exists today evolved from the varied administrative decisions of a colonial government' (France, 1969:174). In Tonga, the indigenous government acted more drastically and officially replaced the customary practices of the early nineteenth century by an entirely new system of land tenure under a constitutional decree promulgated in 1875. In fact, practice was slow to adapt to the constitution (see Chapter 5), but today many people in Tonga feel towards their land rights like those in Fiji who regard the colonial creation as 'immemorial tradition' which 'enshrine[s] the ancient land rights . . . [and] is a powerfully cohesive force in Fijian society' (France, 1969:174–5).

In many countries the idea that the maintenance of 'traditional' forms of land tenure is essential for the integrity of culture and way of life is expressed as a basic article of faith by politicians, planners, and others (Fingleton, 1982). During the nineteenth century, some colonial governments sought to protect indigenous rights to land as these were seen as being vital to the survival of the people as a community (e.g. see Chapter 6). But by codifying 'native tenure' in order to preserve it and give it standing in the new legal structures of colonial states, the nature

LAND TENURE IN THE PACIFIC ISLANDS 37

of that tenure was often fundamentally changed. Other colonial governments rode roughshod over the pre-existing arrangements and rights on the grounds that a 'civilised power on establishing a colony . . . acquires a decisive power over the soil . . . [and] the right to extinguish the primitive title' (Minister of the Navy and Colonies, Paris, 1854. Quoted in Douglas, 1972:369). In New Caledonia and the Solomon Islands, for example, governments claimed for the state what they defined as 'waste and vacant' land. Other land was seized or bought through fair or unfair negotiations, and indigenous people were forced to make way for European settlers (A. Ward, 1982), convict establishments (Saussol, 1979), mining (Newbury, 1972) or other activities. Such actions set up pressures which also helped change the conditions of tenure on land that remained in indigenous hands.

In recent decades both the uncodified and codified tenure arrangements which have continued since the pre-colonial or colonial periods have been placed under new stresses in many island countries. Population pressure has increased and new demands for land have arisen from cash cropping and urbanisation. Land has become a tradeable commodity with a concomitant demand for easy transferability of title. The comparative value of land according to location relative to roads or towns, or to particular assessments of quality, has changed. All these trends have encouraged individuals, groups or governments to adopt new land tenure practices. In many cases these new practices diverge from either 'custom' or codified law, or from both. Although common, these new arrangements rarely receive the explicit sanction of either the government or those who claim to speak for the nation, the people or the culture. Thus much current discussion on land tenure takes the form of rhetorical assertions on the nature and importance of an idealised form of land tenure with limited relationship to the actual practices of land allocation and control.

The divergences between both the codified and 'customary' models of land tenure, and the practices adopted by many islanders, are examined in detail in four island countries in later chapters of this volume. The present chapter outlines the broader characteristics of Pacific Islands land tenure and the general social, economic and political trends which have occurred over the last two centuries. It also provides background for two of the underlying themes of later chapters: what are the reasons for, and what is the extent of, the divergence of practice from 'custom' and from law; and why, given that much of what passes for 'tradition' at present is an invention of the late nineteenth or twentieth century, is such emphasis placed publicly on land tenure as a 'traditional' part of national culture and identity in the face of obvious contradictions

38   LAND, CUSTOM AND PRACTICE IN THE SOUTH PACIFIC

between the idealised models and the reality of contemporary practice and needs?

Land Tenure in the Late Indigenous Era

It is impossible to provide a definitive account of the tenure arrangements in the region at the times when the various Pacific Islands first came into contact with the outside world. The absence of indigenous written languages, the inability of the majority of early outside observers to speak any local language fluently, the restricted range and duration of most early contacts, and the inevitable tendency for outside observers to translate what they saw and heard in terms of their own concepts, rather than those of the islanders, all mean that early accounts must be interpreted with care. Despite the lack of direct evidence on pre-contact land tenure, nineteenth-century and later accounts do provide ample evidence of features of land tenure in the late indigenous era, 'just before it began to be transformed by European influence' (Oliver, 1974:4), which were broadly common to many parts of the region, to specific types of island environments, to particular groups of agricultural systems, or to societies with particular types of social structures.

Throughout the region there is ample evidence that in the pre-commercial and pre-colonial eras land tenure arrangements were generally flexible and pragmatic. They were also subject to the determinations of local cultural situations. Harding notes that in Papua New Guinea:

> Since principles of land tenure are not codified, and since in disputes there was formerly no agency independent of and superior to the litigants themselves that was charged with preserving and interpreting principles, customary rules are subject, to a marked degree, to pressure of circumstances and dominant interests. (1972:606)

This statement is generally true for most of Melanesia, and the elements of pragmatism and the power of particular interests are more widely true. In the more strongly stratified societies of Polynesia, however, there could be chiefs of higher rank than the litigants and they would adjudicate on the basis of their authority derived from rank, descent, political power and, at the highest level, links to the gods. Therefore it must be stressed that the overview presented in this chapter does not purport to show uniformity in detail over the whole region but seeks to highlight some underlying features which did occur widely if not universally. The specifics of any particular area owed much to the local cultural context and its interaction with environmental conditions through technological and economic practicalities.

LAND TENURE IN THE PACIFIC ISLANDS

Ecological and technical practicalities

Many of the common characteristics of land tenure in the late indigenous period stem from fundamental needs which tenure arrangements seek to meet. The user or group of users of a piece of land need security over it for the period the particular use continues, or at least for long enough to benefit from the investment of their labour or capital by harvesting the crop they have planted. For tree crops this period may span decades; for other crops only a few months. Some means are needed for transferring the ownership or usufruct rights from one person or group to another as needs, such as relative size of groups, and political balance change. The different interests of individuals or groups in one piece of ground must be accommodated.

People may require rights of way across the land of others in order to reach their own plots. All members of a community may need access to a single resource such as a fresh water spring. Different individuals or groups may hold rights to the one area for different purposes, such as cultivation, hunting, or gathering wild produce. In some cases one person or group may own the trees on a plot while another owns the root crops growing beneath them. 'Almost invariably there are many different rights in any one parcel of land and they are often held by different parties' (Crocombe, 1972:220).

In the dominantly subsistence economies of most Pacific Island communities before the present century, fulfilment of a community's full range of subsistence needs usually required access to a number of ecological sites. These might be scattered throughout the island or even across a number of islands. In the absence of commercial markets and with limited alternative mechanisms for exchange of daily necessities, most families had to produce the wide variety of their regular needs for themselves. They also had to make provision for times of hardship. Few specialised in one crop or a narrow range of produce. Land tenure arrangements within the territory of each community usually reflected every household's need to hunt, gather food and collect building materials in the forest, and have access to different types of soils for a variety of crops, to fresh water sources, and to areas of lagoon and reef for fishing and gathering shellfish. Access to each type of land or resource would be controlled by specific customary rules governing who could use and retain the land or resources, who could dispose of the property, and how and to whom land might be transferred.

On many high islands the sequence of ecological zones extends from the reef and lagoon, inland across a beach and sandy area backed by swamp, to fertile colluvial soils at the base of steeper slopes rising to the central and often forested ridges of the island. Access to the range of sites

40   LAND, CUSTOM AND PRACTICE IN THE SOUTH PACIFIC

by each lineage or production unit could be achieved by tenure patterns such as those in Lakeba, Fiji, where groups hold wedge-shaped portions of land 'from the coast to the highest part of the interior rather like the slices of a cake' (M. Brookfield, 1979:166). Many other high islands, including Moala (Sahlins, 1957:450), Tubuai (Joralemon, 1983:99), Oahu (Sahlins, 1992:18–9) and Rarotonga (Crocombe, 1964:17) exhibit land divisions like these. Similarly, the raised almost atoll of Atiu, Cook Islands, with its encircling ring of rough upraised coralline limestone (*makatea*), inner circle of swamps and fertile colluvial soils, and core of central ridges is divided into seven wedge-shaped districts with boundaries that radiate from the centre to the outer edge of the fringing reef (Figure 2.1). Districts are further subdivided, in much the same way, with boundaries running from the centre to the coast and the 'highly valued land was further subdivided amongst much smaller groups for exploitation' (Crocombe, 1972:235–6). In the case of Tahiti, each valley system includes a coastal strip at the valley mouth, fronting lagoon, reef and off-shore waters, all backed by a wedge-shaped segment containing the major resources of the island. 'It appears all Tahitians had access to the valley, coastal and marine resource zones contained in the particular valley system in which they lived' and 'there is . . . some evidence that each system, and its inhabitants formed a single political unit within large tribal groups' (Finney, 1973:16). In Samoa the land of each village normally extends from the reef and shore inland to the central ridge of the island, again giving the community a cross-section of the island and its resources.

On larger islands with more interior settlements this simple pattern of land holdings is not practical, but in the pre-commercial era communities still sought to incorporate a variety of ecological sites into their lands whenever possible to maximise the range of crops they could grow, and minimise risks of crop failure or the impact of natural hazards. In cases where such opportunities were limited, kin and social networks and exchange arrangements acted as alternative ways of obtaining the range of products needed for subsistence, thus supplementing land tenure arrangements with alternative means of reaching similar ends.

In atolls where land areas are small and elongated and where the balance between resources and people is delicate, land holdings are generally in the form of a slice across the island extending from the lagoon to the ocean. On the islets of an atoll the ocean shore provides different resources from those of the lagoon. Each household needs access to dry sites for housing and for growing coconuts and other tree crops, to wells which tap the fresh water lens below the centre of the islet, and to those areas where the water table lies close enough to the surface to be reached by pits in which the root crop, *Cyrtosperma chamissonis* (known as *babai* in Kiribati), can be grown. Thus throughout the Marshalls, 'each

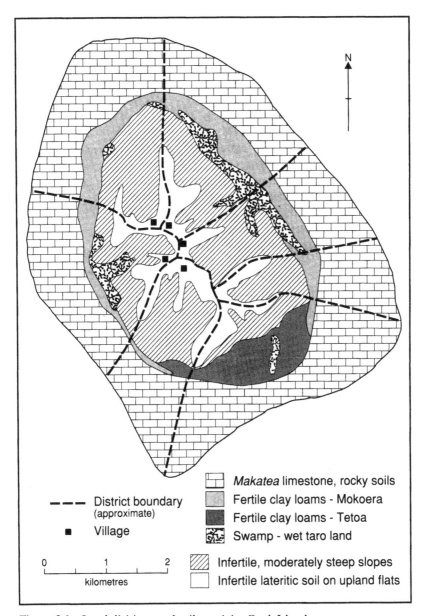

Figure 2.1 Land divisions and soils on Atiu, Cook Islands.
Sources: Crocombe, 1972 for land divisions; Grange and Fox, 1953 for soils.

parcel of land is a transverse section of the islet' and provides the resident 'landholding unit with access to all or most of the resources present in a coral atoll setting' including the variety of marine life, coconut and pandanus trees and living sites on the lagoon strand, and a strip of the

42   LAND, CUSTOM AND PRACTICE IN THE SOUTH PACIFIC

interior of the island for breadfruit trees (Mason, 1987:5). In pre-contact Kiribati boundaries were generally straight and ran from lagoon to reef, thus ensuring that each kin group had access to the range of available resources (Betero, 1987:42). The same was true in Rangiroa in the Tuamotu group (Ottino, 1972:303) and in the three atolls of Tokelau. The Tokelau kin groups also had rights to lots dispersed on different islets around the atoll which increased the chance of having access to at least one productive area at any one time (Hooper and Huntsman, 1987:136). Land divisions on Palmerston Atoll also ran from the beach on the ocean side to the lagoon side, but with no subdivision or restriction of rights to the beaches, reefs or lagoon. Since resources in these latter areas were not considered to be in short supply, there was no need to limit access to them (Crocombe and Marsters, 1987:216).

With limited economic specialisation, and in order to meet both their own needs for sustenance and their ceremonial, exchange or service obligations, most households or kin groups needed to grow most of their own food crops, gather their own firewood and catch their own fish. To grow the variety of crops necessary to provide a satisfactory diet and to cover the risks of pest damage and periods of drought or storm, most households had a number of food garden and tree-crop plots scattered through the community's territory to use different soil types.[1] They commonly included a grove of coconuts near the shore, some breadfruit trees and bananas in a more sheltered site with moister soils, a patch of swamp land re-shaped for beds of taro, and yam gardens on fertile and drier colluvial soils. These plots were often interspersed amongst those of other households. Each household needed the right to use, but not exclusive ownership of, the uncultivated forest or savannah land for gathering firewood and building materials, hunting birds and animals and collecting wild foods.

The tenure arrangements to manage such a system generally involved some form of control over a broad territory by the widest kin group or the residential community. Within the uncultivated and often forested parts of this territory all the member groups could gather produce. Such land, held in the name of the lineage or community as a whole, was not the sole property of any clan, sub-clan, extended or nuclear family or individual. It was a form of commons. When land had been cleared and cultivated, it was generally recognised that the crops thereon were the property of the planter or his or her immediate kin group, and the land would remain under their control for as long as the crops continued to stand. With intercropping of root crops, bananas, and shrubs, such as *Piper methysticum* (kava), this period might extend over several years. Once gardens ceased to produce satisfactory yields under the predominantly swidden system, they were abandoned to allow the land to revert to a scrub or forest fallow for some

LAND TENURE IN THE PACIFIC ISLANDS 43

years, or even decades, until soil fertility was renewed. The previous culti-vators' rights to the former garden sites would gradually wane, or 'grow cold', as the fallow period lengthened. Once the former users had ceased to have or to express an interest in a plot, had moved away from the community, or if their identity had been forgotten, others could clear and take the land into gardens. Thus changes in the relative size of lineages or other production groups and in their consequential land needs could be accommodated over time with clearly sanctioned transfer of usufruct rights. Tree crops such as coconuts might remain in production and under the control of the original planter long after the ground level crops had disappeared and an understorey of shrubs had re-grown. In time the land below the coconuts might be recleared and planted by a person other than the owner of the mature coconuts. Thus a short-term food crop garden might have a different owner from the one of the coconuts sharing the same land.

In some situations a great deal of investment of labour might be involved in land improvement, as when pond fields or irrigated terraces for taro (*Colocasia esculentum*), or mounded gardens in swamp land were constructed. With such wet land cultivation the soil could be used almost permanently because irrigation water, top dressing with mud, or mulching maintained nutrient supply. In places as widely scattered as the swamp lands of the Southern Highlands Province, Papua New Guinea (pers. comm., C. Ballard, 31 January 1994), Prince Frederik-Hendrik Island, southern Irian Jaya (Serpenti, 1965:116), and the Rewa delta of Fiji (Thomson, 1908:370–1); and in the taro terraces or pond fields of Aneityum, southern Vanuatu (pers. comm., M. Spriggs, 16 November 1993), and Vanua Levu (Ward, 1965:288) and Moala (Sahlins, 1962:282) in Fiji, the long-term use and high 'capital' investment in terms of labour inputs often resulted in such plots being regarded almost as the permanent property of the particular lineage, household, or individual responsible for the construction. 'The principle of personal labour creating individual rights obviously applies here' (Serpenti, 1965:116). Somewhat analogous cases occurred in many societies in which house sites were also considered to be the property of the specific family.

Land owners could transfer usufruct or ownership of their land by customary practices in virtually all Pacific Island communities. Apart from the transfer of control of usufruct, or eventual ownership, which could result from a new planter clearing and cultivating fallow land after the passage of an acceptable period of time, land could be transferred to new owners through a number of other customary arrangements. In some societies people with certain kinship relationships to a land holder could have strong grounds for seeking a gift of land. People marrying into and coming to reside in a community might be given land and

44   LAND, CUSTOM AND PRACTICE IN THE SOUTH PACIFIC

assigned a communal affiliation which could eventually grow into clear ownership and membership for the individual or his or her descendants. Land might be given as a reward for special or customary service to a chief or land holder, or group. Refugees might be given protection, shelter and land on which to make gardens, and eventually might be absorbed into the community, even if their origin was remembered through several generations. Land, and other property, could be seized or surrendered in warfare, or as punishment for transgression of customary rules. Above all, communities could divide as a result of internal dispute and either split the land they formerly shared, or move to occupy new and hitherto unoccupied territory.

Who held the authority to exercise dominant control over land, including the power to allocate land for use or transfer, varied across the region. In much of Melanesia where chieftainship was not highly developed and where the area over which a chief might hold sway was usually small, the authority to decide on land matters was usually distributed between the leaders of kinship groups or the 'big men' who had gained influence or power during their own lifetimes. Elsewhere, either hereditary chiefs or elected leaders had the responsibility to act on behalf of their community (and sometimes the strength to turn that into a personal fiefdom). In some situations the control over, and the authority to dispose of, particular areas was clearly acknowledged to be in the hands of specific individuals who were neither big men or chiefs. In the inevitable rivalry for power and influence within and between groups, it was often the control of people, and hence military power, rather than the control of land which was the key to success.

In the Polynesian island groups rights to use and dispose of land were invariably linked with social status, which was determined by the interplay of rank (derived from seniority of descent) and power, both principles being backed by supernatural sanctions. There are many variations to the pattern, and a considerable literature dealing with them. Most scholars would probably agree with Goldman's delineation of three broad ways in which rank and power were associated (1970), if not with his evolutionary scheme for the whole Polynesian area. In the most highly stratified Polynesian social systems such as Hawaii (Kirch and Sahlins, 1992), Tahiti (Oliver, 1974), and Tonga, tracts of land were allocated by a paramount chief to lesser and generally related chiefs. Commoners held their rights from these lesser chiefs to whom they were not normally related by common descent. In other Polynesian systems, status, common descent and land rights were more intimately linked, giving rise to a wide variety of distinctive patterns of cooperation, reciprocity and systems of economic redistribution. Between these two poles were other societies where there were more or less constant struggles for

LAND TENURE IN THE PACIFIC ISLANDS

power between rival descent groups and local alignments in which access to land depended more on the fortunes of war than on any system of abstract principles.

Communalism and reciprocity

The lives of all Pacific Islanders were lived in socio-economic and political contexts in which communalism and reciprocity were core principles based on technological, economic, environmental and social reasons. In the absence of money, labour could not be purchased, but farming operations which had to be performed within a short time span because of seasonal climatic or other conditions might require labour inputs greater than an individual's immediate family could provide alone. For example, dependence on stone, shell, bone or wooden tools meant forest clearance was a slow and laborious task, but cooperation with others in a work group mobilised on the basis of reciprocity made the task feasible within the required time. It was also safer from enemies and evil spirits, as well as more congenial, to be in a group when working on the margins of the community's agricultural land. Other major tasks such as house construction were commonly handled in the same way. Although the immediate kinship group was the basic production unit in most Pacific Island societies, the help of others could be obtained on the basis of reciprocal obligations when needed. At times such group work could be an expression of community and common interests even if it was not a technical necessity.

Cooperation in garden work did not mean that the produce of gardens was communal property, although many outside observers did make this assumption and it still tends to colour the thinking of officials and planners. Conversely, the control by the individual and his or her immediate family of the fruits of their work did not mean that it would be readily practical for an individual to reside outside the normal bounds of the community or to ignore the socio-economic obligations of membership. There were special services or needs apart from labour which had to be repaid by reciprocity in some form. Such services included the help of those with special knowledge of tasks, such as canoe building, or of herbal or magical remedies or spiritual matters. Of prime importance, however, were the social need to be a member of a community, and the need to have physical protection against enemies. Neighbouring communities, often hostile, were organised in the same communal way. Inevitably in this situation, the individual's interests were best served by participation in the communal society. The risk to physical safety and economic and social wellbeing of stepping outside this context as an individual were too high for most.

46 LAND, CUSTOM AND PRACTICE IN THE SOUTH PACIFIC

Land and identity

In communities in which social and economic organisation, the control of land, spiritual beliefs, and the hierarchy of authority are all interrelated, it is not surprising that land, as the source of most material requirements, is viewed as being a pivotal component of the society and its well being. Land is an important component of the cosmology of most peoples. The widespread Polynesian legend of how the god and fisherman, Maui, pulled land from the sea and created island groups is but one example. Mythology often ties ancestors to land and respect for their memory or spirits may require giving care, attention or acknowledgement to the land they once occupied. Land and people were often said to be two parts of the same entity. 'In Marx's classic phrase, the land was the inorganic body of the people. . . . Hawaiians could refer to their ancestral lands as *kula iwi*, the "plain of one's bones," just as they knew themselves as *kama'aina*, "children of the land" which had nurtured them' (Sahlins, 1992:31). A wealth of traditional sayings in many island languages conveys these ideas of integration and words for 'land' can encompass much wider connotations. As Ravuvu points out:

> The Fijian term, *vanua* [land], has physical, social and cultural dimensions which are interrelated. It does not only mean the land area one is identified with, and the vegetation, animal life, and other objects on it, but it also includes . . . the people, their traditions and customs, beliefs and values, and the various other institutions established for the sake of achieving harmony, solidarity and prosperity. . . . It provides a sense of identity and belonging. (1983a:70)

'Thus the concept of *vanua* is an encompassing one; it is the totality of a Fijian community' (Ravuvu, 1987:15). It is in this wider sense that it appears in the name Vanuatu, given to that country on independence. Land can be regarded not only as a stage on which life proceeds, but more widely as a place. 'Cultural identity in Melanesia [and Polynesia] is a geographical identity that flows from the memories and values attached to places. Membership in a clan or social group, individual or collective identity, is inherited through a network of places, the sum total of which constitutes a territory' (Bonnemaison, 1984:117). It is common for communities and people to take as their name, or as a symbol of unity and identity, the name of the land and place they occupy, or in some cases from whence they came.

Nevertheless, in the complex of land, leaders, people and community, the primary linkages are not always directly between land and people. In Tonga prior to the constitutional changes of the nineteenth century, the primary bond, at least from a chiefly viewpoint, appears to have been between the people and their chiefs who had the spiritual and secular rule over the *fonua* (the land and people). The commoners' link to their

LAND TENURE IN THE PACIFIC ISLANDS 47

land stemmed from their association with their chiefs, rather than being a direct tie bonding all people to the land and giving rights to all. Tongan commoners were in a dependent relationship to their chiefs, and the older state of 'being Tongan' seems to have depended more on the social link than on the link to the land. Today some would argue that Tonga's distinctive land tenure system helps give identity, but this is a weaker tie than that often expressed in Fiji or Vanuatu where the right to land is a key factor setting Fijians or ni-Vanuatu off from other peoples who live within the boundaries of the modern states.

With integrated concepts of land, place and people, it is natural that practices adopted for land control and allocation are often seen as core elements of social identity. In more recent years they have been used by politicians and leaders as symbols of national identity. In the constitutions of countries such as Papua New Guinea, the Solomon Islands and Vanuatu, cultural values are stressed and clarification of land issues was a prerequisite to the adoption of these constitutions. In the case of Vanuatu, the constitution itself is 'an instrument to achieve a fundamental reform of land tenure' bringing all land back into the realm of custom (Fingleton, 1982:339).

The Commercial Era

Most of the Pacific Island groups made their initial contact with non-islanders in the late eighteenth and early nineteenth centuries, but in some cases, particularly in inland parts of the larger islands of Melanesia, it was delayed by more than a century. European and American newcomers brought new technologies which allowed individuals to achieve greater output from their own labour; religions which stressed individual salvation and an abandonment of warfare; a monetary basis for exchange of goods and services; and eventually an imposed colonial peace and new levels of overriding government. These gradually provided scope for individuals to find an alternative route to pursuing their personal interests outside the communal way of life.

Not all innovations came directly to islanders from Europeans or Americans. One effect of Western activities was a massive increase in movement around the region by Pacific Islanders as ships' crew, plantation labourers, missionaries and teachers, and sometimes even tourists.[2] It was often these travelling islanders who carried with them new crops, new varieties of old crops, new beliefs and political ideas, and the initial examples of life and work outside the everyday social context of their home communities. Some of the plant and animal introductions had significant effects on agricultural systems and secondarily on land tenure patterns. The introduction of sweet potato (*Ipomoea batatas*) to the

48   LAND, CUSTOM AND PRACTICE IN THE SOUTH PACIFIC

highlands of Papua New Guinea had transformed agriculture at a much earlier time (Yen, 1974), but the rate of plant introduction accelerated rapidly in the nineteenth century. Cassava (*Manihot* spp.) was replacing yams (*Dioscoria* spp.) in parts of Fiji in the 1880s and with its tolerance of low fertility soils and relatively low labour input requirements, it reduced the need for cooperative work and helped change the balance in the relationships between cropping periods, land types and land tenure. Local varieties of indigenous staples were widely transferred. For example, a variety of taro which grew well under dry land conditions, and which was supposedly brought to Fiji from Tanna, Vanuatu, could be grown with less labour input and on a wider range of soils than wet taro. Its ready adoption seems to have contributed to a decline in the cultivation of irrigated taro and the reversion of much of the individual- or family-held irrigated land to broader categories of tenure. More recently, cattle grazing has become a significant factor in the emergence of new tenure practices in some countries because of its requirement for exclusive or segregated use of relatively large areas.

The visits of early explorers, sandalwood collectors (Shineberg, 1967), bêche-de-mer traders (Ward, 1972), and the American and European whalers who followed them seeking 'refreshment' and recruiting islanders for crew, had limited direct impact on land tenure. Their stays on land were short and they did not want sites for settlement. They did, however, introduce firearms and steel tools, and gave people experience of new and usually very hierarchical and authoritarian forms of organising labour and shipboard communities on non-reciprocal bases. By negotiating through chiefs or big men in the specific areas they visited, and by putting firearms into their control, the newcomers helped change the relative power of certain chiefs. Certain localities became favoured by the visitors and some of these places formed the nuclei of the region's first towns. A classic example is provided by the pork trade from Tahiti to New South Wales which had much influence on the rise to overlordship of the Pomare line and the emergence of Papeete as the main centre of Tahiti (Maude, 1959).

Land sales

The missionaries and resident traders who followed did need land and also increased the supplies of tools and other manufactured goods (Pitt, 1970:19). Some early European residents received permissive residence rights similar to those enjoyed by indigenous community members. Others sought more exclusive and long-lasting arrangements which amounted to freehold or fee simple in the view of the purchasers. The donors or sellers may not have always interpreted the arrangements in the

LAND TENURE IN THE PACIFIC ISLANDS

same way. In some cases the vendors did realise that they were transferring the land in perpetuity. In others it is possible that the indigenous people, lacking the concept of land as a commodity which could be sold in perpetuity, thought that they were bestowing some form of permissive occupancy which would lapse when the Europeans involved departed. Some chiefs who sold land either claimed greater rights to do so than their followers (if they had had the chance) would acknowledge, or in fact 'sold' land which did not belong to them or their kin group.

While the initial areas required for church, store and residence sites were small, both individually and in total, the arrival of people seeking land for plantations transformed the situation in many islands. The 1860s saw a rush for land by Europeans in parts of the region, spurred by the high cotton prices which followed the cutting off of supplies from the southern states of USA during the Civil War. In later decades demand for land waxed and waned with world economic conditions and with changing demands for products such as coconut oil, copra or sugar. Prior to the establishment of colonial governments, land dealings were often chaotic and Lewthwaite's comment that 'few among either Samoans or *papalagi* [white people] had clean hands and a pure heart' (1962:141) had much wider application. In the New Hebrides the Compagnie Calédonienne des Nouvelles-Hébrides 'engaged in an orgy of land-buying, in which . . . [speed was more important] than that the alleged vendors should understand the purport of the deeds to which they were affixing their marks, or, indeed, that they should have any right to dispose of the land at all' (Scarr, 1967:199). In Fiji, some 'land dealers and jobbers' kept chiefs 'well supplied with grog' and resorted to 'every subterfuge' in order to get 'land by hook or by crook' (Wilkinson, unpub.). Island leaders, as in the Solomon Islands, often found that the sale of land gave them the means for attaining new forms of wealth and status in the emerging commercial world (Bennett, 1987:116–7). Extensive land sales were mainly confined to the larger islands as most land on the smaller and more densely settled islands was already occupied and, especially in the atolls, the land and soil resources were too limited to attract potential planters.

After the establishment of formal governments, either colonial or indigenous, the administering powers of some territories prohibited, discouraged, or controlled sales of native land. In Tahiti the government of Queen Pomare asserted inalienability in 1842, as did King Taufa'ahau Tupou I of Tonga in the constitution of 1875 and the Land Act of 1882. In the Tahiti case, however, land transfers did take place (Thompson and Adloff, 1971:107). In Fiji, the Assembly of the State of Bua passed a bill in 1866 prohibiting land sales or leases except by the government. Some colonial governments, as in the Gilbert and Ellice Islands, Western

50 LAND, CUSTOM AND PRACTICE IN THE SOUTH PACIFIC

Samoa, Fiji, and the Cook Islands, prohibited sales of native land and decreed that in future non-indigenous people could only obtain land from the indigenous owners under lease.

In contrast, other colonial governments had the goal of making land available for non-indigenous settlers to encourage exports and help finance the administration. In the Solomon Islands the first resident commissioner, C.M. Woodford (1896–1915), encouraged land sales to assist the establishment of British-owned plantations (Bennett, 1987: 126–38). Some governments assumed control of large areas which were supposedly 'waste and vacant'. In 1855 the Governor of New Caledonia proclaimed that Melanesians had rights only to those areas actually under cultivation and that the remainder, that which was *vacante*, belonged to the state (A. Ward, 1982:1). In the territories of Micronesia over which Japan held a mandate after 1918, 'all land not privately owned by natives and others at the time of occupation [by the Japanese] . . . was held to belong to the state' (N.I.D., 1945:498) and this situation was subsequently maintained by the American trusteeship administration. Such measures represented massive dispossessions.

As colonial governments became established they required land for their own functions and to provide sites for ports, towns, and communications. It was also necessary to clarify claims made by European settlers and speculators to have purchased land from the indigenous landholders. Commissions of inquiry were set up in several territories, including Western Samoa, Fiji, New Hebrides, and later the Solomon Islands (Scarr, 1967), to adjudicate on claims. It was a task of great complexity. Claimants commonly identified two points on a shore or river bank and asserted the purchase of all land between two lines at right angles to the shore and extending for several miles inland. Conflicting claims were inevitable (see, for example, Figure 6.4 below). In the New Hebrides one claim of the Société Française des Nouvelles-Hébrides was for '780,600 hectares in a group whose total area was estimated at 1,467,320 hectares' (Scarr, 1967:212–3). A single San Francisco-based syndicate had claims for a total area of 'nearly half of Samoa' (Davidson, 1967:46) and total claims were equivalent to more than double the land area of the whole country (N.I.D., 1945:497). Although the criteria used for assessing the validity of land claims varied, the general result of the commissions' decisions, in conjunction with legislation banning permanent alienation of more land, was to fix the area of freehold land as a rigid component of the tenure pattern of each colony.

Codification and registration of native land

In addition to determining the validity of claims to previous purchases of land and confirming what land belonged to the state, some colonial

LAND TENURE IN THE PACIFIC ISLANDS 51

governments felt it necessary to identify the land that belonged to indigenous owners, whether individuals or groups. The avoidance of inter-group disputes, the wish to identify owners who might later be the appropriate persons with whom to deal in land transfers, the desire to delimit 'waste and vacant' land which might be deemed state land and then allocated for European or other non-indigenous settlers, and a wish to protect the interests of the indigenous people, were all motives for such actions in one or more territories. In Fiji (see Chapter 6) the last of these motives was dominant, as it was in Papua, the Gilbert and Ellice Islands and, after a time, in the Cook Islands and Western Samoa. In contrast the declaration of reserves for the indigenes of New Caledonia was motivated by a desire to free more land for European settlement as well as to provide subsistence resources for the Melanesians (A. Ward, 1982:2). Some legislators found moral justification for such an approach in the common belief that the Melanesians of New Caledonia and elsewhere in the western Pacific, and the Polynesians of the Cook Islands, French Polynesia and other territories, would eventually die out. The declining populations revealed by early missionary counts and late nineteenth-century censuses seemed to support this belief and, therefore, some administrators thought that what was needed were measures to provide for the needs of a declining population until nature took its course and the land became free for Europeans.

Whatever motive governments had in seeking to identify and record indigenous land holdings, the general result of such attempts was to produce legally-recognised models of land tenure which varied considerably from the actual practices followed by islanders prior to codification. As in French Polynesia, they were often 'based on misinterpretations of how the land tenure system worked' (Joralemon, 1983:97). Simplified, standardised, and codified in written law, these colonial land tenure systems often came to be regarded as 'traditional' by officials, and sometimes by islanders themselves. The colonial systems had a number of common features in which they differed from the indigenous arrangements which they supposedly recorded and protected. Land which had been held in a form of common tenure by broad lineages and used for gathering and hunting by lineage members was declared to be 'waste and vacant' and was removed from the category of native land to become state land. Whereas cultivated and recently cultivated land was usually held by relatively small family groups or individuals, the ownership was sometimes registered in the name of larger groups, such as the 'tribe' in New Caledonia (A. Ward, 1982:3–4) or the *mataqali* in Fiji (Chapter 6). The flexibility of pre-colonial arrangements, which allowed the size of a group's domain to increase or decrease as population increased or decreased, was ended in territories such as the Cook Islands (Crocombe, 1964:126–7) and Fiji because boundaries were recorded as

52   LAND, CUSTOM AND PRACTICE IN THE SOUTH PACIFIC

permanent and the names of owners and their descendants registered. Former practices for transfer of land were often banned by oversight or intent. The conditions were established for increasing divergence between the population, and hence land needs, of owning groups and the area of land they held.

Registration also allowed for a steady increase in the number of part-owners of blocks of land. In the pre-literate era, people who left or were banished from their home villages and were eventually absorbed into other communities would in time cease to have any automatic claim to their former ancestral lands (Matheson, 1987; Crocombe, 1964:58–9). Registration by the state now keeps their rights and those of their descendants formally alive, despite the views of those still resident in the home island. A second cause of burgeoning numbers of joint owners arose where, as in the Cook Islands (Crocombe, 1964:126) and French Polynesia (Joralemon, 1983:97), traditional practice normally allowed either patrilateral or matrilateral inheritance of land rights depending on where people took up residence or maintained their communal obligations. Registration, however, was done bilaterally, by both lines of descent, thus inflating the number of recorded joint owners. In the district of Tengatangi on Atiu in the early 1960s an average of 80 living right holders were registered per land section, with sections averaging 6.17 acres (2.5 ha.). Over three-quarters of the right holders were absentees (Crocombe, 1964:127–8). Inevitably, the number of legal co-owners has expanded since that time.

The increase in out-migration from rural areas to towns or overseas has accentuated the absentee effects, not only in the Cook Islands but also in Niue, Western Samoa, and Tonga and in the outer islands of several other island countries. Whereas in pre-commercial times people who migrated far from an area could not maintain their contacts and community obligations, and hence would lose their land rights over time, absentees can now use modern communications to send money as contributions to their kin and community and to maintain links. Some do so with the explicit purpose of keeping open their rights to land in case they should wish to return, and in some situations because of the monetary value of land. Thus multiple ownership of land can be increased much faster than in earlier times, and non-residents may now claim a voice which their forebear equivalents would have lost.

The differences between pre-colonial practice and colonial codified systems can cause disputes, or result in situations in which people simply ignore the law. An example of the first case is found in the differences of opinion which arise between absentees and continuing residents. The former may believe they have rights to land if they or their descendants return to an ancestral island. They may even feel they have preferential rights to compensate for the fact that others have been using 'their' land in their absence. Those who have remained on the island consider that the absentees' rights have expired over the years because they have not maintained their community obligations (Matheson, 1987) and any restoration would depend on new contributions to the resident community. Both sides can claim justification in 'custom' by drawing on different principles.

The second case is exemplified in Tahiti where 'instead of trying to understand the native principles and to adjust them to new conditions, Protectorate policy denied their existence' (Panoff, 1971:50). As a result 'the French metropolitan law has been enforced by French courts for a hundred years without having the intended effect. What the Tahitians in fact do about their land and what rights they recognise in it, are very different from the legal situation' (Crocombe, 1971:30). Two sets of land tenure arrangements based on different premises operate side by side, sometimes conflicting. Those who 'know both sets of rules . . . manipulate them to their own advantage' (Panoff, 1971:53). This is true of many places, as is demonstrated in later chapters.

Changes in land tenure

In countries such as Western Samoa (Chapter 4), Papua New Guinea, Solomon Islands, Tokelau and Vanuatu (Chapter 3), indigenous land tenure practices have never been systematically codified and few surveys of holdings have been made. Nevertheless, changes have occurred over the last century or more and current tenure practices often differ from those of some decades ago. This is equally true where tenure has not been codified as where it has. Quite apart from the results of codification, the changes are consequences of the new technologies, new crops and animals, new agricultural systems, new economic and occupational structures, new migration patterns, and new systems of government which have been introduced in the colonial and post-colonial periods. Although, as is demonstrated in subsequent chapters, details differ from country to country, there are general features which occur in many places.

The adoption of new technology in the form of steel tools was one of the first consequences of contact with European and American traders. The use of steel rather than stone, bone or wooden tools made labour more efficient. Salisbury estimated that among the Siane in the highlands of Papua New Guinea, clearing and fencing gardens took three to four times as long with stone tools in 1933 than doing the work with steel in 1953. Other 'clan work, being mainly axe work, can be estimated as taking two and a half times as long in 1933 as in 1953; lineage work,

54 LAND, CUSTOM AND PRACTICE IN THE SOUTH PACIFIC

involving more repairs, as taking one and a half times as long' (Salisbury, 1962:109). Later studies and experimental work show that the advantage is not normally as great as this, in part because the tasks themselves were changed with the new tools (Golson, n.d. [1981]:52–3). Most experiments comparing stone with steel tools appear to have been done with axes and adzes (Burton, unpub. [1986]) but the almost ubiquitous 'bush knife', or machete, must also have had considerable impact across a range of tasks. Certainly many communities found their subsistence workloads reduced, and the introduction of new crop varieties with lower labour demands also contributed. Reduction in the time taken in subsistence tasks, some of which were often done in groups, allowed individuals or nuclear families to manage larger holdings without assistance from wider kin groups. Land which lay further from the houses could be used economically by allocating the time now saved in clearing or cultivating to travelling between house and gardens.

The initial effects on land tenure of these labour demand changes were limited because there was little need for higher production and the security risk of cultivating far from the settlement was often high. But the potential to re-allocate time was created. Later, the enforcement of peace by colonial governments made it safer to use more distant land, even if people were not travelling and working in a group. Peace also reduced the time which men might have to devote to defence, or warfare generally, and removed one imperative for cooperation in larger groups. More of the land hitherto held in common by the broader lineages could be brought into cultivation without mobilising large work groups and hence could come under the control of individuals or families. Later, when cash cropping was introduced, time had been freed and could be devoted to commercial agriculture if the farmer, as an individual, so wished.

New crop varieties and new species had some effects within the subsistence sector but much more wide-ranging results came from the entry of islanders into commercial farming. The initial provision of food for visiting ships and the small groups of missionaries and resident traders was not very significant, but when missions and traders encouraged the production of coconut oil and later copra for export, land use patterns changed quite dramatically. As a traditional crop, coconuts had been grown in small groves in most settlements, but the area planted expanded dramatically in the second half of the nineteenth century as people saw the opportunity to obtain imported goods from the proceeds of oil or copra sales. Missions encouraged production to assist the church. Some governments, such as Western Samoa and Tahiti, required people to plant to meet taxes levied in cash or, as in Fiji, in kind, and to increase exports. The new coconut areas were usually located near the coast and villages to minimise carriage of the coconuts. As a result new food gardens had to be located further inland on newly cleared land. The average area held by planters and their families was increased and the proportion of a community's land controlled by families rather than by the community as a whole was expanded. The period during which land remained under the control of individuals or households before being returned to fallow and eventually to the category of forest or general community land was lengthened. The life of a coconut plantation could far exceed a generation, whereas few of the subsistence gardens were cultivated for more than a few years before fallowing. Land might now lie in the control of a production unit, whether a nuclear or extended family or an individual, for as long as living memory. The introduction of other tree crops like cocoa or coffee extended these effects, and in recent decades the establishment of pastures, which need no fallow, and in theory may be kept in production indefinitely, have accelerated the processes of increasing the size and duration of land holdings. These changes in land use practices have all taken place without alteration of customary land tenure although the old practices are now being used for non-customary ends, and with new consequences.

The effects of money and commercial farming

Unlike most traditional and perishable products, money earned from the sale of crops not only allowed the purchase of services or goods produced elsewhere, but could provide economic, social and psychological benefits to the individual by being saved rather than by being given away to earn status and accumulate credit in the reciprocal obligations thereby created. The new forms of value which land acquired when Europeans sought to purchase it were reinforced by the potential earnings from cash cropping. Land became a commodity, even if the sale of native land was constrained by government decrees.

Money also helped open the way for individuals to opt out of full participation in communal duties. Labour could be bought with cash rather than exchanged reciprocally. An employer of wage labourers did not have to work for them in return. In the longer term money offered an alternative to the social security hitherto provided by the kinship group and wider community. Cash earned from the sale of crops was not a traditional good in itself and was fungible, whereas most traditional produce was not. As it could be readily held secretly, money allowed people (if they wished) to divert less of the product of their labour to community purposes. New routes to status and wealth were opened but these tended to be based on the ability to farm larger areas than before, and to hold land in individual hands for much longer periods.

56   LAND, CUSTOM AND PRACTICE IN THE SOUTH PACIFIC

The traditional Pacific Island root crops of taro and yam produce high calorific yields both per unit of labour input and per hectare of planted land. Barrau (1958:25) estimated that in most of Melanesia a food crop area of about 0.2 acres (0.08 ha.) per capita was sufficient for subsistence needs. Most of the commercial export crops, and especially tree crops such as coconuts, coffee or cocoa, require significantly larger areas to provide an equivalent return in food purchased with the proceeds of sale of produce. To meet the newer consumer demands of families also requires larger areas to be planted and means that commercial or mixed subsistence–commercial holdings are considerably larger than purely subsistence holdings.

In the case of bananas, a common subsistence and commercial crop using introduced varieties, the extra plantings for export production in Fiji in the 1950s appears to have doubled the area cultivated per capita (Ward, 1964:488–9). Rodman describes the establishment of large holdings by leaders in Vanuatu after the establishment of the copra trade and the imposition of peace (1985b:59; Figure 3.2 this volume). The German administration around the turn of the century required each Samoan adult male to plant 50 coconut palms each year, increasing holdings of kin groups (*aiga*) but also laying the foundation for individuals to begin to claim land as their own (see Chapter 4). In the 1950s in Western Samoa a few individuals began to establish quite large personal holdings on customary lands. One such holding, at Vaisala in western Savai'i, had 200 acres (81 ha.) under cocoa which formed the core of a business enterprise including a store and transport service (Ward, 1962:269). In Tonga, despite the legal norm for 'tax allotments' (see Chapter 5) to be a standard size of 8.25 acres (3.3 ha.), larger holdings remained in the hands of nobles and those who had held chiefly status prior to the nineteenth-century reforms, while in the 1950s others obtained sufficient land to create much larger farms (Maude, 1965:110). This process has accelerated in the last two decades under the stimulus of opportunities to export watermelon, vanilla or pumpkin squash (James, 1993:228). In the late 1950s some Papua New Guineans began to plant coffee plantations near Goroka in emulation of the European-owned plantations established there (Finney, n.d.[1973]:55–6) and others quickly followed. Cattle farms organised by 'cattle bosses' in the Eastern Highlands resulted in areas of up to 100 ha. being enclosed (Grossman, 1984:64). In the Longana area of Aoba, Vanuatu, 'the average landholder . . . controls 7.84 ha. of coconuts' but 5 per cent of the landholders have over 30 ha. each and control 31 per cent of the land (Rodman, 1984:70). Throughout the region inequality in the amount of land controlled by different people has increased and in some instances landlessness has emerged as an actual or potential problem.

LAND TENURE IN THE PACIFIC ISLANDS 57

The increased area cultivated per head or per household and incorporation of a commercial component into mixed subsistence–cash crop systems of production (Yen, 1980) has been widely accompanied by a tendency for commercial or partly commercial holdings to be controlled and claimed by individuals, usually male. In western Melanesia, where women undertake much of the work in the largely traditional subsistence agricultural sector, men tend to concentrate on non-customary cash cropping within which traditional gender-based divisions of labour are not followed. The cash incentive offered by commercial agriculture or grazing attracts individuals, especially males, who see the possibility of boosting their status both within the customary realm with contributions financed from the sale of produce and outside tradition through accumulation of money and the consumer goods to which it gives access. Commercial farmers often try to manage their holdings on an individual or nuclear family basis and resist the demands of kin leaders or government officials for performance of communal work. They frequently prefer to use wage labour and thus avoid having to reciprocate with their own labour for the assistance received from kin or other community members. Such calls can occur at unpredictable times and be disruptive to their own commercial farming schedules.

Commercial farmers are also likely to seek to use customary land for long periods either for long-lived tree crops or for continued cultivation of successive short-term crops. In so doing there is a tendency for them to claim, under the cloak of 'custom', rights which are closer to individual, long-term and outright ownership than tradition or the custom of earlier times would have allowed. They may also wish to bequeath their holdings, and the permanent or semi-permanent improvements thereon, directly to their descendants. This would avoid the possibility of the property being claimed by, or redistributed to, other kin who may have some customary claims over the land, and may be close kin in a classificatory sense but quite distant in terms of biological relationship.

The emergence and acceptance of individualistic ways which cash cropping has fostered also owes it origins to other factors. Missionary teaching about the nature of the Christian family, and in particular the preference for the nuclear family rather than wider family structures, has been influential. In Tahiti 'the missionaries partly succeeded in integrating the extended family and the *'ati* [descent groups] into little domestic units more in accordance with the mission's conception of family' (Panoff, 1971:48–9) than were the older and larger social units. The goal of personal accumulation of monetary and durable forms of wealth is also increasingly widespread. It is a relatively new goal because most traditional forms of wealth were not durable and brought status through their distribution and the consequent accumulation of obligations owed by the

58 LAND, CUSTOM AND PRACTICE IN THE SOUTH PACIFIC

recipients. The rise of a monetised component in the agricultural economy was accentuated by the widening opportunities for wage labour, not only through migration to towns, foreign-owned plantations, or mines, but also in rural areas. The opportunities for work on road construction and maintenance, in stores and transport businesses, and increasingly as paid labour on the land of other villagers, freed more and more rural people from primary dependence on the land, albeit at the risk of loss of longer-term security. Education and service sector employment later accentuated the trend. For some, one consequence has been a changed and economically weaker relationship to the land, which has opened the way for others to adopt new tenure practices.

Differentiation has increased both in the need for land between members of villages or communities, and in the area of land to which people have access. Some people need only small plots to provide modest subsistence supplements to their wage incomes. Others are specialist commercial farmers with little involvement in subsistence cultivation but needing relatively large holdings if their farms are to become economically viable. In places like the Rewa River delta in Fiji, the area west of Apia in Western Samoa, in Tahiti, Tongatabu and Rarotonga, landlessness has become a reality for some people. Although the majority of rural Pacific Islanders engage in a mixed subsistence and cash crop agriculture, all have been affected by the changing balance between market and home consumption. There has been a widespread tendency to grow less of the labour- and fertility-demanding crops, such as yams, and relatively more of less demanding crops, such as sweet potatoes and cassava. Households no longer need to grow such a wide range of crops themselves as the seasonality of production and the need to cater for periods of food shortage or unusual climatic events is met by purchases from markets or stores. It is less necessary for many families to have a scatter of gardens on separated plots of land for different species or seasons. Orientation towards the market has resulted in specialisation on the particular varieties of a species, such as taro, which withstand transport and have the best keeping and marketing qualities. In many areas food crop agriculture has become less varied and less intensive (Brookfield, 1972b).

One consequence of the changes in farming systems is that the advantage of having a single consolidated holding has increased. For many farmers there is advantage in living on these holdings rather than in a nucleated village. The latter might be well located near the 'point of minimum aggregate travel' in relation to a scatter of gardens, but badly located relative to a single holding. Residence on the farm may thus reduce travel time between house and farm as well as help to protect produce from theft. In countries like Western Samoa or on atolls where surface water is rare, the availability of roofing iron and water storage

LAND TENURE IN THE PACIFIC ISLANDS 59

tanks, or piped water supplies, allows residence away from the village, which was often sited close to a spring or other fresh water source.

The factors described above all contribute to the tendency for the fragmented and dispersed holding of households typical of the pre-commercial era to be replaced in many areas by larger and consolidated holdings. As significant parts of these holdings tend to be committed to long-term uses, such as pasture or tree crops, and significant capital may be invested in improvements, such as fencing and on-farm buildings, there is an increase in the likelihood that farmers will come to regard the land as their permanent or virtually permanent property, while other people find they have reduced opportunities to establish farms on the land of their kinship group. Again, these changes have often occurred without breaching the normative principles of land tenure which people would consider to be 'customary'.

Since the 1950s governments have played a much greater role in many aspects of Pacific Island life, particularly in fostering planned rural development. The availability of overseas aid to fund development projects aimed at increasing the participation of Pacific Islanders in commercial development, combined with the general aim of governments to foster economic development for national purposes, has led to a growing number of relatively large-scale farm development projects. In the intellectual climate of recent decades these have almost always been based on the premise that individual holdings specialising in a narrow range of crops are the most likely to be economically successful. Oil palm farms clustered around nucleus estates and processing plants in Papua New Guinea are one example, while the sugar industry of Fiji is a much older case of similar organisation. Cattle farm projects in Fiji provide other examples. Figure 2.2 shows the change in land holding patterns which resulted in such a case in eastern Viti Levu. The registered lands of the various owning *mataqali* have been subdivided into a set of 30-year leases for small cattle farms with an average area of about 38 hectares. Before the land was subdivided into leases, members of the owning group, and people from other groups (see Figure 6.8 below), could cultivate scattered plots across this area under customary arrangements, but the land is now allocated for the exclusive use of the lessees for at least three decades, and probably longer under renewal clauses. Although Pacific Island politicians and their governments usually emphasise the need to maintain traditional land tenure and the ideal community life as key parts of what they describe as 'the Pacific Way', when they promote the individualism of such projects they are helping to accelerate social trends which are changing the nature of tenure on the land involved, and in some respects undermining the customs which their rhetoric states should be preserved.

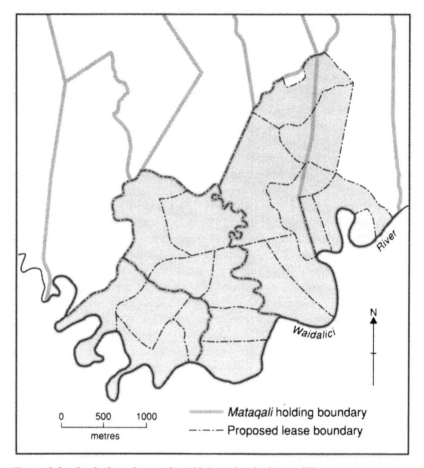

Figure 2.2 Cattle-farm leases, Sote-Naitutu beef scheme, Fiji.
Source: Native Land Trust Board, Suva.

There are two main reasons why the designers of development projects favour individual farms. The first is the common belief of planners and government agricultural staff that communal organisation of commercial agriculture on communally owned land is generally unsuccessful because of the likely conflict of interests between the community members themselves, and between the time schedules of the market and the community's priorities. There is some truth in this, but it is not an inevitable consequence that the land involved must be removed from customary forms of tenure to counter these risks. The assumption that individual non-customary tenure is a prerequisite for successful commercial farming by individuals has often been based on an overestimate

LAND TENURE IN THE PACIFIC ISLANDS 61

of the importance of the broadest level of communal land ownership resting with the maximal lineage, and an underestimate of the extent to which agricultural work and the disposal of its proceeds were traditionally handled at an individual or household level. Traditional land tenure arrangements could, and frequently did, allow patches of land to remain under the control of one farmer and his or her descendants with reasonably long-term security. The examples of coconut groves discussed above illustrate this point.

The second reason for government encouragement of transferable leaseholds, or registration of land titles in the names of individuals, is the assumption that farm credit can only be extended against the security of the land. If the farmer does not have a transferable title to the land, then banks and other credit agencies have often been reluctant to lend funds for farm development. This has been a powerful force behind the encouragement given by government to development schemes based on individual leasehold farms. In recent years some development banks, such as that in Papua New Guinea and the Grameen Bank in Bangladesh, have found alternative means for arranging loans to farmers which avoid the need to take a mortgage over the land, but the assumption that the farmer needs individual title remains common, and development projects are still usually based on individual family farms on which the farmer has some type of transferable land title.

Changes in rural life stemming from one or more of the various forces noted above are reported from many parts of the region. Many of the tendencies recorded provide opportunities, latent or realised, for people to become less economically dependent upon communal activity within their lineage or settlement unit and freer to live and work independently or in small extended families. The adoption of cash cropping is central to the change. Money can free a farmer from personal involvement in reciprocal labour and other obligations and from the need to grow a range of subsistence crops. Agricultural specialisation becomes possible and advantageous for some individuals.

Evidence for these interrelated trends comes from right across the region, but it is necessary to stress that the precise relationships between them are not always clear, and differ in detail from place to place. As Finney warns 'the trend toward nuclear family households [in Mai'ao is not necessarily] . . . a simple epiphenomenon of increased commercialization' (1973:95). On Mai'ao, in French Polynesia, 'use rights to copra lands have been increasingly allocated to individual co-heirs' since the 1930s (Finney, 1973:114) and younger men now consider this 'inevitable and necessary if each co-heir is to maximize his income from copra production' (ibid.:116). But such a strongly commercial, almost uni-causal, view is not always found as multiple causes are clearly operating and have

62   LAND, CUSTOM AND PRACTICE IN THE SOUTH PACIFIC

different weight in different areas. For example, Joralemon shows that in Tubuai individualism in cash cropping continues successfully without formal individual land ownership because individual use rights within the group territory are recognised and secure. The high rate of absenteeism reduces pressure on land and there are some economies of scale for the commercial potato growers of a kin group if they use adjacent plots of land within the group's territory (Joralemon, 1983). However, where pressure is greater and commercialism stronger, as in Tahiti, some people have sought to buy or otherwise acquire land rights and seek legal partition into individual holdings for some decades (Panoff, 1971:56). 'Markets' in customary land have also emerged across the region from the highlands of Papua New Guinea (MacWilliam, 1988:79) to Fiji (Chapter 6) and Tonga (Chapter 5). These may not be legally recognised but they operate to allow land transfers in the context of increasing commodification of land and a changing balance between group and individual interests.

A common result of the trend towards individualisation in agriculture is a tendency for land which was traditionally held in a form of commons to be privatised. The customary practice whereby forest land held in common could be cleared by an individual or small group, and then remain under the control of that person or group while in use, is a common traditional practice. But, as noted above, the ability to keep that control for decades through continuous occupation with tree crops or pasture and thereby, de facto, privatising the land, establishes an entirely different tenurial situation not envisaged in more traditional times. Other devices have also been used to transfer communal land into the control of chiefs, big men, or other individuals. Some mechanisms have been based on government requirements or policies which encourage individualisation of farm activities.

In French Polynesia the French law based on private ownership did not mesh with kin group holdings and, when the land of descent groups ('ati) was registered, 'in many instances the group's trustee [the head of the 'ati] took advantage of the confusion and had the Administration register all his co-members' rights as his own' (Panoff, 1971:50–1). In Papua New Guinea, when cattle farms were being promoted by the government in the 1970s, it was recognised that the land would probably be owned by a group or groups. To meet its own lending requirements, the PNG Development Bank arranged for two representatives of the landowning group to sign a Clan Land Usage Agreement on behalf of the community acknowledging that the farmer, or the 'cattle boss', had the right to use the land during his lifetime. This agreement gave scope for the bank to advance credit. However, one result is that 'rights of commonality have . . . been affected. Cattle bosses restrict access to naturally

LAND TENURE IN THE PACIFIC ISLANDS

occurring resources within the enclosures'. They also 'want their sons to inherit the projects' (Grossman, 1984:106–7). Thus group land has been captured by individual leaders. In the Solomon Islands there is an inherent risk that 'trustees', named to act on behalf of an owning group when land is leased, 'will in time appropriate rights of ownership to themselves' as only their names 'appear on the land register' (Larmour, 1984:8). The 'masters of tradition' described by Rodman (1987:159–61) in Vanuatu captured group land for themselves when they planted considerable areas in coconuts for copra production in the early decades of this century. Parallel cases can be found in other countries and in recent years the process has been quite widespread in Fiji and Western Samoa (Chapters 6 and 4), with the establishment of cattle pasture or long-term tree crops being the mechanism used to bring this about.

Despite the many changes which have been emerging in recent decades, and many academic accounts of these changes, few official statements on land tenure, or reports prepared for development projects, describe anything other than what is assumed to be traditional practice. While many politicians urge the maintenance of 'custom', of which land tenure arrangements have been an integral part, they encourage development programs which use non-customary forms of tenure and generate attitudes and motivations antipathetic to traditional ways. Some reasons for these disjunctions lie in the close relationship between the older structures of Pacific Island societies and the emergence of new political and economic elites. The new elites find it advantageous to cement their status by publicly linking their current roles to those of more traditional times. In some cases this enables them to continue to draw on contributions of labour, produce or valuables, the raison d'etre for which stems from a time when quite direct and short-term reciprocity lay at the core of socio-economic and political relations. Today, some recipients direct the proceeds towards individual and non-reciprocal ends so that the 'reciprocity' becomes increasingly asymmetrical.

In earlier times the feeling of integration between land, people and group identity was usually relatively local in its span. At national levels of discourse, the link between land and people has been used as a plank in the building of wider national identities, but this sometimes depends on greatly simplified or generalised descriptions of land tenure and other customs. Nevertheless it can be a powerful force. The use of such rhetoric, however, could have unpredictable impacts if it does not match current realities reasonably well. If too much reliance is placed on a single model of land tenure (or any other cultural marker) as being the 'real tradition', the assertion could be divisive if people of a particular class, or from a particular part of the country, do not accept that model as applicable to their customs and practice.

64 LAND, CUSTOM AND PRACTICE IN THE SOUTH PACIFIC

In parts of the region there is growing awareness of the discrepancies between custom, law and practice in matters of land tenure. In Western Samoa and Tonga there have been government and cabinet inquiries into land issues although the findings of neither have been made public (see Chapters 4 and 5). Local short-term solutions adjusting land tenure practices to modern economic needs have been worked out for some of the problems specific to a particular place or community. But these have often been successful precisely because they have ignored legal conditions. If further codification or reforms are attempted and are to provide long-term solutions, the great variety that exists in both the so-called 'customary' systems and in the ways they have been modified, ignored, or exploited for non-customary ends will need to be taken into account. The custom of the 1990s is not that of the 1960s, let alone that of the 1860s. If the major changes which have occurred, and which have been necessary to meet late twentieth-century conditions, are not recognised, accepted, and dealt with by formally modifying what can legally be done within 'customary' land tenure systems, the end results of some of the present trends may be unexpected, favourable to a very few, and largely detrimental to many. Subsequent chapters examine some of the detail of changing practice in land tenure in four countries and explore these issues in greater depth.

Notes

1. When the people of Banaba were resettled on the island of Rabi, Fiji, in 1945, agricultural advisers urged that families should consolidate their per capita allocations in a single block. However, some families wanted a scatter of plots 'for economic and social reasons' and achieved this by 'assigning their children to acre allotments in the more distant areas . . . [or] in more than one village area' (Silverman, 1969:100). By so doing they created a tenure pattern analagous to those which were common in the 'late indigenous era'.

2. In 1834 Captain Eagleston took Cokonauto, a leading chief of Rewa, Fiji, to Tahiti in the ship *Emerald*. Eagleston called Cokonauto 'Phillips' after Stephen Phillips of Salem, the owner of the *Emerald*, and on their return he brought back and presented two cattle to Cokonauto. They were the 'first . . . ever introduced among the Fijis'. On being asked by the Fijians what they were, Eagleston 'having some little difficulty in expressing [the] name of each to the natives . . . classed the two in one and called them "Bula ma Cow" which was very readily taken up by the natives whose curiosity was centered on the strange and wonderful Tie Papalonge Bula ma Cow' (Eagleston, unpub.:29). This may be the first use of the common pidgin word *bulamakau* [cattle, and some places by extension, corned beef] in the western Pacific Islands.

CHAPTER 3

Breathing Spaces:
Customary Land Tenure in Vanuatu

Margaret Rodman

In 1980, the newly independent country of Vanuatu abolished all free-hold land ownership and returned the alienated land to its 'custom owners'. To a greater extent than any other island country Vanuatu has emphasised customary land tenure in its constitution and nation building (Fingleton, 1982). In part because of differences in its colonial history, and despite extensive alienation of land to foreigners prior to independence, it has gone further than most Pacific Island states in limiting free market ownership of land. In 1980, Vanuatu became the only Melanesian country to dissolve the colonial dualism of 'customary' (or 'native') land and 'alienated' land (Larmour, 1984:38). Rejecting its twin official colonial names, New Hebrides/Nouvelles-Hébrides, the country took a name which means 'our land'. Through the constitution, ownership of all land reverted to the 'custom owners'. These can be defined as indigenous individuals or groups whose ownership claims are based on customary principles and practices.

Dissolution of the colonial dualism of customary and alienated land is important in two ways. First, it suggests that the idea of land inalienability was as fundamental to the leaders of the independence movement as the idea of land acquisition had been to European colonial involvement in the islands. 'By 1905 one company, the Société Française des Nouvelles Hébrides (SFNH) claimed over . . . fifty-five per cent of the archipelago' (Lane, 1971:257). Although the scale of such claims was unprecedented in islanders' experience, Europeans were not alone in amassing large holdings. Customary warrior leaders took some land from those they vanquished and more from loyal, intimidated followers. The constitution expressed an idea that islanders who lost their land to Europeans or to their own leaders had often asserted: that no matter who controlled the land for the moment, ultimately it was a resource inalienable from the

66   LAND, CUSTOM AND PRACTICE IN THE SOUTH PACIFIC

customary owners. The irony of assertions of inalienability amidst a history of land alienation, and the problematic concepts of both 'customary' and 'ownership', are topics to be explored in this chapter.

Second, the dissolution was part of the process of creating a unified state from a territory which was also split by other divisions arising from the joint administration. The Anglo-French Condominium, which governed the New Hebrides from 1906 until independence, was a comic opera of dualisms, with two systems for almost everything, such as administrative bureaucracies, including police, schooling and medical care. There were even three of some things, notably three national languages (English, French, and the creolised pidgin called Bislama) and three systems of law (English, French, and a local joint-legislation, including a native criminal code). Conflict over land, among European settlers and between settlers and islanders, was central to the history of the Condominium. While the colonial administrations made efforts to maintain a colonial presence throughout the Condominium that included resolution of customary land disputes, this was largely ineffective and islanders were generally left to sort matters out on their own as they always had done.

Customary ownership became important in the colonial era as a concept in opposition to European forms of land tenure. But the identification of idealised forms of traditional culture, including land tenure, by the Bislama term '*kastom*' probably did not occur until the 1950s, possibly in counterpoint to '*bisnis*' (Lindstrom, 1993:499). *Kastom* means 'conspicuous tradition'. In Lindstrom's view, *kastom* has identificatory, regulatory and oppositional capacities. It provides a way of talking about national identity; it is a 'powerful idiom for organising and managing individual behaviour'; but it also 'has the potential to unsettle the state and threaten its order' (ibid.:495–6). Confusingly, *kastom* has more to do with tradition, especially the concept of invented tradition, than with 'custom' in the sense of habitual, cultural practices of social life. Like all traditions, *kastom* operates in the present to create an ideological myth that encodes a relationship with the past (Handler and Linnekin, 1984; Keesing and Tonkinson, 1982; Jolly, 1992). *Kastom* is a discourse about the past that is 'situated in the present and oriented toward the future' (Keesing, 1993:588).

Both *kastom* as an invented tradition and custom as habitual practices have had, and will continue to have, powerful impacts on the Anglo-French colony that became Vanuatu. In Vanuatu, '*kastom* is predicated on a sense of rupture and revival', whereas in Fiji, *vakavanua*, 'the way of the land', expresses 'a sense of continuity between past and present' (Jolly, 1992:330). The proclamation that all land belongs to the custom owners is, in one sense, an appeal to *kastom* in its oppositional role, and

VANUATU

a direct denial of colonial practices of land alienation and of colonial attempts to legislate or police land matters. But the proclamation also created a zone of abandonment by government, in the sense that highly variable customs and the difficulty of identifying custom owners can be glossed over as *kastom* and left alone, beyond state control.

Other chapters in this book draw attention to contradictions between legal or customary land tenure conventions and practice that previously have often been unseen, ignored, or denied. Highlighting contradictions may draw attention to scenarios of conflict, actual or hypothetical. This chapter focuses on the opportunities for operating flexibly and without creating overt dispute between apparently contradictory conventions of custom and practice, as long as they are not brought into open debate as contradictions. The intention here is to draw attention to the 'breathing spaces' within custom, and between what is customary and *kastom*. These are ambiguities of which participants are sometimes unaware but of which they may sometimes take individual advantage. In particular, it is suggested here that recourse to custom as symbol can allow new ways of doing things to seem old, and old ways to seem new, without old and new coming into conflict and without the contradictions between them becoming abrasive. Hobsbawm, in differentiating the dynamic vitality of custom from tradition's invariance, has said that custom serves as both 'motor and fly-wheel', sanctioning change or resistance with precedent and social continuity (1983:2). *Kastom* is used somewhat differently, to assert a break with the colonial past while placing reliance on a customary past that was neither unitary nor amenable to state control.

Case studies central to this chapter explore land tenure with attention, first, to the dynamic qualities of custom and, secondly, to the relationship between custom and *kastom* in Vanuatu. A key characteristic of the process whereby recourse to ideas of custom sanctions change or resistance, or both, is the separation of contradictory principles, laws, or practices (or all of these) so that these contradictions can be ignored. Such separations are central to the nature of contemporary customary land tenure in Vanuatu, as can be demonstrated in detail by consideration of the Longana district of Ambae.

The dynamic qualities of custom are evident in the activities of those men called by this author 'masters of tradition' (Rodman, 1987). They are holders of relatively large areas of land planted in coconuts and their control over this land, while seemingly 'customary', may develop into a new form of social differentiation. In other words, new forms of inequality arise directly from control of larger coconut plantations, but are accepted as old forms of inequality in which leaders acquired large land holdings by virtue of reputations built in their lifetimes. A key difference is that in the old days, large land holdings were a consequence of an

68   LAND, CUSTOM AND PRACTICE IN THE SOUTH PACIFIC

individual's personal renown; now they are the basis for it. Furthermore, the large holdings are proving to be more heritable than were the old reputations of 'big men'.

While in a sense it has been a fiction that these larger land holders conform to the ideal of Melanesian egalitarianism and are just like everybody else, it is a fiction, like many everyday truths, by which people have lived. The fiction provided an opportunity not only to deny change but to some extent to inhibit it and minimise the personal and social risks of dispute. The illusion that the present is not really different from the past is somewhat self-fulfilling so long as copra prices are low and few alternative sources of cash exist. In so far as 'masters of tradition' act like customary 'big men', they redistribute their wealth and allow access to their resources in ways not very different from their traditional predecessors. They continue to play out relations of mutual social obligation, at least until better financial opportunities come along, but they retain long-term control of large land holdings that set them apart from fellow islanders.

The second case study of the relationship between custom and *kastom* deals with the de facto return of authority to the local level and to customary forms of land dispute resolution in the absence of island courts promised by the post-independence government. In this instance, old ways of dealing with land disputes seem new as custom becomes *kastom* Island courts have existed on paper since 1983. One of their main purposes is to resolve land disputes and thereby establish clear title to customary land, but a lack of infrastructure, finance, and legislation for registration of title to customary land are regarded as problems at the national level (Republic of Vanuatu, 1993:123–5). These difficulties, combined with the general recognition that land disputes require local knowledge for effective resolution, have kept island courts from operating effectively in the rural areas. In Longana, the local traditional leaders who received a short training course to become island court magistrates, dealing only with appeals from village meetings (often called 'courts'), instead resolve village land disputes; nothing happens at the level of the island court. They resolve local land disputes, as they have always done, by recourse to customary principles, by consensus, and by the payment of customary fines and compensation. Title is as clear, and as contingent, as it has ever been.

Land and Identity: A Historical Perspective

Customary principles of land tenure

Unlike Samoa and Tonga, where land tenure principles are relatively uniform, and Fiji, where at least in law they have been made uniform, much variety in land tenure principles exists within Vanuatu. This variety is emphasised in the published literature. For example, Barak Sope began his study, *Land and Politics in the New Hebrides* by observing that 'because of the cultural fragmentation of the islands of the New Hebrides, indigenous ideas on land are also fragmented' (1974:6). With more than 80 islands (68 inhabited), more than 100 languages and a population of only 156,500 scattered over a Y-shaped archipelago about 800 km in length (Figure 3.1), variation concerning land tenure is hardly surprising. Considerable variation exists, especially between matrilineal and patrilineal descent rules and between the relative emphasis placed on groups and individuals in land holding. The island of Ambae, for example, is less than 40 km in length, and 12 km in breadth with a population in 1989 of 8,583 (Republic of Vanuatu, 1991:24). Yet patrilineal reckoning of descent and inheritance of land prevails in the western half of the island (Allen, 1969); and in the eastern half, descent and land transmission follow a matrilineal pattern. In north Pentecost and east Ambae matrilineal descent is combined with a principle of virilocal residence. South Pentecost practises patrilineal descent. Patrilineal clans characterised land holding in pre-contact southwest Malakula with well-demarcated territories associated with each landholding kin group, but not with each individual (Van Trease, 1984). Group rules were more important than the rights of individuals to land in the Santo interior, although individuals could gain access to land through a variety of ties to different groups. Descent and marriage were matrilineally organised but land was inherited patrilineally and residence was patrilocal. Generally in the northern part of the group, the rules for acquisition of land rights are described as having been quite flexible (Van Trease, 1984).

Less flexibility was evident in the southern part of the group. In Epi and islands to the south, land holding was associated with titles transmitted between individuals. 'While linked to the larger kin group, these individual rights gave primary right of use and the authority to grant access to other members of the clan. A man without a title in effect had no land' to control, although he would always have use rights to someone else's land (Arutangai, 1987:264). The permutations of lineality, locality, and land acquisition principles clearly resulted in tremendous diversity. Yet, as Tonkinson concludes, 'despite varying descent emphases in different regions, everywhere there was considerable recognition and utilization of both matrilineal and patrilineal principles in institutional structures and everyday behaviour' (1982:75).

Despite apparent diversity, land tenure in the various islands of Vanuatu has much in common with customary land tenure elsewhere in the Pacific. Principles of shared access to land among members of

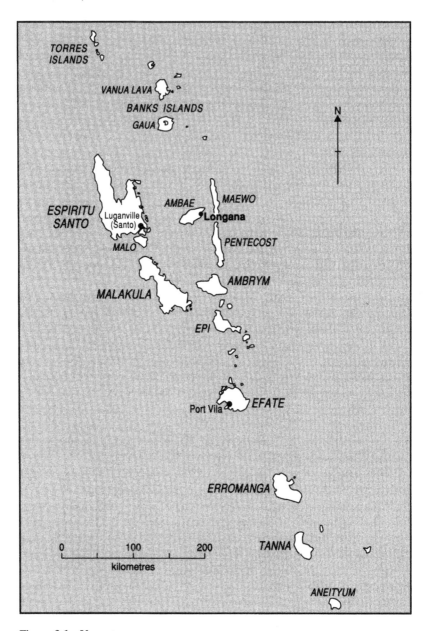

Figure 3.1 Vanuatu.

VANUATU   71

communities or kin groups, or both, are common in Vanuatu, as elsewhere, as is outlined in Chapter 2. Similarly shared is a concern to allow access to an ecologically diverse range of lands for gardening, hunting and gathering building materials. Control of such access and rights of disposal over land, however, is not widely shared in Vanuatu and has tended to rest with senior males.

Throughout Vanuatu, land tenure principles emphasised themes of mobility versus rootedness, and an emphasis on knowledge as the key to power in land tenure matters. As Tonkinson has observed, geographic mobility characterised interactions between local groups as well as residential arrangements in Vanuatu (1982:75). His studies of a relocated Ambrymese community (1977, 1985) and Bedford's (1973) analysis of mobility in transition in the then New Hebrides, provide examples of permanent and circular migration and explore the implication of migration for identity. The relationship between mobility and rootedness also intrigues Bonnemaison (1986), who has shown that the seemingly conflicting metaphors of the tree, a symbol of rootedness in place, and the canoe, a symbol of mobility, pose no paradox for indigenous people in several areas of Vanuatu. On the southern island of Tanna a grid of spatialised social relationships organises movements of things and people (Brunton, 1979:99). A system of hierarchical titles cross-cuts this grid. The titles are linked to particular *nakamals*, a term in Bislama denoting men's meeting places. *Nakamals* range from large buildings in the north of the group to open spaces, often centring on a large tree, in the south. In Tanna, *nakamals* are clearings used for kava drinking and ceremonial dancing, and there are more than 200 of them. The titles associated with these *nakamals* are transmitted patrilineally. They are associated with the allocation of residence rights in hamlets and other land rights, as well as with the distribution of political, economic and magical prerogatives. The abundance of such titles is said to be a problem (Philibert, 1992:103). Brunton reported (1979:103) that Jean Guiart enumerated more than 1,000 titles in 1953. At the time the adult male population was only 1,790. The result was a hierarchical system with almost no social authority or, as Brunton says, putting a twist on Guiart (1956:10, 107), Tanna was 'an atomistic society with a lot of structure' (1979:102).

Bonnemaison (1984, 1986) has clarified the situation by pointing out that the roads (*swatu*) linking *nakamals* are the key to socio-spatial organisation on Tanna (Philibert, 1992:104). Where magical, moving stones stopped, space took form and magical places came into being, according to Tannese tradition. When people later emerged from stones, their social space was already organised for them, divided into territories and criss-crossed by a network of paths that the moving stones had blazed. Thus, land tenure in Tanna is more than a set of relations among

72 LAND, CUSTOM AND PRACTICE IN THE SOUTH PACIFIC

people, for place is believed to have played an active role in shaping human interaction. People's identity arises from the stone, magic place, and territory from which they originated. Individuals, especially men, speak of themselves as rooted in place like trees (Bonnemaison, 1984). Social hierarchies on Tanna are geographically organised and are believed to flow from a hierarchy of places. These social hierarchies are represented metaphorically as canoes, with one titled man at the helm, another to assert power in war and peace, and a third, a magician, for spiritual protection. These social canoes move from their home territory along safe passages to visit allied groups, exchange women and share food.

Lindstrom (1990) also attributes significance to rootedness and mobility in Tannese attachments to land. He identifies geography, or place, as one of three 'disciplines' that organise knowledge on Tanna. The power of individuals and leaders is locally based and covers a restricted spatial range. It is also unequally distributed according to gender, age and, especially, knowledge. Land claims are pressed through the assertion of a 'geographic copyright' which is distinctively Tannese, yet recognisable as one variant of a pattern found throughout the islands. Place also figures prominently in the expression of knowledge in the northern islands of the archipelago, as case material from the Longana district of Ambae will later show.

Tanna provides an extreme example of ways of talking, thinking and acting with regard to land, in terms of mobility, rootedness, and knowledge, that are also found elsewhere in Vanuatu to varying degrees. These are 'geographic societies' in which place is central to identity and knowledge about place is fundamental to acquiring and holding land. Rubinstein's work on the island of Malo documents the importance of what he calls 'placing the self'. Like Layard (1942), Rubinstein found that on Malo men and land are spoken of as sharing 'blood' (1978:175). An individual's personal essence and identity flow into, and come from, the land. Jolly (1991) shows that people's identity is expressed in terms of place on Pentecost. Like Bonnemaison (1986) and Rodman (1987:35–6), she notes the powerful amalgam of person and place in the concept of *man ples*, a person linked through a whole chain of ancestors to a place; or more generally in recent times since independence, a native of Vanuatu is known as a 'ni-Vanuatu'. Bonnemaison emphasises that *man ples* is the only 'true' man, retaining his identity by always returning to his root-place. He quotes a Tannese man as saying that 'men were rooted to the soil but women were like birds who fly above the trees, only descending where they see good fruit' (Bonnemaison, 1984:124). Jolly, however, stresses the importance of the idea of *man ples* for exercising power in a context of social change. The image of *man ples*

VANUATU

not only asserts that the land is 'inalienably attached to the people of the place'; it also proclaims 'local people as rightfully in control of it' (1992:342). Western ways, then, can be likened to women who move between the rooted men, like birds flying between trees. Jolly quotes a Pentecost islander as saying that European custom is just a recently arrived bird, in contrast to indigenous *kastom* which, like a banyan tree, has roots in the past (1982:339–40). The rest of this section looks at that 'recently arrived bird' and its implications for land tenure in Vanuatu.

Europeans and land alienation

Philibert and Rodman (in press) suggested that the first years of contact foreshadowed the colonial history of the Condominium and shaped ni-Vanuatu patterns of interaction with Europeans that continued to be played out almost kaleidoscopically through independence to the present day. In 1606, the Spanish explorer Quiros became the first European to locate the islands, which were later charted by Cook in 1774. But the New Hebrides attracted little European attention until the discovery of sandalwood in the southern islands in 1838. By 1865, commercial extraction of sandalwood had declined as the supply dwindled. But in the intervening years, islanders learned a great deal about how to get what they wanted in exchanges with the traders who needed their cooperation to obtain enough wood. On some occasions, islanders even made traders pay them with pigs and shells, which were traditional valuables, turning the traders into participants in the regional trading system (Shineberg, 1967:159).

During the labour trade in the second half of the nineteenth century, islanders gained further experience with Europeans as they worked in the plantations of New Caledonia, Fiji, and Queensland. By the time of the labour trade

> the balance of power had shifted as Melanesian men and women had nothing to offer but their labour, and this required that they place themselves in the custody of foreigners for at least three years at a time. . . . The result of this period is that ni-Vanuatu saw for themselves what existed beyond their island world and interacted with new categories of people from white employers to fellow islanders belonging to different cultures. (Philibert and Rodman, in press)

During the same period as the labour trade, Christianity became well established in the islands. Competition for souls, like European competition for land and labour, was schismatic, reinforcing indigenous political factionalism and sometimes exacerbating it with sectarian and national rivalries. By 1900, there were more than two dozen Presbyterian missionaries, nine Anglican priests, and eight Catholic priests and nuns

74   LAND, CUSTOM AND PRACTICE IN THE SOUTH PACIFIC

in the New Hebrides. Part of the appeal of conversion to Christianity for islanders lay in the new knowledge that missionaries brought.

> Traditional knowledge – technical, social and religious – could no longer adequately account for a cultural horizon considerably expanded with the arrival of Europeans. Moreover, power (political) and knowledge (religious) are closely linked in Melanesia, so in attempting to assimilate the newcomers' knowledge, often at any cost, people were at the same time seeking moral, economic, and political equality with them. (Philibert and Rodman, in press)

The Havannah Harbour area of Efate was the largest centre of European settlement in the islands with 11 cotton planters living there by 1873 (Morrell, 1960:180). By 1880, the settlers, who were largely British subjects, turned to copra, coffee and cocoa as cash crops. Many encouraged islanders to plant small holdings of coconuts and to exchange, first, freshly shelled coconut and, later, dried coconut meat for trade goods or, less often, for cash. But poor markets, cyclones, and disease (especially malaria) took a toll on white settlement. Further, settlers suffered from Britain's non-interventionist policy in the Western Pacific which meant that they could not establish legal title to land claims nor could they recruit island labour to work their plantations. Meanwhile, French settlement, unconstrained by British policies, increased as did pressure for France to annex the islands. Many British residents on Efate sold their land to the Compagnie Calédonienne des Nouvelles-Hébrides (CCNH), founded by John Higginson, an Irishman who became a naturalised French citizen. CCNH acquired large holdings on other islands as well, and by 1905 it claimed more than 55 per cent of the total land area of the archipelago (Whyte, 1990:95).

Conflicts between European settlers and islanders increased; twenty Europeans were killed between 1882 and 1886 (Ward, 1948:300). In 1887, despite Australian opposition and British reluctance, a Joint British–French Naval Commission was created to maintain order. It was, like the Condominium government that followed, a bizarre and unworkable arrangement. British and French naval commanders were to be on duty in alternate months, except for the six-month cyclone season when neither navy sailed. They were to meet before taking action and never to intervene in land disputes of any kind (Morrell, 1960:204). This was a problem as land was the focus of many disputes in the group. Settlers wanted to establish legal title to their claims. Islanders (and other settlers) regarded many of the claims as dubious. Land sales by people who were not the 'real' custom owners were called into question, as was the intent of islanders who may have thought they were allowing Europeans to use the land rather than alienate it permanently (Whyte, 1990:96).

VANUATU   75

The Convention of 1906 attempted to resolve the land issue. Britain and France declared the New Hebrides to be 'a region of joint influence in which the subjects and citizens of the two Signatory Powers shall enjoy equal rights of residence, personal protection and trade, each of the two Powers retaining jurisdiction over its subjects or citizens and neither exercising a separate control over the Group' (New Hebrides Convention, Article 1, quoted in Scholefield, 1919:377). In other words, Britain and France jointly extended their authority over the New Hebrides without claiming territorial sovereignty or demanding the allegiance of the islanders, who, in fact, could become subjects of neither power, despite being required to obey certain laws of either or both.

The Convention created a Joint Court, consisting of a British and a French judge with a Spanish president. Land claims were to be registered with the Joint Court based on the Australian Torrens system of land registration, which indexed unchallenged land titles to the cadastral map. Numerous conflicting claims were filed, mostly between Société Française des Nouvelles-Hébrides (SFNH, the ex-CCNH) and British claimants, who were mainly the Presbyterian churches and Burns Philp and Company, whose lands, by an agreement with Australia, became in effect 'Commonwealth lands'. Conflicting claims were treated as 'mutual caveats' and had to be published for at least a year before resolution was possible (Ballard, 1976:285; Whyte, 1990:94–8). Explicitly excluded from possible registration were all land deeds registered in Suva, for British claimants, or Nouméa, for French claimants, prior to 1886. The French favoured this provision as it protected their nationals' claims and effectively disallowed those of earlier (mostly English-speaking) settlers. Islanders also were largely powerless to challenge title claims, lacking the necessary legal documentation. However, a private lawyer in Port Vila, Edward Jacomb, travelled throughout the group advising islanders of their rights, gathering information about land disputes, and representing islanders in court. In retribution, the French then cruised the islands arresting 'large numbers of "native agitators"' (MacClancy, 1980:82). Not that there was real cause for concern about competing land rights in the early years of the Joint Court, for it did not register a single land title for almost a quarter of a century.

The Protocol of 1914 superseded the Convention, leaving the land clauses intact but providing for the establishment of a system of native administration, including the creation of native courts. The First World War intervened and the Protocol was not ratified until 1922. Eventually, in 1929, the Joint Court made its first ruling and began to process the 900 requests for freehold land registration pending at the time. The inefficiency, vested nationalism, and legalistic obfuscation evident in the

76   LAND, CUSTOM AND PRACTICE IN THE SOUTH PACIFIC

Table 3.1   Registered land in the New Hebrides, 1976

		Hectares	Hectares
Unregistered Land			951,745
Registered land			
British			
Individuals	*7,062*		
Companies	*11,197*		
Churches/missions	*10,728*		
British government	*211*		
Land Trust Board	*6,403*		
Total British		35,601	
French			
Individuals	*50,231*		
Companies	*44,726*		
Churches/missions	*1,581*		
SFNH	*59,197*		
French government	*21,985*		
Total French		177,720	
Municipalities		15	
Joint administration		530	
Native reserves		12,558	
Native land		9,997	
Total registered land		236,421	236,421
TOTAL AREA			1,188,166

Source: British National Service, 1976: 9.

early years of the Joint Court set the tone for subsequent land problems. In particular, the roots of the land problem that eventually led to independence are evident in the insistence that 'registration of property was one of the essential factors in assessing the validity of any deed' (Philibert and Rodman, in press).

The Joint Court began with land claims on Efate, then slowly worked its way through the southern islands. By the end of the 1930s, all claims had been heard in the islands from Efate southward. In the course of its work, the Joint Court developed three categories of land, and a fourth residual category of 'land under claim'. No provision existed in the Protocol or in law for such categories; rather the court created them 'for its own administrative convenience' (Sope, 1974:18). The first category, 'registered land' (see Table 3.1), had been surveyed, registered, and legally recognised by the Joint Court. Virtually all land in this category was alienated. Although New Hebrideans were allowed to register title to land, almost none did so, for registration seemed unnecessary and complex. Further,

VANUATU 77

it required agreement from other potential holders to allow a particular land holding unit to register title to the exclusion of such potential land holders. Such agreement was hard to obtain. 'Native Reserves' were areas set aside by the Joint Court for use by indigenous people in conjunction with registration of title to nearby land in favour of non-natives. Finally, 'Native land' was all other unregistered land that traditionally belonged to New Hebrideans. Most land held by New Hebrideans under customary tenure was not registered and hence lay outside the Joint Court's classification and jurisdiction. Land disputes between islanders on unregistered native lands and on (registered) Native Reserves were settled 'according to custom' and the two governments became involved only in the few disputes that were brought to them for resolution (British National Service, 1976:9; Sope, 1974:180).

After the turn of the century, islanders increasingly turned to cash cropping on land held according to customary principles. For a variety of reasons they were less willing than before to work for European planters. Working conditions on plantations were hard and often demeaning; missionaries (especially Presbyterians) opposed labour recruiting and exercised considerable influence both over their flock and against Europeans seeking workers; and islanders were able to acquire money and trade goods in ways other than by selling their labour. MacClancy comments that as islanders began harvesting their own coconuts commercially, selling copra to traders, and obtaining desired trade goods, some became traders in their own right.

> Able to pay a good price for copra because of their cheaper standard of living compared to Europeans, they did quite well. By 1930 about one-sixth of all copra exported was produced by ni-Vanuatu and it was common for them to employ other ni-Vanuatu, especially on Aoba. When the price of copra was high people preferred to work their own coconut groves. Only when the price fell drastically did they seek contract employment – the very time planters did not need to hire many labourers. (1981:88)

Faced with dwindling supplies of local workers, French planters began employing indentured labourers from Tonkin, Indochina, in 1913, and by 1925 there were 5,000 in the group. Conditions continued to deteriorate. Copra sacks became more valuable than the dried coconut they contained (MacClancy, 1981:89). The French government gave relief to its nationals through loans, subsidised prices for copra produced by French planters, took over a large portion of SFNH land in order to pay off its creditors, and returned labourers to Indochina at government expense. Even so, 'some 80 per cent of the debts were written off, and with them the last great attempt to establish national colonialism through European rural enterprise in the islands' (Brookfield,

78 LAND, CUSTOM AND PRACTICE IN THE SOUTH PACIFIC

1972a:71). Nevertheless, French settlers fared better than British settlers, and by 1939, the French outnumbered the British in the group by ten to one.

With the outbreak of the Second World War, the Joint Court's work was suspended until the late 1940s. The Second World War was a boom time for the New Hebrides. Major American supply, aviation, and hospital bases on Efate and Santo supported the war effort against the Japanese in the Solomon Islands. As many as 100,000 Americans were on Santo, and a total of half a million allied soldiers passed through the colony. The American forces built the necessary infrastructural airfields, wharfs and roads – expenditures on a scale that the Condominium government could not have contemplated. About 10,000 islanders worked for the Americans during the war. The wartime experience changed their lives. The legendary generosity of American soldiers with PX goods, the ease and friendship with which they treated islanders, and the islanders' discovery that some of the American soldiers were black like themselves, all made the war years a time of stocktaking for many. Never had islanders seen such quantities of Western goods; nor had they seen wealth disposed of in the way the Americans did, as they dumped millions of dollars worth of supplies and vehicles into the sea at the conclusion of the war to protect American markets. The sight of so much 'cargo' being squandered did nothing to discourage millenarian cult activities in the islands. On Tanna in particular, cargo cult activity increased during and after the war as islanders rallied to support the John Frum cult (see Lindstrom, 1993), named after the brother of the god of the island's highest mountain, who was rumoured to have become King of America. The John Frum cult urged followers to resist everything non-traditional and exhorted islanders to throw their money into the sea in anticipation of the millennium. Arrests followed and both missionaries and the government administration sought to suppress such outbreaks. But the tensions, evident in a particularly extreme form in this movement, were widespread among islanders, who were attracted to the ideas and amenities of Western life on the one hand, yet were concerned to maintain traditional values and practices on the other.

The Condominium government was financially unable to maintain the pace of development initiated during the war, nor was it committed to doing so. The colony profited to some extent from the global economic prosperity of the 1950s. This was a kind of 'golden age' for French settlers, without the land disputes or labour problems of earlier years (Henningham, 1992:28). For islanders, however, there was little improvement, especially at a political level. They lacked any formal mechanism for participating in national government until 1957, when the Advisory Council was established. Five seats out of fifteen on the council were reserved for islanders. Gradually the influence of the Advisory Council increased, as did the participation of indigenous people. Seats were filled by election, but islanders made up only half the council as late as 1969 (Henningham, 1992:36). During the 1960s, the Condominium sought to establish local councils throughout the group. In many places islanders greeted these innovations with suspicion, and they resisted both the imposition of taxes and governmental interference in local affairs. Nevertheless such councils flourished with British support in areas such as Malakula and Pentecost, despite muted French opposition.

The structure of the Condominium kept islanders' affairs largely separate from the formalities of government and involvement with the state, and until mid-century this separation applied to land in many parts of the colony. When European land interests began to clash directly with those of the islanders, the latter became increasingly active in their opposition to European land claims. While resistance to land alienation dates back to the nineteenth century, by the 1960s 'it had become the most important political issue and the catalyst for the nationalist movement' that led to independence (Whyte, 1990:98). Land disputes and lack of clear title to property for Europeans had led to the formation of the Condominium; the same kinds of problems led eventually to its dissolution. Although Europeans claimed vast amounts of land in the New Hebrides, most of it was left uncleared and unfenced as 'dark bush'. Such land remained a resource for islanders who made gardens, hunted, and sometimes settled there. Sometimes the islanders, like the Europeans, thought they owned it. In the 1960s, European plantation companies began clearing dark bush on land they claimed, in order to raise cattle on Malakula and Santo. Islanders attempted to prevent registration of such claims in the Joint Court by pulling out survey markers and otherwise disrupting the process. They also resisted the efforts of an American, Eugene Peacock, to develop a 'retirement paradise' on contested plantation and bush land on Santo's east coast and elsewhere.

Nagriamel, a movement formed in the early 1960s and centred on the village of Vanafo on Santo, was the locus of much of the indigenous resistance. It opposed the alienation of customary land, especially dark bush, all of which was said to belong to the *kastom* owners. Nagriamel attracted a following unprecedented in Vanuatu. It brought together pagans and Christians, who had been fragmented by sectarian differences, uniting them in pursuit of their traditional heritage. The reclaiming of land, which many spokesmen argued had never been alienated, was a symbol and key element of opposition to European encroachment. The leader of the movement, which shared roots with the so-called cargo cults that emerged in association with the Second World War, was Jimmy Stevens,

80   LAND, CUSTOM AND PRACTICE IN THE SOUTH PACIFIC

a ni-Vanuatu whose ancestors included a Tongan woman and a British seaman. Ironically, he came to stand for the essence of Vanuatu traditional culture.

Britain and France agreed that land problems were increasing in the New Hebrides, but they disagreed on possible solutions. The British listened to experts who favoured the establishment of a land commission. France, fearing that such a commission might jeopardise land already registered to its nationals, preferred to try to obtain individual settlements in which land holders would give a portion of their dark bush land to islanders in exchange for the latter's acknowledgement of the legitimacy of the Europeans' remaining claim. Few settlers, however, were willing to relinquish such land voluntarily.

By the late 1960s, approximately 90,000 hectares of the total area of cultivable land was in use (out of an estimated 640,000 cultivable hectares and a total land area of about 12,000 square kilometres). The land actually under cultivation was divided more or less equally among Europeans and islanders. However, this distribution was by no means equitable, for New Hebrideans comprised 95 per cent compared with the Europeans' 3 per cent of the 1968 population. 'A Condominium Administration survey published in 1970 on the basis of 1968 figures showed that New Hebrideans hold 64 per cent of the land, largely uncultivated or semi-cultivated land. The French have 31 per cent, the British 4 per cent and the Condominium 1 per cent' (Sope, 1974:19). Emerging New Hebridean leaders recognised the land problem as a fundamentally political matter, and intensified their demands for the return of most alienated land to the customary owners.

In 1971, the Condominium at last legislated against property speculation in the face of much opposition from European settlers. Further, in 1973, the British established a Land Trust Board primarily to control lands that had been acquired from Burns Philp and Company by the Commonwealth of Australia. The intention was to respond to islanders' demands for the return of alienated land to custom owners; to increase rents paid by lessees so that they came closer to market values; and to find solutions to land disputes involving the board's properties (Stober, 1984). Creation of a Land Trust Board, under British auspices, provided a way 'to further the use of such land as is vested in it from time to time for the benefit of the people of the New Hebrides' (cited in Ballard, 1976:286–7).

The 1971 legislation barring land speculation marked another political turning point. The New Hebrides Cultural Association attracted national attention for the first time through a demonstration in Port Vila in August 1971 in support of the new legislation. The Cultural Association was led by Father Walter Lini, an Anglican priest whose first parish was Longana and who went on to become the first Prime Minister

VANUATU 81

of Vanuatu. The Cultural Association was renamed the New Hebrides National Party, later to become the Vanuaku Pati. It was the first political party in the colony.

The Vanuaku Pati stood for the return of all land to the customary owners, and for the immediate independence of the country. It won the pre-independence 1979 elections and, with independence scheduled for 1980, was poised to form the first government of Vanuatu. But neither Nagriamel nor the francophone political parties that had emerged accepted the legitimacy of the election results. In January 1980, while both resident commissioners and a Vanuatu government mission were in Paris discussing the island nation's future, Jimmy Stevens' Nagriamel movement quietly took over Santo town in the name of the independent state of Vemarana. With national independence scheduled for 30 July 1980, the French, British and Vanuatu governments tried to negotiate a settlement, but to no avail. The result was the Santo Rebellion, or 'Coconut War' as it became known in the international press, which continued until the Vanuatu government, led by Prime Minister Walter Lini's Vanuaku Pati, requested troops from Papua New Guinea to bring the conflict to an end about a month after independence (Beasant, 1984).

By the time of independence, the leaders of both Nagriamel and the Vanuaku Pati had had dealings with the United Nations, both had promised to lead their followers to freedom, and both had maintained a fundamental assertion that ni-Vanuatu land was inalienable from its customary owners. Yet, as the Santo Rebellion showed, differences between the two movements were as great as their similarities. These differences were the legacy of the Condominium, of the mistrust that traditionally separated island groups, and of outside influences pursuing their own interests. Thus the Condominium ended in much the same way as it had begun, with the two colonial powers unable to do what needed to be done or to make a graceful exit. For France, the immediate consequence of the Santo Rebellion was one of bitter relations with the anglophone government of Father Walter Lini. Many French settlers and mixed race francophones were expelled from Vanuatu at the time of independence and others, who had already left the country for New Caledonia, were not allowed to return.

The Joint Court made its last decisions in the early months of 1980. 'After 52 years of operation it had handed down over 1400 judgements covering 241,678 hectares of land, or about 20 per cent of the total land area' (Whyte, 1990:100–1). Under the new constitution, except for land the government acquired in the public interest (called public land), all land now belonged to the 'indigenous custom owners and their descendants'; the 'rules of custom' were to 'form the basis of ownership and use of land in the Republic. Only indigenous citizens of the Republic who

82   LAND, CUSTOM AND PRACTICE IN THE SOUTH PACIFIC

have acquired land in accordance with a recognised system of land tenure shall have perpetual ownership of their land' (Vanuatu Constitution, 1979, Chapter 12, Articles 71–73). The constitution had been approved in 1979, and in anticipation of independence the Land Reform Regulation of 1980 was implemented to smooth the way for a national land law.

The immediate problem was to deal with the land held prior to independence by Europeans and indigenous people who were not the custom owners. Provisions were needed for the definition of 'alienators' and for the transition from registered freehold title for such persons or companies to leasehold agreements between them and the custom owners. If leases were not to be arranged, compensation to the alienators for improvements to the land reverting to custom ownership had to be worked out. The Land Reform Regulation of 1980 defined as alienators all persons, whether or not they had registered title, who, on the day before independence, had freehold or perpetual ownership of land, a right to a share in land by inheritance, a life interest or a beneficial interest in land (New Hebrides Representative Assembly, Resolution No. 29 of 1980). Alienators had to be present or have a tenant physically using the land. The alienator had to maintain improvements to the land and pay all taxes due. He or she then had the right to continue to live on the land until an agreement was reached with the custom owners or until compensation for improvements was forthcoming. It was possible for a registered negotiator to deal with customary owners on an alienator's behalf, but in all cases Ministry approval was necessary for agreements between customary owners and non-indigenous persons. This regulation was strengthened by the Alienated Land Act No. 12 of 1982 which clarified the earlier regulation, and by the passage of the Land Leases Act in 1983. The latter provided for maintenance of a register of titles to leases which would serve as proof of land rights. A valuation surveyor was charged with assessing rents payable and the value of improvements under a lease. However, uncertainty over title, disputes about the identity of the true custom owners, and lack of information continued to cause delays in registration (Whyte, 1990:105). These complaints were similar to those which plagued the Joint Court. In the 1990s, hopes have turned to computerisation of land data as a solution to the problem but in 1993 the computer hardware and software were both being blamed for further delays.

On the day of Independence all land owned on the eve of independence by the British government, the French government, the Joint Administration (Condominium) or a municipality became 'public land' held 'for the benefit of the Republic' (Republic of Vanuatu, Land Reform Regulation 1980, Part 6). During the following year, the boundaries of Port Vila and Luganville (Santo) were fixed for the purposes of management and physical planning, although these boundaries continue to be contested by custom owners (Halliburton, 1992:61). Urban land corporations were set up in Vila and in Luganville and the corporation in the former was known by the acronym VULCAN. Both corporations were expected to arrange new leases for what had been freehold urban land prior to independence and to pay a portion of the ensuing rents to the custom owners. VULCAN, however, was amended under pressure from well-placed representatives of customary landholding groups so that the entire amount of rents from the urban leases, less VULCAN's costs, was paid collectively to the three peri-urban villages which were the custom owners (Connell and Lea, 1993:96). Disagreement about how to divide the proceeds and allegations of corruption led to the dissolution of the land corporations and their replacement by two Urban Land Leases Selection Committees.

In urban areas, land titles were converted on independence to automatic leases which, however, rested on the notion of customary ownership and on the assumption that rents from leases would pass, through authorised bodies, to custom owners. The elaborate process, described by Halliburton (1992:62–3), was designed to result in a clear lease which would be 'transferable, subdividable, mortgageable, and inheritable'. It also became possible to obtain a 'negotiator's certificate' from the Minister of Lands to enter into leases with custom owners outside the urban boundaries. Finally, in 1992, an act was passed allowing the Minister of Lands to acquire land 'in any area that is likely to be needed for any public purpose' subject to compensation for damages to the land being paid to the custom owner (Vanuatu Government, Land Acquisition Act No. 5 of 1992).

Land for urban development in Port Vila was in short supply by the early 1990s. Halliburton reports a Ministry of Lands estimate that by 1992 more than 95 per cent of land within the boundaries of Vila was leased and that 'no land will be available for urban development in Port Vila within ten years' (1992:64). Squatter settlements had developed on the outskirts of Vila and informal, extra-legal leases, or no leases at all, characterised the occupation of these areas in 1993.

Negotiators' certificates were hard to obtain and potential lessees have encountered persistent difficulty in obtaining agreement about who is the 'true' custom owner, leading to disputes, frustration, and informal arrangements. Some of the land settled by squatters and extra-legal lessees could now be acquired by the government in the public interest in the aftermath of the 1992 legislation. But a form of customary land registration, and possibly freehold tenure with protection for customary rights, was still seen to be necessary at the national level for effective resolution of the difficulties in obtaining private leases from custom owners (Republic of Vanuatu, 1993:124).

84 LAND, CUSTOM AND PRACTICE IN THE SOUTH PACIFIC

Larmour has observed that local communities have always managed land in Vanuatu (1990:57). He and Ghai (1985) point to the importance of concepts of local communities and custom rather than the state and the market in the land provisions of the Vanuatu constitution. Land, in the context of custom, is a social product; or, perhaps ni-Vanuatu would argue that people are a geographical product. In any event, land is not commoditised under custom as it is in market conditions. Tension exists between custom and the market.

> From the point of view of the market economy, there are various 'problems' with the customary system. There is limited negotiability, since there are so many fetters on alienability. . . . Ownership is not vested exclusively in one person or entity, and since there is no finality in rights of use, there can be no secure title. Since rights depend on actual cultivation, boundaries of land of one's entitlement can fluctuate. Since 'ownership' rights can be so fragmented, dealings in land can be complex. They are complex also because it is not sufficient to deal with the person in actual possession of it. The absence of clear boundaries, the absence of written records and the fluidity of the system produce discord and disputes. (Ghai, 1985:397)

While the colonial administration saw customary land tenure as an obstacle to development, the independence constitution revolutionised land tenure overnight by affirming customary land rights and abolishing land titles held by expatriate individuals and companies in the rural areas. According to Ghai the constitution's chapter on land is 'at odds with the general thrust of the [Vanuatu] Constitution' in that the land provisions imply an alternative paradigm of development, based on communities rather than the state (Ghai, 1985:398). Yet communities alone could not control land development in Vanuatu. There, as elsewhere in Melanesia (and, indeed, globally), communities and the state seem to be in perpetual conflict where land development schemes such as logging or tourism are involved. This is 'a double bind that is as old as colonial history: on the one hand [governments] are supposed to be protecting the custom owners against alienation of their land, and on the other they are supposed to be promoting alienation in the interests of national development' (Larmour, 1984:39). Vanuatu, despite the pre-eminence of custom declared in the constitution, is no exception in this regard. In the post-independence period the government has oriented its development paradigm toward expansion of the economic base in order to achieve self-reliance (Republic of Vanuatu, n.d.:2–3), with emphasis on the market rather than communities and custom. Consequently, the process of regulating land acquisition and use has been one of trying to reconcile highly contradictory interests, especially where land transactions involve custom owners and indigenous citizens or non-indigenous alienators.

VANUATU 85

In sum, with the constitution, Vanuatu overthrew the colonial system of land tenure without calling into question the pre-eminence of the state and the market in other respects. This treatment of land contrasts markedly with the freezing of land tenure principles in Fiji, and with other Pacific Island countries (notably Papua New Guinea, Western Samoa, and the Solomon Islands) where dual systems of customary and alienated land persisted after independence (Larmour, 1984:38). In Fingleton's view, rather than trying to encourage future law reform, 'Vanuatu's approach has been to go behind the whole land tenure system imposed during the colonial era and reinstate the pre-colonial land tenure system' (1982:338). This of course is impossible. There was no system of pre-colonial land tenure per se. Landholding principles were diverse, linked by common but often paradoxical themes (such as rootedness and mobility, matrilineality and patrilineality, communal and individual control) that played out in different ways in particular times and places. Nor, even if there had been a single pre-colonial system, could it have been restored unchanged after so many years. Custom, the key principle informing land tenure in the constitution, is an invented tradition, in Hobsbawm's (1983:1) sense of symbolic practices focused on the inculcation of certain norms and values which try to imply continuity with the past, however spurious. It is not surprising, then, that in addition to the contradictions between land clauses and other aspects of the constitution, others exist between custom as a general principle of land tenure with a fairly recent history at a national level and the workings of customary land holding and dispute resolution in diverse, local communities. But these contradictory aspects of custom seldom collide because of the vagueness of the meaning of 'custom', or *kastom*, at a national level and because the state does not yet exert much influence at the community level with regard to matters of land. These contradictions and the space for action between them can be explored through examination of customary practices, as well as principles, of land tenure in a particular part of Vanuatu, the Longana district of Ambae (previously Aoba) island in the north of the group.

Customary Land Acquisition and Use in Longana, Ambae Island

The island where William Rodman and the author have conducted fieldwork off and on since 1969 has been known by many names, including Lepers' Island, Opa, Aoba and, most recently, Ambae (Rodman and Rodman, 1985). When missionaries and labour recruiters began to visit the island regularly in the 1870s, the residents of the Longana district of Ambae lived mostly in scattered hamlets in the forested, volcanic hills of the island's southeast quadrant. A handful of traders, including a lone

86 LAND, CUSTOM AND PRACTICE IN THE SOUTH PACIFIC

woman, set up small operations along the coast, buying land from local people or simply using it under permissive occupancy. The Anglican Melanesian Mission established a church and, later, a hospital and schools at Lolowai Bay at the eastern end of Longana. Local people say the mission took the land in compensation for the murder of a priest, Charles Godden, in 1906.

In the late nineteenth century islanders did not live on the plain, partly because of the prevalence of mosquito-borne disease in coastal areas. They came down to the sea to fish, collect salt, and hunt on the coastal plain that runs the length of the district. Trips from interior hamlets to the coast were dangerous and continued to be perilous until pacification in the 1930s. During these years, indigenous warfare and violence between islanders and Europeans were part of everyday life. In the grim view of one missionary, these were 'days of never-ending revenge' (Webb, 1922). Small, scattered hamlets seem to have been the peacetime norm. Each hamlet consisted of a few brothers, their wives and children living on land acquired from the men's father, father's brothers, or mother's brothers. When raiding and revenge were most intense, however, people gathered under the protection of relatively powerful leaders to form larger settlements. Palisades of saplings around settlements made it harder for enemy raiders to kill people in their home villages.

To further reduce the risk of attack and to feed themselves in times of warfare, residents maintained small gardens within the palisades. Each household also cultivated taro (*Colocasia esculentum*) outside the palisades in the relatively cool, damp hills above 200 metres., and yams (*Dioscorea* spp.) and bananas (*Musa* spp.) in drier, lower areas. These were, and still are, staples of the diet although now they are supplemented by sweet potato (*Ipomoea batatas*), island cabbage (*Hibiscus manihot*), cassava (*Manihot* spp.), 'Fijian' taro (*Xanthosoma* spp.), and other introduced crops (Bonnemaison, 1974:190–210). Both coastal and inland gardens follow a fallow rotation cycle of about three to seven years. One planting yields a year's harvest for most crops, with bananas and cassava continuing for two or three years.

As in the past, many pigs forage in the bush, but those with the most valuable tusks are carefully nurtured and kept close to home. Male and rare intersex pigs with full circle, or even double circle tusks, remain the focus of ceremonial exchanges and pig killings at marriages, funerals and in ceremonies for attaining higher levels in the graded society (*hungwe*). High rank in the graded society was, and still is, an individual, male, achievement fundamental to leadership, although personal characteristics rather than rank alone determine whether a man will actually emerge as an effective leader. The achievement of rank is a personal triumph, but it has always required extensive cooperation. A rank-taker can kill only a few of his own pigs and must rely on exchange partners to donate most of the animals necessary for a successful ceremony. Consequently, graded society activity was in abeyance during periods of warfare; the ceremonies required peace so that participants could travel and interact in safety.

In the days before missionisation, men often had more than one wife and high ranking leaders might have as many as ten. Each wife, except the tenth, came from the matrilineal moiety opposite to that of her husband. The tenth was not supposed to be a sexual partner, but cooked all of her husband's food to protect him from poisoning and sorcery. Each wife generally had her own dwelling house and detached kitchen. Men and boys from about the age of six lived in a *nakamal*, or men's house, which women could not enter.

Occasional parcels of bush land in Longana were held by named matrilineal clans (*duvi*). Some forest land belonged to individuals, but boundaries were unclear and usually unimportant. Most uncleared land belonged simply to Longana as opposed to the neighbouring districts of Malavung or Lolovenue. Land disputes did not focus on uncultivated land, but rather on garden land in use (*rivurivu*) or fallow (*talu*), or hamlet sites (*tokagi vanue*). Land generically (*tano*) was not something to fight over; but lived-in space (*vanue*) could always be contested. The latter, even in the days before pacification, was the property of individual land holders. This included beaches and waters between a beach and the outer reef slopes.

Acquisition of land

To say that land is, and, as Longanans claim, always has been, individually rather than communally held is somewhat misleading. A land holder has never been alone in exercising a claim to a piece of land. He is rather the pre-eminent right holder for the time being, the tallest tree in a forest of growing competitors. A land holder can be defined in this context as a person who controls other people's access to a piece of land. In principle, and almost always in practice, every adult must have access to land. The statement was made repeatedly that every Longanan must have access to a piece of land and that, therefore, landlessness was inconceivable. 'You won't find a single man who can be said to fly about like a bird with no land under his feet. It is true that if someone comes from somewhere else like Pentecost, he doesn't really have land here. He has to buy land. But those of us who are really "*man ples*" all have land' (interview, 8 May 1979). This informant spoke of men, but women also were assured of access to land although they seldom controlled its allocation. To be

88   LAND, CUSTOM AND PRACTICE IN THE SOUTH PACIFIC

Longanan by definition means having land rights; individual and collective identity is grounded in place. Land is inalienable in that the right to have some is inalienable. The few cases of landlessness that did exist during my fieldwork all involved people whose identity as Longanans was also questionable, and in some respects these individuals were not regarded as belonging to the place.

To have access to land is not necessarily to control it. Fewer people control access to land. Women are rarely land holders in their own right although they are crucial as matrilineal links through which control of land passes. Generally, only women without brothers and some widows hold land in their own names. A land holder's name is identified with the name of his place. The land is said to be 'in his name' or to be 'his place'. The extent of a land holder's individual power, however, depends on the relative influence of close kin, as well as on his knowledge and ability to persuade others of the validity of his account of the history of a piece of land. This is the art of *gaindumu*, which in this context means detailed knowledge of ties between people and land. It is both a mode of evaluation and a means of explanation.

Gaindumu is crucial to understanding how Longanan land distribution worked in the past and does today. People who know *gaindumu* are knowledgeable about the history of land holding. They monitor land acquisition and disputes. They can also manipulate this process, as warrior leaders did in the past and as new 'masters of tradition' have done since pacification. Their knowledge about land is also 'know how', the ability to gain or maintain control over land for the benefit of others or for their own ends, or both. It can also be their undoing, as the following case from Longana fieldwork in 1985 indicates:

> Robert and Oliver were participants in a land dispute in the early 1980s over the true custom ownership of a piece of land where the Longana and Lolovenue districts meet the Melanesian Mission claim at Lolowai. Oliver claimed some of the land; Robert knew the *gaindumu* of the original ownership of the land, and the story he told at the public meeting did not support Oliver's claim. Instead, he supported the Lolovenue people's claim, which also benefited a Longanan named Isaac. One of the leaders who presided over the meeting explained: 'Robert not only knew the histories of land ownership; he could explain them clearly. People took seriously what he had to say. At the meeting he explained why Isaac's family had prior claim to the land that Oliver sought. Strong words were exchanged. Because of his vast knowledge about the origins of land ownership, Robert influenced people to side against Oliver. To dispute a man's story of his family origins is a very serious matter in our custom. It almost always causes trouble because it gives men a heavy burden of shame. When Robert later became sick he was convinced that Oliver had poisoned him because of his involvement in the dispute. And that is why people think that Oliver killed Robert with poison. He killed him because Robert had shamed him in public and because of Robert's knowledge of land. Oliver wanted to silence him. (Interview, 3 December 1985)

VANUATU 89

Control over land is akin to ownership in that it gives the right to allocate its use or to dispose of it. Access to use of land is essentially a right of usufruct, not ownership. The actual distribution of control over land is necessarily a very selective process where anyone has potential rights to many more places than he could really win control of in a dispute or than he could possibly use for subsistence or small-scale coconut production. The places that every Longanan gains access to and that some Longanans control during their lifetime are numerous and varied; the relations between people joined by places are complicated and shifting. Control of every place is identified with chains of individuals in the past, with a network of potential claimants in the future, and with one individual in the present (or, occasionally, siblings acting as a unit). Thus longer term control over land could be obtained in a variety of ways most of which also involved the knowledge and persuasion known as *gaindumu*. The main channels for land acquisition customarily have been through inheritance, through contributions to funerary feasts, through payment, and, if one were sufficiently powerful, through clearing or simply through use. One could always gain access to (or usufruct over) land for agriculture more easily than control over it. Gaining access was usually just a matter of asking the land holder for permission, at least in the days before extensive coconut plantations.

Inheritance

The rights of a man to control a portion of his father's land and his mother's brother's land were equally strong. There is evidence that both patterns of inheritance co-existed and competed for some time prior to European accounts (Codrington, 1969:68), which is not surprising given cross-cutting principles of matrilineality and patrilocality. Rights to a father's land are based on bonds of blood (*dai*) that link a father to his sons and daughters. A person's right to his mother's land is through membership in a matriclan (*duvi*) that is a descent category but not a corporate group (Lovell, 1981: chapter 7). Land held by each grandparent can also be claimed by virtue of the fact that one's father or mother had rights to it. Similarly, siblings of one's parents are a potential source of land because they share a mother and/or a father with the parent. This kind of reckoning based on filiation can extend through one parent–child link after another to tie anyone to almost any piece of land in the district, if – and this is crucial – the claimant excels at *gaindumu*, i.e. he knows enough and has the skills to make the case.

Funerals

The distribution of land to heirs in Longana has customarily taken place as part of a hundred day cycle of *bongi* feasts that follow a person's death,

90 LAND, CUSTOM AND PRACTICE IN THE SOUTH PACIFIC

a practice documented elsewhere in Melanesia and one that continues in Longana and elsewhere in Vanuatu (Epstein, 1969; Ogan, 1972). In Longana, these feasts, held at five day intervals, 'mark and contest boundaries between the living and the dead, between places, and between the conflicting interests of different people' (M. Rodman, 1993:651). The largest, most competitive feast cycles follow the death of a major, male land holder. During the hundred-day period, the dead person's spirit is believed to hover possessively near the tops of fruit trees and coconut palms. The spirit watches as the body is wrapped in pandanus mats and buried. It waits as exchanges of food, mats and gifts take place below. The *bongi* cycle serves as a customary process whereby a dead land holder is slowly detached from his place and others attach themselves to it. The competition is three-way: between the sons of the deceased, male members of the dead person's matriline (e.g. his sisters' sons or his brothers) and more distant kin or even unrelated men who come bearing gifts.

Although speeches at a *bongi* repeatedly emphasise the importance of cooperation, humility, and respect, the feasts are opportunities for people to secure land as individuals at others' expense. Children of the deceased must give mats and pigs to validate their claim to their father's land. If they fail to do so in sufficient quantity they forfeit their claim. They must reciprocate every gift from the father's matriline, and from other donors by giving compensation (*holata*) in the form of pigs or mats. If they cannot repay gifts in this way, they must offer the donor a portion of their dead father's land. This could have had the effect of redistributing land from those whose numbers and customary wealth are declining to those whose numbers and fortunes are improving. Matrilineal kin, with or without relinquishing their claim to some of the land, express their satisfaction with the *holata* payments by presenting the children with a counter gift of pigs, called *vulunqatu*. This releases the dead man's spirit from the trees he has been guarding for a hundred days since death, allowing them to bear fruit again.

Children often need help to defray the expenses of *holata* payments to their father's matriline. Yet such assistance is cautiously solicited or accepted for it too must be reciprocated, and the cost may be measured in land if there are not enough pigs and mats. Sons could reject such an offer of assistance if the *bongi* expenses were within their means. But if there were many debts from their father's participation in the graded society, for example, they might have little choice. Some Longanans amassed large land holdings by investing heavily in *bongi* ceremonies. They spoke of helping others, but this customary rhetoric smoothed over the fact that they were also helping themselves. The trader, Corlette, cited by Ponter (n.d.:10), could as well have been describing

VANUATU 91

Ambae as the islanders who lived near him in Bushman's Bay, Malakula, in 1935. Corlette reported that when a man died and had no near relations at hand, another man might step in and provide the pigs necessary for the funeral feast. If the pigs were not repaid by a relation, he took possession of the deceased's lands. Today, old men and their children take measures to protect against loss of land in this way.

Warfare, payment and acquisition of land by use

In warfare, as in funerals, land could substitute for pigs, as a last resort for compensation payments. No compensation was paid to protagonists; one had to be innocent to receive it. Pigs were the preferred form of *holata* in war as in funerals, and payment of land was not strictly considered to be *holata*; it was not compensation, but it did make people 'feel better' and kept them from complaining. Shrewd men sometimes stood by when a cycle of raiding began, 'helped out' when the fight was well under way, and received pigs or a piece of land for their efforts. As at a funeral, helping others had its personal rewards.

Sale of land is not new in Longana; it is considered to be customary. Land could be bought with cash, pigs, mats, or even kava. If one bought land, it could be passed on to one's sons or one's line just like land acquired in any other way. The fact that land customarily could be sold contrasts *prima facie* with the constitution's assertion that all land belongs to the indigenous custom owners and their descendants. Under the constitution 'only indigenous citizens of the Republic who have acquired their land in accordance with a recognized system of land tenure shall have perpetual ownership of the land' (Chapter 12, Article 73). Freehold ownership and land transfer, as part of a recognised land tenure system, was possible under customary land tenure prior to independence but new freehold acquisitions were initially thought to be no longer allowed. It is doubtful that any such prohibition would make any difference to practice in rural areas. Indeed, local people could argue that sale of land is part of customary tenure, although I know of no post-independence sales of land in the area. Customary purchase of land, however, was not alienation in the sense that the term is used in the constitution. The constitution juxtaposes customary owners and alienators. Customary owners are 'indigenous'; 'alienators' can be non-indigenous citizens of Vanuatu and non-citizens. Therefore the purchase of Longanan land by other indigenous people was a customary practice, albeit one seemingly at odds with the constitution, rather than one of alienation.

Finally, it was possible for warrior leaders in the past to acquire land simply by occupying it. Such men did not take over the land of those they defeated; instead they took over the land of their own supporters.

92   LAND, CUSTOM AND PRACTICE IN THE SOUTH PACIFIC

Those who sought shelter behind the palisades of a warrior leader's large settlement could not complain if he used their land. Followers were indebted to such a man for protection, and they feared his power, for leaders were often assumed to be skilled in sorcery and poisoning. Such men, like leaders today, were knowledgeable about the history of land holding in their area. They were also expert, as are contemporary leaders, in the art of speaking in public to press a claim to disputed land.

Masters of Tradition

By about 1930, Longanans had come to see the Melanesian Mission as an alternative to dependence on the protection of strong leaders. The missionaries tolerated pig killing ceremonies and kava drinking, but they could not endure the endless cycle of raiding. In 1932, Longanans assisted the resident missionary in bringing in Condominium policemen to arrest a leader and two young warriors for the murder of another Longanan. No longer could leaders impose their will with a gun. Yet, even after pacification, leaders retained considerable autonomy. Leaders 'engaged in a kind of dialogue with the state' in which they settled most disputes themselves but referred some disputes to the British or (rarely) French District Agent when it served their purposes (W. Rodman, 1993:61). Larcom reports (1990) similar situations in Malakula. Representatives of the Condominium government rarely appeared in Longana except to deal with murders and serious offences, especially any that involved whites. Leaders continued to resolve land disputes at the local level. Ordinary people still relied on the willingness of leaders to promote their interests through *gaindumu.*

With the end of warfare, an Australian trader encouraged islanders to plant more coconuts as a cash crop. The severe downturn in the copra market during the global depression of the 1930s combined with the difficulty of recruiting island labourers for necessarily low wages led some European traders or companies to encourage the development of small-scale, indigenous copra production. The risks, costs, and labour of production were thus passed on to local people who sold their copra to the trader and spent the proceeds in his store.

With peace prevailing, most people moved away from the larger settlements and returned to a residential pattern of scattered hamlets. They left whatever portions of their land a warrior leader had planted (with the help of his many wives) and settled on another of the several pieces of land available to most households. In the lower hills, which were the most densely populated part of Longana, coconuts were planted in fenced gardens where they continued to grow after the food crops were harvested. A coconut palm was a tree like any other in the days before cash cropping. It belonged to the person who planted it, and to those among that person's heirs who knew of it and claimed the right to use it. With cash cropping, however, coconut palms became inseparable in terms of ownership from the ground in which they grew, for they took it out of circulation not for three to seven years, as a garden did, but for about seventy-five. The land holder, not the planter, became the owner. The fact of having planted palms no longer established an individual's right to the land, rather it was evidence that the person already had that right. To plant coconuts where one's right was questioned precipitated a land dispute, as it would today. In the long run, the effect of cash cropping coconuts on principles of Longanan land holding has been to strengthen the equation of palms with the land itself, as capital under a land holder's control. Coconuts have encouraged individual ownership of land, rather than of crops alone, and a greater degree of exclusivity in rights to particular plots of land.

Coconut holdings planted in food gardens were small and individually-owned parcels were dispersed, following the pattern of the gardens. Figure 3.2 shows the pattern of holdings which arose from this process in the southeastern part of the region. But a few men were able to start relatively large plantations at this time. These were men of high rank and considerable influence. Even after warriors faced gaol sentences for taking the law into their own hands, leaders in the graded society could cross the line between assuming responsibility for law and order in their area and taking control of part of the land itself. Large plantations were created in the numerous gardens that had been acquired from the warrior's followers who had sheltered in his settlement. Others bought large tracts of uninhabited land on the coastal plain from other claimants, using their wealth in pigs, mats and kava, as well as cash from their inland copra plantations. Finally, some simply seized control of land and established plantations far larger than most. They used their *gaindumu* skills to press claims to the lands on the basis of distant relationships to ancestors who had lived on the coast before it was depopulated. Although such men were no longer able to defend their actions with warfare, it was, and still is widely believed that they continued to use violence against those who opposed them with the silent weapons of sorcery and poison. Despite the flimsiness of some of these land claims, they went unchallenged. In this way a handful of men came to control far more plantation land than others. These were the men called by the author 'masters of tradition' (Rodman, 1987). Figure 3.2 shows the larger holdings of such men in a number of localities, but especially in the northeast of the region.

It is clear that 'land tenure in Longana is not a system of rights expressed in action, but a process in which actions are selectively

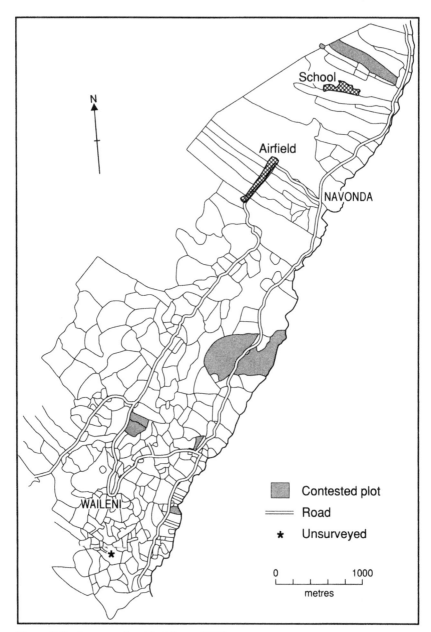

Figure 3.2 Longana land holdings, 1978.
Source: Rodman, 1987:56.

VANUATU 95

validated by rights' (Rodman, 1987:44). During fieldwork in 1978–79, practices of land holding were documented in some detail, particularly those related to land planted in coconuts. Cash cropping coconuts was a major change in land use, yet the principles of customary land holding had seemed unchanged during earlier fieldwork in Longana (1969–71). The central question was how customary land tenure could allow land holding and other social relations to change while appearing in people's statements to remain the same.

By 1978, Longana seemed in aerial photographs to be a carpet of coconut palms, with a patchwork grid of palms in the old gardens inland and long lines of palms filling the coastal plantations. Some Longanans had access to less garden land than they required. Others chose to buy much of their food rather than grow it. Many had no gardens near their inland homes and depended on the generosity of large land holders who allowed them to plant gardens near the coast. Gardens were not made near the villages because pigs generally ran free and damaged any food crops planted near settlements. The problem of 'animals astray' was repeatedly debated and disputed, but not resolved. Longanans frequently told how concerned they were about the lack of garden land, but they persisted in planting coconuts in whatever gardens they could. Had garden land really been in short supply, one suspects that the pigs would have been fenced in and coconut planting would cease. This did not happen largely because of the generosity of large land holders. By allowing access to portions of their land for gardening they helped to fulfil the customary mandate that 'every Longanan must have land' and bolstered their own status by their generosity in sharing what they had accumulated.

In 1978, 314 of these holdings were mapped (Figure 3.2). These were controlled by 140 landholding units. Control of seven of the plantations was contested and these were dropped from the analysis for most purposes. In all, 271 plots, or 88 per cent of Longanan plantations, were held by individuals, 16 of whom were women. Of the 36 cases of shared control over plantation land, 29 involved either siblings or parents and children. Plantation land for which data were available was quite evenly divided along the two moiety lines, with 125 plots for one and 129 for the other. For 245 plots, data on the birth order of the land holder were available; 196 (80 per cent) were eldest or only siblings, including all but one of the eleven female land holders (see Table 3.2).

A comparison of how land was acquired in the current and previous generations pointed to a slight shift away from matrilineal inheritance of land toward father-to-son inheritance (see Table 3.3). Both inheritance patterns remained customary options, as Longanans said they had always been. Purchase of land was important in both the 1978 generation of land holders and the previous generation. For men, wives seemed

96   LAND, CUSTOM AND PRACTICE IN THE SOUTH PACIFIC

Table 3.2   Frequency of eldest and only siblings as land holders
(307 plantation plots)

	Eldest siblings	Only siblings	Other	Plots
Males	136	50	48	234
Females	3	7	1	11
TOTALS	139	57	49	245

Source: Field data, 1978.

Table 3.3   Mode of land acquisition for current land holder and prior
generation

	Current generation		Prior generation	
From:	No.	%	No.	%
Father	122	56	38	46
Matriline	32	14	19	23
Purchase	30	14	15	19
Husband	6	3		
Compensation	5	2	7	9
Wife's kin	15	7	1	1
Mother's father	9	4	2	2
Missing cases	88	c.d.	232	c.d.
Contested	7	c.d.	n.a.	c.d.
TOTALS	314	100	314	100

Note: Missing (n.a.) and contested data (c.d.) are excluded from
percentage calculations.
Source: Field data.

to provide new access to plantation land control in 1978. Another way of
looking at this is that providing plantation land to one's married daughter's husband was increasingly valued as a new expression of the customary emphasis on 'helping'.

Bongi gifts at funerals as a means of acquiring plantation land are
included in Table 3.3 under 'compensation'. Land given for war-related
deaths and land that powerful men planted without payment or claiming kin connections to it also falls into this category. The 'compensation'
category is smaller than might be expected, largely because those who
acquired land as payment for *bongi* gifts or who talked their way into control of it through *gaindumu* justified these acquisitions in terms of kinship. Kin-based categories in Table 3.3 include land holders whose
acquisition of land is based more on skilful action at *bongi* ceremonies
and in public meetings than on kin ties per se. Nevertheless, there is a

VANUATU

noticeable decline (from 9 per cent to 2 per cent) in the compensation category from the previous to the current generation.

Male land holders almost always live on land they control. Only four did not live on their own land in 1978. Of these, one was an immigrant from West Ambae, and two had left home in the process of separating from their wives. The last was a virtually landless man whose father had gradually sold off the family holdings for kava. Hamlets have tended to be small, averaging 16 people living in four households. Larger hamlets, such as Waileni (population about 70) where the author lived, look like villages. Dwelling houses and kitchens cluster around a central clearing. This may be the site of a church and a *nakamal* (no longer reserved for men) which is used for kava and feast food preparation. In the central clearing there may also be a pre-school, community hall, or clinic. As Figures 3.3 and 3.4 show, however, such a settlement is really a collection of hamlets located at the intersection of land holdings. The clearing is on the land of the community leader, and every man lives on his own piece of ground. If every Longanan must have a place in theory, it seems equally true in practice that every adult male Longanan should live on his.

The tendency to live on one's own land would seem to restrict people's residential choices. Given this, the degree of residential mobility between and within hamlets is surprisingly great. During a twelve-year period (1970–82), the number of people who moved into or out of Waileni was more than two-thirds of the settlement's 1982 population. Between 1978 and 1982, more than 80 per cent of the buildings were occupied by new households, were rebuilt, or both. Monthly data, collected in 1978–79, showed that the individuals making up the population changed by more than 20 per cent every month, although the total population of Waileni never varied by more than one person. The residential mobility evident in maps drawn in 1982 and 1993 (see Figures 3.5 and 3.6) can be quite revealing of changing social relationships. It also reflects the impact of cyclone damage on impermanent tropical housing (Rodman, 1985a, 1985b; Rodman and Rodman, n.d.).

Although Longanans continued to maintain that everyone must have land, by 1978 some had much more of it than others. In earlier times, warrior chiefs had held far more land than others. In a sense inequality of land holding in 1978 seemed traditional. With more research, however, it was obvious that the practices had changed while the custom appeared to remain the same. Customary land tenure had both legitimised the concentration of land in the hands of a few people and obscured new consequences of following tradition. Because the validation of action with reference to land rights is so selective, land tenure practices could change considerably while the principles of land tenure – that is, what is customary – stayed the same (cf. Crocombe, 1971:15).

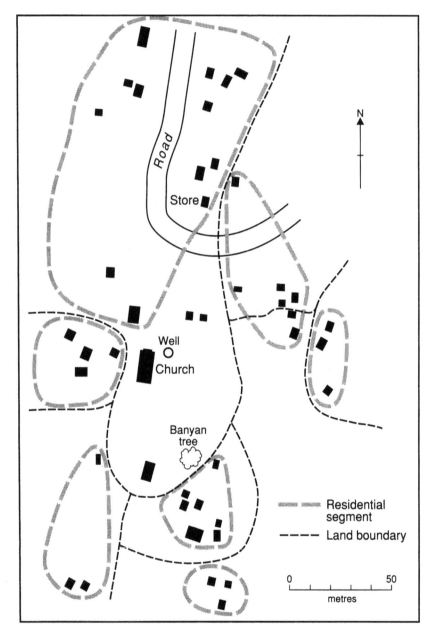

Figure 3.3 Waileni, 1978.
Source: Rodman, 1987:57.

VANUATU

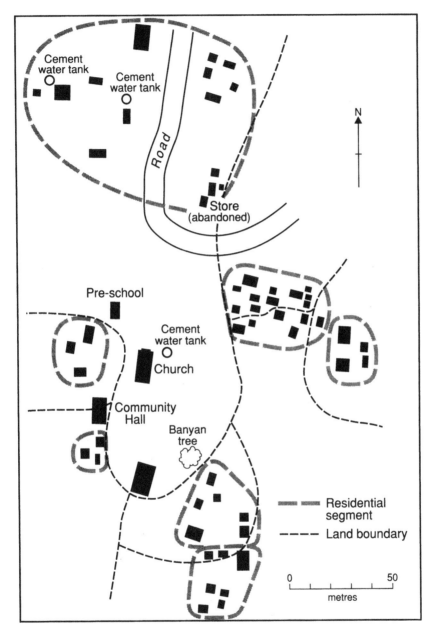

Figure 3.4 Waileni, 1993.
Source: Field data.

100 LAND, CUSTOM AND PRACTICE IN THE SOUTH PACIFIC

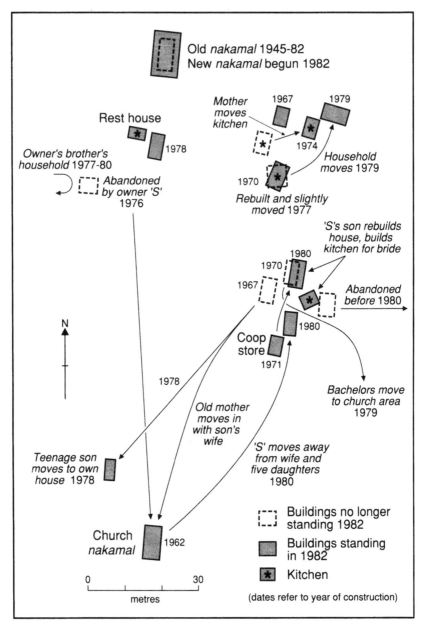

Figure 3.5 The hamlet of Lovatuweliweli, north Waileni, 1982.
Source: Field data.

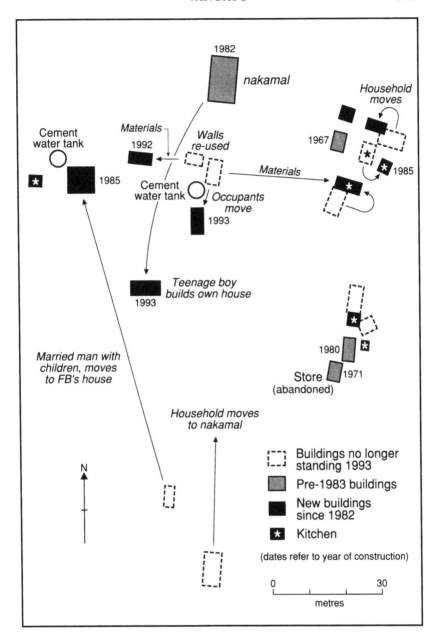

Figure 3.6 The hamlet of Lovatuweliweli, north Waileni, 1993.
Source: Field data.

102 LAND, CUSTOM AND PRACTICE IN THE SOUTH PACIFIC

In brief, 66 per cent of Longanan land holders each held 5 hectares of plantation land or less, controlling between them 21 per cent of the land planted to coconuts. Yet 31 per cent of the plantation land area was controlled by only 5 per cent of the population whose average holding was more than 50 hectares. Large land holders, like the warrior chiefs who had been the fathers of some of them, attract followers, mainly kinsmen who live and work in the plantations. The patterns of using the labour of kin and reciprocating with food are similar to those followed in the old days. Large land holders also hired between five and ten labourers from other islands, mainly Pentecost and Ambrym. These workers were paid $A2 to $A3 per bag of 'green' (un-dried) copra in 1978, depending on whether the price of copra, then much higher than it was by 1993, was over $A200 or $A300 per tonne. Even when one considers the costs of feeding and otherwise maintaining this labour force of kin and employees, the incomes that large land holders were earning in the late 1970s far exceeded the average. For example, one man who in 1978 paid $400 in wages for each pass through his coconut holdings yielding 6 tonnes of copra would earn more than $1,800 gross each time. Clearly both wages and profits depend on the copra price. Eight land holders each earned more than $A5,000 from copra sales in 1978. Their average income from copra was $A9,500, while overall the average copra income per land holder was $A2,300. The annual gross per capita income for people in these households (including dependents) was estimated at $A1,057. For everyone else it was estimated to be only $A202. In other words, large plantation land holders were earning at least five times as much from copra sales as ordinary Longanans. Copra sales were not the only source of their incomes. Such men also had, for example, cattle, cocoa, stores, and trucks. Large land holdings, then, provide the basis for increasing gaps between the incomes of the few and the many.

Rather than acquiring large amounts of land for gardens and pigs because one was a warrior leader, in 1978 some men could use large plantation lands to acquire other forms of wealth and power. In addition to using their monetary income for gaining customary prestige, they also had the opportunity for capital accumulation, purchase of consumer goods, and the establishment of other businesses in trucking or retailing, and could thus gain status in non-customary fields.

Almost half a century after pacification, ordinary Longanans were still afraid to speak out and try to regain land lost to warrior leaders. If one did not know *gaindumu*, one could not win, and there was still the fear of sorcery and poison. Land disputes were frequent, nevertheless; but protagonists often had forgotten details in the history of the land that only leaders seemed to know and which the latter brought to bear in dispute

VANUATU 103

settlement. Leaders, then, continued to 'help' fellow Longanans, who were also somewhat at the mercy of their knowledge.

Calling the large land holders in Longana 'masters of tradition' draws attention to the ways in which, on the one hand, they have followed customary practices to achieve success, but, on the other, their goals and what they have achieved are not really traditional in the sense of being unchanged from those of leaders in the past. In 1978, these relatively wealthy land holders acted so much like customary leaders that it was hard to see that the basis for their pre-eminence was new. If the copra market had continued to thrive, these men could have emerged as capitalists with few commitments to customary social obligations if they so chose. They may yet do so. Meanwhile, the illusion that they were not really any different from older leaders preserved a breathing space between 'development' and 'custom' and avoided overt conflict between ultimately incompatible goals. The illusion, for the moment, has become the truth, both because such men have continued to keep up their social duties and because prospects for increasing differentiation along class lines have diminished since 1978.

In 1993, the copra price was little more than half that of 1978, even with government stabilisation that had not existed before independence. All but the two youngest masters of tradition were dead, and one of those was rumoured to be deeply in debt. Three of the largest plantations had been divided among heirs, but were running cattle as single operations with multiple owners. All the heirs had been pressured to subdivide the plantations but countervailing arguments prevailed, with the owners reasoning that commercial plantations were different from gardens and had to be run as large enterprises. One of the wealthier heirs put a fence around such a partitioned plantation in order to 'help' the owners, of whom he was but one. Some large plantations stayed intact because heirs successfully forestalled *bongi* assistance that might have to be repaid with land. The old masters made sure their debts in the graded society and at the bank were paid off before they died. They let their heirs know their exact wishes, specifying where each son, nephew or other beneficiary would hold the right to cut coconuts. One old leader even insisted on being buried in a coffin instead of mats in order to reduce the *bongi* expenses.

Longanans were not worried about garden land in 1993. They were growing more food crops than before and buying little alcohol because cash was scarce due to low copra prices. Correspondingly they were making less copra, as returns scarcely justified the effort, and were relying more on contributions from the increasing numbers of relatives who had moved to the towns of Port Vila or Santo. There were no longer any wage labourers working on Longana plantations. Throughout the

104 LAND, CUSTOM AND PRACTICE IN THE SOUTH PACIFIC

district, pigs were fenced and for the first time since the authors began fieldwork there in 1969, crops were growing next to the houses. There had been no severe cyclones in a couple of years. People were well fed. They were beginning to replant many of the senescent coconut plantations with better-yielding varieties of palms.

Cross-cutting this idyllic if cash-poor existence were increased fears of sorcery and poison. These were not specifically linked to land claims, but they indicated that people still would be too fearful to try to reclaim land lost to the ancestors of the present large land holders. In sum, the masters of tradition were ensuring that their heirs kept control of the big plantations. While none would emerge as wealthy capitalists in the short run, the land was there, and was theirs. In 1993, large land holders were in a breathing space between the pulls of the market and of tradition, a period in which the contradictory forces of capitalism and custom did not have to come into conflict. For the moment they could continue to act like customary leaders, ensure their own social security by keeping others in their debt, to provide social assistance as required, and to wait for new business opportunities while retaining exclusive control over their land.

Island Courts and Local Land Disputes

The case of 'masters of tradition' draws attention to an interlude during which important changes occur in social relations in the 'customary' realm arising from changes in economic conditions and land tenure, yet are masked by seeming to be the way things have always been. The tensions remain subdued. The lack of action in the establishment of island courts also shows that the contradictions between *kastom* and customary practice can create a similar breathing space, one that benefits both the national government and local interests for the time being.

The Island Courts Act of 1983 was, in the view of one anthropologist, 'a crucial step in the government's attempt to construct and solidify a national cultural identity', and an attempt to reconcile national concerns with *kastom* as a source of national unity with the 'power of Melanesian localism' – i.e. the reliance on consensus among local co-residents 'as the most authoritative influence on dispute settlement and values' (Larcom, 1990:176). Village courts in Papua New Guinea and local courts in the Solomon Islands were the models for Vanuatu's island courts. Three magistrates preside, one of whom must be a 'custom chief residing within the territorial jurisdiction of the court' (Island Courts Act, Section 3.1). The Chief Justice nominates these magistrates and can create or dissolve particular island courts. The mandate of these courts is to deal with civil and criminal matters concerned with the administration of customary law. Their territorial jurisdiction is clear, but legal

VANUATU 105

scholars see the absence of 'any general customary law jurisdiction' as a crucial failing (Weisbrot, 1989:80–1). The courts consequently focus on offences under the Penal Code and minor civil claims; they play no role in the matters over which conflict most often occurs at a village level, so they operate, in effect, more as magistrates courts than as the custom courts they were intended to become. In practice, the island courts' jurisdiction over land disputes is even more disappointing. 'In virtually 100 per cent of cases the unsuccessful litigants in land matters in the island courts exercise their rights of appeal to the Supreme Court' (Weisbrot, 1989:81).

The Second National Development Plan (1987–91) lamented that 'disputes over the ownership of custom land, rather than land availability, are the largest single obstacle to the development of the rural areas of Vanuatu. With seven island courts now established the means to deal with the situation are in place but, due to a lack of trained manpower, the performance of these courts is not good and the backlog of land cases is large' (Republic of Vanuatu, n.d.:154). Assistance that other departments might have provided (e.g. surveying) was not forthcoming, due to lack of funds and staff. In 1989, amendments were made to the Island Courts Act to allow 'a magistrate to preside at every sitting involving a land ownership dispute, but inadequate manpower resources within the Judiciary have prevented this from becoming a reality' (Republic of Vanuatu, 1993:124). Consideration was being given in the Third National Development Plan (1992–96) to vesting more authority in traditional courts (i.e. village meetings to resolve disputes). This would officially recognise the de facto situation existing in Longana, and no doubt elsewhere. In sum, lack of funds and judicial personnel, and the plethora of appeals that had ensued in the few places where island courts actually heard land cases, combined to make the courts more of a problem than a solution.

Added to these problems was the fact that even fewer island courts were really in operation than it seemed. The Ambae court was one of the seven established by 1986, but by 1993 it had never met. Four Longanan leaders had received some training in 1985 to serve as island court magistrates. They were expected to cease resolving local level disputes, handing this responsibility over to other, less experienced but promising leaders in the villages. In the event, nothing happened.

The reasoning behind the implementation of island courts recognised the crucial roles that could be played by customary leaders and by customary practices of dispute resolution. A discussion paper on adjudicating customary land disputes emphasised that 'full use should clearly be made of the existing traditional methods of dealing with land disputes as ideally these disputes should be settled at the lowest possible level'

106   LAND, CUSTOM AND PRACTICE IN THE SOUTH PACIFIC

(Russell, 1982). What is ironic is that traditional methods are being used so thoroughly that, in some places, they substitute for the island courts they are supposed to serve.

The so-called island court magistrates in Longana have continued to mediate and resolve customary disputes in the villages, as they and their forbears have always done. During the colonial era, the Condominium government had imposed legal sanctions in the event of serious criminal offences, such as murder. District Agents worked in tandem, often quite effectively, with local leaders who served as Assessors. Assessors dealt with more customary matters and those deemed less serious by the standards of European law. But before independence came, the 'government had gone' and islanders were left to administer justice themselves (W. Rodman, 1985). Efforts were made to codify customary practice, turning it into *kastom* in a way first evident in cargo cults (Lindstrom, 1993) and popularised by the Vanuaku Pati and Nagriamel as *kastom* that opposed colonial law. Most dispute resolution, while imposing fines set by such codes, has continued to be guided by uncodified customary principles concerned with the power of words and knowledge, as well as people's motives and feelings, or what Larcom has called the 'justice of emotions' (1990:180–4). In mid-1993, customary leaders continued to resolve land disputes using *gaindumu* to trace connections and persuade others of the truth of their knowledge. Land disputes are resolved in the only way they ever have been, by customary leaders using local knowledge at the village level.

Larcom argues that the devolution of authority to the local level signalled the government's failure to create meaning, or values, at a national level (1990:177). In practice, the situation seems somewhat more complex. The plan was to create courts that made judgements in conformity with local customary practice, administratively bridging the gap between cultural and linguistic diversity in the islands and the need for a national law, especially a land law, set in motion by the constitution. Instead of capitulating to localism, as Larcom claims, or bridging the gap between national and local law, as the government intended, island courts are in effect temporarily sheltering behind localism because they lack the wherewithal to do much else. While hardly intentional, this maintains the rhetoric of national *kastom* in Lindstrom's sense of 'regulation' by recourse to largely non-codified, local custom. In effect this creates another breathing space which prevents the contradictions between national and local levels from coming into conflict, allowing 'custom' to exemplify *kastom* and buying time to achieve objectives regarding island courts that would alter customary control of land and people.

The problems island courts face in land issues are solved in the short run by devolving the task to village-level custom. In the longer run, however, old ways of handling land disputes are problematic for the Vanuatu government, given its mandate to develop a national customary land law and increase the productivity of the rural sector. Local solutions to land disputes inevitably are products of vested interest, unevenly distributed knowledge, and differential abilities of speakers in a public forum. Such solutions are not permanent and, as we have seen from the actions of 'masters of tradition', they are not always 'fair' by the standards of Western law, which, although foreign to Vanuatu custom, is what underpins much economic activity of the type in which ni-Vanuatu increasingly are involved.

Another dimension of this space between contradictions concerns land registration. Although land belongs by constitutional right to the custom owners, no provision for registering title to customary land, or transferring customary land to freehold, has yet been legislated. The government claims that absence of registered title inhibits land development in the rural areas (Republic of Vanuatu, 1993:124). This may not be so at present, given that depressed copra prices in themselves inhibit development. But it is certainly the case that custom owners have been promised the option of land title registration from the time of independence, that little or no progress has been made toward achieving this goal, and that it remains important to the national government. It is also possible that the government finds it more palatable to blame rural development problems on the absence of a customary land registration scheme than on other factors. After all, land is a problem that has plagued the islands since the earliest days of the Condominium. 'Land problems' provide an explanation that everyone can accept for why something has not happened, even if the details of those 'land problems' are not specified or understood.

Conclusion

Kastom can only operate at a national level as a vague symbol of unity as it is a symbol predicated on differences in local custom which carry the risk of disunity. An autocratic government might be able to impose a degree of uniformity on the diversity of land tenure principles and practices in the archipelago, as occurred in Fiji. However, Vanuatu politics precludes simple solutions to the problem of drafting legislation to register customary title. Customary solutions to land disputes are most easily found at a local level. The acknowledged control by local people over land dispute settlement allows the national government to buy time to work out the complexities of possible registration and of island courts. Moreover, it allows local people a breathing space in which to continue to sort out land claims in a more flexible way, and with greater local

108 LAND, CUSTOM AND PRACTICE IN THE SOUTH PACIFIC

vested interest, than is likely if registration of customary title were to become possible at a national level. In other words, in post-independence Vanuatu the government has succeeded in its goal of retaining customary tenure as the basis of rural life. But it has done so, at least partly, through the failure to implement laws and practices related to customary land tenure at a higher level.

The changes in land tenure practices elsewhere in the Pacific that seem socially destructive, in Ward's (1993) sense, are less evident in Longana because customary practices there have ridden, and been allowed to ride, waves of change. Principles of customary land holding still provide some access to land for all and an illusion of equality in a situation cross-cut by inequalities of wealth and control over land holdings. There is still a gap between relatively large land holders and the numerous small holders, but social differentiation along these lines has not increased much in the past fifteen years. One reason is increasing inequality between Longana people in urban centres and those in the rural areas; these inequalities are no doubt greater than those within the rural area and follow different lines.

Not only are changes in land tenure in Longana to date, both in terms of 'masters of tradition' and post-independence land law, insufficient to be socially destructive, it is suggested here that it may be inappropriate to consider them in that way. The Longana material lets us see that contradictions within customary tenure and between *kastom* as an invented tradition and customary practices can be productive. They can provide the time in which changes, albeit sometimes unrecognised ones, take shape without necessarily causing conflict between contradictory ideas, institutions, laws, and practices. Land tenure is dynamic, never totally in or entirely out of synchronisation with the rest of social life. It is an ongoing process of negotiation between different interests, a way of seizing or missing different opportunities, and a language for expressing degrees of exclusivity and mutual obligation.

CHAPTER 4

From Corporate to Individual Land Tenure in Western Samoa

J. Tim O'Meara

Individual land tenure is now widely established in Western Samoa, and with it economic individualism. The process has taken well over a century, however, and it has not been easy. Early missionary attempts to instil individualism in the Samoans went unheeded (Meleisea, 1987:18). The missionary, George Turner, lamented that:

> [the] system of common interest in each other's property . . . is still clung to by the Samoans with great tenacity. . . . This communistic system is a sad hindrance to the industrious, and eats like a canker-worm at the roots of individual or national progress. (1884:160)

Speaking of that early era, Meleisea argued that:

> The foundation of the Samoan economy and *fa'a Samoa* [the 'Samoan way'] was subsistence agriculture based on descent group tenure and ownership of land, and for social and political institutions to have changed, the system of land tenure would have had to change. The Samoan system made economic individualism impossible. (1987:18)

Later, the New Zealand administration's attempts to 'press the evolution of land usage toward individualism provoked opposition, even though of their own momentum changes seem to be slowly setting in that direction' (Keesing, 1934:287). On the eve of independence, Marsack warned that 'while the *matai* [chiefly] system still stands in Western Samoa there can necessarily be no individual ownership of small pieces of Samoan customary land or small plantations thereon' (1961:28).

Nevertheless, changes have now set so far in the direction of individualism that the observations of Turner, Meleisea and Marsack can all

110   LAND, CUSTOM AND PRACTICE IN THE SOUTH PACIFIC

be reversed: individual or national progress is now eating at the roots of Samoa's 'communistic system'; Samoans now worry less that the Samoan system will make economic individualism impossible, and more that their economic individualism will make the Samoan system impossible; and Samoans now claim individual ownership of so much customary land that the *matai* system has changed and weakened as a result.

The 'Communistic System' of Old Samoa

During the early to mid-1800s, before 'Old Samoa' had been greatly affected by European intrusion (cf. Stair, 1897; Watters, 1958a; 1958b), corporate extended families, called *'aiga*, owned nearly all residential and agricultural land, as well as houses, canoes, and other resources.[1] Membership in a corporate *'aiga* included anyone who could trace descent through either male or female links to the group's founder, and who participated actively in the family's affairs. Most people maintained full membership in at least the four separate *'aiga* of their respective grandparents, with the strength of their claims in other *'aiga* tailing off gradually, rather than membership being explicitly bounded.

Although some *'aiga* members moved away for marriage or other reasons, the remaining members, together with their spouses and children and perhaps adopted children and occasional hangers-on, all lived on the *'aiga*'s residence site and cooperated in the use of the family's land and other resources, all under the direction of and serving the family *matai*, or 'chief'. Authority, or *pule*, over the use of the corporate family's lands and other resources and over those living on the family's land was vested in a particular *matai* name, or title, which was an office specific to that family. The authority vested in this title was exercised by successive titleholders, but ownership of the land and other resources remained with the corporate *'aiga* in perpetuity. Therefore land that was appurtenant to a *matai* title was never inherited by a person. Thus although Schultz states that 'land is the chief article of inheritance', his subsequent discussion appropriately concerns only principles of *'aiga* membership and succession to the family *matai* title, not the inheritance of land as such (1911:51–2).

Some corporate *'aiga* controlled two or more *matai* titles, in which case one title was superior to the other. The superior title was that of an *ali'i* (high chief), while the subservient title was that of a *tulafale* (orator chief). In such cases a separate plot or plots was usually designated as appurtenant to the subservient title, but the *ali'i* retained ultimate control over the plots and over the subservient titleholder. Some *tulafale* titles controlled families and land in their own right, however, and were not subservient to an *ali'i* title.

WESTERN SAMOA

Titleholders were almost all male and held their titles for life, rarely being deposed or assassinated by their *'aiga*. When near death, a *matai* conferred his title on a successor in a living will called a *mavaega* (Stair, 1897:75). If a chief died without appointing a successor, the *'aiga potopoto*, consisting of the leading members of the corporate *'aiga*, gathered from around Samoa at the official residence site of that title to name a successor. The successor was usually an elder son or younger brother of the previous titleholder, but not necessarily one then residing with the family. Lacking an appropriate cognatic successor, the title might even go to an adopted son, a son-in-law, or under threat even to a complete outsider. In such cases it was the family's intention that the title return to a cognatic member in the following generation, but noncognates 'often succeeded in keeping by force the position only temporarily allotted to them, and in assuring the succession to their own blood relatives' (Schultz, 1911:52–3).

If a chief did not already live at his title's residence site, he soon moved there, took over the principal house as his residence, and began directing family affairs. Once his status was ratified by the other chiefs of the village or district at a special kava ceremony (*saofa'i*), he could exercise the broader authority and responsibility vested in his office, not only assuming internal control over and responsibility for the family and its resources and often directing family religious matters, but also representing the family and advancing its interests in village council meetings and other political, social, and ceremonial affairs.

In old Samoa chiefs possessed 'great power over their relatives and dependents, which they used as they pleased, and were irresponsible to any other authority' (Stair, 1897:76; also Kramer, 1902, 1[2]:17–8). Untitled men 'were ever ready to carry out the commands of their chief, no matter how tyrannical' (Stair, 1897:124). Thus, occupants of family land might be at some risk should the title go to a rival or outsider. Paramount, however, was the family's need to present a strong and united front in the village. Turner emphasised the importance of maintaining 'the numerical strength of family', so that 'if a family is numerically strong, no one dares to injure them' (1884:173, 178, 221). Schultz noted that one family was sometimes 'subjugated by a stronger family', and that:

> quarrels over inheritance are extremely frequent. If it came . . . to deeds of violence, as it often did in earlier days, the victory fell of course not to right but to might. Further instances of . . . 'Might before Right' were given in the countless civic wars of past Samoan history. A rightful heir who belonged to the defeated party had to submit to be dispossessed by a relation who sided with the victors. (Schultz, 1911:52)

112 LAND, CUSTOM AND PRACTICE IN THE SOUTH PACIFIC

Judicial proceedings of a *fono*, or 'council' of chiefs, were usually held by the whole village or district against an offending family, but grievances were sometimes pressed by one family against another 'if the aggrieved party was strong enough', and orders by the *fono* were sometimes resisted, causing wars 'if the culprits felt themselves strong enough to do so' (Stair, 1897:91). Schultz claimed that 'club law' was the ultimate rule (1911:52).

The role of villages, districts, and larger alliances in the control of land

While corporate *'aiga* claimed ownership of plots developed by their residents, the village *fono* and its paramount titles protected and exercised eminent domain over all village lands. These usually included all the territory from the offshore reefs fronting the village residence sites to the forested peaks high above their garden lands. Villages 'considered themselves perfectly distinct from each other, quite independent, and at liberty to act as they pleased on their own ground, and in their own affairs' (Turner, 1884:180). A village acted as a unit primarily to maintain peace and harmony between its constituent families and to defend its members and territory.

Eight or ten related villages 'united by common consent . . . for mutual protection' to form districts, or *itumalo* (Turner, 1884:180). Districts played little or no role in the internal control or management of land, but if members of a different district threatened or encroached upon a constituent village's land, the threat was countered by all the villages of the district acting under district leadership.

Territorial and family alliances larger or more widespread than a district once fought together in large-scale wars to defend their combined populations and territories or lay waste to others. Upolu and Savaii islands each had three semi-permanent territorial alliances. In addition to or overlapping these territorial alliances, 'close blood relationships of one chiefly family to places often quite remote led to treaties of mutual assistance in warfare' (Kramer, 1902 1[2]:24).

The paramount title(s) of each *'aiga*, village, district, and territorial alliance thus organised and led the protection of all lands at their respective hierarchical levels. This authority to intercede against an outside threat is known as *pule fa'amalumalu* (sometimes *pule fa'amamalu* or *pule fa'amalu*), which literally means 'protective authority'.

'The holder of a *pule fa'amamalu* will not normally interfere in any way with the management of the land by any of the *matais* under whose immediate *pule* it has been placed, provided that *pule* is exercised according to the rules' (Marsack, 1961:24). If an outsider attempts to interfere, however, the *pule fa'amamalu* holder steps in to defend the lands, but 'then retires and leaves the management of the lands to the holder of

WESTERN SAMOA 113

the immediate *pule'* (Marsack, 1961:24; see also Keesing, 1934:270). *Pule fa'amalumalu* was thus an integral part of the strategic hierarchy of alliances developed during ancient times, when disputes over land were causes of 'the frequent and bloody wars in which the natives so constantly engaged' (Stair, 1897:57).

Individual land ownership in Old Samoa

Particular households or individuals within an *'aiga* often worked their own designated plots or sections (Williamson, 1924:240), but everyone contributed to a common resource pool controlled by the *matai*. These designated subdivisions of family land were often carried over from one generation to the next, but they could be revoked by the *matai* at any time and so did not constitute individual ownership regardless of the duration of occupation (Williamson, 1924:261).

Reports from the early 1800s to the early 1900s indicate that some individuals did own and inherit particular plots of land on occasion in Old Samoa. Such cases were rare, however, and usually lasted only until the owner could acquire a *matai* title and establish a new corporate family based on that land. Thus, the 'personal rights of some individuals to certain sites and lands were recognised, but as a general rule the lands belonged to the family as a whole, though the recognised head of the family exercised a supreme right' (Williamson, 1924:239). Schultz states that 'land that anyone has received by inheritance, or as the gift of a third party, or has acquired with his own means – the payment consists in mats, pigs, etc., and lately also in money – is private property and subject to no family control' (1911:44). According to Mead, 'individual ownership of land is rare and sporadic', and she describes one case in which a new corporate *'aiga* was founded on land that had been individually owned for one generation (1930:71–2).

While individual ownership of land was well outside the norm in Old Samoa, it could follow from the recognised powers or discretion of chiefs, the limits of whose authority were more pragmatic than principled. Land and Titles Commission records mention an instance in Vaega, for example, when land was given to an individual as *togiola*, literally 'payment to live'. The vicious warrior priest, Tamafaiga, had threatened to kill all the women of a local *'aiga* after one of them stole a ceremonial fine mat intended for him. Massacre was only averted when the offending family gave a prime coastal residence site to one of Tamafaiga's daughters. According to court testimony this must have occurred in the 1820s and the plot is still individually owned by heirs of Tamafaiga's daughter today, although it was formally divided by the commission in the early 1900s to halt bickering among the heirs.

114 LAND, CUSTOM AND PRACTICE IN THE SOUTH PACIFIC

Permanent transfer of land

Developed land could be legitimately transferred from one owner to another in Old Samoa. Steubel records that transfers were 'justified' to repay a variety of favours, and he notes that such land 'will belong to the new owner forever' (1987:177). Mead reports that 'a piece of land may constitute either dowry or bride price' (1930:70). In the research villages of Vaega, Neiafu and Malie, plots have been transferred as: dowry; gift to support a son who had been adopted out; trade for a more conveniently located plot; repayment for the gift of a pig or fine mat; repayment of a cash loan; 'pawn' to acquire money; payment for food and for armaments in time of war; and as *togiola*.

Europeans investigating land tenure in Old Samoa concentrated their inquiries on the possibility of permanent sale or gift of land (see Williamson, 1924:241–4). Common opinion (e.g. Turner, 1884:176–7) was that a *matai* could legitimately alienate part of his title lands with the concurrence of leading family members, and village lands could be alienated with the concurrence (and for the benefit) of all resident families:

> An ideal *matai* will control his regiment in patriarchal style, and in important family affairs will undertake nothing without first consulting with his family or his own branch of it. A legal limitation [i.e. one enforced by the Land and Titles Commission] of his power (*pule*) exists with respect to his authority over the land – *fanua lau'ele'ele* – which belongs to the family. (Schultz, 1911:43–4)

Given the ubiquitous testaments to the 'tyrannical' powers of chiefs in Old Samoa, many chiefs presumably strayed from this ideal of consultation.

Temporal continuity and geographical uniformity of land tenure customs

Available evidence indicates broad geographical uniformity in land tenure and other customs throughout Old Samoa, with a 'uniformity of customs and language' prevailing from 'one end of the group to the other' (Turner, 1884:166). Regional differences in land tenure were not reported in Old Samoa, nor do contemporary Samoans believe there were (or are) such differences. Instead, a uniform set of formal practices and principles known as *aganu'u* were and are recognised throughout Samoa. Political intrigues of particular families and villages sometimes resulted in minor, local variations, called *agaifanua*, which provided historical charters for a new status quo. However, these local variations resulted from the same general social processes and prerogatives found elsewhere. Thus, *aganu'u* and *agaifanua* both imply formal practices of

WESTERN SAMOA

relatively ancient derivation. Both are equally 'traditional' in the sense of being old and accepted aspects of village life. Both serve as *fa'avae*, meaning 'foundation' or 'charter', for their respective social groups and are therefore accepted by the contemporary Land and Titles Court.

Samoans today describe as their customary land tenure a set of principles and practices which closely match those reported by Europeans in the nineteenth century, those recorded in early Land and Titles Commission records, and those elicited by researchers throughout the twentieth century (e.g. LTC, 1903–1906; Schultz, 1911; Mead, 1930; Keesing, 1934; Nayacakalou, 1960; Marsack, 1961; Farrell and Ward, 1962; Holmes, 1971; Sutter, 1971; S. Tiffany, 1974, 1980; W. Tiffany, 1975; O'Meara, 1987, 1990).

Not all land holding practices conform to *aganu'u* and *agaifanua*, of course, either in Old Samoa or today. Particular claims were, and are, disputed. Accepted *agaifanua* or even *aganu'u* were sometimes transgressed and new ones established. Nevertheless, adult villagers, especially *matai*, distinguish between the principles of customary land tenure, about which there is wide agreement, and deviations from those customary principles that appear in their own practices or in those of the Land and Titles Court. Thus, the orthodox land tenure principles and practices of Old Samoan *aganu'u* and *agaifanua* are still well known today even though not always followed. If such deviations stand for three or four generations, the span of personal observation of any living person, they can gain the imprimatur of local tradition, and if they also become widespread enough, they would eventually become accepted as part of 'Samoan custom'. The contemporary changes in land tenure practice described below have not yet reached that stage.

Attempts to change and then to maintain the land tenure of Old Samoa

Colonists arriving in Old Samoa were always interested in acquiring land. During the 1860s land speculation accelerated, leading Germany, Great Britain, and the USA to the brink of war in 1889, before a treaty between these 'great powers' banned further sales of land and set up a tripartite Land Commission to settle disputes over previous sales. Claims then amounted to more than double the entire land area of the archipelago. The commission eventually registered as freehold only eight per cent of the area claimed, although two-thirds of the claims were wholly or partially confirmed (Gilson, 1970:410–1). Land not recognised as freehold or claimed later by the German administration remained as 'customary land' and now makes up about 80 per cent of the land area of Western Samoa, including nearly all the residential and agricultural lands of rural villages (see Figure 4.1). Sixteen per cent of all land is

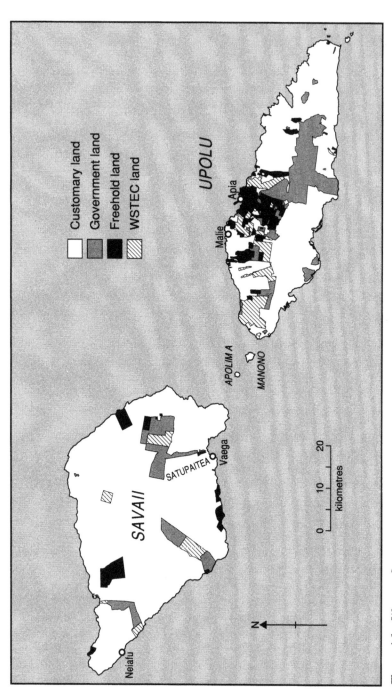

Figure 4.1 Western Samoa.

WESTERN SAMOA 117

'government' or public land, mostly in mountainous areas or in the Western Samoa Trust Estates Corporation (WSTEC) lands which were taken by the New Zealand government as war reparations after the First World War. Only about four per cent of all land is privately held 'freehold', and most of that is concentrated in the Apia town area and along the commercial plantation belt of northwest Upolu.

In Old Samoa disputes over land and *matai* titles often turned violent, as there was 'an ever-present willingness to test the rights of any dispute by force' (Keesing, 1934:269). In 1899, however, the three great powers granted exclusive control over the western group of islands to Germany, and the German administration quickly halted the violence which, although endemic to Old Samoa, had been fuelled by recent colonial intrigues. Following the success of the Land Commission and German pacification, Samoans sometimes took their disputes over land and *matai* titles to the colonial government (or had them brought before it) for peaceful resolution. In 1903 the Governor, Dr Solf, set up a formal administrative tribunal called the 'Land and Titles Commission', with himself as head. In settling disputes, the commission 'followed as closely as possible the Samoan usage' (Keesing, 1934:277), meaning as closely as was amenable to the operation of an administrative tribunal and to broader German colonial interests.

When New Zealand forces took Western Samoa from Germany at the outbreak of the First World War, the new administration carried over the Land and Titles Commission and the rest of the German colonial bureaucracy virtually unchanged (Meleisea, 1987:102–3, 118–9). Ten years later the New Zealand administration attempted to individualise Samoan land tenure in two stages. In 1924 the New Zealand Administrator stated in his annual report:

> I am convinced that the existing native land laws or customs will retard [Samoans'] development, and therefore, in their own interests, as well as in the interests of the Territory, these laws should be changed. To change the system of land-tenure will be by far the most difficult problem in Samoa. Those interested in retaining the present system are the chiefs and leaders of the people . . . who are very jealous of their rights to exercise authority over their lands. (Quoted in Keesing, 1934:279)

The administration first convinced the pliant *Fono* of *Faipule*, the local Samoan legislature, to institute a system of individual leasehold similar to that operating in Tonga (see Chapter 5), except that allocations were to be made voluntarily by village *fono* from their forest lands (Keesing, 1934:280). Such allotments were not to be sold or subleased, and the individual holder was to remain under the control of his *matai*. Furthermore, when the holder died, the land was to revert to the control

118 LAND, CUSTOM AND PRACTICE IN THE SOUTH PACIFIC

of the *fono*, and the holder's heirs were not to succeed to it if they had equivalent land elsewhere. The administration's proposal was, in effect, to create 'two recognised forms of native land ownership in Samoa, the older *fa'aSamoa* kind of title, which would still continue to apply to the existing cultivations [and residence sites], and the new more individualistic title' (Keesing, 1934:280).

The surveying and registering of leases progressed very slowly under the New Zealand plan for lack of funds. Nevertheless, during the first three years about one-third of all villages proceeded on their own to allot 'areas of approximately the prescribed size to young men without property' (Keesing, 1934:280-1).

> Such a move, though in the direction of individualism and tending to undermine the integrity of the communal or family group, was no great violation of Samoan usage. It merely stimulated and gave formal recognition to the older custom by which the *matai* or *tapanu'u* [high chiefly title(s) overseeing village lands], by virtue of his *pule*, allowed eligible people to take up uncultivated land or occupy a house lot in the village. (Keesing, 1934:281)

Allocations of forest land may have been made on occasion in Old Samoa, but probably only to chiefs. Lands of corporate *'aiga* were often allocated internally to separate households or even individuals, but the early literature does not indicate the allocation of forest land to untitled men, who had very low status. Stair describes them as a 'useful class' of warriors, farmers, fishermen, and cooks who 'smarted under the tyranny of their masters' and whose lot was 'little if any better than slavery' (1897:74-5). Von Bulow says that untitled men were bondsmen and were called 'stinking pigs', and that while a high chief might make a bondsman an orator chief and give him a piece of land as a way of rewarding or soliciting a follower, the high chief could later take back the property and kill or drive away the bondsman (cited in Williamson, 1924:248). Thus, the sweeping allocations of forest land to untitled men in the 1920s show how much Samoa had already changed from the first days of European contact.

Keesing provides no clue as to why village councils made individual allotments of forest land in the 1920s. Judging from practices today, however, their motive was probably to reduce conflict among farmers competing for land as they expanded cash cropping. The individual allocation of forest areas – called *fua*, or 'measurements' – is now standard practice in villages which have dwindling reserves of forest land. Such allotments are usually made to all *matai* who head economically independent households, though untitled men who head independent households sometimes receive allotments as well. *Matai* may claim the developed plots by their respective titles in the customary manner, but

WESTERN SAMOA 119

most claim individual ownership instead. Untitled men necessarily claim their allotments by individual ownership. Individual *fua* are not often designated in villages which have an abundance of forest land, but newly cleared plots in such villages are nevertheless almost always owned by the individual (or individuals) who develop them. As a result, individual ownership has come to exist alongside what Keesing called 'the older *fa'aSamoa* kind of title', just as the New Zealand administration envisaged in the 1920s. This did not come to pass immediately.

> When . . . at a *Fono* of May 1926, the authorities proposed that a system of direct inheritance of land be instituted under which the Samoans were to be 'empowered to bequeath their cultivated areas of land to their next-of-kin, or near relatives, in lieu of the present system, which provides for the clan or whole of the members of the family selecting a successor to the deceased head of the family, who thereby acquired the control of the family land,' even the acquiescent *Faipules* [legislators] refused to take action. In reality such a regulation would for all intents and purposes negate the existing *pules*, allow the individual holders to be free of family control of the *matai* in which this is vested, and indeed involve a revolution not only in land usage, but also in the entire family and social system. (Keesing, 1934:281)

Most Samoans bitterly opposed the administration's proposed 'revolution'. Their resistance to colonial rule was strengthened because individualisation of their land tenure would have greatly disrupted their society, further weakened the traditional authority of the *matai*, increased the risk of exploitation by foreigners, and because it was imposed from outside and did not appear to be in their own interests in the economic conditions of the time. By 1936 the Samoans had won substantial concessions toward local self-government, including the Native Land and Titles Protection Ordinance of 1934, which guaranteed that customary land would continue to be held 'according to the customs and usages of the Samoan race'. This legislation 'provided an official barrier to too-rapid acculturation', but at the same time it 'has hampered changes that the Samoan people may have wished to make of their own volition. It has not entirely stopped evolutionary processes, but it has certainly retarded their development' (Farrell and Ward, 1962:195).

In spite of the concessions, Samoan leaders did not trust New Zealand, with its heritage of presumptive individual rights, to protect Samoan customary land from individualisation (Tuiatua Tupua Tamasese, 1992a:24). Recognising that the viability of *fa'aSamoa* depended on *matai* control of their title lands, Samoan leaders thus sought political independence from New Zealand not only to free Samoa from outside control (and to assert their own), but also to preserve *matai* control over family land and thereby to maintain *fa'aSamoa* (ibid.:25). As

120 LAND, CUSTOM AND PRACTICE IN THE SOUTH PACIFIC

Nayacakalou observed, 'there is in Western Samoa an extremely close integration of the system of land tenure with the social and political systems; they are interdependent, so that a change in land tenure must closely affect the entire social order' (1960:120).

Resistance culminated in 1962, when Western Samoa achieved political independence, with a constitution Articles 100 and 101 of which declare that the new nation is to be based on 'Samoan custom and tradition' and that customary land is to be 'held in accordance with Samoan custom and usage and with the law relating to Samoan custom and usage'. With these guarantees, the continuity of *fa'aSamoa* and the control of *matai* over their *'aiga's* lands might seem assured. But the guarantees were compromised at the outset by the constitution itself, which abridges chiefly control over customary land by maintaining the colonial-era ban on its permanent alienation or transfer, by continuing the state's tight control over leases, by numerous other abridgments of *matai* authority in favour of state authority, and by continuing operations of the Land and Titles Court, which was carried over virtually unchanged from the colonial era.

Court-induced changes

From its inception the official role of the court was to settle disputes peacefully, to protect customary lands and titles from illicit claims, and to register rightful claims in order to improve the security of tenure and thus enhance development. The Samoan leadership later promoted the court 'as a neo-traditional bulwark of Samoan custom, and . . . the Court is now regarded as a mechanism integral to the maintenance of chiefship' (Powles, 1986:206). But successive administrations have also employed the court to protect individuals from the sometimes authoritarian rule of chiefs and to generally undermine or usurp the traditional powers of family chiefs, village councils, and the once-powerful *Pule* and *Tumua* alliances of orator chiefs (Meleisea, 1987:83–4, 103; Tuiatua Tupua Tamasese, 1992b:1, 13). Court records and widespread public testimony also suggest that it has been used on occasion to reward government or *'aiga* supporters and harass opponents.

Though the commission was renamed a 'court' in 1934, it has continued to operate more as an administrative tribunal than as a court of law (Marsack, 1961:4; Va'ai, 1993). The only major change from Governor Solf's days is that disputants now argue before a panel of respected *matai* appointed by the Samoan government. Disputants still argue their claims without legal representation (though lawyers help prepare major cases), and there is no cross examination of witnesses. The Court has no written codes or statutes to guide its deliberations, nor does it present

WESTERN SAMOA

written or verbal opinions which might constitute a body of legal precedent. Instead, judges and other senior court officers say that each case is decided 'on its own merits' (pers. comm. 1983, 1984, 1993).

Even some of the court's administrative policies undermine Samoan 'customs and usages'. The broad social change toward individualism has been spurred by a seemingly innocuous administrative rule in the 1934 Ordinance (amended as the Land and Titles Act 1981), which requires the registrar to act upon a petition, oral or written, presented by 'any interested Samoan' (Section 82). Registrars have consistently interpreted 'any interested Samoan' to mean anyone who claims a connection with the land, title, or people involved, and the registrar almost always acts by ordering a halt to the protested activity until the matter can be sorted out. The practical effect of such support for individual rights is not only to open the court to all manner of spurious or malicious suits (O'Meara, 1987:142–3), but also to revoke virtually all but token *matai* authority over family members and family lands.

The current registrar states that when the customary *pule* over lands and titles is unclear or when the family cannot reach a consensus, 'the court decides' who will hold the disputed plot or title and how they will act (Galumalemana N. Schmidt, pers. comm. 1993; also court records). But because of the changes described in this chapter, customary *pule* is now rarely clear, and disputants rarely reach a lasting consensus. With the number of disputes before the court continually rising, the lion's share of *pule* has thus come to lie with the court itself: *'E pule le Fa'amasinoga.*

Grassroots changes

Changes to Samoan land tenure have also come from the grassroots level. Evidence gathered from hundreds of petitions and court cases in the archives of the Land and Titles Court, from early ethnographic reports, from discussions with elders who participated in the changes of the early 1900s, and from scores of family histories recounted by a younger generation all show that the de facto individualisation of land tenure was well under way as the new constitution was being debated. Even at the height of the *Mau* resistance 30 years earlier, Keesing found that profound changes were apparent under the surface traditionalism.

> A casual student of land matters in the modern Samoa might well think that little change has taken place. He would find, so far as he was able to penetrate behind the jealous veil of secrecy, that old land customs and ideas are still alive, and that the Samoans display little desire to take over those of the white man. Nevertheless, deeper study will show that in the last century the Samoan land system has been vastly modified: there have been factors at work that have tended on the one hand to stabilise and on the other to disorganise it. (Keesing, 1934:273)

122 LAND, CUSTOM AND PRACTICE IN THE SOUTH PACIFIC

Reflecting on the pre-independence era, many Samoans recall that they lived then as members of large extended families which still owned land and operated as corporate units under the autocratic control of their *matai*, with *tasi le suafa, tasi le umu, tasi le tagatupe, tasi le fa'aputuga 'ie toga* – 'one chief, one cooking oven, one money purse, one collection of ceremonial fine mats'. Court records show, however, that splitting and sharing *matai* titles was already common immediately after German pacification, and shortly after mid-century a combination of political and economic motives initiated more than three decades of wholesale splitting, sharing, and creating of titles (S. Tiffany, 1975; Powles, 1979:8–9; O'Meara, 1990:151–6). As a result, nearly all men (and many women) are chiefs today, and virtually every household has its own cooking oven, money purse, and collection of fine mats.[2]

In addition, by accepted village principles and practices, individuals now own most plots of land, houses, and other resources which they use primarily for the direct benefit of themselves and their nuclear families. The traditional 'Samoan desire for permanence in the relationship of title to land' (Powles, 1979:9) has been erased. Both ownership and *pule* are now usually inherited by the children of the former owners without regard to the particular *matai* titles any of them might hold, and increasingly within the last 10 years even without regard to whether they hold *matai* status at all. Thus, individuals have replaced corporate *'aiga* as the primary land-owning units, nuclear family households have replaced multi-household extended families as the primary socio-economic units, and economic individualism has largely replaced the 'communistic system' of Old Samoa.

Case Studies of Land Tenure in Modern Samoa

Detailed evidence of contemporary land tenure principles and practices is available from three villages, including Vaega and Neiafu on Savaii, and Malie on Upolu (see Figure 4.1). The most complete data were gathered from Vaega during two research periods – the first covering about 10 months during 1982 and 1983, which was part of a broader research project covering 34 months between 1979 and 1984 (O'Meara, 1986; 1990), and the second during nearly four months of field research in 1993. Comparative data for Neiafu and Malie were collected during four months of field research in 1984 (O'Meara, 1987). All Land and Titles Court cases and petitions concerning land were read for the district of Satupaitea, in which Vaega is located, and for the villages of Neiafu and Malie. Informal inquiries were also made in other villages between 1981 and 1994.

WESTERN SAMOA

Vaega lands in 1983

In 1982–83 the author mapped Vaega's 195 agricultural plots (totalling 522 hectares) and 36 residence sites, interviewed all 32 resident *matai* and several untitled men and women and attended numerous court cases, village *fono* deliberations, and informal discussions on land matters in the village. Interviews were in colloquial Samoan and covered a range of questions concerning the history of use, ownership, and *pule* of every plot in which the interviewee claimed some interest. Questionable interview claims were checked with third parties and with court records when necessary, but no attempt was made to determine which of conflicting claims was 'correct'. Instead, the most conservative claim was used as the basis for cataloguing plots according to tenure type (see Figures 4.3 and 4.4). Thus, if the court or any member of the family claimed that a plot was held according to orthodox custom, the plot was logged accordingly.

Village residents habitually distinguish between plots they claim under orthodox customary tenure and plots they claim under contemporary individual tenure. They commonly label lands under customary tenure as *fanua fa'aleaganu'u*, literally 'customary lands', and they describe the older of these as *fanua fa'avae* – the 'foundation lands' of a corporate *'aiga*. Plots under individual tenure are *fanua sa'oloto* ('free lands') or *fanua totino* ('one's own land'), or more descriptively, *fanua o a'u lava*, 'land belonging only to me'. Similarly, a chief identifies lands owned by the corporate *'aiga* to which his title belongs as *fanua o lo'u suafa*, 'lands of my title', in contrast to *fanua o lo'u tino*, 'lands of my body', which he owns as an individual person.

Lands held under orthodox customary tenure are also called *fanua fai tele*, 'lands used by many'. Individually-owned lands may come to be 'used by many' after a generation or two of direct inheritance by the owner's offspring, but such lands are easily distinguished by further questioning. People say that 'foundation lands' are 'owned' by corporate *'aiga*, so asking 'who owns' such a plot, *'O ai e ona lea fanua?*, yields a response such as 'The Family of the Saua Title', *Sa Saua*. Asking 'who owns' a plot with multiple individual owners, on the other hand, yields a response such as 'Only my brothers and I', *Na'o matou ma o'u uso*.

Many agricultural plots and residence sites have been informally apportioned or divided for use by different households or individuals, and everyday authority is often delegated to those who occupy and work the land. Villagers are quick to distinguish this limited *pule o le fa'ato'aga*, 'authority over the garden', from the more fundamental and overriding *pule o le fanua*, 'authority over the land'. They describe temporary allocations of land with such phrases as *'Ua tufa fa'ato'aga, 'ae le'i tufa le pule*,

124 LAND, CUSTOM AND PRACTICE IN THE SOUTH PACIFIC

'the gardens have been distributed, but not the authority'; or *'Ua vaevae fanua, 'ae le'i vae motu,* 'the lands have been divided, but not completely broken off'.

Family title lands are sometimes divided permanently among individual heirs, however, in which case they are described as *vae motu,* 'divided completely broken off', or *tufa motu,* 'distributed completely broken off'. When the heirs of a corporate *'aiga* formally divide the family lands, 'each person gets their own piece of land', *'E tofu le tagata ia ma lana fasi fanua.*[3] Heirs then virtually always claim their respective shares under individual tenure. Such permanent divisions of *'aiga* land require the consent of all branches of the *'aiga potopoto* at a formal meeting, usually held at the title's official residence site. The residence site itself is rarely divided formally – that being expressly prohibited by the Court – but informal and essentially permanent divisions are very common.

In 1983 over three-quarters of residence sites in Vaega were still held more or less according to orthodox corporate tenure ('Old tenure' on Figure 4.2). The remaining residence sites included two small sections recently reclaimed from the sea which were classed as 'New tenure', four plots which had been given over to 'Church or school', and a few others classed as 'Changed to new' tenure by virtue of having been formally distributed to individual heirs. In contrast, only one-third of the 195 agricultural plots (22 per cent by area) were still owned by corporate *'aiga* in more or less the customary manner (see Figure 4.3). Forty per cent of all agricultural plots (58 per cent by area) had been owned individually under 'New tenure' since first being cleared, beginning about 1923 or 1924. Another quarter of all agricultural plots (14 per cent by area) were once held according to custom, but had been formally apportioned by the corporate *'aiga* among their respective heirs, who then owned the plots as individuals under 'Changed to new' tenure. Two-thirds of all agricultural plots (72 per cent by area) were thus claimed under individual tenure in 1983 in the two categories of 'New' and 'Changed to new' tenure. Seven other agricultural plots (six per cent by area) supported the local church and village schools.

Neiafu lands in 1984

In 1984, the author interviewed 31 *matai* (including one woman) in Neiafu village, or just under half of all resident *matai*, plus three untitled men, and assorted family members who attended some interviews (O'Meara, 1987:99–101). The histories of use, ownership, and *pule* of 167 plots, probably half of all village plots, were recorded.

As in Vaega, nearly three-quarters of the house sites recorded in Neiafu were still held by corporate *'aiga,* the rest having been formally

WESTERN SAMOA 125

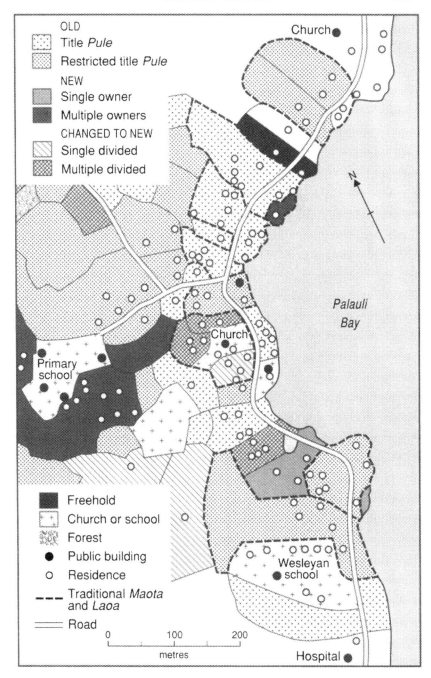

Figure 4.2 Type of tenure within Vaega village, 1993.
Source: Field survey. Boundaries of coastal residence sites are approximate only.

126 LAND, CUSTOM AND PRACTICE IN THE SOUTH PACIFIC

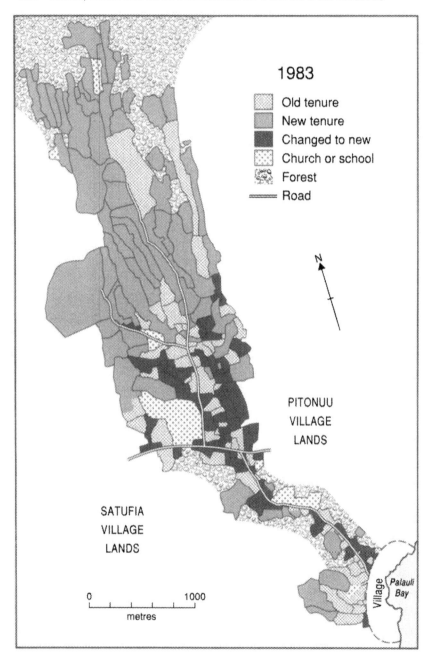

Figure 4.3 Type of tenure of agricultural plots, Vaega village, 1983.
Source: Field survey. Map based on O'Meara, 1987:86.

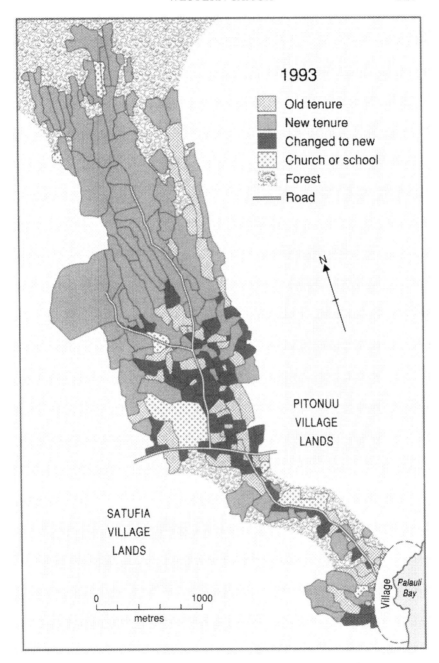

Figure 4.4 Type of tenure of agricultural plots, Vaega village, 1993.
Source: Field survey.

128 LAND, CUSTOM AND PRACTICE IN THE SOUTH PACIFIC

apportioned or divided among individual heirs. Several apportioned sites were former agricultural lands along the new inland road, which are much easier to apportion among heirs than title residence sites. Only one-third of all agricultural plots recorded were still held according to customary tenure, while two-thirds were held under individual tenure. Almost half of all recorded agricultural plots were cleared from the forest after the Second World War, and virtually all of these plots have been held under individual tenure from the beginning. The earliest use of individual tenure recorded was about 1928. Nearly one-quarter of all recorded agricultural plots had once been held communally, but had then been formally apportioned among heirs and thereafter owned individually.

Although Neiafu is somewhat more remote and traditional than Vaega, agricultural lands in Neiafu are individually owned and used somewhat more often than in Vaega. The higher incidence of individual tenure in Neiafu is apparently due to three reasons. First, Neiafu's main cash crop, cocoa, is much more valuable than Vaega's main cash crop, copra. Consequently, people have a greater economic incentive to restrict land ownership and use in Neiafu. Even those cocoa lands that are still owned by corporate *'aiga* are almost always divided internally between individual planters who jealously guard their respective trees. Second, Neiafu's forest reserves have facilitated the rapid adoption of individual tenure by providing abundant new land to clear. Third, cocoa is faster maturing and requires less labour than coconuts, which makes it more feasible to develop and maintain new, individually-owned lands.

Malie lands in 1984

Preliminary investigations on Upolu confirmed the trend to individual tenure on that island. Malie, near Apia on the heavily populated north-west coast of Upolu, is short of land and was chosen for study as this shortage might have inhibited the adoption of individual tenure. Fourteen *matai*, nearly one-third of those resident in the village, plus one elderly widow who was head of a household, were interviewed. Information was recorded on 86 plantation and residence plots, probably half of the village total (O'Meara, 1987:101–4). Malie is unusual in that a survey was made of its lands in the 1930s and the map is held in the Department of Lands, Survey, and Environment, Apia. Information was also gathered in Malie in the 1960s by Pitt (1970).

In 1984 two-thirds of the residence sites recorded in Malie were held under corporate *'aiga* tenure; just over one-quarter had been formally divided among heirs and were held individually; and several others were under freehold – a somewhat less traditional pattern than the other two research villages. As in Vaega and Neiafu, only one-fourth of recorded

WESTERN SAMOA   129

agricultural plots in Malie were held according to orthodox customary tenure. Even though Malie is outwardly more Westernised than the Savaii villages, only one-fourth of the agricultural plots recorded were under individual tenure. The remaining half fell in between old and new. Residents said that these plots *tau*, or 'pertain to', a particular *matai* title that has a demonstrated historical relationship with the plot – which accords with orthodox custom – but they denied that anyone other than a resident member of their immediate family could succeed to the title. If someone else did succeed to the title, the residents would then consider it a 'different title' having no authority over the land they themselves occupied. This practice of restricting a title or its recognition to the heirs of the current occupants is directly contrary to custom and, when carried to the extreme, has nearly the same practical effect as claiming individual ownership and inheritance of the land.

Many of the in-between lands had already been divided when family *matai* titles were split or re-split between contenders, thus forming newly independent, land-owning branches of each family. This process also occurred in the other research villages, but less commonly. Such title splitting is sometimes due to the growth and fissioning of *'aiga*, but this is not always the case. Early court records show that title-splitting was already fairly common in the first two decades of this century when Samoa's population had fallen to a low ebb. The freelance survey map of Malie lands made during the 1930s provides similar evidence.

The map lists an estimated population of only 350 people divided into 32 named (but not necessarily corporate) families, including those of the pastor and five part-Europeans. The 32 families consisted of about 70 households. Twenty-one *matai* are shown as controlling specific plots. Seven others are not identified with any plot, but six of these hold titles from other villages, and those titles cannot control land in Malie. The seventh *matai* shares a Malie title with five other men, but unlike them he is not identified as controlling any plots. Three other land holders share another *matai* name in common, but each of them is shown as controlling his own separate plot or plots. One of these three is shown as controlling three agricultural plots while residing on land listed under the name of another title or titleholder. All this suggests de facto individual tenure, or at least that the two titles in question and their corresponding *'aiga* had divided into eight independent branches, each most probably composed of a single household.[4]

Comparison of the 1930s survey map, a 1964 sketch map (Pitt, 1970:101), and the 1984 interview data reveals that where particular plots could be identified in a later period, some had been subdivided. More importantly, some identifiable plots had passed to the control of people who held different *matai* titles than those identified earlier with

130 LAND, CUSTOM AND PRACTICE IN THE SOUTH PACIFIC

the same plots. This indicates de facto individual ownership and inheritance of these plots rather than corporate *'aiga* ownership.[5]

The somewhat different contemporary land tenure pattern in Malie is explained by the absence or reduction of four conditions which have helped cause or facilitate the change to individual tenure in Vaega and Neiafu. First, individual clearing and planting of land is the fastest and surest method of claiming individual ownership, but this avenue has generally not been open to Malie residents because of a severe land shortage throughout most of this century. Early court records and the 1930s map show that in the first decades of this century, Malie residents were moving toward de facto individual tenure until the village ran out of new land to clear just before the Second World War. Significantly, of the recorded plots that have been developed since the government made some additional land available to Malie in the late 1970s, all five are individually owned.

Second, an increase in the number of *matai* titles bestowed in most other villages has greatly facilitated the spread of individual tenure because *matai* status was considered necessary for claiming *pule* even over individually-owned land. But Malie has experienced a shortage of titles as well. From the first legislative elections in 1957 until the introduction of universal suffrage in 1991, only *matai* were allowed to vote, which provided a powerful new incentive for handing out titles.[6] Malie is the Upolu residence of the great Malietoa title, the current holder of which is Western Samoa's head of state. Consequently Malie banned the creation of new titles in order to avoid the unseemly wholesale distribution of titles for election purposes which became common in other villages. Nevertheless, some title splitting and sharing has continued. As a result of the ban on title creation, there were only 45 resident *matai* among Malie's population of 1,825 in 1984, or only one *matai* for every 41 people (including men, women, and children). This compares to one resident *matai* for every 11 people in Vaega and one for every 12 people in Neiafu, which was about the national average. Malie's relatively low number of *matai* titles has limited the number of people gaining *matai* status, which in turn has limited the feasibility of claiming individual ownership of land.

Third, Malie became involved with the Land and Titles Court much earlier and to a greater extent than Vaega and Neiafu, primarily because of its proximity to the court and because of its heavy involvement with the Land Commission in the early 1890s. The mapping of Malie lands in the 1930s had the similar effect of fixing on paper the ownership and *pule* at that time, making later adaptation difficult. Since one of the main purposes of the court was to increase security of tenure by registering ownership and *pule*, it is ironic that by registering them in customary form, the court has impeded the indigenous development of individual tenure whereby people increase their personal security of tenure by severely restricting who may claim usufruct of a plot, who may own and inherit it, and who may exercise *pule* over its use and its produce.

Finally, residents of Vaega and Neiafu explicitly cite disputes over cash crops as the primary catalyst in the break-up of corporate *'aiga* lands, but because of Malie's land shortage, high rate of in-migration, and greater access to wage employment, most agricultural land in Malie is planted in food crops. Food crops and the land on which they are grown are much more likely to be shared than cash crops and cash-crop land. Moreover, Malie's high population – more than three times that of Vaega or Neiafu – includes many relatives who have migrated to Malie from villages that are more distant from Apia. Thus, people living on the same title land in Malie would be much less closely related than in villages where population growth has been by natural reproduction attenuated by out-migration. This dilution of kin ties in Malie would make it more difficult to divide existing title lands among resident heirs or to allocate scarce forest lands for individual clearing and ownership. Immigrant relatives would also have a strong incentive to support orthodox customary tenure, on which they base their residence claims.

Vaega lands in 1993

Formal interviews were conducted in 1993 with the 55 *matai* residing in Vaega, plus several untitled men and women who were heads of households, and other family members who attended interviews. Field maps were updated and new court records for Satupaitea were examined.

Residence sites: Only two changes since 1983 were noted in the formal ownership of residence sites. One unused site was donated to the adjacent church-sponsored secondary school in 1993. The second change concerned the *ali'i* of a recognised corporate *'aiga* who, a decade earlier, had claimed title *pule* over a combined residence and agricultural plot, although this was disputed by the many members of his *'aiga* living on the site. They claimed individual ownership as heirs of their father and grandfather who, they maintained, had first developed the plot, perhaps with the help of the *ali'i*'s own father. In 1993 the *ali'i* conceded that the plot was not under his title *pule*, which thus reclassified the plot from 'Old' to 'New tenure'.

Informal divisions had become more apparent since 1983, including new stone walls and hedges established to publicly mark internal boundaries. Figure 4.2 also shows that some residence sites are claimed quasi-traditionally by 'Restricted title' tenure, where a plot is claimed by title in

132 LAND, CUSTOM AND PRACTICE IN THE SOUTH PACIFIC

the customary way, but title succession or recognition is itself restricted to only close cognatic kin of the current occupants.

Vaega residents recognise eight traditional corporate *'aiga* in their village (Figure 4.2), each with its own *matai* title or (in five cases) branch of a title, its own official residence site (called either *maota* or *laoa*) and one or more other residential and agricultural plots. One of these *'aiga* originated in the nineteenth century when a Vaega man returned with a *matai* title from another village. Another *'aiga* originated about 1900 with the splitting of an existing title.[7] The other six *'aiga* are considerably more ancient.

About 1900, all but one of the developed plots in Vaega were owned by these eight *'aiga* and were subject to the respective authorities of their eight *matai* titles plus four or so subsidiary titles.[8] Each title was held by a single incumbent. Each incumbent of the eight major titles lived on the official residence site of his title, and each incumbent of a subsidiary title lived on a site belonging to the higher title which he served, although the subservient *matai* had some degree of authority over that site and the garden lands he and his family worked. Vaega then had about 225 residents (Pirie, 1964, vol. 2, Figure 4; Jupp, 1956; McArthur, 1967), half today's population of 550, and the village probably cultivated about one-quarter of the land it does now.

The eight traditional corporate *'aiga* in Vaega no longer act as corporate entities for either production or everyday consumption. Several continue, at least nominally, to hold their title residence sites and some other plots more or less according to custom. All eight still function with varying degrees of cohesiveness in important family and village ceremonies and in village political affairs. A major difference now is that most *matai* titles which head these traditional *'aiga* are shared by many individuals, most of whom do not reside on their title's residence site. Many do not reside in the village. Many resident *matai* hold newly-created titles, most of which are shared by several incumbents and have no lands or corporate *'aiga* appurtenant to them.

If the doubling of population during this century were the only factor at work, the number of corporate *'aiga* owning residence sites in the village might have risen from eight to 16. Instead, up to 34 families now have formal or de facto control over their own residence sites (Figure 4.2). In other words, the number of families controlling their own residence sites has grown twice as fast as the population. If economic independence (O'Meara 1990:176–7) rather than ownership of a residence site were the criterion, the roster would include about 60 independent families today, an increase nearly four times that of population growth.

WESTERN SAMOA   133

Agricultural lands: Many agricultural plots have been enlarged since 1983, but no new plots were opened up. Most of the higher gardens were abandoned after the devastating cyclones of late 1990 and early 1992, and others were abandoned in 1993 because of the newly-introduced taro leaf blight.

Interviews in 1993 uncovered 27 changes in the tenure classification of agricultural plots since the 1983 interviews. Twenty of those 27 changes resulted in plots being moved or added to the number of individually-owned plots, which include those of 'New' and 'Changed to new' tenure.[9] Only seven of the 27 changes resulted in plots reverting from individual to corporate ownership.[10] In sum, the 1993 data for Vaega thus show a net increase of 13 agricultural plots (6 per cent) claimed under individual ownership in the decade since 1983. Excluding church and school plots, nearly three-quarters of all agricultural plots in Vaega are now owned by individuals. In addition to these changes in ownership, a more dramatic change has occurred in authority.

New claims of authority for untitled people: In 1983 no one claimed that untitled people could legitimately exercise *pule* over land in their own name, even if the person was recognised as the individual owner or part-owner of a plot. Everyone maintained that *pule* over an untitled person's land was properly exercised by that individual owner's husband, brother, or other relative who held *matai* status. In 1993, however, many people freely asserted that untitled people can, should, or do have legitimate authority over individually owned land. The great majority of those expressing this view were themselves *matai*. Representative statements include:

> *'E le afaina lo'u suafa i le pule. Pe matai pe le matai, e pule ai a'u.* 'My title is irrelevant to the authority. Whether chief or not, I exercise the authority.'

> *'O le fanua lea, o le fanua lava o a'u. Sa se isi o le 'aiga. 'Oti a'u, e pule fa'atasi la'u fanau, tama ma teine, pe matai pe leai.* 'This land is the land of me alone. Other members of the extended family are prohibited. When I die, my children will exercise the authority together, boys and girls, whether chief or not.'

> *'O le fanua lea 'o le fanua lava 'o le tino 'o lo'u tama. . . . 'O le pule 'e fa'asolo i suli 'o lo'u tama.* 'This land is the land just of the body of my father. . . . The authority over the land passes along to the heirs of my father.'

> *'E le afaina le suafa 'a'o le suli.* 'Not the title but the heir matters.'

> *'E le afaina pe suafa pe le suafa, e pule ai a'u fanau.* 'It doesn't matter whether they are titled or untitled, my children will have the authority.'

> *'E pule ai la'u fanau e nofo i le 'aiga.* 'My children who live with the family will exercise the authority.'

> *'E pule ai lo'u atali'i . . . ona o le atali'i o a'u. Pe suafa pe le suafa 'a'o le suli.* 'My son will exercise the authority . . . because he is my son. Whether titled or untitled, he is the heir.'

134 LAND, CUSTOM AND PRACTICE IN THE SOUTH PACIFIC

Only one person, an *ali'i*, volunteered an explicit justification for this important change, saying that 'the paramount title exercises authority over everything. But who knows, these days when I work and I chop down the forest, I should have the authority. We have universal suffrage now' (in translation). A structured poll on the question was not formulated but, when stating their claims by plot, about one-third of people attending interviews expressed their outright support for untitled owners exercising direct *pule* over their lands. The majority opinion was only slightly more conservative. As a middle-aged woman explained, when her aged father, Vagana Sola, passed away, all his children would inherit his lands and would exercise the *pule* together, with resident members having more say than non-residents; but once the siblings reached a joint decision, the *matai* among them would represent the heirs in public: *'E fai [le pule] i luga o le malilie e tasi [o le fanau], ona oso ai lea le matai e fai mea e fai e matai*, '[The authority] will be exercised on the agreement of all [the children], then the chief(s) [among them] will come forward to do what chiefs do' (i.e. make speeches).

Vagana's children still recognise the *pule fa'amalumalu*, or 'protective authority', of the other *matai* titles (not just the *ali'i* title) of their corporate *'aiga* over six of his eight plots (the other two being *fua* in his name), but they said that those titleholders could only support Vagana and his heirs against outside threat, not dispute them. If the *ali'i* of the family tried to block a lease or claim rent from one of Vagana's lands, the judges at the Land and Titles Court would know that the *ali'i* was only being 'greedy', and Vagana was sure to 'win'. On the other hand, support by the other chiefs of the corporate *'aiga* could always be helpful. Demonstrating one's claim to land requires a recitation of the history of the plot, showing how it has come to be in one's hands, and those individuals and their corporate *'aiga* were centrally involved in the history of six of Vagana's lands. Vagana had come from another village to reside permanently with his wife's family, and the residence site he and his wife occupied and five of his seven agricultural plots had been permanently distributed to him and his wife in the formal division of her *'aiga's* lands 20 years earlier.

In another noteworthy case, a non-*matai* who was not a member or resident of Vaega was granted a *fua* to clear from the forest. The man does have a remote cognatic connection and a close marital connection in the village, and had served the village well in previous years as headmaster of a nearby school. He intended to hire casual workers to grow taro for export, and had a large area cleared and sparsely planted. The land was soon abandoned, however, and neither the man nor any of his immediate family now reside in the village. Nevertheless, the people of Vaega maintain that he 'owns' the land and has authority over it, and they

WESTERN SAMOA

maintain that his children will inherit the land when he dies, regardless of their own *matai* status.

Distinguishing Superficial Similarities Between Individual and Corporate Tenure

The classification of agricultural land reported above divides plots into only three types ('Old', 'New', and 'Changed to new'). These types are each subdivided below in order to distinguish the new individual claims from superficially similar claims under corporate ownership, and to show that even some claims that technically fall under 'Old tenure' have the same practical effect as individual tenure.

'Old tenure'

The basic criteria for 'Old tenure' are that ownership is claimed in the name of a corporate *'aiga* and authority is vested in that *'aiga*'s *matai* title. Practices relating to *matai* titles have changed greatly over the last 100 years, however, giving people the opportunity to practice de facto individual tenure while fulfilling many of the technical requirements of custom. This strategy was described as 'restricted title' tenure in the discussion of Malie lands, above. The prevalence of the strategy in Vaega is illustrated in Figure 4.5, which shows Vaega agricultural plots held under 'Old tenure' broken down into three sub-types according to how restricted succession is to the title that is said to hold *pule* over the plot.

In the sub-type of 'Title *Pule*', the plot is owned by a corporate *'aiga* or recognised branch of an *'aiga* (not necessarily one of the first eight) and is subject to the *pule* of that *'aiga*'s or branch's title. No restriction is made on which members may accede to the title. This is the closest sub-type to orthodox customary tenure, the major difference being that most of the titles are now shared by more than one person.

Under 'Restricted title *Pule*', people claim that the plot is owned by a branch of a corporate *'aiga* and that *pule* is exercised only by titleholders of that branch, but subdivision of the *'aiga* is not accepted either by other members of the family or by the court. Such claims indicate growing pressure to break up a corporate *'aiga*.

'Very restricted title *Pule*' applies to a plot when the current occupants claim that it is under the *pule* of a title (and hence is owned by that title's corporate *'aiga*), but the title can only be held by members of the immediate household or nuclear family of the occupants. This is usually a charade, covering up what amounts to individual tenure, and people sometimes laughed about it when this was pointed out in interviews.

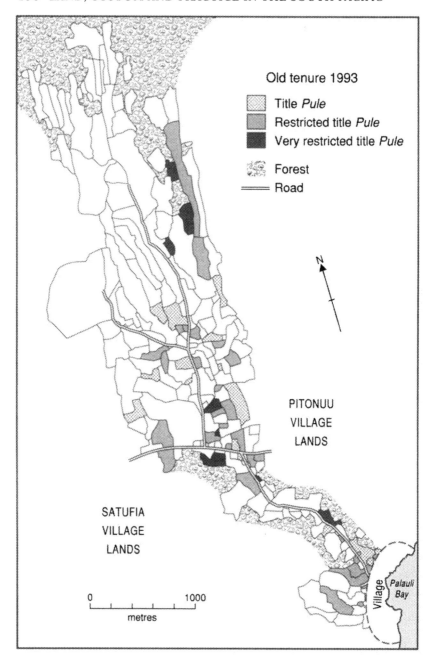

Figure 4.5 Sub-types of 'Old tenure', Vaega village, 1993.
Source: Field survey.

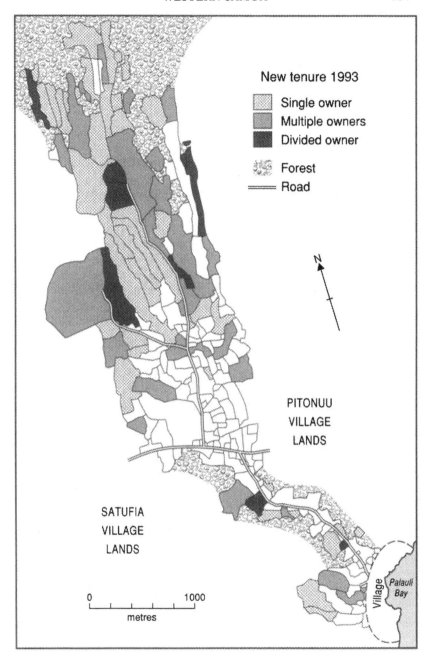

Figure 4.6 Sub-types of 'New tenure', Vaega village, 1993.
Source: Field survey.

138 LAND, CUSTOM AND PRACTICE IN THE SOUTH PACIFIC

'New tenure'

Most plots claimed under 'New tenure' have only one owner because they are relatively new and because the forest areas from which they were cleared were assigned to individuals by the village *fono*. Some allotments were assigned to two or more brothers, however, in which case the initial ownership was by more than one individual. When the initial owner or owners die, the land is inherited by all of their children. When there are two or more owners, the offspring of each inherit their parents' share. Thus, either initially or by inheritance, individually owned plots under 'New tenure' may be owned by more than one person – as 'freehold' land may be. Plots under 'New tenure' are shown by sub-type in Figure 4.6 according to whether the number of owners is single or multiple, together with the plot's history of single or multiple ownership. This highlights the important distinction between ownership of a plot by more than one individual and ownership by a corporate *'aiga* (whose membership includes several individuals). The subdivision also shows the continual pressure to reduce ownership to a single individual.

'Single owner' plots are those which are now and have always been owned by a single individual. Plots with 'Multiple owners' currently have two or more people sharing individual ownership (though not necessarily use). This may arise either from the joint allocation or clearing of land or from inheritance. Most such plots are informally apportioned or divided internally, presaging a subsequent move to the following sub-type. 'Divided owner' plots were formerly under 'Multiple' ownership, but have since been formally and permanently divided among those owners so that each plot or part of a plot is now owned by a single individual.

'Changed to new tenure'

Lands that have been changed from corporate to individual tenure are categorised and shown in Figure 4.7 according to whether the number of owners is single or multiple, together with the plot's history of single or multiple ownership. The purpose is to illustrate again the tendency to reduce the number of owners to a single individual.

Land is classed as 'Single divided' if it was formerly under corporate tenure, but was then formally divided or distributed to a single heir who now claims individual ownership. A plot that was formerly under corporate tenure is classed as 'Multiple divided' if it was distributed to a single heir whose multiple offspring have since inherited the plot. Current ownership of 'Single' and 'Multiple divided' plots is thus identical to the 'Single owner' and 'Multiple owners' sub-types of 'New tenure' respectively, though their histories differ. Land is classed as 'Re-divided' if it was

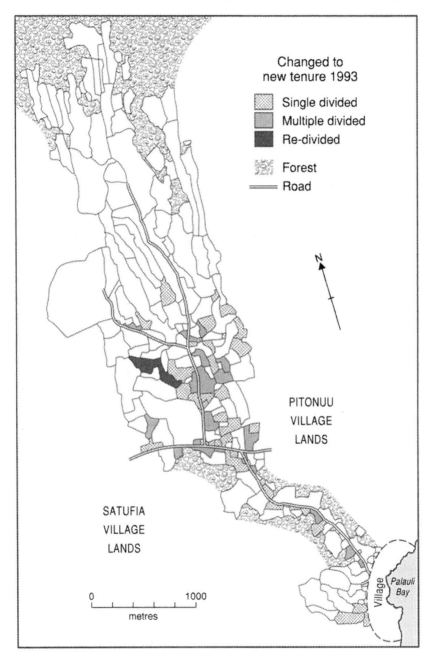

Figure 4.7 Sub-types of 'Changed to new tenure', Vaega village, 1993.
Source: Field survey.

140 LAND, CUSTOM AND PRACTICE IN THE SOUTH PACIFIC

once held under 'Multiple divided' ownership, as above, but has since been re-divided or apportioned between heirs so that each part is now owned by a single individual.

Problems arising from multiple inheritance

The tendency to divide or re-divide plots among individual heirs shows that difficulties can arise under individual ownership as heirs multiply. Multiple inheritance has not yet become a widespread problem, however, even though some plots are now in the third generation of individual ownership. Outmigration to Apia or overseas, together with a modest increase in local wage jobs, has kept the number of people actively working the land from rising dramatically. Most villages have also had adequate forest land available so that people could clear new lands, which they could claim as individuals as soon as they secured a *matai* title. Stagnation of the rural economy has also reduced the likelihood of problems arising from multiple inheritance, as there is comparatively little economic cause for argument among multiple owners. If economic conditions dramatically increased the value of land or its produce, as has happened in Tonga (Chapter 5), the problems arising from multiple inheritance and lack of a land market would intensify. Finally, whatever problems might arise from inheritance by multiple owners, they are less severe than those arising from ownership by a larger and more dispersed corporate *'aiga*, whose membership is not entirely bounded and whose *matai* title may now be shared by many people.

Even in their individual tenure, villagers have generally maintained the customary principle that people who leave their family's land (and so in more traditional times came to serve another *matai*) relinquish their right to use the land without special permission and also lose any direct say in its management. This principle is compromised today when family members live in Apia or overseas, serving no other *matai* and often sending remittances home. But the rarity with which migrants return to re-settle in the village has meant that problems rarely arise from this compromise. More serious is the court's recent policy by which all heirs, no matter how distant genealogically or geographically, are accorded an equal say in family land and title matters (Galumalemana, 1994:173). This threatens to plunge Samoan land tenure into the same chaos found in Tahiti and the Cook Islands (see Chapter 2).

Explaining the Change to Individual Tenure

Samoans and outside observers tend to think of changes such as the individualisation of land tenure as processes of 'Westernisation' and

WESTERN SAMOA   141

explain them as Samoans mimicking higher-status ways of Westerners. Samoans derogatorily label such behaviour *fia palagi*, literally 'wanting to be like Europeans'. However, *fia palagi* motives have little significance in explaining the land tenure changes described here. Samoans are adopting individual land tenure not because they want to be like *palagi* (ambivalence of attraction and repulsion being nearly equally balanced), but because they share the same human nature, increasingly live in similar circumstances and face similar obstacles and opportunities with similar information and resources, and have recently come to accept some similar beliefs, values, and goals in addition to those they already shared. As a result of these similarities, many of the changes in land tenure and society that Samoans have made are similar to those that people in Asia, Africa, and Europe have also made. As Turner remarked on comparing Samoan games and other customs with those of Europe: 'What a surprising unity of thought and feeling is discoverable among the various races of mankind from a comparison of such customs as these!' (1884:134).

The people of Old Samoa developed their characteristic social relations (which among other things ordered their use of land) out of considerations that were far broader than their immediate interests in land or its products. In conditions of endemic warfare and feuding, the motives and strategies for which were also played out in public status displays and competition, people needed the solidarity and protection of groups. With little superordinate political control or support, they relied primarily on devoted kin groups. As kinship ties became more remote, however, solidarity could turn to competition, so that localised kin groups remained largely autonomous. Belief in personal *mana* and numerous other supernatural agencies (Kramer, 1902 1[2]:284–5; Turner, 1884) tipped the balance of power within those kin groups toward autocratic control by chiefs.

People also wanted a large and well coordinated labour force so that different farming tasks as well as fishing, construction works, crafts, household chores, child rearing, care for the elderly, and important social and political activities could be carried out in concert. Infant mortality approached two-thirds, however, and adult mortality was high from hostilities, especially among males, resulting in very low population growth, relatively low population density, and a small total population (Turner, 1884:83, 134–6; Jupp, 1956; Pirie, 1964; McArthur, 1967). Nuclear families were frequently small and incomplete. Building a sizeable labour and defence force in such risky demographic conditions was achieved by the organisation of multiple-extended families.

Each localised kin group was nearly self-sufficient, in accord with its political autonomy. Technology was simple, and few tasks required much

142 LAND, CUSTOM AND PRACTICE IN THE SOUTH PACIFIC

direct supervision. The few elaborate crafts such as tattooing and major house or canoe constructions were carried out by specialists contracted by the family *matai*. The ability to store or transport foods after harvest was limited, and competition between kin groups meant that significant help was sought from other kin, not from neighbours or the village at large. People thus expended great efforts maintaining their ties with dispersed kin and maintaining the ideological importance of such ties. In return, distant kin were allowed to maintain a voice in local family affairs, including access to the group's *matai* title and the personal authority, respect, and service due to it.

Generally bountiful food crops allowed nearly year-round production, with only modest effort applied intermittently in both the production and processing phases, so people had considerable time for social and political activities (Turner, 1884:171). To take advantage of micro-ecological diversity, agricultural plots were scattered inland. Except during periods of intense raiding, shoreline residence was preferred to exploit marine resources and coastal fresh water springs, and to take advantage of sea transportation. Land for agriculture and for house sites was generally abundant, and only relatively minor improvements were made to most plots. Neither land nor its products had much value in themselves as commodities, as stores of food, or even as stores of wealth without considerable labour input. Thus, labour was the scarcer and more important resource.

Under these conditions, securing exclusive 'ownership' of and control over the use of specific tracts of land was only one concern among many, and it was toward the wider set of goals that people ordered their kinship and other social relations. Consequently, adherence to rigid and explicitly defined rules of land ownership, authority, and use was rarely a high priority except in the competitive relations between *'aiga* and between villages. At those levels of socio-political organisation, Samoan custom defines highly explicit rules of tenure which cannot be transgressed without opposition. But within the smaller and more cooperative groups of the *'aiga* (and to a much lesser extent the village), where status and authority differences between individuals overshadowed the need for such rules, there was less reason to draw rigid lines defining specific land rights for occupants, chiefs, and the wider membership of the *'aiga*. There was consequently some leeway in how particular groups apportioned those roles internally (Williamson, 1924). Thus, some variation in landholding arrangements occurred within relatively autonomous groups as the result of piecemeal accommodations to particular circumstances, personalities, and power struggles in conditions where nominal ownership of and authority over particular sections of land was less important than the organisation, loyalty, and control of people

WESTERN SAMOA

operating over a broad array of activities, notably including endemic warfare.

In the non-market conditions of Old Samoa there was relatively little reason beyond the clash of personalities for an untitled person or low-ranking chief to dispute his superior *matai*'s management of family gardens and their produce or his allocation of sites. One way or another, individual efforts went to support the needs of the *'aiga*, which included maintaining a strong and prestigious *matai* as its leader. At the same time, an untitled person or low-ranking chief did have very significant supernatural, personal-safety, and economic-security reasons to heed the superior *matai*'s orders and to work together with the group under his leadership. Personal independence was not a reasonable or attractive alternative.

Matai no longer provide the strategic leadership in warfare and feuding nor command the supernatural awe that once justified their status. Today, new economic incentives tempt *matai* at all levels of the hierarchy to use their traditional positions of authority and respect for personal economic gain, causing frequent complaints in villages. The same economic incentives now tempt the rank-and-file to expend their own efforts and resources on themselves and their nuclear families. As a result, working a garden allotment under the direction of the extended family's *matai* is no longer an acceptable arrangement.

In addition, labour-saving technologies and market goods as modest as steel machetes, corrugated iron roofs, and tinned herring have reduced the need for a large and coordinated pool of home labour just when the size of nuclear families has risen dramatically. The greatest economic returns for village households now come from urban and overseas remittances (O'Meara, 1990:184–7), and at such distances an emotionally close-knit nuclear family has a clear advantage over an old-style extended family living under the autocratic control of a *matai*. In short, new motivations which cause large extended families to fly apart are increasing just when many of the older motivations which held them together are decreasing. Thus, Samoans now have many different options and weigh them differently than their ancestors did.

While the variations found in landholding practices in modern Samoa are similar to those of Old Samoa, the degree and frequency of variation is very different. Most significantly, individual ownership, which was an uncommon and usually temporary extreme in Old Samoa, is now the accepted and preferred norm, and owners want it to be permanent. Just as the reasons for diverging from orthodox custom have changed, so have the reasons for adhering to it.

Villagers themselves are explicit about their reasons for changing to individual tenure. Their primary reasons are increased access to

144 LAND, CUSTOM AND PRACTICE IN THE SOUTH PACIFIC

income from cash cropping, their corresponding desire for more secure and independent control over those incomes, and the hostilities that arise when those desires are not met. They also desire more secure and independent control over relatively expensive European-style houses, which people build almost exclusively with remittances or local wage incomes earned by the nuclear family. Under corporate family ownership, the current occupants would always be at some risk because numerous and quite distant relatives could claim access, and in the next generation the *pule* over the current occupants' lands could pass to a person who was neither closely related nor sympathetic to the current occupants.

Some of the circumstances which once made extended-family communalism an attractive alternative still remain, however. Cash incomes are still too low and too insecure, and government services are still too meagre for most households to disregard the broader security net that extended families provide. Some households need that security net more than others. In 1993 the only person I found in Vaega who rejected individual land tenure was a middle-aged *matai* of no social status whose wife had recently left him, and who was then sole provider for the poorest household in the village. He alone declared that individual land ownership was 'bad' and that living only for oneself and one's children was *ola faufau*, 'living selfishly'. He pointed out that such a life would be very risky because there would be no one to care for him or his children when he grows old or falls ill.

Similarly, the only *matai* in Vaega who said he would defer to the wishes of his paramount chief if someone wanted to lease his own land was also one of the most vulnerable people in the village. Neither of the man's parents were Samoan, though he had lived *fa'aSamoa* almost all his life. He had married into Vaega and had no relatives of his own there or elsewhere in Samoa. The paramount chief of the village had given him a newly created title nearly 20 years earlier as a way to attract another follower. Now of advancing age and very modest means, the man had no other support than his wife's family and the paramount chief he served.

Convenience is another reason for maintaining some plots in corporate ownership. Many of the agricultural plots still held communally in Vaega and in Neiafu are tiny bits of land with rocky, exhausted soils lying immediately behind the coastal residence sites. Even when corporate families divide their other plots among individual heirs, they often keep these tiny plots under corporate ownership to provide a convenient source of coconuts, firewood and pandanus leaves. Consequently, no family wants to lose access to such plots. On the other hand, the plots provide too few coconuts or cocoa to become a source of dispute over cash crops.

WESTERN SAMOA 145

Finally, the Land and Titles Court has acted as a conservative influence in some respects, as court decisions have tended to ossify land claims in more or less customary form, although the court's position has been ambiguous during changing times.

The role of the Land and Titles Court

Dissatisfaction with the Land and Titles Court is so widespread among Samoans today that it is difficult to find people who claim to *talitonu*, 'trust' or 'believe in', the court. Complaints stem directly from alleged irregularities, inconsistencies, and other problems in court operations, but more fundamental problems lie in the court's charter. The Land and Titles Court is charged with an impossible task, attempting to settle disputes fairly, maintain or restore family and village peace and harmony, protect individual rights according to some unspecified conception of 'natural justice' (Marsack, 1961:28), and at the same time uphold custom. No court or tribunal could achieve all of the court's current goals simultaneously.

Contemporary Samoans do not live in ways that accord well with the premises behind customary land tenure principles, so that customary norms do not provide clear standards for dispute resolution or adjudication. No court of law could uphold or preserve intact customary principles and practices which reigned in an era of competitive and often violent pursuit of status and power. As Samoa's economy has become more market-oriented and its population larger, land and its products have become scarcer and more valuable. Economic activity has come to centre on the household or even the individual, rather than on the extended family. In these circumstances, the inherent vagueness of custom on the relative powers of individual occupants has combined with a rising conflict of economic interests between those occupants and their family chiefs and other family members to produce fertile ground for conflict. Thus, Samoans increasingly want rules concerning the ownership and occupancy of land and the disposition of its products to be more explicit, more individualised, and more secure.

Even when particular people or the court want to follow the *aganu'u*, the unmodified principles and practices of ancient custom no longer provide clear or acceptable guides in the very different conditions of contemporary life. Multiple titleholders and claimants are now scattered over half the globe, and the constituent households of a title family no longer own their resources together, produce together, consume together, act together in mutual self-defence, or have any other earthly incentive to put their competitive differences aside. And traditional processes of decision-making by consensus are severely strained when

146 LAND, CUSTOM AND PRACTICE IN THE SOUTH PACIFIC

the ultimate consensus builders of Old Samoa – supernatural sanctions and brute force – are no longer available.

Western-style court adjudication ideally protects specified and publicly agreed upon 'rights' accorded to individuals or groups, with contrasting or conflicting 'rights' in any particular instance being weighed impartially against each other and against specified benefits accruing to the wider society. To the degree that such an ideal legal process was carried out, it would be inimical to the power politics which provides the motivational foundation for *fa'aSamoa* practice in both its ancient and contemporary forms, and so could not serve to maintain that custom. In particular, a court of law is antithetical to the autocratic powers of chiefs, and the Land and Titles Court has in fact steadily eroded those customary powers. To the extent that the court operates as a court of law, it will fail to preserve and protect much ancient Samoan custom and usage. To the extent that it continues to operate more as an administrative tribunal than a court of law, it will remain an arena for power politics.

Changing 'customs and usages'

The court's mandate to settle struggles over land and titles peacefully and equitably 'according to the customs and usages of the Samoan people' is inherently vague. No specification has ever been made as to what those 'customs and usages' might be, how they might be ranked, how contradictions might be accommodated and whether 'customs and usages' might be taken to have changed. Even if these matters were specified, the ancient 'customs and usages' are themselves vague on critical points, including the respective powers of chiefs, individual occupants, and other family members.

The role of the court thus hinges on interpretation of the central phrase of its charter, but it has never said explicitly what it takes either the English or Samoan versions of the phrase – 'customs and usages' and *tu ma aganu'u* – to mean. An earlier assumption (O'Meara, 1987; 1990) that 'customs' referred to prescriptive norms of ancient derivation, while 'usages' referred more descriptively to actual practices, and that by implication ancient 'customs' might differ from contemporary 'usages', may be too clear-cut. Both Samoan terms may be translated as 'customs' (Pratt, 1893; Milner, 1966) and the legal scholar, Guy Powles, suggests that no distinction may have been intended, with the two terms simply giving added weight to the phraseology (pers. comm. 1993).

Senior members of the court have indicated that it is their official duty to defend ancient custom from the corrosive effects of contemporary individualistic practices (Marsack, 1961:28; O'Meara, 1990:147; pers.

WESTERN SAMOA 147

comm. 1983, 1984, 1993). The 1975 *Report on Matai Titles, Customary Land and the Land and Titles Court* is inconsistent with that conservative view when it states that 'customs and usages' means those 'accepted as being in force at the time when the matter arises' (GWS, 1975:12). The report also states the contrary view that 'although custom can and does change gradually . . . custom . . . is a conservative force and changes more slowly than the community' (1975:93).

Furthermore, the report states that 'the Court will not recognise a change in custom unless it is satisfied that the change is accepted by the community in general as having the force of law' (1975:93), which implies that the court only follows public opinion. The registrar states similarly that 'Departures from those principles [of custom and usage] in the decision-making of the present Court must be attributed to the changes in values that have taken place' (Galumalemana, 1994:173). However, the court itself has been instrumental in pushing along those changes in values. It has always interpreted its mandate to include the protection of 'individual rights' against the authoritarian (but customary) powers that chiefs formerly exercised. It does not allow chiefs to bequeath land or titles in a spoken last will and testament (Marsack, 1961:13–14), and the present court does not recognise the customary distinction between close and distant heirs (Galumalemana, 1994:173), which was recognised by Marsack's court. Thus, the court sometimes deliberately contravenes the widely accepted customary powers of chiefs in order to act as 'an equalising agent' (ibid.:180).

The court has explicitly avoided developing a body of legal precedents, or necessarily adhering to such general precedents as might be extracted from its earlier decisions, and there is little justification for assuming that Samoan 'customs and usages' in themselves constitute a body of 'Samoan common law' as suggested in the 1975 Report (GWS, 1975:91–4). Consequently, there is little secure foundation for interpreting the court's mandate as allowing it to change its standards of dispute resolution when it believes that community sentiment and practices have changed. That the court has changed some of its standards along with or ahead of community sentiment and practice is no doubt to its credit, but the legal justification appears slim.

On the rare occasions when disputes concerning individually owned customary lands come before it, the court's decisions often support individual tenure rather than adhering to orthodox custom. But in addition to interview and other statements by senior court officials, the court's records show that it is reluctant to explicitly endorse contemporary practice when that practice contradicts orthodox custom. Instead, the court and those arguing before it mask the contradiction of supporting individual tenure while trying to adhere to custom by dressing individual

148 LAND, CUSTOM AND PRACTICE IN THE SOUTH PACIFIC

tenure in customary phrases. Recent examples from the court records for Satupaitea district illustrate this habit.

In one case the court's decision describes land as being 'appurtenant to the title [sic] of Sasa Vao', thereby inserting the name of an individual into the customary phrasing where only a *matai* title belongs. In another case, two related men who held the unrelated *matai* titles of Lafo and Vele disputed the ownership of a plot. The court determined that both had equal claims as surviving heirs of the previous owners, thus recognising the legitimacy of individual ownership and inheritance, but the court couched this un-customary decision in a customary phrase, declaring that the plot was 'appurtenant to the titles of Lafo and Vele', which is impossible in custom because the two titles belong to different corporate families.

Another dispute concerned the agricultural lands of a *matai* in Vaega who, in interviews over a 13-year period, had claimed individual ownership over this land 'by his body' rather than by his title of Fiamamafa. This claim was confirmed by his neighbours and relatives, who make similar claims to their own lands. Nevertheless, the court listed the lands as being 'appurtenant to the title Fiamamafa', thereby implying the land was not held individually, but by the title Fiamamafa. The respondent in the case claimed not to be using Fiamamafa's lands, but only those 'appurtenant to the title [sic] Laufa'i Pona', which also signifies an individual. Thus, both court and respondent used traditional phrasing appropriate for land claimed by title, but actually signified ownership by an individual (i.e. Laufa'i Pona) rather than a *matai* title (i.e. Laufa'i). In a fourth case the court abandoned any pretence of upholding custom, declaring simply that the customary land in question belonged to a man named Pili Manulele, without suggesting that the plot was appurtenant to his or any other title.

While the court does sometimes make 'allowances for the realities of modern Samoa' (Galumalemana, 1994:80), there is no mechanism for it to document or necessarily even find out about those realities, nor to determine when a change has become 'accepted by the community in general as having the force of law'. Neither is there any mechanism to ensure that the court's determinations are consistently applied, as it has no higher court of appeal.

Thus, there are no explicit standards of ancient custom, codified law, or legal precedent against which the public might judge either its own actions or those of the court, no mechanisms for determining when the implicit standards have changed, and no mechanisms for independent review of court decisions. Operating as an administrative tribunal, the court has been left largely to its own discretion – in effect legislating, interpreting, and adjudicating some of the nation's most important

WESTERN SAMOA   149

matters behind closed doors. This lack of explicit standards and mechanisms increases both public dispute over land and titles matters and public suspicion over the court's decision-making process.

From title to titleholder

Until universal suffrage replaced *matai*-only suffrage in 1991, villagers compromised with custom and with the court by restricting the *pule* over individually owned plots to only those owners who had gained *matai* status. According to this compromise, non-*matai* still inherited land as individuals, but they usually could not control its use, at least publicly, and non-*matai* usually could not own land they had cleared themselves until they gained *matai* status (O'Meara, 1987:95; 1990:147–8). Under this compromise, however, neither ownership of nor *pule* over individually owned land was connected in any way to a particular *matai* title or to a corporate descent group, as is the case in orthodox customary tenure. The registrar's objection that in such cases the court 'still vests the pule of land in the matai' (Galumalemana, 1994:179) indicates a need to clarify this point and its relation to court policy and practice.

The statement implies that vesting the *pule* of land 'in the *matai*' accords with Samoan custom. Instead, it accords with the court's common practice of supporting individual 'rights' against the authoritarian exercise of customary powers by family chiefs. As Galumalemana recognises (1994:173, 179), Samoan custom does not 'vest' authority over land 'in the *matai*', who is a person, but rather in a particular *matai* title, which is an office. According to custom, the current holder of a title office temporarily exercises the *pule* which is permanently vested in that title. This distinction between title and titleholder might be glossed over in discussing the conditions of Old Samoa because almost all lands were then owned by corporate *'aiga* and were thus appurtenant to that *'aiga*'s particular *matai* title, which was in turn held by a single person. But the distinction cannot be glossed over today because most lands are owned by individuals, most existing *matai* titles have been split among several branches of their respective *'aiga* and then each split title shared by several incumbents, and many newly created titles belong to no corporate *'aiga* at all. This splitting, sharing, and creation of titles hopelessly confuses customary tenure, which is an important reason in itself why people now want individual ownership of the lands they occupy. On the other hand, people's desires for individual ownership and for broader economic independence are important motivations for seeking or accepting their own *matai* titles in the first place.

The apparent conflation of titles and titleholders extends to the court's current interpretation of *pulefa'amau*, meaning to 'fix' or 'register

150 LAND, CUSTOM AND PRACTICE IN THE SOUTH PACIFIC

authority' over land or titles, which provides another indication of the court's implicit support of individualism. Galumalemana states that:

> Other than the fact that ownership has to be registered under the owner's title, pulefaamau is similar to the concept of individual ownership in so far as it legally excludes occupation and usage of land by any other owner or his heirs (1994:174). The nearest Samoan term to the Western concept of individual ownership of land is pulefaamau (registered pule i.e., registered in Court) of a section of land by a titleholder whose heirs may, without question, inherit their father's land. (ibid.:179)

Pulefa'amau is just the registration of ownership and *pule*, wherever they might lie. Under orthodox custom, ownership and *pule* lie with a corporate *'aiga* and its *matai* title, not with any individual. Thus, 'upon the death of the *matai*, or relinquishment of his title, the *pule* over the family lands descends not to his heirs of the body but to his successor in title' (Marsack, 1961:22). The registrar's statements cited above confirm what court records show, however, that the court now often vests both ownership and *pule* in a person – an 'owner', 'titleholder', or '*matai*' – rather than in a corporate *'aiga* and its title office. Contrary to the fundamental principles of orthodox customary tenure, the court now accepts that the 'heirs' of the present 'owner' may 'inherit' exclusive 'ownership' and *pule* of 'their father's land'.

Urban Perceptions of Rural Land Tenure Practices

Rural residents today not only commonly claim individual ownership of plots, they fully intend this ownership to be permanent. They do not see individual tenure as an outgrowth of Samoan custom, but instead say that it is a *mea fou*, or 'new thing', having been adopted progressively since the time of their parents or grandparents. In addition, villagers explicitly assert that the individual tenure they now practise is contrary to what they regard as their *aganu'u moni*, meaning 'true' or 'legitimate custom'.

In Apia, people in government and public circles not only consider individual land tenure contrary to Samoan custom, but also therefore contrary to the constitution, to subsequent legislation, and to official policy of the Land and Titles Court. People usually keep their claims of individual ownership in low profile outside their home villages, however, not only to avoid problems with the court, but also to avoid problems with urban relatives who would be less impressed with the family titles bestowed on them if they knew that acquiring the titles now gives them little or no say over village lands. The court itself has not even recognised, at least publicly, that most of the 'customary lands' it oversees are

WESTERN SAMOA

no longer held according to orthodox custom and usage. Individual tenure is never mentioned in government reports (e.g. GWS, 1975; 1991). In spite of the court's implicit support for individual tenure in specific cases, extensive discussions with court officers elicited more official denial and rejection of individual tenure than recognition and acceptance. Nevertheless, at least some of the high-ranking members of the Land and Titles Court who still reside in rural areas claim individual ownership of customary land in their private affairs, even though they are called on to defend orthodox custom in their official posts (pers. comm. 1984 and 1993).

Marsack noted that claims to individual ownership of customary land had come before the court. He apparently believed, however, that such claims merely resulted from what he called 'confusion' or 'misunderstandings' among the Samoans as to their own customs.

> Although in most cases the devolution of Samoan customary lands to the successor of the previous title-holder is fairly well understood in the villages, the confusion of European and Samoan ideas in the vicinity of Apia has led to many misunderstandings on the subject of succession to Samoan customary lands in that area. Several cases have come before the Court in which it has appeared that, though the land in dispute is Samoan customary land, it has for some generations been occupied by heirs of the body of the original title-holder; and the present holder of the title is not only not exercising a *pule* over the land but is not even claiming the *pule*. (Marsack, 1961:22)

In such cases it was and often still is the court's practice to declare that the *pule* over the land remains with the title, but then to forbid the title-holder from exercising that *pule* over the occupants (e.g. Marsack, 1961:22–3). The court has consistently supported the individual's 'right' of continued occupation against claims by an overbearing *matai*, subject only to the occupant performing some minimal *tautua*, or service, to the *matai*, at least until the trouble simmers down. The court thus supports de facto individual tenure while adhering to the letter of orthodox custom. Marsack concludes with this advice: 'One of the most important lessons that young Samoans of today have to learn is that while the law regarding land tenure stands as it is, no Samoan can claim the fee simple of any Samoan customary land' (1961:23).

Most urban Samoans seem to be unaware of the change to individual ownership in rural areas.[11] Even those who are aware of it in their own family or from working at the court are usually unaware of its prevalence. Some who reside permanently in Apia or overseas may be reluctant to acknowledge individual tenure because of its implications for the continuation of traditional Samoan culture, with which migrants often identify strongly even though they have left its everyday practice to their rural

152 LAND, CUSTOM AND PRACTICE IN THE SOUTH PACIFIC

relatives. Some urban residents may also be reluctant to acknowledge the prevalence of individual tenure because it implies a marked reduction in the dignity and authority of family *matai* titles that they hold or to which they aspire. Many people also appear to believe that rural Samoans have an inherent conservatism which – buttressed by British-style national law – would make their shift to individual land tenure impossible. *'E le fa'apena le fa'aSamoa*, they say, 'That is not the Samoan way'.

Nevertheless, the vast majority of both rural and urban Samoans have embraced individual tenure as they adapt piecemeal and opportunistically to changing economic, political, and demographic circumstances. Village *fono* across Western Samoa have also supported and even initiated steps toward individual tenure. Thus, what on the national level is publicly unacknowledged and officially illegal is in perfect accord with the accepted strategies of village life and with the unwritten laws of semi-autonomous village *fono*.

Market Demand for Freehold Land

Further evidence of the popularity of individual tenure is the high demand for freehold land. Village pastors, for example, commonly use the relatively large cash incomes they receive – WS$25,000 (US$8,000) per annum was not unusual in 1993 – to purchase freehold land around Apia and build European-style residences in preparation for retirement. Urban salary earners do the same.

Against such demand, the scarce supply of freehold land results in severe price distortions (leaving some land owners with a vested interest in maintaining the distortion). Unimproved residential land in suburban villages on the outskirts of Apia commonly sold for around WS$15,000 (US$6,000) for 0.1 hectare in 1993 – three to five times the annual take-home pay of a mid-level wage earner. Inflated prices impede housing construction and business development even where freehold land exists. It also makes urban planning very difficult, as both prospective home owners and business entrepreneurs are often forced to build wherever they happen to hold land. Occasional public sales or long-term leases of WSTEC land are the only additions on the supply side of the market. These offerings are heavily oversubscribed, with winners being selected by lottery during the 1980s and more recently by competitive bids.

Over the years several land-short villages were granted tracts of WSTEC land at token rates. The village councils generally allocated surveyed blocks to individuals as small homesteads, with separate blocks going to different individuals who held the same *matai* title and even to some individuals who did not hold titles.[12] Some of these villages have now petitioned the government to convert the leased tracts to freehold,

WESTERN SAMOA   153

to be owned outright by the current occupants, who are themselves 'heirs of the body' of those individuals who were first granted the plots. Since WSTEC land is technically freehold, there is no legal impediment to such transformations, and one (at Manono-Uta) has been completed recently (pers. comm. Leiataua Dr Kilifoti Eteuati, 1993).

Many migrant families wish they could sell all or part of their individually owned 'customary land' or their share of corporate *'aiga* land to finance a house or small business in Apia or overseas, rather than leave the land and its improvements to their relatives. Customary land may be leased by *matai* for up to 30 years, but the process can be very lengthy and difficult. The intention to lease must first be announced in the government newspaper for three months and then any objections dealt with through the court. This places the owner-occupants at risk from all sorts of spurious claims and delays to which the Land and Titles Court is subject. The court backlog now amounts to 25 years on Savaii and eight years on Upolu, even without considering delaying tactics commonly employed by petitioners (GWS, 1991:11 and Appendix II). Even successful lessors often find that rents are only paid for a year or two, and collection of back rents is difficult or impossible, especially when the lessors are overseas.

In late 1992 Cabinet prepared a new Land Registration bill (No. 24), which would facilitate the development of customary land by channelling leases through the government, in much the same way the Native Land Trust Board operates in Fiji (see Chapter 6). The immediate purpose of the bill is to make leases of customary land more secure and equitable for both parties (pers. comm. Leiataua Dr Kilifoti Eteuati, 1993). Whether it will work in practice is not yet known, but it is unlikely to be attractive for small-scale transactions.

Most people who remain in the villages express little interest in selling their customary land, partly because such sales are illegal, but also because land is their one productive asset and guarantee of future security. Some village residents from various rungs of the economic ladder said during interviews that they would sell some or all of their customary land if they could. One especially prosperous man from Savaii wished he could convert his large, individually held customary estate to freehold so he could develop and then sell it. He noted, however, that the social and economic risks of allowing the sale of customary land may not be justified.

If sales of customary land were legalised, it would no doubt remain illegal for non-citizens to own land, so any risk of monopolisation would come primarily from wealthy Samoans rather than from foreigners. Economic standing is by no means egalitarian in Western Samoa, even within a single village (O'Meara, 1990:190), and many Samoans are

154 LAND, CUSTOM AND PRACTICE IN THE SOUTH PACIFIC

appropriately concerned that legalising the sale of customary land would compound existing inequalities. On the other hand, the economic and social costs of prohibiting such sales are also substantial.

In the meantime, more and more Samoans are electing to live on the limited freehold or leasehold land around Apia, or overseas. Ironically, they not only gain greater independence for themselves by doing so, they also gain an incentive for wanting customary tenure to continue in the villages they have left. That way urban residents can have their freehold land and their share of *'aiga* land too – a point not lost on their rural kin.

Conclusion

A genuine attachment to traditional values and practices does not necessarily prevent Samoans from choosing new paths. Like everyone, Samoans have an assortment of goals, values, and beliefs which may come into conflict in certain circumstances, especially in changing circumstances. Thus, the notable pride that the vast majority of Samoans feel in being Samoan and in their *fa'aSamoa* is not necessarily accompanied by traditionalism in a particular action. In resolving land and other practical matters, they tend to give very little weight to the long-term or cumulative effects their actions might have on traditional practices. They more often seek ways to bend tradition to their immediate purposes. As worthy as cultural preservation is, other goals are also worthy.

Samoans have been individualising their land tenure on their own terms and at their own, accelerating pace for at least a century. Ironically, the individualistic principles and practices that villagers embrace today are almost precisely those against which their grandparents rebelled in 1926. It is more ironic still that with *fa'aSamoa* now protected against interference from outside, it must now be protected against interference from inside. Where a colonial government once tried to impose individual tenure on people who resisted in the name of custom, a Samoan government now employs a quasi-European court system to maintain quasi-customary tenure as people shift of their own accord to individual tenure.

Meleisea observes that 'there is no law of history . . . which decrees that the fundamental institutions of the Samoan nation must pass away, merely because similar institutions have been eclipsed in other parts of the world' (1987:234–5). Neither is there a law of history which decrees that people will continue to follow those institutions when conditions change. The only inevitability is that people will continue to choose from among the options open to them, based on their current beliefs, values, and goals.

WESTERN SAMOA

Notes

1. Use of the English verb 'own' here corresponds to the Samoan verbal pronoun *ona*, which only coincidentally sounds similar (Pratt, 1893). It would unduly stretch the similarities, however, to say that in Old Samoa people controlled access to things in ways that correspond precisely to those implied by the English term (see Williamson, 1924:233–7, 254–5, for a summary of English usages in early reports). The Samoan term formerly indicated only a generalised possession of and more-or-less exclusive control over things, without the special legal and commodity implications of the English verb. As economic conditions have changed, however, Samoan usages of *ona* have broadened to include the possibility of legal and commodity ownership.

2. Just under 75 per cent of all males aged 21 years and over residing in Savaii were *matai* in 1988 (O'Meara, 1990:151) and the number of registered *matai* has increased about 15 per cent since then (LTC, 1993) with little change of population.

3. This and some other statements reported are not entirely correct grammatically but are direct quotations.

4. A similar pattern is revealed in the maps of Satalo and Asaga villages presented by Farrell and Ward (1962:193–5).

5. An early court map from Vaega provides similar evidence.

6. The increase in *matai* titles began decades before the constitution institutionalised *matai*-only balloting and has continued after universal suffrage in 1991. In addition to political advantage, the desire for individual ownership of land and for other aspects of economic independence has also fuelled the spread of *matai* titles and made it more acceptable (O'Meara, 1990:149–53).

7. Vaega's *fa'alupega*, the honorific recitation of the village's social and political charter, mentions only three titles specifically, plus three groups of titles. New titles are conveniently classed with one of these three groups without disturbing the *fa'alupega*.

8. The exception is the individually owned residence plot received as *togiola*, mentioned above.

9. Eleven 'Old tenure' plots or sections of plots had been formally divided among individual heirs, thus moving them to 'Changed to new' tenure. New evidence or changed testimony placed four other plots in the 'New tenure' category which had been listed previously under 'Old tenure'. Two tiny plots that had been missed in the earlier mapping and interviews were both added under 'Changed to new' tenure. Finally, three extensions had been hived off as separate plots and were listed for the first time in 1993 under 'New' or 'Changed to new' tenure as appropriate. Eight other 'New' or 'Changed to new' plots had been apportioned among individual heirs since 1983, but since these plots remained individually owned, their inheritance did not result in a change of tenure type.

10. One plot moved from 'New' to 'Old tenure' and another six plots (owned by only two families) moved from 'Changed' back to 'Old tenure'. Five of those seven plots had reverted to 'Old tenure' when one *matai*'s intent to bequeath land to his children was blocked after his death by a resident cousin who was short of land. [In contrast to these five, 25 plots that were claimed under individual ownership in 1983 had been inherited successfully by the children or spouse of the previous owners by 1993.] The other two plots that reverted to 'Old tenure' were claimed under corporate *'aiga*

156 LAND, CUSTOM AND PRACTICE IN THE SOUTH PACIFIC

ownership in 1993 by the same man who had claimed them under individual ownership in 1983. He had recently acceded to the paramount title of his *'aiga* and had then found it convenient to claim the plots by that title even though he had successfully claimed them by his 'body' under individual ownership. This new claim by title was superfluous, but it added some importance to his title succession.

11. I draw this conclusion from recent published reports (e.g. Aiavao, 1993:23), from my own extensive discussions with Samoan government officers and members of the public (1979, 1981–83, 1984, 1985, 1988, 1992, 1993, 1994), from responses to two public lectures I gave on the subject in Apia (1983, 1993), and from reported comments by leading Samoans on my earlier findings (O'Meara, 1986; 1987).

12. See, for example, maps of Satapuala and Fagali'i-Uta, Department of Lands, Survey and Environment, Apia.

CHAPTER 5

Right and Privilege in Tongan Land Tenure

Kerry James

In the closing decades of the nineteenth century, as international rivalries and ambitions drew the whole South Pacific into a web of protectorates and annexations by European colonial powers, Tonga proclaimed its own written constitution and declared itself an independent monarchy (Figure 5.1). This move set the nation on an historical course quite different from its neighbours. Tonga was never colonised. Furthermore, the first monarch, Tupou I, in order to consolidate his authority and lessen the power of strong rival chiefs, instituted reforms which gave all males individual rights to land. Tongan commoners were set free 'from serfdom, and all vassalage' and the other powers Tongan chiefs had over their people's lives and property; instead, chiefs were told to 'allot portions of land to the people' (quoted from the 1862 Code of Laws by Lātūkefu, 1975:34–5).

Elsewhere in the Pacific, land rights underwent changes which clearly reflected outside interests. Colonial governments rapidly established a distinction between freehold and customary or native title. This duality involved a further contrast between individual alienable rights, which were taken up by settlers and commercial interests, and communal, inalienable rights intended to protect the integrity of the 'native society' and the livelihood of the indigenous population. The Tongan constitution of 1875 allowed no such dualities. No land was alienated to outsiders and customary rights were superseded. All land became the property of the Crown and was divided into royal, government, and noble estates. From these estates, all adult men were entitled to the permanent hereditary usufruct of an individual holding of garden land, known as a tax allotment (*'api tukuhau*), and a smaller house site, known as a town allotment (*'api kolo*). Upon the registration of an allotment with the Minister of Lands, the land was to remain with a man and his

157

158 LAND, CUSTOM AND PRACTICE IN THE SOUTH PACIFIC

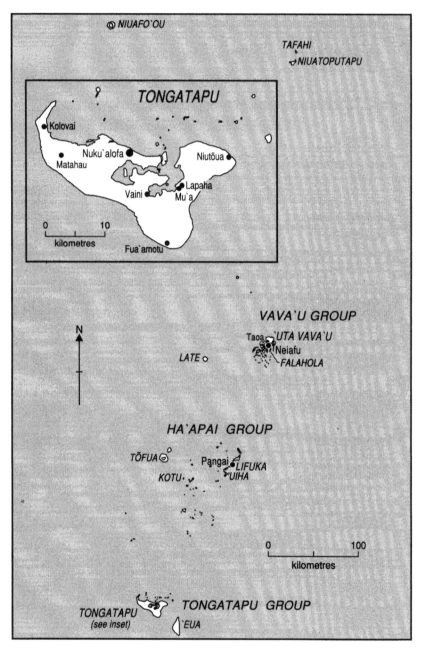

Figure 5.1 Tonga.
Note: The southern island of 'Ata is not shown.

TONGA   159

male heirs so long as rent was paid to the estate holder and taxes to the government.

Tupou I's levelling reforms, by which he reduced the power of most of the existing chiefly lines, were modified for political reasons when he selected the most powerful 20 chiefly titles to become a modern landed nobility (Lātūkefu, 1974:211; Ma'afu, 1975:1). Each noble title was granted an impartible estate, heritable by male primogeniture. He also conferred estates on six *matāpūle* (ceremonial attendants of chiefs). As the independent smallholdings were to be drawn from the hereditary estates, however, the law was clearly intended to protect the wellbeing of commoners rather than protect the privileges of nobles in the matter of land (Marcus, 1978:517).

Consequently, the history of land tenure in Tonga is concerned less with a movement towards individual land rights in the face of laws intended to buttress communalism than with changes in relations between social strata. It is concerned also with changes in the nature of the value of land. The legal provisions regarding land have not been perfectly implemented in the century since their inception. The subsequent disparities in Tongan land tenure between law and practice give rise to four major historical themes. The first is the very gradual, indeed, hesitant way in which the common people began to take advantage of the emancipatory provisions of the constitution and to exercise their legal right to land by applying for allotments and registering them with the Minister of Lands. The second is the increase in the population which by the late 1950s made it impossible for every Tongan man to acquire his constitutional right to land from Tonga's limited land base, although much arable land lay unused, bound in the hereditary legal entitlements granted to nobles and male commoners. The third theme is the government's resistance to major changes in the original land measures, partly because of their significance as reforms arising from the foundation of an enlightened Christian monarchy, and partly because specific provisions were in the interests of the nobility and expanding numbers of commoners as they established increasingly diverse types of land holding and use (Marcus, 1978:510). The fourth theme arises from the constitutional prohibition of the sale of land and the appearance since the end of the Second World War of an informal land market composed of extra-legal payments for the lease or use of land. Since the 1970s, the illegal land market has grown rapidly in volume and value as a response to increasing monetisation, the modern incentives of commoditisation, and the increasing rationalisation of commercial ventures. The market has also grown through the input of remittances received from emigrants settled or working overseas.

160 LAND, CUSTOM AND PRACTICE IN THE SOUTH PACIFIC

The Institution of Reform

Pre-reform land holding

The pre-reform political system was a highly stratified, typically Polynesian form of hierarchical social organisation. Chiefs were ranked in relation to one another by their seniority of descent from major titles which meant, in effect, their genealogical proximity to the sacred Tu'i Tonga line. Chiefs had various degrees of authority over the people living on their hereditary tracts of land (*'eiki ma'u tofi'a*), which they held by conquest or through their allegiance to a higher chief (Marcus, 1978:514; Bott with Tavi, 1982:69–70). There was no communal land in Tonga, except the *mala'e*, or 'green', near the chief's house, which was used for meetings, chiefly installations, ceremonies, or for 'dances, and entertainments, such as boxing or wrestling' (Gifford, 1929:176). The chiefs allocated parts of their land to lesser chiefs, who apportioned it among their *matāpūle*, 'ceremonial attendants'. These in turn apportioned smaller areas within the *kāinga* (the extended families or political support groups) by allocating plots to the *'ulumotu'a*, the 'heads' of extended families which gardened the land. The populace was often called simply *kai fonua*, 'eaters of the soil'. The term, *fonua*, also refers collectively to both the land and its people (Wood Ellem, 1981:x). The *ngatae* (coral tree, *Erythrina variegata*) was often planted around gardens as a boundary marker because it grew so quickly (Gifford, 1929:176). The Tongan expression, *vaha 'a ngatae*, 'a boundary of coral trees', served also as a metaphor to indicate the responsibility of tribute (*fatongia*), which the cultivating groups had regularly to give to the chief whose land they used (S. Lātūkefu, pers. comm. September 1993).

The chiefly system ideally functioned by reciprocity. A chief's supporters, his *kāinga*, composed of kinsmen, tenants and political followers, provided him and his retinue with food, goods, labour, and service in warfare. The chief provided leadership, settled disputes, and judged tenants' complaints against lesser chiefs. The highest-ranking aristocrats (*'eiki*), were believed to have affinity with the gods and, thereby, to provide spiritual protection. The annual presentation of the *'inasi*, 'first fruits', by the Tu'i Tonga to the deity of fertility and harvest spared the land from her divine wrath and ensured prosperity for the coming year (Lātūkefu, 1975:8–9). The respect due to chiefs at all times was deeply instilled into the people by various *tapu* (prohibitions) surrounding the titled chiefs and aristocrats, and by the physical and moral enforcement of behaviour considered appropriate to their god-like presence.

At a formal level, hierarchical chiefly control implies a uniform pattern of land tenure throughout the polity; but it also implies the possibility of significant local variation depending on the whim, birth rank,

TONGA 161

local power and status, political goals, and temperament of a particular chief. Chiefs had the authority to specify cultivation, prohibit the consumption of certain ceremonially-important crops, and demand either light or heavy services and tribute from their subject people, including the Europeans to whom they gave protection (Martin, 1817:165). Successful and generous cultivators could get more land from the chief, while others could be dispossessed if they displeased the chief by their lack of productivity or generosity. Moreover, the land may not have been distributed or worked in exactly the same fashion in every part of the country. In the 1770s, Cook noted that gardens established in heavily populated areas, such as the western district of Tongatapu, were neatly fenced with reeds and divided by narrow paths (Bott with Tavi, 1982:15). Vason, a renegade missionary in western Tongatapu, recalled that in the early nineteenth century he:

> became very desirous of a portion of land to myself, that by my own industry, I might render myself independent. At this time, a neighbouring chief wished to dispose of a tract of land; my chief Mulkaamair, purchased the estate for me, with a spade, an axe, a small native canoe, and a couple of knives. . . . It contained about fifteen acres. . . . With what joy did I contemplate its little pendant groves . . . diversified by little habitations, which contained the peaceful natives, who now became my subjects and labourers to cultivate my fields for their own subsistence and mine! . . . It may appear surprising that an estate as small as fifteen acres should contain the cottages of labourers: but it should be considered that Tongataboo was throughout cultivated like a garden, and that the cocoa-nut and plantain trees, upon a small extent of ground, were sufficient to support many inhabitants. (Orange, 1840:138–9)

Subsequent accounts suggest that the eastern part of Tongatapu was not nearly so well tended, and that the cultivation Cook and Vason witnessed in the western districts was the result of a long period of peace and prosperity. Cultivation was severely disrupted when garden labourers were drawn into the widespread fighting which began at the end of the eighteenth century. It has been estimated that at the time of Cook's visits, Tonga's population was probably stable at around 30,000, and land was plentiful. By 1830 wars, famine, and disease had reduced the number of people in the archipelago by at least a third (Bakker, 1979:8; McArthur, 1967:72). By that time probably 'not more than half of Tongatapu was cultivated' (Wood Ellem, 1981:58–9). In 1852, when the fighting ceased, 'the population was probably not much above 20,000' and had not increased significantly by 1875 (McArthur, 1967:73–5). Queen Sālote, an authority on Tongan history, emphasised repeatedly that people, not land, were the chiefs' most valued resource (Bott with Tavi, 1982:69). The control of land was just one form of chiefly control of political supporters (Marcus, 1978:516).

162 LAND, CUSTOM AND PRACTICE IN THE SOUTH PACIFIC

Tupou I's reforms

Tāufa'āhau, when he became the first monarch of the present Tupou dynasty in 1845, needed to consolidate his tenuous authority. In order to reduce the commoners' dependence on the chiefs and the chiefs' power over them, he intended to make the people tenants of allotments of land by the sole authority of the Crown. Following his legal codes of 1839 and 1850, and the Emancipation Act of 1862, the king, with the aid of a Wesleyan missionary, promulgated a constitution in 1875. This was done partly to avoid colonisation by European powers such as had occurred in Samoa, Fiji, Tahiti, and Hawaii. Rather than concede Tonga to Europeans, he is said to have given Tonga to God and the motto *Koe Otua mo Tonga ko hoku Tofi'a*, 'God and Tonga are my Heritage', inscribed on the royal coat of arms, has become that of succeeding generations of Tongans (Tongilava, 1993:3). Tonga's independence of action was manifest in the land law as outlined in the constitution and specified in the Land Act of 1882 which was to be the basis of other provisions for individual rights and freedoms (Marcus, 1978:516).

According to the 1882 Tongan Land Act, urban and beach land, including a zone extending 50 feet (15.4 metres) inshore from the high water mark, together with a large amount of non-arable rural land, became government estate. With the permission of Cabinet, Tongans and foreigners were allowed to lease land from the government for up to 99 years for the purpose of establishing stores, churches, schools, jetties and wharves. The remaining land was divided into hereditary estates distributed among members of the royal family and other male title holders. The king finally chose 30 chiefs to become *nōpele*, a term adopted from the English 'noble'. His successors have added only three additional titles which, together with the six hereditary *matāpule* estates, make a total of 39 hereditary titled estates throughout the kingdom.[1] The major feature of the act of 1882 was the acquisition and inheritance of land by individual commoner men. The law gave every male aged sixteen years and over the right to receive from his noble's or royal title holder's estate a town allotment of 0.4 acres (0.16 ha.) as a house site and a tax allotment of 8.25 acres (3.3 ha.). On the smaller islands and in the densely populated western region of Tongatapu tax allotments were only half that size. If an allotment holder died without legitimate male issue the land reverted to the estate. In the unlikely event of a man having a female as his sole heir, she inherited only a life interest in his land as long as she remained unmarried and celibate (Adsett, 1989:31–2). Women were rather poorly served in the matter of formal land rights because it was assumed that men, in their roles as husbands, brothers and fathers, would continue to look after them. Widows were given a life interest in their deceased husband's land,

TONGA

163

so long as they did not remarry or cohabit with a man, and unmarried daughters and sisters had the right to be supported for life from their fathers' or brothers' land.

No early map of Tonga shows the noble and *matāpūle* estates. It is likely that they comprised parcels of land held in different parts of the kingdom by chiefs allied to the superior title and who were ruling the land at the time the superior chief was given a noble title. When boundary surveys began at the turn of the century, the surveyors' field books and the original master plans showed large individual tracts of land still held within the hereditary estates by the extended family groups of former chiefs (who were often called petty chiefs, *'eiki si'i*) and their commoner supporters (*kāinga*) whose rights to the land had been superseded by the provisions of the constitution (Tongilava, 1993:3). Within his estate, each noble was granted an *'api fakatofi'a*, a piece of land which was to be held exclusively by the title holder for his own benefit. The size of each noble's personal holding was never precisely determined by the Land Act, but was most likely to have been the estate (*tofi'a*) he held formerly by his chiefly title.

Hindrances to Reform

Few commercial incentives

The constitution was published in Tongan but its immediate impact on patterns of land holding was slight. There were no legal or bureaucratic mechanisms in place to enforce the new regulations and most people either did not know about them or ignored them. The nobility, who were legally dependent upon the monarch and the constitution for their titles, lands, and positions in government, and former chiefs, who had acquired perforce the same legal status as commoners, thus continued to enjoy the tribute and other forms of customary respect rendered by those who lived on their lands (Lātūkefu, 1975:26; Marcus, 1978:524; Morgan, 1985). In addition, there were few incentives from the 1850s to the 1890s for Tongans to acquire cash. European traders and planters bought copra and coconut oil, but Tongan producers concentrated on subsistence production. They did not seek wage labour, and 'engaged in cash cropping only to meet the limited monetary demands' of the Wesleyan Church and the government (Marcus, 1978:526). After the British Protectorate was established in 1900 with the power to review Tonga's financial and foreign affairs,[2] Tongans further reacted against European influence and showed even less interest in commercial production which was almost solely in the hands of a few Europeans and their part-European descendants.

164 LAND, CUSTOM AND PRACTICE IN THE SOUTH PACIFIC

The commoners' registration of tax allotments proceeded slowly and met a further hurdle in 1915 when the Tongan parliament gave nobles the right to be consulted over all applications to register land from their hereditary estates (Lātūkefu, 1975:77). Most nobles chose to interpret the right of consultation as the right to select their tenants and to delay the registration of the allotments. Commoners had always had to have permission from chiefs to use their land, so the 1915 legal revision merely strengthened the general perception that applicants for land must be particularly generous with their gifts in order to be successful (Lātūkefu, 1974:212). In this way, the nobles retained some of their power over the people. In some cases, they have abused this power and caused hardship to commoners who have worked an allotment for years and given gifts of food, kava, and, increasingly, money to the estate holder, only to be denied secure legal tenure of the land. Nobles were ready enough to allocate land from their estates in order to ensure a steady supply of tribute from cultivators, but they were reluctant to allow registration. Once a man paid a small fee and formally registered his allotment with the Ministry of Lands, the land legally passed out of the control of the estate holder (Maude, 1965:105). The estate holder's decision to reject or delay an application for registration could be overturned by the Minister of Lands. But the minister was invariably a noble, and no commoner would think of challenging the authority of one noble by going to another although, on occasion, a noble might speak to another noble on behalf of a tenant (Lātūkefu, 1974:211). Indeed, until well into the 1950s, commoners rarely approached a noble directly but would use an intermediary, a *matāpūle*, a town officer, or a person of pre-reform chiefly rank to take their requests and placatory gifts to the noble (Maude, 1965:103).

In 1927, a new land act was devised by Queen Sālote to improve agricultural productivity. It allowed women to lease land and permitted male tax payers to register 12.25-acre (5.0-ha.) allotments instead of their allotment of statutory size (3.3 ha.). Only a few of such larger tax allotments were registered. The queen also strongly emphasised the value of Tongan traditions based not on money but on family ties and loyalty to social superiors. In the matter of European ways, she advised her people 'to take things slowly' (Tonga, 1948:128). Throughout most of Sālote's reign most Tongan farmers continued to concentrate on subsistence gardening. Only a few who had a pressing need for cash ventured into commercial cultivation. Their efforts were constrained by the still widespread distrust of European-controlled mercantile ventures, combined with fluctuating prices for copra on the world market and difficulties in producing and transporting sufficient bananas of requisite quality to fill Tonga's export quota to New Zealand.

TONGA   165

The lack of involvement of Tonga's almost wholly agrarian economy
with commercial markets meant there was little stimulus for implementation of land reforms. The first registration of land was recorded in
1898, but few others followed (Lātūkefu, 1974:212). Before the first com-
petent and comprehensive survey of land began in 1957, only 2,564
allotments of the statutory 8.25 acres (3.3 ha.) had been marked out.
The retention in many areas of irregularly sized customary holdings,
both surveyed and unsurveyed, frequently hindered subdivision into
statutory allotments (Maude, 1965:101). Many nobles resisted having
their estates surveyed because it would have prevented them from any
further vigorous shifting of their boundaries (Gifford, 1929:176). Land
was not a scarce resource, and most was worked by commoners in a customary fashion for two or three generations after the legislation was
passed. The commoner families used large or small areas as determined
by their chiefs, but with no legal guarantee of tenure (Campbell,
1992:82).

Customary forms of land holding

Many customary forms of land holding and land transfer lingered simply
because there was no legal mechanism to remove them. There was, for
example, no way of immediately removing the petty chiefs' control of
hereditary tracts of land, even though they had been constitutionally
dispossessed of them. Many chiefs were close relatives of the new nobles,
within whose estates their land now lay, and were frequently their supporters in national political struggles. As a result, many nobles left the
local allocation of their land to the lesser chiefs so that its use rights
passed down the traditional hierarchy of authority much as before. The
alternative would have been to subdivide their estates and register the
allotments to commoners, but estate holders were reluctant to do this
because of the loss of influence and tribute it would entail.

In addition, the system established for the surveying and registration
of land plots was itself inadequate and cumbersome. The number and
names of the former chiefs and hereditary land holders were not
recorded in the nineteenth century and remained as indeterminate as
the extent of their lands. The chiefs in pre-reform Tonga were said to
have numbered 'hundreds', but 50 years after the constitution, a mere
75 were recorded by Gifford (1929:132–40). Because both chiefly titles
and lands were customary or 'extra-legal', being neither provided for
nor made illegal by the land law, Gifford's finding may reflect the low
profile that chiefs presented to outsiders as a mark of their respect and
allegiance to the nobles, or it may show that many minor chiefs had
become less widely recognised. After 1927, the Lands Office records

166 LAND, CUSTOM AND PRACTICE IN THE SOUTH PACIFIC

show only the nobles' estates and registered tax and town allotments (Maude, 1965:107–8). Such information as exists about customary holdings comes from oral accounts and local studies. Some 'petty chiefs' continued to hold large tracts of land within noble estates for more than 80 years after the 1882 legislation. The following accounts of two of them, 'Ahio and Lātūkefu, from the western district of Tongatapu, help to explain how many former chiefs who were not made nobles were finally able legally to secure much and sometimes all of their land.

'Ahio, Ata, 'Ahome'e, and Lātūkefu were among the many pre-reform chiefs who had occupied estates in densely populated western Tongatapu. Only Ata and 'Ahome'e were given noble titles and estates although 'Ahio was the highest-ranking of the four (Gifford, 1929:132). His huge tract of customarily-held land stretched from Kolovai in the west (now part of the noble Ata's estate following the 1882 reforms) to south-eastern Tongatapu around the Fua'amotu area, which now lay within the estate of the noble Tungī, Queen Sālote's consort. After the 1934 amendment to the Land Act of 1927, Tungī had encouraged his Fua'amotu tenants to register 15-acre (6-ha.) allotments. Many of these tenants and their families were intelligent, well-educated, and hardworking people whom Tungī had relocated from the soil-poor Ha'apai islands to give a positive example to his more indolent Tongatapu tenants.[3] Another noble, whose estate 'Ahio's land crossed, also wanted more land in hand for his tenants. Accordingly, Prince Tungī told 'Ahio to supervise the land near Fua'amotu, or it would be subdivided. To do this, 'Ahio moved from Kolovai to Fua'amotu in the 1930s. After Prince Tungī's death in 1941, his eldest son, the present king, inherited his estates. Determined to modernise Tonga, he then insisted that 'Ahio's land which lay within the Tungī estate be subdivided into 6-hectare plots. The 'mutual respect and honour' (*feveitokai'aki*) that existed between the two, however, 60 or more years after legislation, had led to one chiefly line becoming royal and the other commoner; the Crown Prince gave 'Ahio's close male relatives first choice of the allotments and they subsequently registered the best plots in their own names. Because of the customary respect (*faka'apa'apa*) granted by chiefs to their sisters and to their sisters' children, the male relatives endowed included 'Ahio's sister's sons, some of whom lived in Nuku'alofa. Thus, all 'Ahio's close family members were able to legally register large allotments from his customary land long after he had been legally dispossessed of it. His land was so extensive, furthermore, that after his numerous relations received six-hectare lots in the 1940s, many other men were also able to register statutory 3.3-hectare allotments from his land.

The junior title of the four was Lātūkefu, who held a smaller tract of land near Kolovai (Gifford, 1929:134). Ata, his senior in terms of title

TONGA 167

and the noble within whose estate Lātūkefu's land lay, never attempted to evict either him or 'Ahio, showing again the courtesy extended to petty chiefs by their noble relatives. In fact, 'Ahio was cash cropping the richer Kolovai land to provide his household at Fua'amotu with a small income. However, he still permitted the children of his sister, who had married Lātūkefu, the customary rights of *fahu* ('above the law'), which allowed them to take produce from his farms in the Kolovai area in the 1950s despite his farm manager's annoyance. Money was very scarce in Tonga at the time, but 'Ahio never complained to his sister concerning her children's rights. In the early 1960s, following the completion of the cadastral survey of Tonga, the noble Ata still did not want to issue orders to his junior kin but, at that point, the then Minister of Lands, Tu'i Pelehake, the king's younger brother, politely asked Lātūkefu to register his land's subdivisions. All the land was subsequently registered in 3.3-hectare allotments by Lātūkefu's sons and brothers.

Petty chiefly families also had a distinct advantage compared with other commoners in the allocation of town allotments. For example, 'Ahio had a town allotment in Kolovai of almost 1.2 hectares, far larger than the statutory limits, on which his sister, her husband Lātūkefu and their family also lived. In the 1960s, the Kolovai Town Officer, a commoner not of chiefly descent, challenged the validity of this large town allotment. But Ata, the noble of Kolovai, overrode the objections in favour of his 'Ahio and Lātūkefu relatives. The two families later subdivided the land to provide town allotments for several of their younger members. In these ways, chiefly families were able to retain, exchange among themselves, and legally register large amounts of the customarily-held land of which they had been constitutionally dispossessed (S. Lātūkefu, pers. comm. September 1993).

Customary holdings

The term 'customary holding' refers to plots of land that are generally recognised to have been with certain families for generations. Early surveyors identified the boundaries of customary holdings demarcated by trees, stones and other landmarks, by asking the heads of neighbouring holdings where the survey lines should be pegged (Tongilava, 1993:3). Such holdings could be registered as tax allotments if the Minister of Lands was satisfied that the boundaries were clearly established and agreed upon by both the estate holder and prospective tenant. In the case of disputes, the minister might order a survey of the boundaries (Adsett, 1989:14). Until the completion of the cadastral survey in 1962 permitted greater regulation, a large number of customary holdings remained unsurveyed. In the early 1960s, before the completion of the

168 LAND, CUSTOM AND PRACTICE IN THE SOUTH PACIFIC

cadastral survey which began in 1957, Maude found customary holdings, both surveyed and unsurveyed, registered and unregistered, to be prevalent in the four estates he studied and in other places studied by others. For example, only a small part of the 1,907-hectare estate of the noble Ma'afu in central Tongatapu had been surveyed into 3.3-hectare allotments; over half was still divided into customary holdings of between 4 and 53 hectares (Maude, 1965:111).

Customary holdings also tended to predominate in other areas of long-established settlement and cultivation where local conditions overrode the constitutional provisions. On the noble 'Ahome'e's 138-hectare estate in western Tongatapu, early surveyors had merely defined the boundaries of the existing holdings, which varied from 0.7 to 6.3 hectares. As elsewhere, land tenure was complicated because some residents held land outside the estate, and men living in other villages but who 'belonged' by kinship to 'Ahome'e held land from him. Except for one section near the village of Matahau, the estate had never been subdivided into 3.3-hectare lots (Maude, 1965:109). Similarly, in 1952 when Koch studied the small island of 'Uiha in Ha'apai, 5.4 square kilometres in area, its customary holdings had not been surveyed (Maude, 1965:113–4). The cadastral survey on 'Uiha defined customary boundaries of allotments ranging in size between less than 0.4 and 10 hectares, the same range as on 'Ahome'e's western Tongatapu estate. Most plots were small, and the ideal of 3.3 hectares for tax allotments was never realised. 'Uiha was more finely subdivided than 'Ahome'e's estate and there were relatively more allotments available on 'Uiha in relation to the number of residents. On the other hand, the people on Tongatapu had opportunities of obtaining land outside the estate which gave those within it more chance of having sizeable holdings; whereas the people of 'Uiha were limited to their small island alone (Maude, 1965:113–4).

After the cadastral survey, customary holdings larger than the statutory size were required to be subdivided into 3.3-hectare allotments (Maude, 1965:99). The allotments that resulted were usually registered by close relatives of the original customary holder, as in the case of 'Ahio's and Lātūkefu's land. But registration of allotments meant that land which had been held by extended kin groups and controlled by their head was now held by individuals. Family heads ('ulumotu'a) preferred land held by custom because the tracts were often much larger than the statutory size and the senior kinsman of an extended family had a great deal of discretionary power in allocating parts of the land to particular households for cultivation. They could make tenurial arrangements and land transfers, which were directed more toward discharging customary obligations to wider kin and nobles than to the use of the land for personal gain (Marcus, 1978:526). The cadastral survey sub-

TONGA 169

divided and enabled the registration of thousands of allotments. The significant increase in registration weakened smallholders' allegiance to extended family groupings and moved them further toward the goals of individualism and economic independence which underlay the initial reform, processes which had begun with the emancipatory ideas of the mid-nineteenth century (Maude, 1965:121; Marcus, 1978:526). Without explicit direction as to what the law should do in the case of surviving customs, however, many former practices had been maintained outside the law rather than in direct contradiction to it (cf. Marcus, 1977:229). The accommodation of law and customary practice can be traced over several generations in the case study of one small island community.

Customary practice

Falahola Island (a pseudonym) is 1.24 sq. km. in area and lies 3 km. off 'Uta Vava'u, the principal island of Tonga's main northern group (Figure 5.2). For most of this century, the distribution and control of tax allotments on the island has involved broader sets of kin than is implied by legally defined individual land tenure. Older brothers frequently shared their inheritance rights to registered allotments with younger brothers, and also with male cousins who are classificatory brothers in the Tongan kinship system. Where possible, allotment holders also provided land for females and for illegitimate and fostered male relatives, all of whom had been excluded by legal provisions from the inheritance of land allotments but who by custom required provision. These irregular illegal or extra-legal transactions were countenanced and managed by three successive noble estate holders who, unlike many other nobles in the twentieth century, had resided continuously on their estate. The noble title was first granted in 1880, but the dates of neither the first noble's death nor of his son's succession are recorded in the palace office. The second title holder lived on Falahola until his death in 1934. He was succeeded in 1935 by his oldest son, who died in 1971. The earlier nobles appear to have used their legal prerogatives to structure the island community; they did not permit men from elsewhere to register land on Falahola, although some in-marrying men were allowed small gardens (cf. Adsett, 1989:16).

The first three nobles exercised a great deal of discretionary power over the disbursement of allotments and transfers of tenure between island families. This was arranged primarily through the legal reversion of allotments to the estate after the death of a land holder and their reallocation by the noble, or by asking an absentee holder to surrender his allotment to the estate for reallocation to another resident islander. Since the death of the old noble in 1971, there has been a markedly

170 LAND, CUSTOM AND PRACTICE IN THE SOUTH PACIFIC

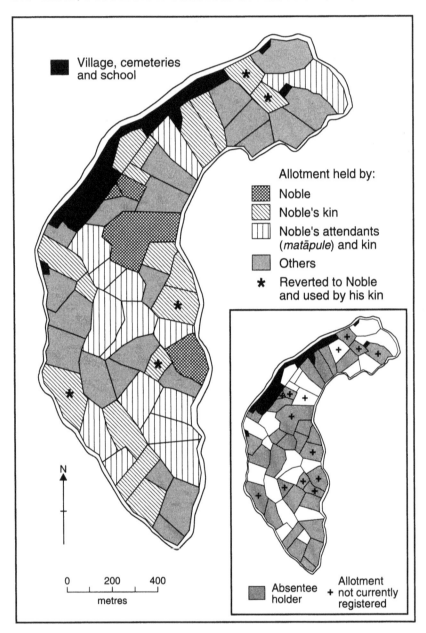

Figure 5.2 'Falahola' Island.
Sources: Field enquiries and land registration records, Ministry of Lands, Survey and Natural Resources.

TONGA   171

greater emphasis on allotments as individual property subject to individual control. Before then, allotments tended to be controlled for the good of a wider set of kin and of the island community as a whole as it was represented by the noble. The title was vacant from 1971 until 1974 because the heir, the previous noble's oldest son, had not returned from the United States. He then briefly held the title from 1974 until his untimely death in 1977. During that time he converted some garden land next to the village into town allotments for his own kin, reputedly for bribes. (The result of this irregular transaction is not classed on Figure 5.2 as part of the village, and the two small 'noble's tax allotments' are shown as garden land abutting the village.) The last noble was not well regarded because of these and other irregular actions. The title again remained vacant from 1977 until 1993 through the lack of a direct legitimate male heir. In 1993 the oldest son of the last noble's eldest sister was appointed by the king to the title. The appointment is too recent, however, to alter the present account.

The population of Falahola was not enumerated until the census of 1956, when it had 212 people and a relatively high population density of 170 people per square kilometre, comparable to that of 186 on 'Uiha in Ha'apai and 178 on 'Ahome'e's estate in Tongatapu (Maude, 1965: 68, 69, 108). The population had increased to 270 by 1966 and remained the same in 1976, but then fell to 218 in 1986. In 1993, the author counted only 170 people resident on the island. The population may have been more numerous in previous decades because the island was for generations the noble's seat and included members of his large extended family, his two *matāpūle* and their extended families, and numerous supporters and affines. Despite a high degree of recent out-migration, the island has retained its identity as a community because of the cohesion provided by numerous overlapping kinship ties between the residents. When tracing people's relationships over generations, it became increasingly difficult to decide from whose standpoint a person was 'close' or 'distant' kin. The relative hardship of life on an outer island has increasingly limited Falahola people's choice of marriage partners and many have married within the island in direct contravention of the Tongan custom that forbids commoners to marry anyone to whom they can trace any relationship. In the 1980s, people on Falahola wryly admitted that they are 'pretty much all related to one another', frequently in several different ways. By the 1990s, the islanders lived mainly by fishing and subsistence gardening, supplemented by wage labour in Neiafu, Vava'u's main town, and remittances of goods and money sent from overseas (James, 1991). Falahola has generally poor soil and few cultivators have attempted to grow cash crops. By 1993, because of migration, there were in any case only 30 able-bodied men to care for 140 other people on the island. Most of the island's

172 LAND, CUSTOM AND PRACTICE IN THE SOUTH PACIFIC

residents were either very old or very young, as is the case on most other outer islands in Tonga.

Not all of the island's 124 hectares is arable land. About 18.6 hectares is government estate. The village occupies 8 hectares and a further 10.5 hectares is taken up in steep cliffs at the northern and southern ends of the island and the rocky foreshores between seven beaches, which are also government land, including a zone extending 15.4 metres above high water mark. The 59 tax allotments occupy 105 hectares. Tax allotments on the island began to be registered from 1908, ten years after the country's earliest recorded registration. By 1928, 47 of the present 59 tax allotments were registered. All but the two allotments that the last noble converted into town allotments had been registered by individuals at some time. Two of three small allotments which had reverted to the estate became sites for cemeteries and one became the site for the government primary school (Figure 5.2). Among the 56 remaining arable tax allotments, 17 allotments are not currently registered. In 1962, at the completion of the cadastral survey, the allotments ranged in area from less than 0.4 up to 5.7 hectares. The average tax allotment was 1.7 hectares, just over half the statutory size. The mode was a little over 2 hectares and the median was minimally above the mean. Many of the tax allotments had been formed by amalgamating two or three older gardens each of which was named, usually for a flowering plant or a landmark. Since 47 per cent of the present tax allotments are only 1.2 to 2.4 hectares in area and only one, the noble's 5.3-hectare *'api fakatofi'a* (the land belonging to the title), is larger than 3.6 hectares, most of the older gardens must have been less than 0.75 hectares in size. Thus, Falahola was even more finely divided than 'Uiha, being less than a quarter its size. It was also known locally as 'the most [active] fishing village in Vava'u' because of the rich reefs that lay nearby. It is likely that marine resources formed the greater part of the people's diet and that the sea was once as great a part of their life as the land.

Absentees hold 34 allotments, accounting for 65 hectares. In 1993, only 12 of these allotments were out of date in their registration. Interestingly, five allotments which are at least two or three generations out of current registration are occupied by close kin of the former noble. Although each of the allotments once was registered, the land would have reverted to the estate. Thus, the noble's kin have been using the land 'at his will' in a form of tenure by customary right (cf. Maude, 1965:107). It is not clear why the users have not registered the allotments. The noble estate holders may not have encouraged their close agnates to register land in order to keep some control over them, or the occupiers may simply have felt quite secure in their tenure because they were close relatives of the estate holder. Their tenure is, in fact, secure

TONGA 173

because of their long recognised continuous use of the land. Should a dispute over these allotments arise with the new noble, the court would almost certainly decide in favour of the five who are using the land in the second and third generation even without formal registration, because, on several occasions, the Land Court has decided that 'registration is not the only test of ownership' (Hunter, 1963:104–6,121–5; Maude and Sevele, 1987:126). This type of customary tenure is becoming rare today, however, especially in prime cash cropping areas, which do not include Falahola. It is quite different from the more casual use of the second largest block of 'noble's land' (Figure 5.2), only part of which is occasionally cultivated by a distant kinsman of the last noble. There is not the same permanence and certainly no security of tenure regarding this form of 'permissive occupancy' which occurs from time to time on Falahola on other allotments held by absentees, or on allotments whose registered holders are deceased and whose heirs are relatives of the users (cf. Maude, 1965:107).

By 1990 the vacant title held just over 18 hectares of island land directly. This included the title's *'api fakatofi'a* of 5.5 hectares, a tax allotment of 2.3 hectares registered successively by each noble in his own name, and the two small unregistered allotments amounting to 1.1 hectares next to the village which were converted into town allotments in the mid-1970s. These four allotments in the noble's direct control amounted to 8.9 hectares. In addition, almost 9.3 hectares of estate land was allocated in the five allotments customarily held by close kinsmen. When these 18.2 hectares in nine allotments were added to the 18 hectares registered by the noble's kin in a further 12 allotments, a total of just over 36 hectares, over a third of the island's arable land, was held in the early 1990s in 21 allotments by the title holder and his kin. Members of the noble's two *matāpūle*'s families held between them another 30.8 hectares in 14 allotments. Over 38 hectares, 36 per cent, of the island's garden land was held in 21 allotments by other people.

The majority of the 51 transmissions of land recorded by the author on Falahola were from father to son. Although the 'father' frequently proved to be the father's brother or father's father's brother, or an even more distant agnate, the transactions were within the law and also satisfied the customary obligations to provide for relatives. In several cases, however, processes other than legalisms were more clearly at work. Legal succession to an allotment cannot be traced through a female, so a man has no claim to his mother's father's land. But these rules do not follow Tongan custom, and in Falahola nine of the 51 transmissions were through women; three from a father to his daughter's son, one from a father to his widowed daughter for her life interest, one from a widow to her brother's son, and four from mother's brothers to their sisters' sons.

174 LAND, CUSTOM AND PRACTICE IN THE SOUTH PACIFIC

Many of these variations are acknowledged in practice in Tonga, for 'where there are no heirs through males, estate-holders and the Minister of Lands usually permit the nearest male relative to register the land' (Maude and Sevele, 1987:123). So, the law itself is often modified in its formal practice. It is certain that in these Falahola cases there was no direct male heir on the island. One could not be sure that an heir did not exist elsewhere in Tonga or overseas, but from the viewpoint of the islanders an 'extra-legal' inheritance by a current resident had priority. The noble estate holders clearly gave preference to island residents rather than to remote legal heirs who were unlikely to make any contribution to island life. Heirs were either not contacted or were asked by the noble to relinquish their claim in favour of a relative on the island.

Islanders insisted that 'the two families of parents are free to give land to their daughter's children if they love them'. They recounted also cases in which men had 'given land to their sisters'. When it was suggested that they could not do this, because of the legal provisions, the people merely shrugged and said, 'This is our island, and our noble can do what he wants'. The tension between the customary and legal forms of inheritance showed in two cases where land passed from an older to a younger brother rather than to the older brother's oldest son, and another four cases in which land passed to a foster son. These were practices of long standing in pre-reform custom but both became forbidden by law (Marcus, 1977:235–8; Urbanowicz, 1973:118–9). The constitution also made the inheritance by foster children illegal. But the nobles of Falahola continued the practice as a means of providing for families and households excluded from the inheritance of land. In the early decades of this century, there were two cases on Falahola of foster children (sister's sons given to their mother's brothers) receiving their foster fathers' land, through its reversion to the estate upon the death of the foster father and its subsequent reallocation by the noble to the foster son. In the same way, the noble provided allotments for both his youngest brother, who was an illegitimate son of his father, and for one of his own illegitimate sons by 'fostering' them with childless land holders. The nobles usually did not seek to subvert the law, but they exercised power as estate holders to choose how it would work.

Two case studies show how individual male land holders' continuing responsibility for their wider kin was translated with the help of the noble into the transmission of people and land. By fostering heirs to landless relatives, the land holders provided their kin with both land and a 'son' to work it. In the first case (Figure 5.3), a man [4] inherited land from his deceased father [2]. His father's sister [3] never married and was therefore entitled by law to provision from her father's and brother's land. [3] was [4]'s *mehekitanga* (his father's sister), customarily the most

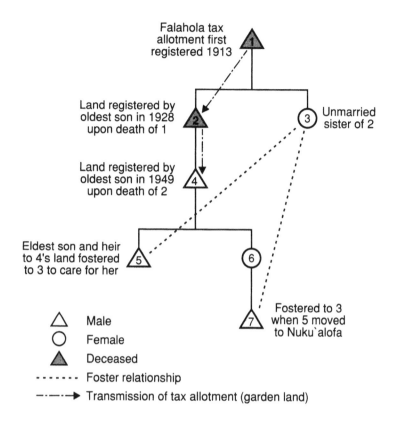

Figure 5.3 Transmission of land and people on 'Falahola': case I.
Sources: Field enquiries and land registration records, Ministry of Lands, Survey and Natural Resources.

honoured person in the Tongan extended family. Accordingly, [4] gave to [3] his heir [5] as a foster child so that [3] according to custom had control over both her brother's child and sustenance from his land (cf. Rogers, 1977:162). After [4]'s death, however, the land will pass to [5] according to the law. When [5] left the island to take a job in Nuku'alofa, his sister [6], who also lives in Nuku'alofa, sent her son [7] back to [3], to honour her by giving her a 'son' to work for her and to 'keep her company'. [4] provides food for both [3] and [7], and [7] helps [4] garden.

The second, more complex, case probably evolved less as a grand plan than as a series of ad hoc arrangements and shows how land and children were shared among a set of siblings for three generations (Figure 5.4).

An older brother [1] and his younger brother [2] both registered allotments on Falahola in 1913. [1]'s only son [6] died without issue in

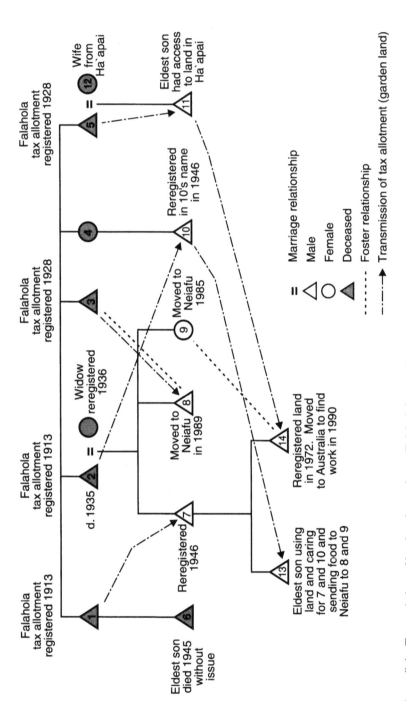

Figure 5.4 Transmission of land and people on 'Falahola': case II.
Sources: Field enquiries and land registration records, Ministry of Lands, Survey and Natural Resources.

TONGA 177

1945 so [1]'s land passed to his brother [2]'s eldest son [7]. In 1993, [7] was old and was being cared for by his sons [13] and [14], who jointly garden [7]'s land, which will be inherited by [13]. In the original sibling set, a third brother [3] and a fourth brother [5] were also able to register small allotments, each of less than 4 acres, in 1928. [3] did not marry, but was given a foster son and namesake, [8], who was the second son of his older brother [2]. According to custom, the child [8] had been named for [3] by his sister [4], [8]'s father's sister (his *mehekitanga*). Also, following Tongan custom but not the law, the foster son [8] 'inherited' his foster father [3]'s allotment. The second brother [2], it was said, 'loved [4] his only sister so much that he gave his *'api* to her'. Actually, [2]'s *'api* passed to his sister [4]'s son [10]. As the registrations show, [1] had provided for [2]'s eldest son [7]; so [2] had given his second son [8] to his brother [3] in order to help him and so the boy would obtain [3]'s land as an 'inheritance'. When [2] died in 1936, the life interest in his land passed to his widow, who registered it in her name. When she died ten years later, however, since both sons [7] and [8] were provided with land, [2]'s land did, indeed, pass to [10], who registered it in his name in 1946. [7]'s land was re-registered, from [1]'s to his name, in the same year. This suggests that [1] and [2]'s plots had probably been worked by [7] and [10] for the benefit of the original holders' families, until the death of [2]'s widow, when each man registered his inheritance and [7] formally transferred his father's allotment to his cousin [10].

The principle of inheritance through males rather than through females reasserted itself in the next generation, however, because, by the 1980s, [13] was using his future inheritance. Thus, [2] might well have loved his sister so much that he gave his land to her son but, when her son dies, the allotment will return to [2]'s oldest son [7]'s oldest son [13] according to the legal provision of inheritance through male primogeniture. Since [13] will inherit from [7] and [13]'s eldest son from [13], [10]'s land may pass to a younger son of [13] or [14] because both these men have adult sons living on the island and, together, working the allotments as a unit (see below).

In the third generation, another example occurs of a child [14], who was heir to land, being given as 'foster child' to [9], his father's sister, who had no land. In the first generation, the youngest brother of the set [5], who registered land on Falahola in 1928, married a Ha'apai woman and went to live with her people. His eldest son [11] married in Ha'apai and received land there. Accordingly, [11] surrendered his tax allotment on Falahola in favour of [14], who was his father [5]'s brother [2]'s son [7]'s son but who, by becoming [9]'s foster son, had become, in the Tongan classificatory system, [11]'s 'sister's son' and, therefore, of higher status than him in the family. Since [13] would legally inherit

178 LAND, CUSTOM AND PRACTICE IN THE SOUTH PACIFIC

[7]'s allotment and would also receive one from [10], [7] fostered his second son [14] with his sister [9] so that she should have a son and the use of the land that [14] would obtain from [11]. The sister [9] later married a man with land but they had no children.

By the fourth generation, which is not detailed here or shown in Figure 5.4, much of the land has passed by law to heirs who have migrated and are not likely to return to Falahola and, yet, jealously guard their land rights on the island for themselves and their heirs. Among these men are several who registered land only after the former noble's death in 1971. They included the son of [14] who registered [9]'s husband's land, to which he has no right in law, but which was possible because of the enduring bonds that exist between [14] and [9]. [14] gave his daughter to [9] as a foster child because she has no children of her own, as he himself had been given to her. As a widow, [9] had the life interest in her husband's allotment, which is now being used by another foster daughter and her husband because [14]'s son, who registered the *'api*, emigrated to Australia in the 1970s.

Many heirs are keen to secure land rights on Falahola, although they have salaried employment elsewhere. Increased commercial activity in Tonga in the 1970s, combined with increasing migration and commercialisation, has made people more aware of the value of land rights as a commodity. The earlier suggestion that successive estate holders managed the distribution of land on Falahola is supported indirectly by the fact that only three re-registrations of land by heirs took place between 1948 and 1970, but there have been 16 since then; eight of which occurred in 1971–2, immediately after the death of the last long-established noble of Falahola.

One might speculate that people who had held land 'at the pleasure' of the old noble because they either felt secure with him or, alternately, were not permitted by him to re-register the allotments, quickly registered them in their own names once he died, especially as his heir did not immediately succeed him to the title. It is difficult to say whether or not successive noble estate holders achieved a harmonious distribution of people and land because, presumably, alienated or frustrated islanders and those who had other aspirations left Falahola. By the early 1980s, when I first visited the island, land holding was potentially a divisive issue. Land had achieved a monetary value and had also become a marker of social status in the new order (cf. Marcus, 1977:223–4). Land holders on Falahola had become more reluctant than previously to share use rights with siblings. Nine of the 34 'absentee' holders on Falahola (Figure 5.2) had moved too long ago to be traced. The other 25, known

TONGA 179

to live in other parts of Tonga or overseas, hold almost one-third of the arable acreage. Only three of the 25 have wholly, even though informally, made over land to the use of younger brothers; all three are church ministers and said to be 'Christian' and 'generous'. Only 14 registered land holders reside on the island; another 18 male residents, who are heads of households, cannot get title to land because they are younger sons or originate from elsewhere. In 1993, 15 of the 18 had permissive occupancy of land through women; they used their widowed mother's, married sister's husband's, or wife's family's land. In 1993, new town allotments were unobtainable, although 12 houses, representing a third of the town allotments, were vacant because their owners had emigrated. The notion of personal, individual 'ownership' is now very strong and Falahola people confine their activities within the bounds of their own land or that of their close relatives but only with their permission.

Provision for family members without land rights has been recorded elsewhere, and may be found throughout Tonga. Van der Grijp's study in the late 1980s of the changing fortunes of an extended family in the prosperous, vanilla-growing village of Taoa in western 'Uta Vava'u showed senior men 'expected to help their sisters and their children', and also their junior male kin (Van der Grijp, 1993a; 1993b:245). He concluded that shared use arrangements:

> indicate a partial return to the pre-Constitution system, when all the males in the *maison* [local kin group] had access to (the use of) land. Land is now officially transferred from father to oldest son but, in practice, the use of the land, and in some cases, even the inheritance rights, are shared between younger brothers and other relatives. (Van der Grijp, 1993b:246)

These modern cooperative arrangements, however, are qualitatively different from pre-constitutional ones in which all the men of an extended family or *kāinga* gardened together, under the leadership of the *'ulumotu'a*, their senior kinsman or chief, in a situation where each extended family had to provide its own subsistence and a surplus as tribute for the superior chief, and where other means of support were virtually unknown. In Van der Grijp's example, however, the land is held legally by individuals and not on behalf of the whole *kāinga*. The individual holders can choose with whom to share land and, as a consequence, Van der Grijp's conclusion is contradicted by his own data when he notes that the younger members of the shallow patrilines that garden the allotments held by senior males were uncertain of their future and that 'a growing number of young men emigrate to the capital or abroad in the search for an income for themselves and their households' (Van

180 LAND, CUSTOM AND PRACTICE IN THE SOUTH PACIFIC

der Grijp, 1993b:246). On Falahola some young men also cultivate subsistence gardens with their fathers because they have no other livelihood, but many others, who have no chance of inheritance and insufficient education to find salaried employment in Tonga, have emigrated, as have the young people from Van der Grijp's study site Taoa.

The work groups of close relatives in Tongan cultivation in the 1980s can be explained not in terms of atavistic tendencies to pre-reform modes of production, but by the relative shortage of land, especially commercially-productive land, and the paucity of other sources of income. In the late 1980s, the profit from an allotment well planted with vanilla in Taoa was likely to be between T$20,000 and T$24,000, sufficient to provide a cash income for several nuclear families. Similar cooperation between related male cultivators has also occurred in other productive cash cropping areas, such as on Kotu Island in Ha'apai, where men regularly travelled 35 km, or five hours each way by boat, to cultivate kava in the rich volcanic soil of the neighbouring uninhabited island, Tōfua (Perminow, 1993). In the 1990s, male (and female) relatives working together in commercial or subsistence agriculture does not disguise the fact that the land itself is in the hands of an individual, who may welcome relatives as co-workers when many hands are needed, but who can also legally deny them access to land. A registered allotment holder has the same rights over the land as a noble and many, it is said, 'act like little chiefs'. Since the 1960s, commercial land holding in fact has become much less like the pre-reform situation. The control of land has become more individualised, and its use more exclusive where lucrative commercial ventures developed. Cash has become an increasingly vital factor in land use arrangements, in which growers pay relatives for the use of land and also pay for the labour of family members. In Tongatapu, particularly in areas where squash is cultivated, family workers who are not paid are likely to offer their labour to another grower for payment, as the demand for adequate labour and land has far outstripped its availability, and the values of land holders have altered.

Population Growth and Increasing Commercialisation

Population increase

It is ironic that in 1957, the very year in which a comprehensive cadastral survey of the country began, the rapidly expanding population surpassed the point at which it would have been possible for every Tongan man to have his statutory right to land. The population grew rapidly after 1921 and more than trebled between 1931 and 1976 with an increase from 27,700 to 90,085 people. Since the 1930s, the population

TONGA 181

density within the total land area of 669 sq. km. increased from 41 persons per sq. km to more than 135 persons per sq. km. Since about 1980, the population has remained around 95,000 because of emigration overseas. But emigration does not necessarily free up land, and it was estimated in the 1980s that at least 10 per cent of registered allotments were held by people living overseas who were under no legal obligation to allow other people to use their land in their absence (Maude and Sevele, 1987:128).

Internal migration has brought about an increasing divergence between the distribution of population and the distribution of arable land. In 1990, the Tongatapu group (Figure 5.1) had 52 per cent of Tonga's land but 67 per cent of the population, most of whom lived on Tongatapu, an island of 260 sq. km., or less than 40 per cent of the country's land area. Almost a third of Tonga's population, about 30,000 people, were crowded into the capital Nuku'alofa. Nearby villages contained another 15,000 people, many of whom commute daily to Nuku'alofa. As a result, by the 1990s very nearly half the total population was concentrated in or around the capital. Fewer than 20,000 people lived on the 180 sq. km. of land in Vava'u, the northern group, and only a few hundred of them on the northern outliers, Niuatoputapu, Niuafo'ou, and Tafahi. Fewer still, only 9,000, were in Ha'apai. The middle group has the most restricted resource base of the three main groups with 119 sq. km. of land scattered between 36 islands composed mainly of atolls.

Land distribution

The 471 square kilometres of arable land in Tonga (71 per cent of the total land area) allows a maximum subdivision of 14,470 tax allotments of statutory size (Maude, 1965:22,196n25). Before 1960, most government land had been surveyed but only a comparatively small area, amounting to 2,564 allotments, had been registered. The government estate of Niutōua, 769 hectares in area, which Maude studied, was among the first estates to be subdivided into 3.3-hectare lots. Located at the eastern tip of Tongatapu, Niutōua reflected most nearly the intention of the initial land reforms: only 3 per cent of households in Maude's sample had no land, 66 per cent had the regulation allotment, and 31 per cent had 6.5 hectares because two taxpayers in each household had an allotment. But even here the problems of land distribution that accelerated in the following years already existed, since 17 per cent of male taxpayers on the estate had no land because all the allotments were occupied, and 33 per cent of those registered as land holders at Niutōua actually lived elsewhere in Tonga (Maude, 1965:112).

182 LAND, CUSTOM AND PRACTICE IN THE SOUTH PACIFIC

In the early 1960s, 60 per cent of the population resided on nobles' estates, where the situation was much less straightforward than on government land. Comparatively little of the nobles' land was surveyed. 'In 1962 over half the title-holders had not fully registered their estates and some had not registered any of their land at all' (Maude, 1965:100). In 1961, only 7,585 tax allotments were registered (5,000 more than before the cadastral survey began), of which approximately 1,100 were held by widows. At the time, 11,485 men, or 64 per cent of the 17,970 males aged 16 and over who were entitled to land, did not have a registered holding (Maude, 1965:117). After the cadastral survey was completed, in mid-1962, there were 12,950 surveyed allotments but possibly as many as 18,400 male tax payers 16 years and over who were legally entitled to land and about 1,500 widows, who were entitled to a life interest in an allotment. In all, there were about 7,000 Tongans eligible for land in excess of the number of allotments (Maude, 1965:180–2). The government had little more land to distribute and, by 1966, the majority of the newly-surveyed allotments on noble estates had been allocated to tenants, although it is not clear how much of the land from noble estates was securely registered, or how evenly it was distributed between different households (Needs, 1988:59).[4]

Most of the figures given for the 1950s and 1960s are derived from Maude's estimates. The Tongan government did not produce regular reports on land holding until the end of 1971, when almost 41 per cent of the total land area had been granted as tax and town allotments and, 'the Crown and nobility retained either absolute or very strong control over almost 50 per cent of the total land area' (Needs, 1988:59). Nearly 30 per cent of the land, over 20,000 hectares, was designated as nobles' estates at a time when it was calculated that 14,000 taxable males were without registered allotments (Taliai, 1975:23). Figures such as these, angrily quoted by militant churchmen and others, were among the reasons that in 1974 the government, composed largely of nobles, reclassified three quarters of the land previously categorised as 'hereditary noble estates' as 'allotments not yet registered but already allocated'. The magnitude of the nobles' holdings was thus statistically altered from just over 27 per cent of the total land area in 1973 to under 7 per cent in 1974 (Needs, 1988:60). The 19,843 hectares, 'already allocated' but not registered in the name of the user, continued to produce a stream of gifts from farmers to their noble landlords. A further five per cent of Tongan land was leased to churches, schools, companies, non-Tongans and other land users. Finally, the government held 22 per cent of the total land area, but this was mainly in the form of uninhabited islands and land not suitable for agriculture (Tonga Census, 1976, I:3). By 1984–5, most usable land was in some form of private tenure but the number of eligible tax payers was 28,372, almost

TONGA 183

double the number of the 14,471 existing tax allotment holders (Maude and Sevele, 1987:137). Another 2,000 to 3,000 'allocated' acres were registered as allotments as the trend towards individual control continued. By 1989, town and tax allotments held by tax payers accounted for 62 per cent of all land, of which almost 45 per cent was registered and over 17 per cent was 'allocated' (see Table 5.1).

By the 1990s, the proportion of men eligible for land in Tonga who held a registered allotment had fallen, perhaps to less than one quarter. It was estimated in the mid-1980s that 'by the year 2000 the number of eligible tax payers in Tonga is likely to exceed 40,000' (Maude and Sevele, 1987:137). If widows and emigrant men eligible for land were added, the number of claimants would exceed 55,000, but even were all the remaining arable land to be allocated 'the number of tax allotments would not exceed 16,000' (ibid.). If all the emigrants were to return home, Tonga could provide less than a third of the number of allotments required to fulfil the statutory provisions. Given this situation, it was ironic that at the time so much arable land lay idle, bound up in registered holdings by men who had moved overseas or chosen not to farm. In 1984, when cash cropping was still largely confined to coconuts and bananas, it was estimated that only 37 per cent of arable land in Tongatapu was in use, allowing for the pattern of shifting cultivation that left parts of allotments fallow for one to three years (quoted in Maude and Sevele, 1987:135). In the late 1980s and early 1990s, pumpkin squash was introduced for export to Japan. The success of the squash as a commercial crop in addition to the growth of the vanilla market placed an even higher demand on land suitable for cultivation. These developments led to previously unused land being made available for cropping through formal or informal arrangements, especially in Tongatapu.

Increasing commercialisation

Because Maude's fieldwork ended in 1962, when the cadastral subdivision had created many new allotments, he was able to look forward optimistically to their future allocation and registration. He wrote then of 'equality overtaking privilege' because, 'the current re-allocation should . . . markedly alter the distribution of land' (Maude, 1965:101). But by then there were already more men than allotments. The increasing numbers of landless men meant that land holding itself became a form of 'privilege'. Many government employees, whose jobs brought them social prestige but low salaries, were also part-time cultivators (cf. Marcus, 1978:526–7). The pattern which emerged was far from Maude's vision of 'equality', and also very different from Tupou I's ideal of all male tax payers having land.

184 LAND, CUSTOM AND PRACTICE IN THE SOUTH PACIFIC

Table 5.1   Land holding in Tonga, 1989

	Area (acres)	Hectares	%
Registered tax and town allotments			
to Tongans	82,523	33,397	44.7
Allotments 'allocated', but not yet			
registered	31,997	12,949	17.3
Land of hereditary nobles	12,824	5,190	6.9
Land leased by:			
Government	2,063	835	1.1
Churches	5,651	2,287	3.1
Statutory Boards	580	235	0.3
Tongan Nationals	3,485	1,410	1.9
Foreigners	5,120	2,072	2.8
(Number of lease holders is 3,064)			
Government land (uninhabited land, forest			
reserves, volcanic islands etc.)	21,019	8,506	11.4
Other government estate (water bodies,			
lakes, etc.)	19,413	7,856	10.5
TOTAL	184,675	74,737	100.0

Source: Government of Tonga, *Statistical Abstract*, 1989:141–2.

Tongans' desire for cash had grown markedly after the Second World War with their increased knowledge of the outside world and a greater desire for education and overseas travel to enable the younger generation to take their place in the modern world (Bollard, 1974). Progress in education and the economy quickened in the 1940s after the return to Tonga of the Crown Prince. The first Tongan to gain a university degree overseas, he became Minister of Education and, in 1949, Premier. A boost in the world copra market in the 1950s, followed by a boom in the market for bananas in the 1960s, encouraged Tongan farmers to produce cash crops. After the cadastral survey, more farmers formally registered allotments and became reluctant to share land intended for commercial farming. Maude noted in the early 1960s the increasing difficulty of borrowing land for commercial production and the growing number of cases in which a cash payment or gifts were given for the use of land, especially in cash cropping areas of Tongatapu. He also observed that the great majority of non-commercial producers were able to borrow land for the cultivation of subsistence crops through informal arrangements with senior kin, for which no direct payment was made (Maude, 1965:119–20). Further increases in population and in the value of land, however, hardened the attitudes of registered allotment holders. Their own production of food and a monetary income permitted them to favour their nuclear

TONGA

families above the claims of wider kin (Marcus, 1978:526). If they wished they could now operate with a greater degree of individual independence from wider familial obligations. Meanwhile, junior kin became more conscious of the limitations of being legally landless.

In 1965 the present king, Tupou IV, succeeded his mother Queen Sālote. By that time most Tongans wanted a steady source of cash income beyond periodic cash needs for the church and other forms of non-commercial payments. Increased revenue from overseas aid, in addition to increased exports, had 'enabled the Government to develop education, medical, and other services', and to build up financial reserves, develop shipping, vanilla production, fisheries, building construction, and light manufacturing industries (Maude, 1965:44–5). The king steadily promoted modernisation. The civil service expanded with the influx of overseas aid, and the church became a particularly important sector in Tonga's economy, also with aid from overseas. Since the 1970s, remittances of money sent by Tongan emigrants have been injected into the informal and formal economy 'including transactions in the subsistence sector and traditional exchanges' and 'stimulating the demand for imports' (Marcus, 1978:527–8).

Most people prefer positions in the commercial or government sector for themselves or their children but non-agricultural employment opportunities, although they have increased rapidly since the 1970s, have not matched population growth. The success of large-scale commercial farming during good marketing conditions, however, has also become extremely prestigious. Land holders with some education and positions in government or church bureaucracies, or in the small but increasing number of businesses, have accumulated capital from agriculture or remittances. Many acquired commercial holdings larger than the statutory allotments, mostly on Tongatapu, by informal arrangements with customary and statutory holders, and began to hire agricultural labourers (Marcus, 1978:527–8; James, 1993:217, 224–5). Thus, close personal connections exist between many bureaucrats, business people, and commercial farmers. Landholding urbanites frequently inject capital into their land and have other village-based kinsmen, who also hold land of their own, manage the whole of the combined acreage in expansionist agricultural ventures. Nobles were rarely involved directly in commercial agriculture until the pumpkin squash bonanza began at the end of the 1980s. Most relied primarily for income on their monopoly of government positions, the rents from government, church and business leases, and declining amounts of tribute from their tenants (Marcus, 1978:527). The noble Ma'afu, for example, derived rent and gifts from his tenants, rent from the government's lease of his land for the prison and for the Ministry of Agriculture's experimental farm at

186 LAND, CUSTOM AND PRACTICE IN THE SOUTH PACIFIC

Vaini, from a lease for a church college, and from several coconut plantations leased by church organisations and foreign companies. The leases occupied a quarter of Ma'afu's 1,907-hectare estate in central Tongatapu in the early 1960s (Maude, 1965:111).

Attempts at Land Reform

In the late 1960s, commoners' complaints about the inequitable distribution of land increased. The situation was most acute in Tongatapu because of the limited amount of land left to distribute, and because estate holders were under no legal obligation to give land to the immigrants who had flocked to Nuku'alofa. In 1964, a sample survey found that only 49 per cent of households in the capital had a tax allotment on Tongatapu, sometimes miles from the town, and only another six per cent had land elsewhere in Tonga (Walsh, 1964:63). By the 1966 census, only 33 per cent of the tax payers in Nuku'alofa said that they had a tax allotment (Maude and Sevele, 1987:134). Since then, the ratio of people to land on Tongatapu has grown even higher. The early 1970s were marked by generally poor economic development. Immigrants to Tongatapu found themselves increasingly under stress from the limited employment opportunities available and their lack of access to garden or town land.

Church action

In 1975, the Tonga Council of Churches organised a seminar on land and migration which aired many contentious issues. Nobles were blamed for not releasing more land for registration from their estates and for increasing their demands for gifts and services from their tenants as land became more difficult to acquire. One noble admitted that he knew of these practices (Ma'afu, 1975:1–3). The original legislation was intended to give every man enough land 'for his family', but the increasing tendency for decisions regarding land to be made solely by the individual male holder meant that neither his sister and her children, nor the head, *'ulumotu'a*, of his extended family were being given the respect due to them in matters of land affecting the extended family 'as a whole' (Fifita, 1975:34). However, the government refused all major land reform, and continued to hope that non-agricultural jobs would be provided for those without land.

Amendments to the Land Act

In the late 1970s, in an effort to develop commercial agriculture, the government passed two amendments to the Land Act, thereby making it

TONGA   187

possible for farmers to acquire holdings larger than the statutory allotment. The first amendment permitted the mortgaging of land to the Bank of Tonga (BT) and the Tonga Development Bank (TDB) as collateral to secure loans to 'improve' the land over which the mortgage was granted (Adsett, 1989:35ff.). The land that could be mortgaged included registered tax and town allotments, leases, and hereditary estates. The mortgage period was limited initially to 10 years but, in 1980, the term was increased to 30 years. The second important amendment permitted tax allotment holders (except widows who had only a life interest in their deceased husband's allotment) to lease the allotment for 10 years. Lessees could lease up to five tax allotments at any one time. With Cabinet approval a town allotment of between 0.2 and 0.4 acres could be leased for up to 99 years, and for over 99 years with the permission of Privy Council, which is composed of the monarch and the Cabinet. No individual was to hold more than five town leases at any one time. A further amendment in 1978 permitted an individual to lease up to 10 tax allotments (totalling 33.3 ha) for agricultural purposes for a maximum period of 20 years (Maude and Sevele, 1987:121–2). Under special conditions, 50-year leases could be made with the approval of the Minister of Lands and Cabinet (Adsett, 1989:35). Long leases, however, required the consent of the heir, who might otherwise return to Tonga from overseas on the death of his father to find that he had no land (Fonua, 1991:18).

In sum, since 1984 people can legally hold land in Tonga in the following ways. Land can be held as hereditary estates, by the royal family, nobles, and six *matāpūle* titles, or by male tax payers as a tax or a town allotment from either hereditary or government estates by virtue of the Land Act of 1882. Once an individual registers a tax allotment from an hereditary estate, the security of his interest in the land is similar to that of the noble or *matāpūle* estate holder, and is not one 'of proprietorship but rather of permanent hereditary usufruct' (Marcus, 1978:518). This interest can change hands either by the surrender of the allotment by the tenant to the estate holder and its re-registration by another tax payer, a practice which was resorted to frequently on Falahola Island, or allotment holders can exchange town or tax allotments with one another (Adsett, 1989:24). Land can be also leased from the Crown under of the Land Act of 1882. Finally, through the amendments of 1978 and 1984, registered tax allotments or land leased by a taxpayer can be leased to another Tongan, including women, for up to 20 years subject to Cabinet approval or for up to 50 years with permission from the Privy Council. Hereditary town allotments can be leased by men or women for up to 99 years with Cabinet approval and for over 99 years with the approval of the Privy Council, provided in both cases that permission for the lease is received from the heir to the land.

188 LAND, CUSTOM AND PRACTICE IN THE SOUTH PACIFIC

A Royal Commission

In 1983, a Royal Commission into Land was established in response to increasing public pressure for reform. One of its terms of reference, as reported in the *Tonga Chronicle*, was whether the basis of land tenure should be altered from a life interest in usufruct to freehold tenure. Succession to land would be limited to members of the holder's immediate family. Freeholding land would result in the abolition of rents payable to estate holders, of 80 cents per annum for a 3.3-hectare allotment, and other privileges, which consist of large payments or presents of money, items of traditional wealth, and food. It was suggested that new forms of compensation to the estate holder be introduced (*Tonga Chronicle*, 26 August, 1983:2).

The findings of the commission have not been made public, and nor has the basic issue of the redistribution of Tongan land been addressed officially. A strong belief still exists in the initial 1882 legislation as the mainstay of Tongan rights of citizenship and the guardian of Tongan land. In 1991, a leading parliamentary representative for the people in Tongatapu, 'Akilisi Pohiva, petitioned the king to rescind leases held by people who had emigrated, but no action was taken. More recent attempts to impose penalty taxes to induce absentee land holders to release their lands have also met with government resistance. The emigrants protested that land rights are integral to their citizenship and an emblem of their enduring bonds to the land. Many people in Tonga feared that money and goods remitted by these same absentees might cease once their land rights were removed (James, 1993:221, 224). It has also been argued that to take tax allotments from emigrants may only cause more hardship for wives and children left in Tonga who rely on the land for subsistence (Fifita, 1975:33, 41).

The Inflation of the Informal Land Market

Payments of money by applicants for land to estate holders to secure their agreement to registration may have begun before the Second World War, even though there was not a great deal of cash in Tonga at that time (Van der Grijp, 1993b:248). The payments increased as land became scarcer and cash more readily available until money became the 'principal arbiter' of the access to land (Needs, 1988:62). Since at least the early 1980s, Tongans speaking in English have readily used the terms 'pay', 'buy', 'sell', and 'price' with regard to acquiring land. They have no illusions as to what they are doing. 'Selling land is illegal in Tonga,' they say, 'but it goes on all the time'. In reality, no land is sold because freehold does not exist, but people give cash and goods for the privilege

TONGA

of acquiring a lease or permission for the informal short-term or long-term use of land.

The informal land market received a considerable boost from the 1970s laws permitting commoners to lease their town and tax allotments because commoners could then act as land 'brokers' in the same way, if on a lesser scale, as noble hereditary estate holders. The Land Act amendments of 1978 and 1984 set the rent for the lease of a tax allotment at T$10 an acre (0.4 ha.) (Adsett, 1989:25).[5] Surveying fees range from T$17.50 for parcels under two hectares to T$28.00 for surveying from 2 to 8 hectares, and registration of leases costs T$10.50 and subleases T$5.25 (Adsett, 1989:60). Thus, the government obtains very little revenue from the new leases, but extra-legal 'payments' to lessors are usually far in excess of the official figures.

The extra-legal negotiations are officially ignored and are conducted usually within the ideology of the gift traditionally given to the land holder from the person wishing to use his land (Van der Grijp, 1993b:248). The ideological mystification of the material bases of land transactions became the subject of a lively exchange in the Tongan parliament in 1986 between the people's representative for Ha'apai, Teisino Fuko, and several 'Honourable' nobles' representatives, which was summarised as follows in the *Tonga Parliamentary Bulletin*:

> Fuko: spoke of how land has been sold even though it was illegal to do so . . . because land could be sold it was only people with money and foreigners who bought land . . . and . . . most of the people who were selling land were people with tax allotments.
>
> Chairman: reminded the MP of the traditional way of acquiring land, that is, that you take a kava and a gift to the noble.
>
> Fuko: agreed, but he said that only foreigners grow the particular kind of kava that was required. According to the Constitution, land could be attained without even kava.
>
> Acting Minister of Lands: proposed the deletion of a reference made regarding the sales of land, and replace it with the traditional means of presenting kava and a gift.
>
> Fuko: said that whatever term was used it still meant the same thing.
>
> Noble Fusitu'a: explained that the word 'sale' could be used on a number of occasions including the sale of land, but on each of these occasions there was a more appropriate word for the presenting of kava and gifts.
>
> Fuko: stressed that people have lost their rights because of the sales of land.
>
> Chairman: said that it was virtually impossible for anybody to get any land for nothing. He said that he had given a woman T$3,800 in exchange for a piece of land in town.
>
> Acting Minister of Lands: stressed that it was illegal and, if he knew of anybody selling land, he would take him to court. (*Tonga Parliamentary Bulletin* III,

190 LAND, CUSTOM AND PRACTICE IN THE SOUTH PACIFIC

pp. 189–90, 25 September, and p.195, 30 September, 1986; quoted in Van der Grijp, 1993b:246–7).

The amount of money paid for the use of agricultural land increased in all cash cropping areas throughout the 1980s as export crops fetched consistently high prices, but it also varied depending upon the demand, the fertility of the soil, and its location. In 1980, for example, a grower in a vanilla-producing area of western Vava'u gave T$600 'as a donation' to the estate holder for the registration of a 2.4-hectare tax allotment. In 1981, another grower gave T$4,000 to register a statutory-sized (3.3 ha.) plot and, in 1982, another paid T$6,000 (T$1,818 per ha.) to register the same amount of land from the same noble estate (Van der Grijp, 1993b:247).

By the late 1980s the success of pumpkin squash, which went on to net T$15 million for Tongan growers in 1992–3, had increased the price of land rents, especially in Tongatapu where most squash was grown. In 1989 3.3 hectares of 'good garden land on Tongatapu' cost around T$8,000 for its registration (Van der Grijp, 1993b:248). By 1993, however, squash growers on Tongatapu were paying between T$2,500 and T$4,000 per hectare to lease land in the fertile western region and also in the overused central area near Vaini for the short, three-month, squash-growing season. 'Virgin' land or land that has lain fallow for many years fetched the highest price because the grower did not have to use much artificial fertiliser. The prime arable areas are those in which soil quality is good and roads give easy access to agricultural supplies and labour, to the Ministry of Agriculture's experimental farm at Vaini for checks on quality and advice on pest control, and to the wharves at Nuku'alofa for shipment. Tax allotments far from the capital generally cost between T$20,000 and T$30,000 for long-term lease or registration (Tonga, 1990:26). In 1993, less fertile and less accessible land in the eastern districts around Lapaha and Mu'a was acquired for less money, around T$800 an acre, for the three-month growing season.

As a result of the extremely profitable squash harvest, land leased late in 1993 for the 1994 growing season fetched higher prices than the previous year, reaching T$5,000 per hectare in prime areas. A tax allotment in Tongatapu was potentially much more profitable than one in Ha'apai, where there were no squash quotas. A man holding a tax allotment in Ha'apai, who wanted to make a legal exchange for an allotment in Tongatapu, might have had to 'give' T$2,000 or more to close the deal. Similarly, Tongatapu squash producers offered cash as an inducement to exchange more remote allotments for land nearer to roads, labour, and transport. Should squash returns fall, however, so too would the asking price for the use of land because land holders tend to propose a

TONGA

rental based on the expected productivity of the land. Similarly, in 1993–4, agricultural labour in Tonga was expensive, and related to potential returns, but it may not remain so.[6]

Commercial land use

The Bank of Tonga (BT) and the Tonga Development Bank (TDB) prefer to lend money to people with registered land or to lessees who hold legally binding leases. In the interests of economic development, however, they have been instructed by the government to lend money for commercial, industrial and agricultural purposes also to people using land through informal arrangements. If the borrower defaults, the bank can take control of the land over which the loan has been granted for the unexpired term of the loan or mortgage, whether the land was formally leased and mortgaged or whether money for it has been borrowed informally (Adsett, 1989:42). Once the debt is discharged, however, the land returns to the registered land holder, who never loses his superior right of hereditary usufruct. For example, a land holder near Nuku'alofa borrowed money to start a tourist resort. The venture failed, and the Tonga Development Bank sub-leased the property to a local church for the unexpired term of the mortgage or until the loan was repaid, or both. The property then returned to the land holder, who has since leased it to a developer.

Many allotment holders avoid formal leases because the control of their land temporarily passes out of their hands. They prefer to make informal arrangements regarding land use, and these may vary widely. Allotments of 3.3 hectares have been leased for T$250 for a year, because the holder needed urgently to repay a debt, or for T$600, the cost of a return air fare to New Zealand. People borrow land from relatives, or from others outside the family, with mere oral agreements for recompense in cash or goods, or for no recompense at all. In vanilla-growing areas in Vava'u and squash-growing areas in the Tongatapu group, people increasingly 'borrow' land without either the knowledge or permission of the registered holder. This non-permissive occupancy, or encroaching, can occur on tax allotments, government land, and hereditary estates if they are not carefully protected and watched.

The increased profitability of export crops during the 1980s and 1990s encouraged many people who were primarily subsistence growers to enter the market and previously successful commercial growers to increase significantly the area under cash crops. Commercial agriculture also received a boost from the local market, which expanded in response to demand from the increasing urban population. These developments enlivened the extra-legal land market. For example, Tongans are not

192 LAND, CUSTOM AND PRACTICE IN THE SOUTH PACIFIC

permitted by law to mortgage or sell growing crops (Adsett, 1989:11). However, sharefarming arrangements became increasingly common, arrangements under which a grower could plant another's allotment with squash after clearing, ploughing, and preparing the ground with fertiliser, herbicides and pesticides and purchasing seed from the Japanese squash buyers for T$250 per kilo. After a few weeks, the share farmer would give half the plants to the land holder, and keep the other half. 'Naturally,' said one man, 'the share farmer doesn't put quite so much fertiliser on the land holder's half of the crop as on his own'. The increasing individualism in land holding and the exclusivity of its use has undoubtedly been encouraged by squash cultivation, which requires land to be cleared and ploughed to the very borders of the *'api*. Radio messages are more and more frequently broadcast to the effect that a particular *'api* has been leased, and that members of the land holder's family are no longer permitted to take produce from the land.

The government's resistance to land reform has meant that amendments to the land law have never threatened its basic tenets of the inalienability of Tongan land and of permanent, inheritable, individual usufruct. The existence of informal or extra-legal arrangements alongside formal tenurial conditions permits more flexibility in land practice, so that, by the 1990s, a typical Tongan smallholding was a plot of land whose use was sanctioned by complicated tenancy and use-right agreements. Litigation over land increased with most cases before the Land Court involving the attempted eviction of a temporary occupier by the land holder. The court almost always decided in favour of the registered holder. However, there have been cases of male land holders who evicted married sisters from houses that the sisters had built on their brother's land, and widows pressured by their husbands' families to release land before their life interest expired, for the use of the male heir (Crown Law Officer, pers. comm., 1993). Individualised land holding was only slowly adopted, but, by the 1990s, it was seen in many parts of Tonga as an exclusive right.

Urban Land

The informal land market has grown most rapidly in urban areas, especially in Nuku'alofa because of the demand from both immigrants and commercial developers. In the late 1980s town allotments in villages could be acquired for a few hundred *pa'anga*, T$300 being quoted as a 'going price' for a village allotment in Vava'u (Van der Grijp, 1993b:248). Villages in Tongatapu have all experienced a significant increase in their population and in many places, as even on relatively remote Falahola, tax allotments on village peripheries have been subdivided to provide more town allotments. Prices of town allotments in Neiafu, the main town of Vava'u, and Pangai in Ha'apai, were generally still well below T$1,000, but the tourism potential in Neiafu in the late 1980s had pushed up the price of bayside allotments with good views to T$2,000, and further increases were expected. In the capital, prices were already much higher.

The original urban area of Nuku'alofa is located on the north coast of Tongatapu on government land, almost all of which has been distributed or is being reserved for industrial and other commercial development (Figure 5.5). The town was extended to the east to include part of a noble estate, Ma'ufanga. In 1993, four hectares of prime residential land in Ma'ufanga was leased for 60 years for T$268,000. The 1.6 hectares with a sea frontage were to be developed into 0.1-hectare home sites, as were the remaining 2.4 hectares in bushland. A larger Ma'ufanga site of 6.5 hectares was offered at the same time for T$385,000. Quarter-acre (0.1 ha.) blocks on the edge of the lagoon at the south side of Ma'ufanga were acquired from registered holders or from the noble landlord for around T$6,000; those inland fetched T$4,000. Holders of tax allotments in Ma'ufanga were said to be 'like little nobles or little kings, and they know it'. If each of their 3.3-hectare tax allotments were to be subdivided into 0.1-hectare house sites and each of these sold for T$4,000, the tax allotment holder would gain around T$130,000 – enough to invest T$100,000 in a house in Ma'ufanga and to secure a tax allotment in perpetuity, for example, near Vaini, a fast-growing village in a squash-growing area of central Tongatapu. This is a very comfortable scenario in Tongan eyes. Many people who hold tax allotments within the expanded urban area 'are just putting a fence around them and waiting for prices to rise'.[7]

The limited amount of urban land and its high price, however, make it more difficult for the young, the landless, and immigrants to acquire town allotments. In an effort to provide home sites, the government subdivided new areas to the east and to the west of the old town (Figure 5.5). The demand is high for the new subdivisions despite the fact that they are on wet, marshy ground or mangroves and unsuitable for residential areas (James, 1993:225–6). After a cyclone flooded some parts of Nuku'alofa in 1982, the government re-zoned 13 hectares as residential land (in the triangular-shaped new Popua subdivision toward the eastern end of Popua peninsula) and created 396 town allotments there in which to relocate only 600 people (Figure 5.5). By 1990 some 100 to 120 sites, less than one third of the partially-reclaimed water-logged 760 sq. m lots, had homes built on them. At the time of the new subdivision, many home owners in Nuku'alofa also acquired lots in Popua, not for building but for speculation. In 1990, it was estimated that to lease

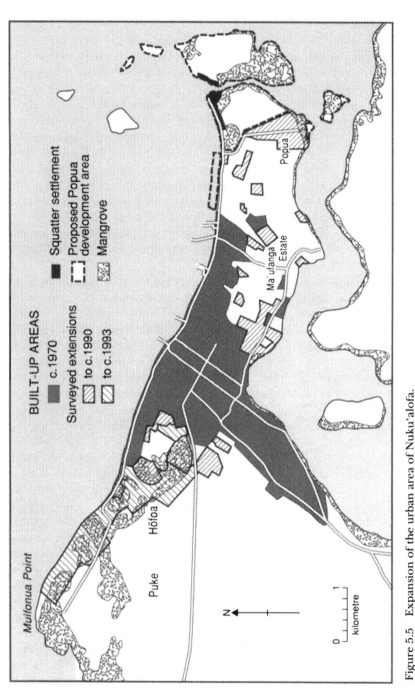

Figure 5.5 Expansion of the urban area of Nuku'alofa.
Sources: Field work; maps from Ministry of Lands, Survey and Natural Resources, Tonga, 1990; and data from D. Seiler.

TONGA 195

even the poorly-serviced Popua lots would cost between T$4,000 and T$5,000 (Tonga, 1990:26, 42). Flooding to a depth of 20 cm. is common in the area, and even the houses built on stilts have water at floor level several times a year. Leaking plastic water pipes lie in stagnant water polluted by pigs, dogs, humans, and the nearby rubbish dump. By 1991 some 200 squatters had moved to the northeast point of Popua peninsula (Figure 5.5), along the sea road next to mangrove swamps, and built shanties from materials scavenged from the nearby town dump. Other squatters live on Nukunukumotu Island and in nearby marshlands. None of them have rights to the land, and they subsist mainly by fishing and gleaning nearby reefs. Some of the illegal residents are government officers, who are saving their small salaries in the hope of one day being able to buy a town allotment. There is, however, a large tourist resort development planned for the Popua peninsula (Figure 5.5). The planners consider the expense of reclaiming the land to be far less than the cost of acquiring a sufficient amount of land for development from presently registered town allotments or tax 'api within the urban area (Tonga, 1990:1, 2, 43).

In 1993, re-registration from existing holders of town allotments of 760 sq. m in Puke or Hōfoa, the largely water-logged subdivisions immediately to the west of the built-up area (Figure 5.5), would cost at least T$3,000, and to fill the land with coral from distant quarries, to form a house foundation, a further T$5,000 to T$6,000 (Tonga, 1990:26). In 1993, a built-up corner allotment in one of these subdivisions was offered for T$10,000. After 1982 the government declared that it had no more land to distribute. Later, it abandoned plans to relocate the town dump at the western extreme of the northern seafront, amidst marshes and mangroves toward Muifonua Point. By 1993, all this land had been subdivided and registered as town allotments, including an 8.1-hectare area of 1.6-hectare town blocks created by halving the tax allotments surveyed in 1962. Much of the land, as in Popua, was registered by prominent urbanites. A senior bureaucrat said that people 'survey and register the land for T$27, pay annual taxes on it, a total yearly cost of about T$67, then sell the lease to some needy person for around T$4,000'. The price of reclaimed lots in these areas is likely to increase.

Nuku'alofa, like Pangai and Neiafu, is marked by a lack of town planning or zoning. Attempts by the town planner to introduce a plan for Nuku'alofa have been rejected by parliament on the grounds that re-zoning would involve revoking individuals' rights to particular town allotments and would 'be unconstitutional'. High-ranking office holders, perhaps, do not want to be controlled by a mere meritocracy of urban planners. On the other hand, the Cabinet has rejected plans, which came from highly placed persons in the kingdom, to reclaim parts

196 LAND, CUSTOM AND PRACTICE IN THE SOUTH PACIFIC

of the lagoons for urban development, as it did previous proposals put forward in the 1980s to dump toxic waste from the United States on some of the more remote Tongan islands.

Land transactions involving Tongans did not cause the same degree of friction as those involving land passing to foreigners. In 1993, it was widely rumoured that two leases in central Nuku'alofa had passed for an undisclosed figure from the king to Hong Kong Chinese businessmen, without the permission of Cabinet. The action was believed to reveal the increased power of the king, upon whom most nobles depend increasingly for their parliamentary positions and salaries. The rumour helped divert attention from the numbers of commoners who have also leased land in central Nuku'alofa to Chinese, Taiwanese, and people of other nationalities who bought Tongan national passports during the 1980s (James, 1994). The people's Tongatapu parliamentary representative, Pohiva, complained that foreigners should not be allowed into Tonga when the businesses could be run by locals (Fonua, 1993:20). The statutory right to land has clearly helped to promote a strong sense of individualism and entrepreneurial spirit in Tonga, even if some of the results of this spirit are contrary to some of the restrictive conditions of that right.

Conclusion

The original (1882) Land Act has never been completely implemented; neither has it been abrogated. When individualised land holding became law, land had little or no commercial value for commoners. The cash derived from cultivation, mostly from sales of copra, was appropriated for many years in the same way as tribute given to the former chiefs except that it passed to the new lords of the land: the nobles, the government, and the church. For many decades after the passage of the 1882 Land Act, people continued to live much as they had before; a small number of individual allotments were registered, but they were used by groups of kin.

By the 1960s, several factors, including the completion of the cadastral survey, the increased allocation and registration of allotments, the present king's moves toward modernisation, and improvements in international markets for Tongan products, gave horticultural land more commercial value. A lively extra-legal land market developed in response to increased demand for land arising from a larger population, urban development, and the increasing commercialisation of agriculture. Nevertheless, Tongans continue to revere the constitution, which gave them individual rights to land (Lātūkefu, 1975:88–9; Tonga, 1990:25). Land practice has never been in step with the legal code but

TONGA

the law has exerted the most profound influence on practice. Despite the disproportionate influence of a powerful elite over land matters, thousands of commoners now have legal rights to land in perpetuity that they never possessed formerly and of which they cannot be legally dispossessed. As a result, they rarely confront the disparities between land law and practice but mediate them through the metaphor of the gift, an ideology which serves to mystify the increasingly materialist bases of land transactions.

In Tonga, as in Vanuatu, 'the illusion that the present is not really different from the past' (Rodman, Chapter 3) has become more difficult to preserve as commercial activity leads to a greater assertion of individual land rights. The increasingly exclusive use of allotments by the registered holder or lessee frequently clashes with customary practice. In increasing numbers of cases, extended family members may no longer use the land if its registered holders produce for the commercial market. Growers who see farming as a business fulfil a more restricted set of family obligations in order to maintain both their business and their family ties, and prefer to pay family workers rather than accept the continuing relations of traditional reciprocity (Ritterbush, 1988:151). Land holders of both hereditary estates and tax allotments, by excluding certain relatives from the use of land and paying others for their land or labour contributions, have moved toward the more impersonal relations of production that typify Western-style capitalism. This movement may well prove irrevocable.

Notes

1. Some titled lines have failed or merged. In some cases, two or three titles have been acquired by a single noble, and other titles lie vacant. At any one time, there are usually between 25 and 30 nobles incumbent.
2. The Protectorate was finally removed in 1970.
3. From case histories of families recorded in the field in the 1980s.
4. It was not very evenly distributed, if Maude's earlier study is an indication.
5. In 1992–3, the value of the Tongan $ (*pa'anga*) was approximately US$0.75.
6. In 1993, the regular rate for a day labourer in Tongatapu was T$15 or, at the height of the squash season, between T$20 to T$25 for an 8-hour day, plus bonuses of food, transport, cigarettes, and cash.
7. Data derived from discussions with local developers in Nuku'alofa in 1993.

CHAPTER 6

Land, Law and Custom:
Diverging Realities in Fiji

R. Gerard Ward

During the last century and a half, Fijians have made great changes to the ways they allocate and control land. Some changes now have the sanction of 'custom' or government law. Some current practices are sanctioned by either custom or law, or both; others by neither. Government land and labour policies of the 1870s and 1880s were designed to protect Fijians from loss of their land and from the social disruption which, it was thought, would follow such loss. These policies, which codified a quasi-traditional order, ran the risk of creating a strait jacket preventing adjustment to new social, political and economic situations. The longer-term consequences have not been as serious a constraint on socio-economic change as they might, largely because people have simply ignored the regulations and their intent. Older flexible practices of land allocation and use continued, or new practices emerged which, though unsanctioned by 'custom' and sometimes illegal, have met new needs. What is often assumed to be a 'traditional' land tenure system now differs from the practices followed prior to codification of Fijian land tenure by the colonial government. Major discrepancies now exist between those registered as owners of land held under 'customary' tenure, legally called 'native land', and those who use it; and between legally sanctioned means of allocating use of native land to non-Fijians[1] and the way much native land is made available to such people. These discrepancies are rarely acknowledged publicly in policy-making circles. Land issues in Fiji are politically charged, especially in relation to differential access to land between the Fijian and Indian communities, and risks to political and social stability exist in either not acknowledging the discrepancies, or in attempting to deal with them.

FIJI

The Deed of Cession and After

Fiji became a Crown Colony in 1874 under a Deed of Cession signed by leading chiefs, and in particular by Cakobau who, with the help of resident Europeans, had established the Kingdom of Fiji in 1871. Article 4 of the Deed states:

> That the absolute proprietorship of all lands not shown to be now alienated so as to have become bona fide the property of Europeans or other foreigners or not now in the actual use or occupation of some Chief or tribe or not actually required for the probable future support and maintenance of some chief or tribe shall be and is hereby declared to be vested in Her said Majesty her heirs and successors. (Quoted in Derrick, 1957:II)

Nevertheless, the first substantive governor, Sir Arthur Gordon, later Lord Stanmore, asserted that Queen Victoria had asked that the surplus lands, which Article 4 said should become Crown land, be returned to the Fijians and thus remain in Fijian hands (France, 1969:158). It is doubtful whether this was the Crown's intent and a later governor, Im Thurn, could not find any evidence for the reported undertaking. Nevertheless, Gordon's view meant that relatively little land was deemed to be not in actual occupation by Fijians and thus the area which became Crown land was relatively small (Table 6.1). Gordon's wish to protect Fijians from the

Table 6.1 Distribution of land by class of tenure

	Area (km^2)	Per cent of total area
State land (excluding mangrove)	1726.06	9.45
Freehold	1490.85	8.17
Native land	15,036.62	82.38
TOTAL	18,253.53	100.00
Of Native land:		
Reserve land	5508.47	36.63
(Of which leased 31/6/93	*816.43*	*14.82)*
Unreserved land	9528.15	63.37
(Of which leased 31/6/93	*3869.31*	*40.61)*

Notes: Land tenure figures issued by different agencies differ considerably. Reserve land can only be leased (under 'Class J' leases) to Fijians, 'Fijian entities' such as the Methodist Church, the Native Land Development Corporation, or to 'quasi-Fijians' such as the Fiji Development Bank. Before 1987 'State land' was 'Crown land'.

Source: Native Land Trust Board.

200 LAND, CUSTOM AND PRACTICE IN THE SOUTH PACIFIC

risk of losing the bulk of their land stemmed in part from his belief that if a 'native race' were 'to be preserved . . . it must be permitted to retain its lands' (Gordon, 1880:23; Legge, 1958:197). The belief was strengthened by his knowledge of the New Zealand land wars and the social impact on the Maori of the loss of their land (Thomas, 1990:149). Furthermore, in the face of very limited financial resources it was the intention to govern Fiji through a system of indirect rule. This required that the power of the chiefs be maintained and thus the colonial government sought to maintain and incorporate Fijian leadership structures (albeit in modified forms in parts of the country) into the administrative system to avoid the introduction of a costly bureaucracy. Maintaining the coherence of Fijian society, and in particular the link between the chiefs, the people and the land, was seen as central to the goal of indirect and economical rule, and the assumption of inalienability of native land was basic to that task, at least for the time being (Legge, 1958:201).

More than a century after Cession, 82 per cent of Fiji's land remains 'native land' (Table 6.1) and Gordon's aims have been fulfilled in broad terms. If the quality of land is considered, the position is not as favourable as this statistic might suggest. Although recent accurate data are not available, in 1959 35.6 per cent of the first-class arable land and 17.7 per cent of the first-class pastoral land of Viti Levu, Vanua Levu and Taveuni were under freehold or Crown tenure. Of the native land, one-third of the first-class arable and 13 per cent of the first-class pastoral land was leased by 1959, the majority to non-Fijians (Ward, 1985:31).

The current standardised, orthodox hierarchy of social groups is described in much the same terms by different authorities, and the following statement is drawn from Ravuvu's recent description (1987:16–17). At the apex is the *vanua*, formed of the agnatic descendants of a common ancestor or ancestral god living in the same general area. Each *vanua* would have one or more *yavusa*, the members again agnatically related. The *yavusa* is composed of several *mataqali* whose members are in turn the agnatic descendants of a son of the *yavusa* founder. Within each *mataqali* are one or more extended families, or *toka-toka*, whose core members would be related according to the same principles. Although common descent provides the basis of membership at all levels, others can be included 'socially or legally' in the group to the extent that 'some people consider themselves to belong to one *mataqali* for traditional reasons, even though they are registered officially as members of another *mataqali*'.

This generalised description of social organisation became the officially recognised model (e.g. Roth, 1953:54; Lasaqa, 1984:18–19). When used as a basis for assumptions about land ownership it became an integral part of the 'orthodox' version of the land tenure system in

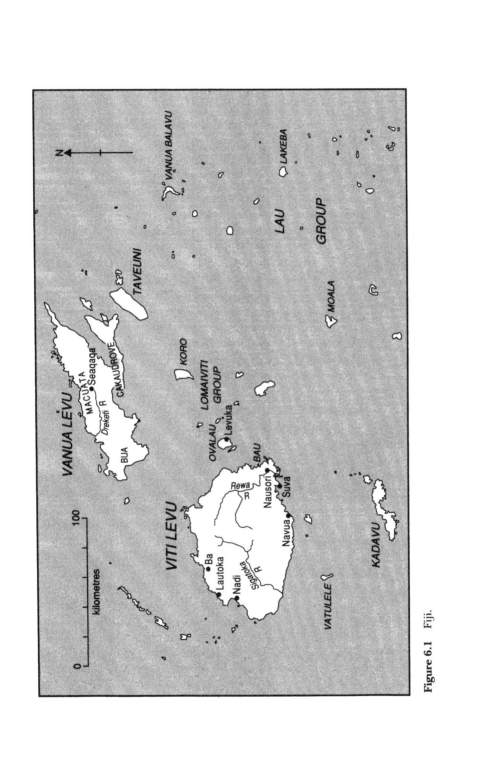

Figure 6.1 Fiji.

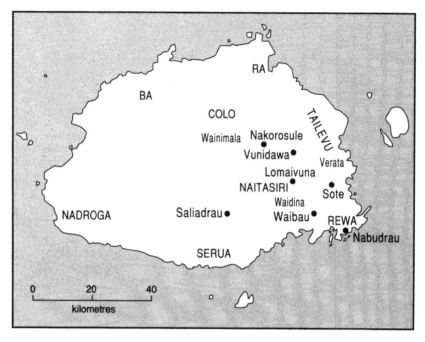

Figure 6.2 Viti Levu. Places referred to in the text.

France's term (1969:102–28). The orthodox model does not allow for the considerable variation reported in earlier periods, and which still occurs de facto. In western Vanua Levu some societies were matrilineal with some land rights also following the matrilineal relationship (Quain, 1948:182–4). The 1896 report of the commission on the decline of population considered the *yavusa* to be a division of the *mataqali* (Report, 1896:92) and this order applied in part of northern Lau (Walter, 1978a:93). In the Wainimala area 'the *tokatoka* sub-unit is hardly recognised' and when the Native Lands Commission (NLC) held its hearings in the area in the period 1912–1914, the local unit of the *bure* ('house') was sometimes classed as *tokatoka* and sometimes as *mataqali* (Ravuvu, 1987:15–17). Nayacakalou (1965) records cases from Kadavu, Nadroga, Naitasiri and Tailevu where village practice differs from the official NLC records in classifying groups as either *yavusa* or *mataqali*. He states that in most villages he knew, the primary divisions of the village 'would be referred to as *mataqali*, whether they were in fact *mataqali* or *yavusa*' (1965:132). Many other field researchers have made similar observations (e.g. Belshaw quoted in Spate, 1959:10; Ravuvu, 1988:94–8; Sahlins, 1962:239; Ward, 1965:7; Watters, 1969:52; Rutz, 1978:23). The discrepancies between practice in villages and the official record is one reason why many Fijians appear uncertain when asked to which *mataqali* they belong, or would give different answers if the questions were framed in relation to land registration or social and ceremonial practice in the village (Rutz, 1978:24; Walter, 1978b:357). For socio-political activities in the village, people may combine into what they term *mataqali* groups, the membership and names of which differ from those recorded by the NLC. Thus there 'are now two parallel sets of classification: one based on the commission's records and the other on the socio-political organisation of the village as it is known to the people' (Nayacakalou, 1975:14).

The 'Orthodox Model' and Older Realities

The discrepancies between the orthodox model of the Fijian land tenure system and current practice reflect not only the socio-economic changes which have taken place in Fiji since the late nineteenth century but also the gap between that model and the realities of actual practice prior to and after Cession.

It is now impossible to reconstruct with any precision the pre-contact land tenure practices or changing patterns of land holdings of the Fijians. There are no written records from the pre-contact period and oral tradition is partial in nature and in its temporal and spatial span. In addition the evidence presented to, and recorded by, the NLC in the earlier decades of the present century was no doubt often partisan, although tested by the questioning of neighbours present at the hearings (France, 1969:133). Nevertheless, sufficient material exists in the NLC reports and other sources to make clear certain important characteristics of Fijian land tenure arrangements prior to significant alterations from outside forces.

The most striking discrepancies between what became the orthodox, codified model of 'traditional' Fijian tenure and pre-Cession practice are the degree of change which evidently occurred prior to 1874, and the degree of variation found from place to place. As Chapelle shows, the argument 'often heard before the Native Lands Commission' that the present patterns of land allocation are the result of occupation 'since time immemorial' cannot be sustained (Chapelle, 1978:85). Mid-nineteenth-century practice differed from the orthodox model in three main aspects – mobility of people, alienability or transferability of land, and the level within the social hierarchy at which land was 'owned'.

Mobility of people

During the nineteenth century, and no doubt in previous centuries, the population was very mobile. The *tukutuku raraba*, the histories of groups of people recorded by the Native Lands Commission, tell of frequent moves from one settlement site to another, the splitting of *yavusa* or

204 LAND, CUSTOM AND PRACTICE IN THE SOUTH PACIFIC

mataqali, the relocation of the different parts, and the coming together of groups which may or may not have had prior kinship links. The distances involved in these moves were often considerable and took people into areas where they did not have prior land claims but where they obtained land by a variety of mechanisms. Examples include the i Sokula lineage of the Tui Cakau, which moved from Verata to Cakaudrove (Sayes, 1982:39–51), or groups of Tongans who settled in the Lau Islands, in Vatulele (Geddes, 1959:209) and in southwest Viti Levu (Derrick, 1957:6).

Figure 6.3 shows the settlement sites which the four *mataqali* living in the village of Sote on Viti Levu in the late 1950s occupied in the remembered past. Some of these sites are recorded as deserted villages on the 1931 Native Lands Commission maps of the registered *mataqali* holdings for the area. Others were identified when the information was recorded during fieldwork in 1959. All four *mataqali* of the *yavusa* Vuanisaqiwa once lived at Natakali, on land registered by the NLC in the name of *mataqali* 'B', and all moved to Delaikurukuru on the boundary between the present lands of *mataqali* 'C' and 'D'. Disputes between *mataqali* leaders led to division and the *mataqali* followed different settlement paths until the late nineteenth century when people moved to the riverside sites of Nalolawa and Bulu before rejoining at Sote. A total of 26 historical links between individual *mataqali* and particular settlement sites was recorded, of which 17 were cases of a *mataqali* living on and using, and presumably claiming rights to, the surrounding land which the NLC registered in the name of some other *mataqali*. Two sites, Nakorola and Bulu, are on land registered in the name of *mataqali* which are not part of Sote village. At least three sites lie on or very close to the boundaries of current Sote *mataqali* holdings. In earlier times of potential warfare people would be unlikely to live outside or on the vulnerable borders of the lands they claimed. It can be assumed that when these sites were occupied, the ancestors of the Sote people used and held land beyond today's boundaries. The case of Sote shows that over the period covered by the village's oral tradition, considerable movement, segmentation and recombination of the groups as settlement units took place. If land holdings had been recorded at different times, the patterns of ownership would have varied greatly from those recorded and fixed by the NLC.

The causes of mobility were those common to many small-scale societies dependent primarily on subsistence agriculture using shifting cultivation techniques. Each such community would use extensive areas for long periods at a low level of overall intensity with short cropping periods and long bush fallows. Such communities might expand or shrink in numbers with the vagaries of demographic processes and their land needs would vary accordingly. Where land was not in short supply

FIJI   205

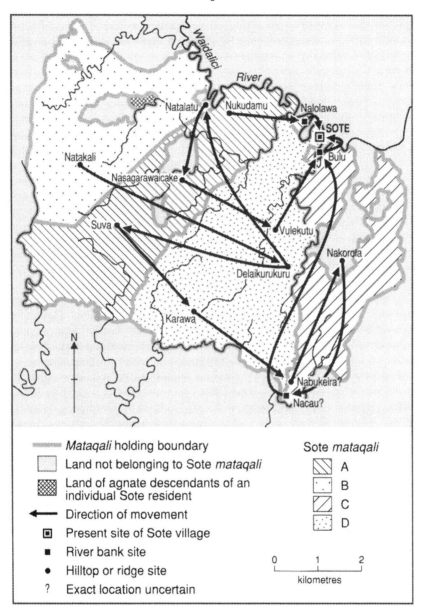

Figure 6.3 Former settlement sites of Sote village *mataqali*.
Sources: Field enquiries and Native Lands Commission maps.

206 LAND, CUSTOM AND PRACTICE IN THE SOUTH PACIFIC

few problems would arise. Where land was limited and population increased, fallows might be shortened, soils depleted and a community or some members of it might move to a new location where unoccupied land was available. If differential growth of adjacent groups occurred, one group's land requirements could press on a neighbour's land. The pressure might be relieved by agreement or force, but in either case land could change hands and a group might move to other areas. Other moves might result from disputes within a community leading to a split and to one or both parties moving to new sites. Ambitious leaders might seek to expand their power over others by force. Groups might combine to share one territory for defensive reasons, or a band of refugees might seek support and asylum from another more powerful group, perhaps in exchange for accepting a subordinate service role to the more powerful hosts. Thus the 'ancient boundaries of lands were continually contracting and extending, in accordance with the military strength of the tribe' although diplomacy rather than fighting might provide the means of adjustment (Thomson, 1908:360).

Accounts by Europeans who spent extensive periods in Fiji in the latter half of last century support the oral history evidence of the fluidity of settlement patterns. The British consul reported in 1866 that in 'the interior of Fiji . . . traces of ruined villages and abandoned cultivation everywhere abound. There can be little doubt that this desolation is entirely due to the ferocious character of the tribal wars' (Jones, 1866:64). Brewster, who lived in Fiji for 40 years from 1870 and was Assistant Resident Commissioner and later Resident Commissioner in various parts of interior Viti Levu in the 1880s and 1890s, collected 'the histories of the principal hill tribes' covering 'nearly three hundred years' and states that 'life in the hills in the olden times was like a huge game of hide and seek' (1922:59). Thomson, one of the early Native Land Commissioners, asserts that the 'Fijians had no territorial roots. It is not too much to say that no tribe now occupies the land held by its fathers two centuries ago. They are united by consanguinity, not by the joint ownership of the soil' (1908:355). The time depth of oral tradition is much less than the two millennia of occupation of Fiji under such conditions, but the frequency of movement was such that 'of over six hundred *tukutuku raraba* recorded in Viti Levu and adjacent islands, only twenty-one tell of a tribe which claims to occupy the site on which it was founded' (France, 1969:13).

Alienation

The frequency and widespread nature of the movement of people and settlements also indicates that land was transferred temporarily or alienated permanently in pre-contact times. Force of arms was one, but by no means the only mechanism. If a group moved away from an area leaving it abandoned, in due course another group might move in and come to consider the land their own. Thomson (1908) gives a number of customary practices involving the intentional transfer of both use and ownership rights. The evidence accumulated by the Land Claims Commission (LCC), when seeking to assess the validity of claims to land by Europeans, also showed that in many parts of the country the appropriate chief could transfer and sell land to others, Fijian or non-Fijian, if he so wished, and that such actions were accepted as legitimate by his people. Despite the assertion in the record of the Council of Chiefs meeting in December 1877 that Fijian land 'cannot be absolutely alienated' (Notes, 1877:35), this was patently not the case before Cession, as the sale of lands by many of the same chiefs and the acceptance of such actions by their followers had shown. The government had also accepted the fact of alienability in recognising the legitimacy of many of the claims by Europeans to have purchased land from Fijians. As Ratu Sir Lala Sukuna wrote later, 'ownership was acknowledged to be destructible' and land could be alienated (1932:117).

Gordon's belief that it was essential to protect land rights meant that the idea of inalienability of native land was basic to his policy. In accepting this assumption he followed the argument set out in an influential lecture on the topic by Lorimer Fison, in Levuka in April 1880 (Fison, 1881). A missionary and long term resident of Fiji, Fison had studied kinship and land tenure. His views were shaped by the theories of Lewis H. Morgan who claimed that at the stage of social development which Fison considered the Fijians to have attained, land would be held communally and be inalienable, even by the chiefs (Fison, 1881:351; France, 1969:117–8).

When it came time to put matters relating to native land into law, Section 3(iii) of the Native Lands Ordinance No. 21 of 1880 declared that 'all native land shall be inalienable from the native owners to any person not a native Fijian except through the Crown and the said lands shall be alienable to the Crown only in the cases and under the restrictions hereinafter set forth'. The possibility of alienating land to another Fijian allowed by this ordinance was certainly in accord with pre-Cession practice. Furthermore, the preamble to the ordinance stated that the 'ancient customs' would be maintained 'until the native race be ripe for a division of such community rights among individuals'. It was envisaged that the ban on alienation would be temporary, and the ordinance did permit landowners, if they wished, to divide their holdings amongst the individuals of their group. These individuals would then be issued with a 'Native Certificate of Title' over their portions. After a Fijian had held

208   LAND, CUSTOM AND PRACTICE IN THE SOUTH PACIFIC

a certificate for five years, a Crown grant could be issued to the holder, thus converting the land to freehold. If subsequently sold, the freehold could pass into non-Fijian hands. This latitude was rarely if ever used and was removed in Ordinance No. 21 of 1892.

In 1905, Governor Im Thurn's Ordinance No. 11 repealed that of 1892 and direct alienation to non-Fijians was permitted with the approval of the Governor in Council. The demand for land from Indians who had completed their terms of indenture and elected to remain in Fiji, and from Europeans, had increased and it was hoped that the new freedom would release land not required by the Fijians for settlement by others. Under this new ordinance, 104,142 acres were alienated to freehold, 65,892 acres of it to the Crown, 30,039 acres to Europeans, and 5,542 acres to Fijians (Ward, 1965:116–7). Reaction developed against this trend in Fiji and in England, not least from Gordon (now Lord Stanmore), who attacked the policy in the House of Lords in 1907 and 1908. That he took such a strong line when his own ordinance had allowed a process of change to occur may have been due to his resentment of Im Thurn's criticism of the earlier policy voiced in a dispatch which was shown to Gordon (France, 1969:157–63). In April 1908 alienation was again banned and this was confirmed in Ordinance No. 3 of 1912, with the sole exception that land could be alienated to the government. The concept of inalienability from Fijian ownership, having been invented in the 1870s, was enshrined by the 1912 Ordinance. It has been continued with only minor changes of wording in subsequent land acts (Fa, 1989). European theory and convenience as much as Fijian practice came to guide policy and provide the principles for codification of 'customary' land law.

Who owned the land?

Early European observers often noted differences between their own concepts of 'ownership' and those of Fijians. In 1865 the British consul, H. M. Jones, stated that Fijians thought unoccupied land was not worth claiming; that land was a man's as long as he planted it; but that after a garden was abandoned it was free for someone else to use (Jones, 1865:604). Later authors provided more complex and more accurate outlines, with Thomson in particular recognising many of the key features of the various tenure arrangements found in Fiji. He also had a more sophisticated understanding of the different levels of rights over land which exist in most places and pointed out that there was 'no more absolute ownership known to the Fijian customary law than there is to the English', where a person may hold an estate in land but not absolute ownership because other parties, such as the Crown, will always retain some overriding rights

FIJI
209

(1908:359). Furthermore, in Fiji 'land as land had no value. Its value arose only from its potential produce' (Thomson, 1908:364).

Thomson recorded three basic categories of land to which different types of rights might be held by different groups or individuals (1908:358–65). Others have given similar descriptions and the same broad categories are recognised as having been reinforced by the authority of the NLC (e.g. France, 1969:14–16; Ravuvu, 1983a:71–5). The *veikau*, or forest, within a group's sphere of influence was considered to be the domain of the broadest social or settlement unit, often now equated with the *yavusa*. Any member of the group would have the right to hunt in or collect from the *veikau*. The intensity with which the *yavusa* would assert its claim over the *veikau* would decline with distance from the village (Ravuvu, 1983a:74). Once cleared for cultivation, usually with the explicit approval of the chief, a patch of former *veikau* came into the class of *qele* or *qele ni teitei* (garden land). In Thomson's view it then 'descends according to the fixed laws of inheritance' (1908:358–9) and would remain in the hands of the person (or extended family) who cleared it as long as it continued to be used. Once abandoned to fallow, the rights of the previous user were not immediately extinguished, but grew weaker with time. Rutz (1978) describes in detail how in the Waidina area fallow land is classified as *veimada* and the previous user continues to hold the prime right of re-use as long as the intention to do so in the foreseeable future is made known.[2] Such rights are jealously guarded for the more fertile land on alluvial riverside terraces, for which there is most competition and where fallows are shortest, but are not so strongly asserted over the less intensively used hill slopes (Rutz, 1978:27–8). Earlier observers recorded similar usage elsewhere, and in particular the fact that the clearest form of ownership lay primarily with the crop, the product of labour, and not with land per se except in areas where land was in short supply. Thomson described the situation with some precision in saying that the 'owner of the *nkele* [*qele*] had over his land a little less than *dominium* and a little more than *usufruct*' (1908:359).

Whereas the boundaries of the *veikau* of a community might be ill-defined for much of the time, those of the *qele* were not. And while the *veikau* was deemed to be held in the name of the broad *yavusa*, the *qele* was recognised as belonging to the extended family or the individual who had cleared and planted it and it lay under their authority while crops and *veimada* rights remained. Usage was a strong marker and component of ownership. Thus 'if the council of the tribe determined to lay claim to a boundary enclosing a strip of debatable land, they sent men to acquire and plant gardens as near the projected boundary as possible. These gardens became the property of the men who planted them, and of their heirs, unless of course the neighbours resented the intrusion, and drove

210   LAND, CUSTOM AND PRACTICE IN THE SOUTH PACIFIC

them back' (Thomson, 1908:360). When the Native Lands Commission was known to be about to visit an area, and as people became fully aware that its decisions would be permanent, 'every tribe begins extending its forest boundaries. The claims invariably overlap, and when the surveyor visits the spot, he finds newly-made plantations overlapping one another for several furlongs in inextricable confusion' (Thomson, 1908:361). By converting border lands from *veikau* to *qele*, people sought to make their ownership firmer and wider, and the boundaries less open to dispute. Such a flurry of planting and intermixing of gardens would have been unlikely in earlier times as it could lead to fighting but, with colonial pacification, disputes which did occur following the commission-induced planting would be argued out before the commission.

The third type of land was that which was recognised as being individually held. House sites (*yavu*) were held even more firmly by families or individuals than the *qele*, and house sites within the village were generally recognised as belonging to the occupying family. Individual tenure was also found on agricultural land on which considerable labour had been expended. This might apply to terraces or pond fields constructed and irrigated for taro, to constructions such as fish traps, and to raised garden beds constructed in swampy land. A clear case of the last occurred in the lower Rewa River delta.

> Over a large portion of these flats the land is broken up into little plots, surrounded by ditches, in which grow *via* [*Cyrtosperma chamissonis*] and *taro* [*Colocasia esculentum*], while the higher ground included by them is covered with fruit trees, and yams and plantains. Each of these plots has an owner; but the owners of contiguous ground are not usually men of the same tribe [e.g. *mataqali* or *yavusa*]. We [the NLC] found it quite impossible to set a boundary to the land of any particular tribe, for the holdings of the individuals were scattered about the country, among the holdings of other tribes, in hopeless confusion. (Thomson, 1908:370)

The explanation of 'this remarkable *morcellement*' was found in the fact that ditching, mounding, and other techniques had been used to trap sediment from floods and to raise planting land above the water table. The expenditure of such labour meant that the land itself was an artifact and 'followed the customary law of the inheritance of chattel property – that is to say, it descended to the eldest surviving son, or, failing a son, to the eldest surviving brother' (Thomson, 1908:370–1). Similar individual rights to specific plots existed elsewhere, as was the case on taro terraces at Sasa in 1960 (Ward, 1965:287–8).

Individual ownership, and transfers of land could also arise from other causes. Under Thomson, the NLC made detailed inquiries about the customs under which land might be transferred. They included gifts of land as rewards for bravery, friendship, performance of specific

FIJI

ceremonial duties, or as a dowry. Land might be seized as a punishment, or as the spoils of war. In the Rewa area and nearby parts of Tailevu Thomson also reports forms of tenancy or 'leasehold' called *cokovaki*, in which chiefs allocated land in return for 'rent'. Similar arrangements were found in eastern Kadavu (Thomson, 1908:372–81).

Under tenure arrangements such as those described above, any piece of land could change from one category, such as *veikau*, to another through time. *Veikau*, held under the general control of a broad group became virtually the property of an individual or extended family when cleared, cultivated, and converted to *qele*, and it remained so through a period of *veimada*. Eventually, when the use or intention to re-use was not maintained, the land could revert to forest, become *veikau*, and once more revert to the general control of the maximal lineage group whence it could again be separated for use as *qele*. Such flexible arrangements could adjust land allocations to changes in population and subsistence requirements. They had the advantages of providing the security of occupation required by the cultivators for as long as they wished to use the land; of recognising the right of the cultivators to the fruits of their labour; of transferability; and of allowing cultivators to have access to the full range of ecological sites within the group's broad domain.

It is obvious that under such conditions it is often difficult to define who 'owned' a particular piece of land in any absolute terms but the right, or absence of right, to use it was usually clear. Rights to use land normally stemmed from membership in the relevant group, but rights might be of limited duration in the case of certain types of gift, or be constrained by overriding rights of others. Membership was normally gained at birth through descent, but others could come into the group on marriage or by invitation. Continued membership would depend on participation in group ceremonial and economic activities, and where appropriate on giving service to chiefs or community or on the presentation of tribute (*sevu*).

Social and political status did not necessarily equate with the size of land holdings. For example, the 'Chiefs of Nasavusavu are hereditarily of very high rank [but] . . . their rank and position bears no comparison with the smallness of their territory' (Wilkinson, unpub.). The power of chiefs came from their authority over people as a labour force and a fighting force and this could be managed through diplomacy, alliances, the power of personality and leadership ability rather than through control of land per se. Nevertheless, an association with traditions of mythical or legendary events and sacred places linked to the land could help bolster the validity of chiefly claims to authority even if, as in the Cakaudrove cases which Sayes examines (1982:39ff), the chiefs were an immigrant group and the link to local land or to local gods was a recent

212 LAND, CUSTOM AND PRACTICE IN THE SOUTH PACIFIC

adoption or invention. Myth and tradition linking people to place could be moulded to fit current realities.

It is clear that there was no uniform system of ownership in the pre-Cession era. Groups of different size or status, and individuals, could own land, and different people or groups had the power to transfer or alienate land in a variety of circumstances.

Sales of Land and the Land Claims Commission

Following the early nineteenth-century incursions of sandalwood and bêche-de-mer traders into Fiji (Shineberg, 1967; Ward, 1972), missionaries and then planters arrived and sought land for long-term occupation. For plantations they preferred land with good soils and near the coast so that export crops could be shipped easily. They sought ownership on their own terms, which implied not only permanent rights to occupy and use the land, but also the right to exclude others from that land even if it were not in use.

Initial purchases were generally small lots for house, store or church sites on Ovalau and other outer islands and along the lower Rewa River (Figure 6.1). With occupation following quickly on the sale, any differences in concepts of ownership were of little moment as the traditional recognition of the validity of permissive occupancy would allow the newcomers to remain whether or not the Fijians considered they had sold the land in perpetuity. Despite some disputes, there was relatively little serious trouble where the purchasers occupied and planted crops on the land.

In 1860 and 1861 much larger blocks were purchased as Europeans sought to establish cotton plantations to take advantage of the high prices offering due to the interruption in cotton supplies to Europe by the American Civil War. On the Fijian side, the desire to obtain arms was a prime motive for selling land, but the chiefs also sold to pay off debts, to attract European settlers who, it was imagined, would bring other benefits, to obtain liquor, or even to punish recalcitrant followers. Neither sellers nor purchasers were above trickery. Land was sold more than once; sellers did not always have the right to sell the land they offered; buyers went about with already prepared documents collecting whatever signatures they could. The Chief Justice was moved to write in November 1876 in a 'Particularly Private and Interim Confidential Report':

> The planter came with his land claim,
> He swore that white was black;
> The pious missionary, too,
> Swore black was white, – alack; . . .

We heard of heroes of the past
Koroi – Serou – Kalao;
Of Ratu Ebenezer's 'deeds',
That Rewa planters knew. . . .

And when the oaths had all been sworn,
The lies in form recorded;
What could we do but make report,
That men were mean and sordid? (Quoted in Gordon 1897, II:195–6)

The cotton boom was followed by depression and many plantations were abandoned. By the time of Cession in 1874 there was less active land dealing than previously and many who remained on their plantations were existing on a partly-subsistence basis while seeking new export crops (Ward, 1969).

The Deed of Cession acknowledged that some lands had 'become bona fide the property of Europeans or other foreigners' and the determination of which lands these were was an important step in protecting Fijian land interests. A Land Claims Commission (LCC) was established in 1875 and over the next six years considered more than 1600 claims and made over 1300 reports. Many claims were rejected as being based on fraudulent or unjust 'sales'. The extent of the commission's problems is clear from Figure 6.4 showing the competing claims made for part of the Macuata coast and Dreketi River area. Only 517 claims were granted as claimed, although another 390 were disallowed as of right but allowed ex gratia because local people had accepted the presence and farming activities of the settlers (Ward, 1969). Thus Fijian concepts of usufruct rights were accepted by the commission and the Governor in Council as justification for a freehold grant. The areas over which Crown grants were issued became the core of the present freehold land of Fiji. The only significant additions were made when alienation was again permitted in the period 1905 to 1908. The location of the freehold land became a major determinant of where rural commercial development by non-Fijians took place. For some decades its boundaries also marked the divide between different agricultural systems, different social and cultural worlds, and between communalism on the one side and individualism on the other. Although Gordon foresaw that in future Fijians might move towards individualism, for many decades the contrasting forms of land tenure were a barrier to this transition.

The 'fixing' of native land tenure

Having established the process for clarifying European land claims, the government moved to settle questions of native land ownership. This was necessary both to secure the protection Gordon sought for the Fijians

Figure 6.4 Conflicting land claims, Dreketi River area.
Source: Map in [C3584], 1883.

FIJI   215

and because the Deed of Cession envisaged that land not occupied or required by Fijians would fall to the Crown (Legge, 1958:188). The questions were, what land did the Fijians own, occupy and require, what groups or individuals owned it, and how could it be registered to guarantee continued ownership and rights? Gordon began by establishing a Native Council (later the Council of Chiefs) and asking it, at its first meeting, to set out the customary land tenure practices. The assumption, based on the advice of authorities like Thurston (1874, published 1886) and Fison, and on Gordon's own preconceptions, was that a form of communal tenure would be described. It must have been startling for him to find leading chiefs from Ba, Bua and Lau advocating that the land be 'divided in portions to the people individually' so that 'each individual would have his own allotment'. The council also went further and resolved that 'the land be divided among the occupants of it according to the families of the land holders' (Notes, 1876:22–3). Not only were the chiefs looking to future needs while Gordon sought to protect a supposed status quo, but the council discussions over several years show that there was little uniformity in the way land was owned from one part of the country to another. There was no real consensus as to the appropriate social group in whose name land was held or should be registered. Ma'afu, the Tongan who was the ruler of Lau pre-Cession and after Cession was appointed Roko Tui Lau, described how the existing division of land in Lau into individual holdings, which he had introduced following the new Tongan model, 'is a good thing' and therefore 'we in Lau have no very great interest in this discussion . . . [on] the division of lands' (Notes, 1876:23).

The government would not accept the council's proposal for individual holdings as it was considered contrary to the intention to maintain custom which was mistakenly assumed to require communal tenure. In fact the chiefs' proposal was closer in a number of respects to contemporary practice of land allocation and use at that time, and to 'ownership' in a European sense, than was Gordon's communal ideal. At subsequent meetings the Native Council was again asked to describe the customary system which existed prior to Cession, but lengthy debate again showed clearly there was no single 'system' per se. In 1878 the Buli Serua asserted that his father, himself, and his son all belonged to different *mataqali* (Notes, 1878:50), an impossibility under what later became the orthodox model of agnatic *mataqali*. Chiefs from other areas pointed out that they had no units called *tokatoka* (Notes, 1878:53). After these descriptions by Fijians of a great variety of practices in different regions, the record of the meeting purports to show agreement by them that the *mataqali* was the unit in which land ownership was vested. One suspects the hand of Wilkinson as translator and recorder in this part of

216 LAND, CUSTOM AND PRACTICE IN THE SOUTH PACIFIC

the 1878 resolution. Considerable pressure may have been brought to bear to get the chiefs to state a compromise view.[3] Despite the reported 'agreement', the resolution in 1878 goes on to say that:

> All persons over sixteen years of age are entitled to a piece of land, and each mataqali shall decide, and give and [sic] portion to each male in the mataqali who is sixteen years of age a piece of land, and assist him to plant it according to the custom of the land, and then he shall be the absolute owner of such land, and his family or relations after him. (Notes, 1878:52)

Eventually, at the 1879 meeting, the chiefs declared that the true ownership lay with the *mataqali* (France, 1969:113), despite all the debate in earlier meetings which had pointed to smaller units or even individuals (as in Lau) being the prime landholding units. In 1880 the first Native Lands Ordinance (No. 21 of 1880) was gazetted and the first version of the orthodox model was enshrined in law. Like all models, it was a simplified representation of reality, not a portrayal of the diversity of reality. It ignored regional variation and in general allowed ownership to rest at only one level of social group. It bore more similarity to the ideas of Fison (or perhaps to Gordon's ideas of society in the Highlands of Scotland some centuries earlier) than to the varied and sometimes contradictory practices which the chiefs themselves had described (France, 1969:110–30; Notes, 1876; Notes, 1877). However, in one respect it was closer to the reality of pre-Cession practice than later ordinances as it did allow for some changes if specific *mataqali* or individuals wished.

The ordinance also provided for the appointment of commissioners to 'ascertain' what land was the property of the *mataqali* or other groups, and for the leasing of native land 'to persons of European descent or others'. The commissioners' initial attempts to register land were unsuccessful. There was resistance. Fijian councils charged with assisting were unwilling to do so as registration of land could remove one of their main roles – adjudicating on land disputes (France, 1969:130–1). Over several decades commissioners often reported that people wanted holdings to be registered in the name of *tokatoka* or its local equivalents rather than *mataqali*, but this was still resisted by the government which felt it would take too long and be too costly. Eventually, by the 1910s, various commissioners and their assistants had registered holdings in a number of provinces under the names of *mataqali*. Some of the earlier work had to be redone and at times pressure was needed to squeeze the structures described in evidence into the orthodox model. For example, in a report made convoluted by the divergence between what the orthodox model decreed and the reality in the islands, Commissioner Maxwell argued that in Lau, prior to Ma'afu's re-allocation of land to individuals with a 'Tongan method',

FIJI 217

rights had rested with the *batinilovo*, a small group roughly equivalent to the *tokatoka*. However, many of the people holding allocations from Ma'afu were of Tongan descent and thus 'not Fijians'. It was doubtful whether they could be dealt with under the ordinance. He concluded that registration should be by *batinilovo*, but that Ma'afu's allocations to individuals should also stand unless a line of descendants died out. The land would then revert to the relevant *batinilovo*. Legislation would be needed to deal with the Tongans and with some aspects of overriding Ma'afu's allocations which the people had accepted as valid (Maxwell, 1913b).

Earlier in the year Maxwell had also struggled with the complexities of the interior province of Colo West (Maxwell, 1913a). In his attempts to make clear the orthodox social hierarchy, he produced the first branching diagram of the *vanua, yavusa, mataqali,* and *tokatoka (bitu)* system. France reproduces the diagram and comments that 'Maxwell was clearly not a man to be distracted by detail' (1969:166). While recognising that in some cases the *bitu* would be the appropriate unit, Maxwell argued that there was no individual ownership in the European sense in Colo West, and asserted that 'once the claimants have been classified, and the various yavusa, mataqali, and tokatoka set out in order and their origin and history obtained, the boundaries of their lands are obtained without difficulty and the disputes are easy to settle.... The conspiracies and perjury which stand revealed from time to time are simply appalling' (Maxwell, 1913a:3). One suspects that if people's evidence did not fit the classification, the process of registration made the fit and that at least some of the 'perjury' simply represented evidence which Maxwell felt had to be ignored in adhering to the *mataqali* as the owning unit. In the face of demands for more land for non-Fijians, the pressure to get the registration done expeditiously was considerable, even at the cost of over-generalisation. Because it was relatively large, it would be cheaper as well as quicker to use the *mataqali* as the unit for registration, even if it did not accord with usage or with what people on the land wished.

Although in theory the holdings to be recorded by the commissioners were those applying at the time of Cession (Maxwell, 1913a:4), both the Lau and Colo West reports show that this was not always the case. In Lau, Ma'afu's allocations stood and were accepted at the time of Cession but were to be partially overturned in order to fit the model. In the Colo West case, many of the people living on the eastern side of the middle and upper Sigatoka valley at the time of Cession occupied a chain of fortified settlements on ridge tops close to the boundary between the western grasslands and the eastern forests. Aerial photographs show extensive flights of stone-faced and irrigated taro terraces in the area (e.g. see Ward, 1965, Plate 4). Judging from evidence from other areas, it is likely that the ownership of these intensively used plots would have

218 LAND, CUSTOM AND PRACTICE IN THE SOUTH PACIFIC

been complex and may have rested with smaller units than *mataqali*. Nevertheless the NLC registers and maps of the area show no complexity. By the time the commission hearings took place almost 40 years after Cession, these areas had been abandoned. Peace had been imposed and the people had moved (or been moved by government decree) to villages near the river with its fertile alluvial flats, water supply, and easier access for government officials. Presumably the witnesses before the commission did not think it worth bringing up the detail of past ownership in the now remote hill country. The old terraces had reverted to *veikau* and were simply subsumed into the broad *mataqali* holdings which were recorded in that area. The same seems to have happened in other areas, as at Nakorosule on the Wainimala River where former terraces can be found under forest but are not recorded on NLC maps. Thus Maxwell did not record the situation as at Cession, but rather a pattern which he determined 40 years later.

Apart from the more rapid progress of the NLC under Maxwell, the other major change of the 1910s was the imposition of further restrictions on the alienation of native land. The 1905 Ordinance had allowed sales, but these were suspended in 1908. The 1912 Ordinance formalised this by stating that 'Native land shall not be alienated by native owners whether by sale grant or exchange except to the Government of the Colony'. This was a much tighter formulation than earlier ones and, in addition to stopping direct sales to non-Fijians, the ordinance seems to have removed the legal scope for allocations under customary mechanisms between Fijians of different *mataqali* (Fa, 1989:117–9). The registration process was to take several more decades to complete, but the orthodox model was now firmly established in law. Government officials were taught about Fijian land tenure in terms of the model and official publications and 'authorities' on Fijian matters came to describe it as if it were the immemorial tradition. In time this became the common belief, at least at the level of public discourse. The orthodox model became one of the icons marking the distinctiveness of Fijian culture, and part of the ideology of being Fijian.

The fixing of the boundaries of the land which the NLC decided belonged to each *mataqali*, and the registration of the names of members of each owning group, legally removed the flexibility of older arrangements. If a *mataqali* increased or declined in size, the land area it owned could not change. If the group died out, its land would revert to the Crown. This was a major change as formerly the land of an extinct *mataqali* would have become available for use by other people in the area. Over the years since registration, inequality of land area owned in relation to the population of *mataqali* has increased. People who moved away from their home area and did not maintain their links and obligations with the home

FIJI   219

community would formerly have found that eventually their land rights had weakened or even disappeared. Now their names remained on the record and legally their rights remained sound. Other traditional mechanisms for flexibility became illegal, including some of the traditional gift arrangements and, of course, transfer by conquest.

Underlying the whole process of registration and survey by *mataqali* units was the assumption that the registered owners of the land would also be the users. In part this stemmed from European concepts of ownership and their application to a situation in which ownership of the land was often separated traditionally from the ownership of the trees or the crops upon the land. In fact ownership and use were often not in accord. This discrepancy came to have increasing importance in later decades, although in the initial years after registration it was of little moment.

The 1920s and 1930s

New trends emerged in the 1920s and 1930s, many of which affected the demand for land from Fijian, Indian and European farmers and from companies. The Fijian population had been increasing after the major decline of the late nineteenth century, but was set back by the influenza pandemic of 1919. Thereafter, with improved public health measures, Fijian numbers increased by 15 per cent between 1921 and 1936 but the Indian population grew faster – by 40 per cent over the same period – even though it was no longer supplemented by indentured immigrants. The sugar industry was adjusting to the ending of the indenture system. The sugar mill at Navua closed leaving a demand for smallholder rice farms for former mill and plantation workers. Elsewhere the Colonial Sugar Refining Company (CSR) converted most of its plantations into smallholder tenant farms. The CSR also bought cane from growers other than its own tenants and the area harvested increased by something over 10 per cent between 1925 and 1940 (Ward, 1965:36). Although still largely subsistence farmers, Fijians were growing cash crops in those areas where they had access to local markets or to shipping for their copra or bananas.

In the early years of the century, the demand for land from those Indians who had completed their indentures and elected to stay in Fiji rather than return to India was partly met by the establishment of leasehold settlements on Crown land. Rice farming settlements were established in Viti Levu and Vanua Levu but sugar cane farming was more attractive because of its higher returns. Increasingly through the 1920s and 1930s, Indian cane farmers leased land directly from Fijians, particularly in western Viti Levu. This was possible under the Native Land Ordinances of 1905 and 1912, provided the lessees negotiated with

220 LAND, CUSTOM AND PRACTICE IN THE SOUTH PACIFIC

members of the owning *mataqali* and the lease was then approved by the Commissioner of Lands. The process was almost entirely a matter for individual negotiation. There was no planning of the leasehold areas for provision of services, or to ensure economic-sized holdings or conservation measures. Lessees frequently sought out small patches of arable land but did not lease the adjacent grassland slopes where they grazed their livestock as if it were common land (see Ward, 1965:131, Figure 5.5). Leases were often given for very short periods. Even the early rice settlements on Crown land only gave annual tenancies. The lack of long-term interest in the land reduced farmers' willingness to make improvements or conserve soil and severe erosion on slopes adjacent to the arable land was common.

Reserves and the Native Land Trust Board

Towards the end of the 1930s, as the demand for land continued and the suitable areas of available Crown land shrank, concern grew about the amount of native land being leased. The risk that some communities would have insufficient land for subsistence and commercial needs was clear, and erosion damage and problems of insecure tenure were recognised by the government and it moved to put land matters on a new basis. The Native Land Trust Act of 1940 was modelled in part on the Native Lands Ordinance 1927 of the Gold Coast (Ghana) as amended in 1931 (Brobby, unpub. [1984–5]:3). It sought to regulate the leasing of native land, make more land available to non-Fijians (or to Fijians who wished to farm on land over which an individual lease title was registered), and to reserve sufficient land solely for Fijian use to ensure that communities could continue to maintain their existing life style. The permanent inalienability of native land was confirmed and the Native Lands Commission began the process of delimiting native reserves.

Reserved land would be for the use of Fijians only and would guarantee sufficient land to support the owning units in the future. Native land which was surplus to these requirements, and thus not in reserve, could be leased to non-Fijians and Fijians. The Native Land Trust Board (NLTB) was established to manage the leasing of native land. To this end, section 4(i) of the act stated that the 'control of all native land shall be vested in the Board and all such land shall be administered by the Board for the benefit of the Fijian owners'. It became illegal to lease native land except through the NLTB.

The delimiting of reserves proceeded over the next three decades, with attention being given first to those areas where pressure for land was greatest. When the process was complete, 36.6 per cent of native land was reserved. Once reserves were set in an area, the NLTB could

FIJI 221

lease the unreserved native land. Under the new act many of the poorly laid out lease holdings were rationalised and for many years the supply of land for non-Fijians was improved although the slow rate of delimiting the reserves in some areas was a constraint. NLTB leases had longer terms than had been normal previously, and they included clauses to ensure sound land husbandry. In more recent years the latter clauses have not been systematically enforced.

The level of rents for NLTB leases are related to the purpose of the lease but should not exceed 6 per cent of the unimproved value of the land (Brobby, unpub. [1984–5]:8–9) and thus are not closely related to market valuations. The divergence between the rents paid for NLTB leases and those set by the market for leases of freehold land has become marked in recent years. Dissatisfaction amongst Fijians with the returns they receive from NLTB leases is one motive for people to rent their land outside the legally approved system.

Of the total rent received by the NLTB for a lease, the board may retain up to 25 per cent for administrative costs. A lower percentage could be levied, but 25 per cent is the norm. Of the remainder of the rent (normally 75 per cent of the total) specified shares go to the three principal chiefs of the owning group – 5 per cent to the *turaga i taukei*, 10 per cent to the *turaga ni qali*, and 15 per cent to the *turaga ni mataqali*. The rest is paid to the other members of the *mataqali* (or *tokatoka* where land is registered in the name of *tokatoka* rather than *mataqali*). Thus in terms of the total rent, the NLTB takes 25 per cent, the three chiefs of the upper levels of the social hierarchy get 22.5 per cent between them, and the remaining members of the *mataqali* share 52.5 per cent.[4] If the NLTB were to charge less than its permitted maximum (25 per cent) the shares going to the chiefs and other landowners would increase.

As a person may hold more than one of the three chiefly positions, some individuals in areas where much of the *mataqali* land is leased may accumulate considerable wealth. Traditionally a share of the produce from land would recognise the service and obligations a chief would be expected to render to the members of his group and would often be redistributed to followers. But where the economy and social activities of the community are no longer based primarily on reciprocity, there is often little contribution to the wider group from the 22.5 per cent of the total rent received by the three leaders. Conditional receipts in recognition of obligations have often become personal and unconditional income as the obligations are no longer felt or met. Lloyd has argued that the pattern of rent distribution has sustained and reinforced 'the political role of the chiefs' and 'had a disastrous effect on the economic attitude of the *mataqali* owners . . . [and] served as a disincentive to Fijian development of the lands they own'. When the 52.5 per cent 'was divided equally

222 LAND, CUSTOM AND PRACTICE IN THE SOUTH PACIFIC

amongst . . . [the remainder of the *mataqali*] it amounted to a mere pittance and was certainly not sufficient to induce them to do other than spend it on consumer goods' (Lloyd, 1982:221). Spate puts the matter more sharply in commenting that the 'possibilities of riotous living for the rank-and-file seem limited', whereas the unearned income 'for the head of the *vanua*, whose normal needs are met within the village and whose house can be built by personal service (*lala*) due to him, is a distinct disincentive. This is the real problem: the chiefs, the natural leaders of society, have often in sober truth been debauched by easy money, while most people receive a pittance scarcely worth saving' (Spate, 1959:17).

As different demands for land arose, for example for tourist hotel developments, the board developed new leasing arrangements for such land (Nayacakalou, 1972:155–7). For Fijians who needed leases over reserve land in order to have security against which banks might offer loans, a new type of agricultural lease (Class J) was introduced. The problem of reserve land not being able to be held by non-Fijians, and thus a bank not being able to foreclose in the case of a defaulting loan, was met by deeming the Fiji Development Bank (FDB) to be a 'Fijian entity'. With this status the FDB could foreclose on a Class J lease and then lease the block to another Fijian. Thus the NLTB has adjusted its land management practices to adapt to some new economic conditions, including the desire of Fijians to become more fully involved in the monetary sector.

Commercialism, Government Policy and Individualism

Since the Second World War, which saw Fijian troops serve overseas in the armed forces and experience different ways of life, there have been major changes in the economy and the social life of rural Fiji. This has not occurred uniformly across the country. From early in the present century, people in villages near towns could find wage labour without shifting residence, and in the sugar growing districts cane farming or cane cutting were avenues for earning cash. Monetisation of the rural economy spread gradually to all parts of the country. Copra was the mainstay for coastal villages, and bananas were grown for export by villagers living along the main rivers of southeast Viti Levu. In the 1950s and 1960s new aid-funded roads allowed interior villages to grow cash crops for the steadily expanding urban markets. By the early 1950s apathy towards unpaid communal village work was often apparent on the part of those in wage employment. Money replaced reciprocity in some villages as the means of mobilising labour for tasks such as house building and some agricultural work (Nayacakalou, 1978:31–7). More recently, commercially available weedicides and modern tools and

FIJI 223

equipment have allowed individuals to carry out most agricultural and other tasks which formerly required the mobilisation of the kin group. The course and implications of these tendencies towards greater monetisation and individualisation of work have been described by many observers (Spate, 1959; Belshaw, 1964; Frazer, 1973; Nayacakalou, 1978; Ravuvu, 1983b and 1988; Lasaqa, 1984; Ward, 1987) although the implications for land management have not always been emphasised.

In the 1950s government policy became more oriented towards development. Expansion of commercial farming and greater involvement of Fijians in commercial activity became related goals. A common view, particularly in development-oriented departments such as agriculture, was that the communal character of Fijian society was a hindrance to development in Fijian villages. This belief was held by many non-Fijians who thought that because the official orthodox model said land was held communally by *mataqali*, therefore land use, agriculture, and the disposal of produce were also managed communally. Some agricultural activities such as major land clearing did involve the mobilisation of a wider group of kinsfolk to work together, but most garden work was done by family members in their own gardens and the crops they grew were clearly the property of the individual and his or her household. Neither was the disposal of agricultural produce usually communal apart from ceremonial prestations. In opposition to those who argued that communalism was a constraint, others, including leading Fijian officials such as Ratu Sir Lala Sukuna and Ratu K.K.T. Mara, argued that the communal environment with its 'tribal discipline' protected Fijians from the risks of urban areas or being in a floating population (quoted in Overton, 1989:26–7) and should be preserved.

In two situations there was justification in the 1950s for the view that communalism was a constraining factor in agriculture. First, without individual, or at least negotiable title to land, a farmer could not obtain credit against the security of the land. Banks were not prepared to lend on the basis of a Fijian farmer's 'sweat capital', as institutions such as the Papua New Guinea Development Bank or the Grameen Bank of Bangladesh were later prepared to do. Secondly, a farmer's obligations to the community could disrupt the successful operation of a commercial holding. Frazer (1973:89) reports that in Ra Province in 1959 this was the main complaint expressed about the communal life of the village by those who had chosen to live outside it. A cattle farmer with only a few cows might be asked to supply beasts for feasts at an unsustainable rate. Key farming tasks which had to be completed at a particular time to meet market or agronomic requirements might be interrupted by the need to spend time in community work, ceremonies or socio-political activities. Non-compliance or non-involvement could put a person's

224 LAND, CUSTOM AND PRACTICE IN THE SOUTH PACIFIC

community standing at risk. The aspiring commercial farmer had to make a trade-off between the chance of commercial success and personal economic gain on the one hand, and community standing, personal status and social wellbeing on the other.

Movement away from one's home village and residence outside the village, even if on one's own *mataqali* land, had been limited by Fijian administration regulations for several decades prior to the late 1940s. Nevertheless there were government attempts to encourage Fijian farmers to establish individual smallholdings on land of their own *mataqali* and in 1941 about 1,500 Fijians held 'occupancy leases' on which they operated small farms (Coulter, 1942:51). As more Fijians wished to farm independently outside the village context, or to work more permanently in towns, the policy which allowed people to be exempted from communal duties was revised in 1948. A person who could demonstrate to an official the capacity to live outside the village, could pay a commutation tax to compensate the community for the loss of his labour in communal tasks. The payers of commutation tax, called *galala*, could live and farm independently outside the village and be excused their communal obligations. The authoritarian character and communal orientation of the *galala* regulations was typical of 'native policy' which lagged behind the changes taking place in rural areas. As Nayacakalou pointed out in 1959, the 'administration's view that independent farming should not be allowed to advance at the expense of the village system needs revision so that the order of priority is the other way round' (unpub.). Although the commutation tax and related regulations were abandoned in the late 1960s, the term *galala* remains in use for someone living outside the village (Overton, 1988a).

In the 1950s and later years, the colonial government commissioned several reports (e.g. Spate, 1959; Burns, 1960) which advocated greater individualisation for Fijians in economic affairs. Individualisation was actively encouraged through agricultural development projects on which the farmers were *galala* and held formal leases over their farms. Since independence, the same development policies have continued, though perhaps with less explicit public advocacy of individualism. The tasks of nation building, the securing of Fijian primacy in the polity, and the fostering of Fijian identity and ethnic and political distinctiveness have been seen to require rhetorical support for communalism. Nevertheless, most cattle projects, the Lomaivuna banana and Waibau mixed crop projects in eastern Viti Levu, the Seaqaqa sugar cane project in Vanua Levu, and the coconut replanting project have all been designed for individual farmers with title to leasehold properties. NLTB data suggests that by 1982 'about 20 per cent of Fijian farmers (excluding farm labourers) were farming outside the village system' (Ward,

FIJI 225

1985:38). Many such farmers hold NLTB leases, sometimes over land belonging to their own *mataqali*, and thus use land which has been removed formally from the 'communal' sector. Many others who still live within villages also operate their farms as individual holdings although they use native land of their own or other *mataqali*, to which their usufruct rights remain within the domain of *vakavanua* (the customary way).

Although many Fijians now live away from their home villages, and dispersed settlement patterns are common, this does not mean that such people have severed all social contacts with their home community or village, or their *yavusa*, *mataqali* or *tokatoka*. The contacts may no longer be daily, but reciprocal obligations remain and are observed even if cash, rather than kind, forms a large part of the gifts or prestations and land holdings are individual rather than communal. It is also clear that:

> While the pre-contact land tenure system served subsistence needs well, the present system adopted during the colonial era could neither serve effectively . . . the subsistence needs of the people, nor satisfy the aspirations of those who wanted to be more fully involved in market production and the demands of the new socio-economic order. (Ravuvu, 1988:127)

Law and Practice – The Increasing Divergence

In the late 1950s and 1960s evidence emerged from studies in villages throughout the country that Fijians frequently used land which was not officially owned by their own *mataqali* (e.g. Nayacakalou, 1955:37, 112; Ward, 1960 and 1965; Sahlins, 1962:273; Lasaqa, 1963; Frazer, 1964:152; Watters, 1969:116). This was counter to the official acceptance of the orthodox model of 'customary' land tenure; to the registration of *mataqali* holdings and recording of *mataqali* members according to this model; and to assumptions by officials that the orthodox model was followed in the villages. In the more formal sector evidence also emerged that the legal requirements for leasing native land were often ignored.

Practice in villages

In former times it was customary for non-owners to seek permission to use the land of another owning group, especially if the area had not reverted to *veikau*. First fruits would normally be presented to the owners. In the 1950s people in some areas would use the land of other *mataqali* without any explicit request or permission. Lasaqa (1963:102) provides examples from northeast Tailevu and the tendency was confirmed by this author's field inquiries in 1958–60 and by Frazer (1964:152), especially if the proposed use were for food gardens. When

226 LAND, CUSTOM AND PRACTICE IN THE SOUTH PACIFIC

the planting of cash crops was involved and where agricultural land was scarce, members of land owning groups were, and still are, less willing to permit non-members of the owning *mataqali* to plant on their land.

In 1958–60, the author conducted surveys of land use in six villages and restudied three of them in 1983. Fully comparable data are available for only four of the villages studied in 1958–60, and for the three re-studied in 1983. In 1958–60, in areas which were not close to towns or not involved in long-term commercial farming, a very high proportion of gardens were not sited on the land of the planter's own *mataqali* (Table 6.2). The changes between the late 1950s and 1983 were not uniform in the three villages which were re-studied, but the differences can be explained largely in terms of the changing relative importance of cash cropping and the amount of land available to the particular *mataqali* or village. Studies of other areas reveal similar trends stemming from similar causes (e.g. Frazer, 1964; Thomas, 1981; Overton, 1989).

In the late 1950s, the only cash crop in isolated Saliadrau village was a limited amount of *yaqona* (kava – *Piper methysticum*) and land suitable for swidden cultivation was plentiful. Informants stated that 'provided no other gardens used by the landowners were in the vicinity, a villager of another *mataqali* might go ahead and establish a garden without making any formal request for permission to do so. If gardens were already established nearby then a request, perhaps supported by the presentation of a *tabua* (whale's tooth), would be made' (Ward, 1965:276). This set of practices ensured that, regardless of formal ownership, each household could utilise the different land and soil types within the village's territory by having several gardens scattered to take advantage of the variety of ecological sites available. Many of these gardens were located on the land which belonged formally to *mataqali* whose members were resident in another village (Figure 6.5).

Nabudrau village, located in the lower Rewa River delta and without road or direct water access, had no cash cropping in 1959 and almost all gardens were located on land which did not belong to the planter according to the NLC records (Table 6.2). In both Saliadrau and Nabudrau households planted with regard to ecological conditions and accessibility rather than ownership, a point also made by Belshaw (1964:186) for the Sigatoka Valley. Even at Nakorosule on the Wainimala River where bananas were grown for export in 1958, only one of the 14 *mataqali* had all its members' gardens on its own land. Four used none of their own land (Ward, 1965:278).

At Sote, where bananas were grown for export in the 1950s and 1960s, there was ample land and little pressure to confine gardens to one's own registered holdings. At Sasa, however, coconuts had been a cash crop for decades and occupied much of the village's cultivable land. Here com-

FIJI

227

Table 6.2 Relationship between garden and land ownership

Village	Percentage of gardens not on the planter's land 1958–60	1983
Saliadrau 1958		
Total gardens used	76	67
Gardens on village land	69	46
Sote 1959	70	37
Sasa 1960	31	n.a.
Nabudrau 1959	88	88

Source: Field data.

mercialism and land shortage for food crops were discouraging owners from allowing others to use their registered land.

Rutz gives a detailed account of how, in the Waidina valley, rights to use of an area of garden land are maintained by a planter through the period and practice of *veimada*, or fallow, and how these rights can be inherited (1978:26–9). Thus, even if the land is not recorded under the name of the last planter's *mataqali*, it could remain linked to that planter or his descendants as long as they maintained its *veimada* status. Where it is possible to recultivate after short fallows, as on well-drained alluvial flats along the major rivers of the eastern interior of Viti Levu, very long periods of occupation can be maintained with alternating cultivation and *veimada*. Watters records that in 1958–9, alluvial land at Lutu village had been used by at least three generations of the same family so that 'close identification of plots of land with individual households suggests that gradual transition of ownership to an individual or household basis may be occurring' (Watters, 1969:90).

An alternative to this explanation may be offered, one which allows for the fact that prior to the registration of land in the name of the *mataqali*, the *tokatoka* (or its equivalent) or the family unit was widely recognised as the customary landholding unit and land was inheritable within that unit. It is suggested here that what occurred in many villages such as Saliadrau, Sote, Nabudrau, and in villages like Nakorosule and Lutu, especially in relation to their non-commercial agriculture, was a continuation of pre-registration practice. Individuals or households cleared the *veikau* to which they had common rights as *yavusa* or village members, established their individual or household rights to the *qele* (garden land) thus created, and continued to hold rights to the particular garden area through the custom of *veimada*. Rather than a new process of individualisation, there was continuity (in these non-commercial periods and situations) of the older custom of *qele* being owned and inherited through *veimada* by the smaller groups of *tokatoka*, *bure* or *bito*. As Ravuvu says, 'even after land had

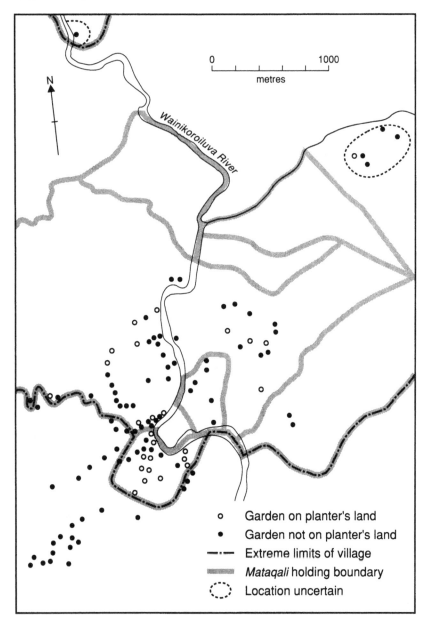

Figure 6.5 Garden and land ownership, Saliadrau village, 1958.
Source: Field survey.

FIJI 229

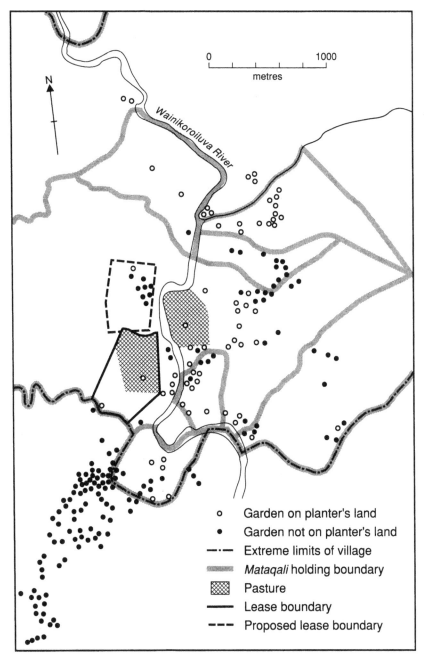

Figure 6.6 Garden and land ownership, Saliadrau village, 1983.
Source: Field survey.

230 LAND, CUSTOM AND PRACTICE IN THE SOUTH PACIFIC

been registered under the title of a particular group, customary practices continued' (1988:130). The orthodox model did not fit practice, past or current, and was ignored by farmers. This was usually acceptable to the formal landowners in areas which were primarily concerned with subsistence cropping, where there was little competition for land for food gardening, and where a demand for leasing land did not exist.

In such areas, both before and after the registration of *mataqali* holdings, members of a family have tended to plant their gardens, and particularly food gardens, close to each other or in relatively contiguous blocks (Sahlins, 1957:454; Ravuvu, 1983a:72–3). The fact of planting and holding land through a series of *veimada* periods could give rise to some merging of the concepts of ownership of the crop and the rights to the land (cf. Rutz, 1978:24–5). As the Chinese proverb states, 'long tenancy becomes property' (Elvin, 1970:107). It will be recalled that when the NLC was about to investigate land claims in an area, the people would often plant new gardens to mark land as their own (Thomson, 1908:361). Figure 6.7 provides a hypothetical example of the pattern of *mataqali* ownership which might be registered if the NLC were to revisit an area three decades after the first survey and to re-survey 'ownership' on similar principles to those applied at the time of the original determination. The memory of the history of use, and hence 'ownership' and the continued right to the use of particular blocks of *qele* is neither infallible nor timeless, and in any case surrender of *veimada* rights allows land to revert to *veikau* and eventually to be taken up as *qele* by others to whom 'ownership' would pass. The contrast between the official map of land holdings as mapped about 1930 and the hypothetical map for 1959 (Figure 6.7) demonstrates the extent to which the flexible processes of adjustment to changing relative needs has gone on over the last half-century, regardless of the formally registered ownership. Such discrepancies between the holdings recorded in the NLC's determinations and current *qele* holdings could be replicated for many villages.

Exclusivity and individuality versus communality

In recent years other discrepancies have arisen between the legal situation and common practice and derive from quite different causes. These have far-reaching implications for settlement forms, land use patterns, and the village economy and society. Even in the mid-1950s, attitudes towards land and who might use it were very different in villages close to urban centres from those in villages like Saliadrau. In Nailaga, in the midst of the sugar cane growing region and close to the town of Ba, land had become commoditised by the late 1950s. Much of the village land was leased to Indian farmers through the NLTB, but some was 'rented' to Indian farmers informally, or used under share cropping arrangements. Although several

FIJI 231

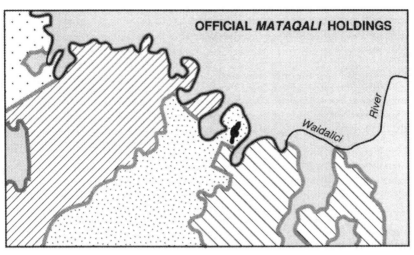

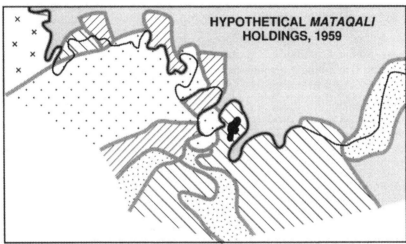

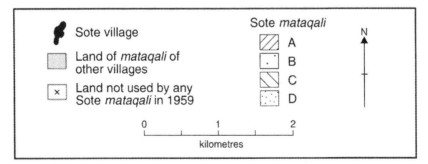

Figure 6.7 Registered and hypothetical land ownership, Sote village.
Source: Native Lands Commission maps for official holdings; hypothetical holdings based on field survey data (see Figure 6.8).

232 LAND, CUSTOM AND PRACTICE IN THE SOUTH PACIFIC

mataqali and *tokatoka* had insufficient land to form economic holdings, and others had land lying idle because they were not interested in farming, the old practices of using others' land freely for food cropping were no longer followed. In 1953, one-third of the land of Draubuta, within the commuting zone of Suva, was leased to Indian farmers through the NLTB and some *mataqali* had little land for either subsistence or cash crops (Spate, 1959:12). As noted above, at Sasa village, on the northwest coast of Vanua Levu, where coconuts had provided the main cash crop for many years, and only a limited area of cultivable land was available near the village, only 31 per cent of the gardens were not on the planter's own *mataqali* land in 1960 (see Table 6.2 above). Under commercial farming and with land having commodity value, the orthodox model had become a barrier against temporary and informal amelioration of the land shortage faced by some villagers. The fencing of individual plots of land in Nailaga seemed symbolic of the new and different attitude.

The reluctance of people to allow members of their own community from different *mataqali* to use land, if the intention were to plant either cash crops or long-term crops, was evident in other areas. At Nacamaki, Koro Island, in 1958, 'with growing cash consciousness *mataqali* with little land were not always freely allowed to use valuable land of other *mataqali*', and one land-short *mataqali* had been told to 'get off' land they had used (Watters, 1969:116). In the Wainimala area, where bananas, cocoa or *yaqona* are planted as cash crops, 'it is wise to grow them in areas where one has the rights of control' (Ravuvu, 1983a:73). Rutz reports that in villages close to the road in the Waidina valley, where root crops, bananas and cattle have been farmed for the market, 'there is a marked tendency on the part of owners to invoke communal against veimada claims. This eliminates the rights of non-communal [e.g. non-*mataqali*] owners . . . [so that] the effective boundaries of the veimada rules in some cases have shrunk from village to lineage' (Rutz, 1978:30–1). The fall in the proportion of gardens not on the planter's own *mataqali* land in Sote village from 70 to 37 per cent between 1959 and 1983 demonstrates this trend (Table 6.2; Figures 6.8 and 6.9). Planters have withdrawn from the land to the north of the river which belongs to non-Sote *mataqali*, in part because of the establishment of a beef cattle development project where farmers hold formal leases. Even within Sote village land fewer planters use land which does not belong to their own *mataqali*. In Saliadrau, which was reached by road only in the early 1980s, the increased interest in cash crops was having a similar effect in 1983. The effect was masked by continued use of land owned by but rather inaccessible to another village, but Table 6.2 shows that on Saliadrau's own land the proportion of gardens on land belonging to other *mataqali* fell from 69 to 46 per cent between 1958 and 1983.

Increasing reluctance to allow non-members to use *mataqali* land, where there is pressure from population or from commercial aspirations, brings to the fore inequalities in the ratio of land to population between different *mataqali*. The formal freezing of land holdings and landowning units (Nayacakalou, 1971:213) by NLC registration made the older mechanisms for redistribution of land extra-legal. Although traditional methods continued to operate in the subsistence context, once commercial interests become dominant, legally registered status can become the guiding principle. *Mataqali* with large holdings but declining membership may live beside others with limited land but burgeoning numbers. The resulting inequalities are now less likely to be eased by customary means. The risks of some people having insufficient land for subsistence needs has increased, and differential access to land has become an increasingly important factor leading to inequalities of wealth and opportunity in Fijian villages (Ward, 1987; Overton, 1992).

The growing tendency for Fijians to favour exclusivity and individuality of ownership of native land are also seen in the increasing use by Fijians of non-customary or extra-legal categories of individual holdings on native land. The first category consists of formal leaseholds issued by the NLTB. The second includes various arrangements which have some basis in custom but are extra-legal or illegal, and in which the intentions of land owners and farmers are not customary.

Formal leaseholds held by Fijians in rural areas are of two types. Almost 3,000 Fijian farmers hold standard NLTB agricultural leases over non-reserved land, with major concentrations at Seaqaqa for sugar cane farms; on mixed crop farms at Waibau and Lomaivuna; and on cattle farming projects in the eastern Sigatoka valley, eastern Viti Levu and elsewhere. Such leases are normally for 30 years. The land is removed from the realm of custom for that period with the lease holder normally having both exclusive rights to its use and the power to sell the lease without the consent of the owning group, or groups. The leasehold can be used as security for raising loan capital, and a lending agency could foreclose on the lease if loan repayments and charges were not maintained.

The second type is the NLTB Class J leases which are generally similar to the standard agricultural leases but apply only to native reserve land and thus can be held only by Fijians. However, organisations such as the Methodist Church, the Fiji Development Bank and the Native Lands Development Corporation (NLDC) can hold such leases through their status as 'Fijian entities'. In mid-1993, 3,228 Class J leases were current, covering an area of 81,643 hectares, of which almost a quarter (95 leases) were under the control of 'Fijian entities'. The combined total of Class J leases and standard agricultural leases held by Fijians, fell from 7,071 in 1982 (Ward, 1985:34) to 6,085 in 1993 because of cancellation of leases

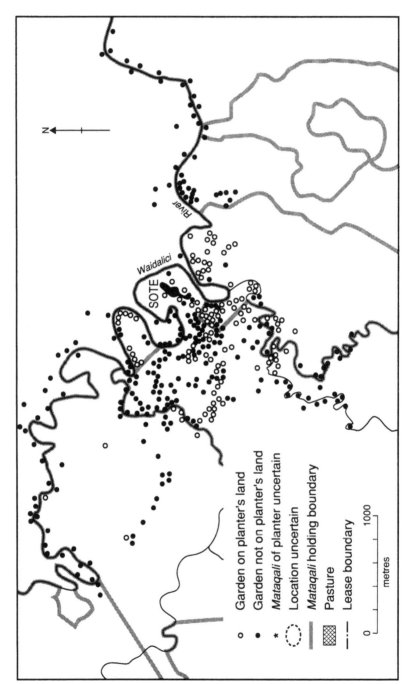

Figure 6.8 Garden and land ownership, Sote village, 1959.
Source: Field survey.

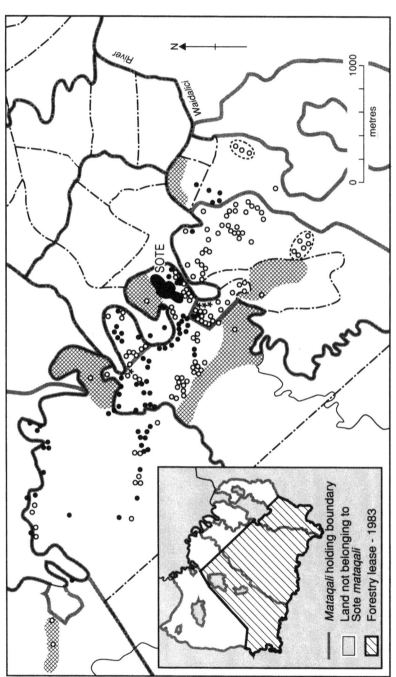

Figure 6.9 Garden and land ownership, Sote village, 1983. (For full key see Figure 6.8.)
Source: Field survey.

236 LAND, CUSTOM AND PRACTICE IN THE SOUTH PACIFIC

by the NLTB when repayments were in arrears (pers. comm. General Manager, NLTB, 11 November 1993). A considerable number of these cancellations related to leases taken out by coconut growers over land of their own *mataqali* in order to get a loan under a British aid project for coconut rehabilitation and replanting.

The need for a lease in order to obtain a loan from a finance agency is a prime reason for a Fijian farmer to take out a lease over part of his or her own *mataqali* land, even when the right to continued use already exists. In the case of the coconut replanting scheme, after the grants had been paid many recipients were reluctant to continue paying rent for land which they could use by customary right without payment. As coconuts are a very long term crop, the planter's rights to continued use of the produce is not threatened by lack of a lease. Neither is the right to pass it on to heirs threatened while the coconuts remain standing. In other cases the reasons for taking out a lease lie in the long-term exclusivity and transferability which a lease provides, and the prospect of capital gain.

The second category of individual holdings on native land, those that are non-customary or extra-legal, includes cases of relatively large farms being established by individuals without formal leases being taken out. In many instances these are on the land of the farmer's own *mataqali* and usufruct rights are established simply by clearing *veikau*. As long as the farmer continues to use the land or maintain *veimada* rights continued occupation is secure. Many such holdings are far larger than would ever have been the case in more traditional times. Increasing numbers of such holdings are not on the farmer's own land.

The general principles which have governed the allocation and use of native land (other than leasehold) since before Cession were based primarily on the production of short-term crops for direct subsistence or local ceremonial use. When land is locked up in the hands of individuals under customary usufruct rights for long periods, as in the case of coconut groves or other tree crops, or pasture, other members of the owning group can become dissatisfied. Their chances of using that land when their subsistence needs increase are clearly constrained and they may be unable to find sufficient land for their own cash cropping ambitions. One person's use of land near the village for a large area of pasture may force others to grow their cash crops at an unreasonable distance from the village. Ravuvu describes the current situation as follows:

> Increasing population, coupled with increasing wants and demands, the shortage and mis-utilization of good gardening land close to the village all limit the ambitious and entrepreneurial gardener. However, in order to satisfy his aspirations, the entrepreneurial gardener either shifts away and settles on a new site or leases another area in order to have sole control over it. If he is one of those who have ownership rights over the area, he might exert these

FIJI 237

rights in ways which could drive other users away from the areas he wants to garden. Such action often leads to conflict . . . with those affected and normal communication is difficult to maintain. (1983b:23)

Figures 6.6 and 6.9 (above) provide examples of how, by 1983, significant areas of land in two Viti Levu villages had become the exclusive preserves of individuals both through leasing land from their own *mataqali* or clearing and holding large blocks under pasture. In the case of Saliadrau, one person had planted a private mahogany plantation without a lease and taken out a lease over another area for pasture. Another person was negotiating for a lease and a third had fenced an area for grazing. In Sote, three leases had been issued and four other areas had been fenced, put under pasture, and thereby turned into long-term holdings which no longer go back into the cycle of reversion to *veikau* with its potential for re-allocation. In addition, a very large area had been leased to the government for forestry plantations. Land use maps of eastern Viti Levu for 1958, 1968 and 1978 show a great increase in the area under pasture, particularly in the 1968–78 decade.[5] Some of this land has been cleared from forest and grassed as part of Native Lands Development Corporation or other cattle development projects, but considerable areas represent small-scale individual enterprises, as in Sote and Saliadrau. Many of the grazing enterprises return relatively little to the farmers, and many show little sign of attempts to make them economically successful. Gaining long-term control of the land itself seems to be an important motive for the activity.

Staking personal long-term claim to land is not a 'traditional' custom. It is an increasingly common practice. It uses customary mechanisms, such as converting *veikau* to *qele* and thereby gaining individual or household authority over the land, for non-customary purposes, namely long-term individual and exclusive access which can be passed directly to one's heirs. Such land is not only taken out of the common pool, it is often managed in ways which bypass those communal elements of agricultural activity which were part of the cement of village socio-economic life. With modern agricultural technology, the farmer has less need to call on kin for help in particular tasks. When extra labour is required, it is often obtained by payment of cash. Wage labour may be easier to arrange when the job needs to be done, and it also means that the farmer does not accumulate reciprocal obligations which he might be called upon to fulfil at times inconvenient to his own farming schedules. Changes in settlement patterns also result. As people leave the nucleated village with its surrounding scatter of gardens to live in a homestead on their own consolidated farm, a dispersed settlement pattern results which is not dissimilar in form to that of Indian-settled rural areas. The individual holdings

238 LAND, CUSTOM AND PRACTICE IN THE SOUTH PACIFIC

usually represent a much larger area controlled per household than was the case in the older subsistence and shifting cultivation systems, thus increasing the risk of others being left without adequate land.

Customary, or *vakavanua*, mechanisms are also used by some land owners to allocate native land to Fijian migrants from other areas. The migrant will normally ask the landowning group, or some member(s) of it, for permission to occupy and plant a block of unused land. Custom does sanction such transfers, even though current ordinances may not. In some cases the owners limit the use to which the land may be put, for example by specifying that cash crops shall not be grown. This is not always the case. The allocation of a block of land may be made with the agreement of a majority of the members of the owning *mataqali*, but in many cases it may be done by the individual 'land controller' (in Eaton's (1988:23) phrase) who holds the *veimada* rights.

In the early 1960s, a new road was built through unoccupied forest country from Saweni to Vunidawa in eastern Viti Levu. Most of the owners lived in villages located some distance away, closer to the main river which hitherto had been the main means of communication. Migrants from Lau made *vakavanua* arrangements with the owners and took up considerable areas of land along the road. Some have remained in occupation ever since. The process was repeated when the road was extended inland to the hydroelectric station at Monosavu in the late 1970s (Chung, 1988). In the Waibau area, near the southern end of the road, the original *vakavanua* and extra-legal holdings were placed under formal NLTB leases and the Department of Agriculture planned new farm layouts to create the Waibau settlement (Ward, 1965:183–6; Overton, 1988b). In so doing the direct control of the Waibau land was removed from the land owners. Elsewhere the land remains under *vakavanua*, even though most settlers have few, if any, of the traditional links with the land owners, which would have been the usual situation in former customary times.

There are advantages for land owners in allowing their land to be used *vakavanua* by 'strangers' rather than having it leased through the NLTB. First, they may retain more control over its use. Second, they may extract higher rents. Third, none of the rent goes to the NLTB or, if the arrangement is made only by the *mataqali* members who hold the *veimada* rights, to other members of the *mataqali*. Fourth, the arrangement need not conform to the conditions of NLTB or other formal leases which ensure that tenants have reasonable security of tenure. Tenants may, of course be less favourably treated than if they could obtain an NLTB lease over the same land, but the shortage of good land for leasing through the NLTB ensures that people will be willing to take up *vakavanua* blocks under arrangements which are, at least in part, illegal. *Vakavanua*

FIJI   239

arrangements can also have deleterious results on the land as short-term, insecure tenancies often discourage farmers from taking conservation or other long-term measures to preserve soil fertility and reduce erosion. They may also be discouraged from making investments in general improvements, the benefits of which they may be denied at a later date.

Law and practice in land dealings with non-Fijians

Whereas it can be argued that *vakavanua* arrangements are customary and possibly in accord with the ordinances when made between Fijians, this is certainly not so for such arrangements between Fijian land owners and non-Fijians. Although, as noted above, examples did occur in the nineteenth century when Europeans were permitted to settle on native land and land owners probably considered the occupation to be a form of *vakavanua* permissive occupancy, such arrangements have been illegal under most of the relevant ordinances operative since Cession. Nevertheless, manuscript maps of the sugar cane areas in the 1880s show land occupied by Indian smallholders which may well have been held *vakavanua* and Anderson (1974:18) reports such arrangements in the same period. The prevalence of the practice in the earlier decades of the present century was one of the factors leading to the Native Land Trust Act 1940 and the establishment of the NLTB. But neither the 1940 law nor the regulation of leasing through the NLTB stopped the practice, and it has become increasingly common regardless of the law.

Much of the tobacco produced in the Nadi and Sigatoka areas in the 1980s was grown by Indians on native land under agreements negotiated directly with land owners (Eaton, 1988:23–4). When given a contract to supply a specified quantity of leaf, a Fijian or Indian farmer who did not have sufficient suitable land would negotiate privately with Fijian land owners for permission to use a piece of high quality alluvial land for the season. The practical authority of individuals or units at below *mataqali* level in land tenure matters is indicated by the fact that 'in some thousands of *vakavanua* arrangements of which [Eaton] has experience, none was negotiated on a *mataqali* basis and none came to grief due to *mataqali* interference' (Eaton, 1988:23–4). In other words, *mataqali* members recognised the rights of individuals amongst them to allocate to others the use of specific areas within the *mataqali* lands. The permissive occupancy was illegal, but both land owners and growers saw it to be in their own interests to follow this course. For the land owners, much higher rents may be obtained, and Eaton records an Indian tobacco grower paying F$350 per hectare – ten times the amount paid for a similar area under his sugar cane lease from the NLTB (1988:28). In

240 LAND, CUSTOM AND PRACTICE IN THE SOUTH PACIFIC

addition, the Fijian owners lose the use of a smaller area of their land for a shorter time than if a normal 30-year NLTB lease were involved. The advantages for the Indian growers lie both in the speedier arrangements which are possible in private deals compared with negotiations for a NLTB lease, and in gaining access to better quality land. Most of the uncommitted alluvial land in these districts is reserve land which cannot be leased legally to non-Fijians, and any new NLTB leases are likely to be on much poorer land. Furthermore, for a crop for which the grower has a guaranteed market for only one season, the short term of these arrangements may not be a constraint.

Of a total of 690 farmers who grew tobacco in the Sabeto area near Nadi in the years 1980–85, 72 per cent did so on land which they held *vakavanua*, and over one-third of these *vakavanua* arrangements were made with Indian growers (Eaton, 1988:28). Such arrangements are common in other areas and for other types of farming, including sugar cane and grazing in western Viti Levu and ginger, rice and vegetable growing in eastern Viti Levu (Overton, 1989). In some cases land formerly used for cane farms by Indians has reverted to Fijian control on the expiry of NLTB leases, but has then been rented *vakavanua* to Indian farmers – sometimes to the same people who formerly held the NLTB leases (Eaton, 1988:25).

Another *vakavanua* arrangement which bypasses the leasing system is that of sharecropping, whereby Fijian land owners allow someone else to carry out one or more of the farming operations in return for an agreed share of the output, rather than a rental payment for the land. In the Raki Raki area of northern Viti Levu a significant proportion of the cane farms which supply cane under contracts issued to Fijians are operated by Indian farmers on a sharecropping basis (pers. comm. S. Prasad, 12 November 1993). The practice has also been reported on cane farms near Ba in the 1960s (Eaton, 1988:25) and in the Nadi and Momi areas in the 1980s (Prasad, 1984); on Chinese-managed and Fijian-owned ginger farms at Waibau, eastern Viti Levu; and on rice farms in the lower Rewa Valley (Overton, 1989:40, 47–8). Like other *vakavanua* arrangements, sharecropping is widespread, but its legal status is unclear as the wording of each particular agreement would determine whether or not it represented dealing in native land itself or merely in the proceeds from the land. The former would contravene the Native Land Trust Act 1940; the latter would not (Fa, 1989:105–6).

Urban areas

In recent decades the pressure on land for urban use has also increased rapidly. The urban population grew from 18.3 per cent of the total in

1956 (McArthur, 1958:9) to 38.8 per cent in 1986 and 22 per cent of the country's total population then lived in the Suva–Nausori urban zone (Bedford, 1988:184–5). Squatter settlements on land held *vakavanua* had appeared on the fringes of Suva in the mid-1950s, and market gardening, often by Chinese growers, was also practised on *vakavanua* holdings on the hilly land between Suva and Nausori. Since then much of this land has been given over to urban housing under a variety of tenurial conditions, including extra-legal or illegal arrangements like those found in farming areas.

An example of *vakavanua* arrangements in a non-agricultural context is provided by a long-established, semi-urban settlement on the highway between Nadi and Lautoka. It has the appearance of an established suburb, is named on topographic maps, but is located on reserve land which has been rented to the Indian residents. Permissive occupancy was given by those members of the *mataqali* who had *veimada*-type rights to the particular segment of *mataqali* land. If the occupation of the land were to be legalised, the land would first have to be de-reserved, and then formal NLTB leases issued. To de-reserve land is within the power of the NLC but might not be politically acceptable. When the case was considered informally some years ago within the NLTB, it was clear that those owners who had given permission did not want any such change to occur. If it did occur, their income would be reduced for the reasons noted above, and because of the ceiling of 6 per cent of the unimproved value placed on rents charged by the NLTB. On their side, the Indian residents were not anxious to have any change in the status quo. They saw a risk that members of the *mataqali* who did not receive a share of the rents (because the land was not in their *veimada* area) and were opposed to the settlement might object and prevent leases being issued. While the arrangement masqueraded under a facade of *veimada* 'custom', however distorted by use for non-customary purposes, it had some customary validity. Those who did not share the rents, or who disapproved for other reasons, were therefore constrained in the extent of public opposition which it would be socially acceptable for them to voice. The question of legalisation was quietly dropped (pers. comm. J. Kamikamica, 12 November, 1993).

It is not surprising that where the pressure for land is greatest, in the urban areas, disputes are common. Rutz (1987) describes the variety of tenure arrangements which occur in the Fijian settlements of the Suva urban area, including *vakavanua* transactions of almost every possible type. But as they are applied in the context of increasing land shortage, rising land values, and a wage rather than a reciprocal exchange economy, 'there is genuine confusion about the obligations and duties of Fijians towards each other, about what constitutes proper conduct in general, and, in particular, with regard to land value and the moral

242 LAND, CUSTOM AND PRACTICE IN THE SOUTH PACIFIC

order for transactions ... [T]he market does represent a different morality and novel social arrangements fundamentally in contradiction to the oppositions that define social relations cemented by reciprocal exchange within the moral economy' (Rutz, 1987:555). *Vakavanua* is not a suitable basis for land transactions in such a context in the longer term and land problems in the urban area are at the base of a 'strong undercurrent of resentment and discontent' (Rutz, 1987:534).

Tensions arise because *vakavanua* arrangements are unfairly exploited by both land owners and migrants from other areas who occupy the land. Early migrants to an area who negotiated the original agreement are often followed by much larger numbers of their kin by 'chain entry'. 'The settlement of Qauia ... began as a *vakavanua* request to the lineage head, through his wife who was a woman from Lau. By 1982, there were nearly a thousand people in Qauia, the majority of whom were Lauans who were distant relatives or strangers and had no *vakavanua* status with the landowners' (Rutz, 1987:547). Thus land owners may find that far more people arrive and use far more land than they had intended. On the other hand, land owners may 'extort money from occupiers for drink and gambling' or other expenses in a form of 'parasitic landlordism' (1987:548).

The NLTB and who owns native land

Some of the discontent reported by Rutz arises from the powers vested in the NLTB and the way these have been exercised in the last two decades. In one case near Suva, all land owners accepted an NLTB offer to lease land for an NLDC subdivision despite it having been occupied *vakavanua* by migrants for more than a decade. This earlier *vakavanua* agreement had no legal standing and the occupants were faced with eviction (Rutz, 1987:549–50). In another much publicised case in 1979 at Delainavesi, near Suva, some members of the owning *yavusa* occupied some of its land, but found that other members had agreed to a lease for NLDC subdivision despite their occupation. The court held that permission was not required from all land owners and that the lease was valid despite the protests of some members (Matahau, unpub.[1986]). Fa (1989) provides other examples in which courts have held that ownership really rests with the NLTB, and *mataqali* or other registered group members have limited scope for redress if their land is leased without their agreement.

It has always been a role of the NLTB to foster 'development' in Fiji by making land which was not in use or needed in the foreseeable future by the Fijian owners available to non-Fijians, or to Fijians who were not members of the owning group. In 1936 Ratu Sir Lala Sukuna sought to

FIJI 243

persuade the Council of Chiefs that 'it is our duty to use our influence, our power, to open up waste Mataqali lands for agricultural purposes; whether they be taken up by Europeans, Indians or Fijians' (Sukuna, 1936:216). Section 4(1) of the Native Land Trust Act 1940, which was passed to give effect to this wish, states that 'control of all native land shall be vested in the Board and all such land shall be administered by the Board for the benefit of the Fijian owners'. After independence in 1971, fostering economic development and greater participation by Fijians in commercially-oriented development became more important goals. Former colonial government policies, which aimed to protect Fijian society from the stresses and risks of rapid economic change, became less evident in practice if not in rhetoric. Presumably it could be taken as self-evident that a Fijian-dominated and democratically elected government would be working to benefit the Fijian people. To enhance the development role of the NLTB, the Native Land Development Corporation was established as a wholly-owned company of the NLTB and started operations in 1975. Endowed with the privileges of being a 'Fijian entity', its role was to develop and manage projects on Fijian land and thereby to benefit the Fijian people. While its initial activities involved mainly rural projects, such as the management of the Seaqaqa cane scheme and the promotion of the cattle projects, it later moved into the urban sphere as the agency for establishing residential or industrial subdivisions on native land.

The national development thrust led the NLTB and the NLDC to a much more activist role, and it has been argued that this led the board to use a more literal interpretation of its powers to control all native land, and to interpret the 'benefit of the Fijian owners' in broad rather than specific terms (e.g. Fa, 1989; Matahau, unpub. [1986]; Brobby, unpub. [1984–5]). Whereas in its earlier years the board had generally had extensive discussions with and sought general agreement from land owners prior to leasing a particular area, in the 1970s there seems to have been less consultation. Matahau asserts that in the 1980s 'it is not uncommon for the executives to inform the Fijian owners that the Board does not need to obtain the owner's consent in dealing with native land except if such land is "reserved land"' (Matahau, unpub. [1986]:21). Even in the 1960s, when Nayacakalou asked who interpreted 'the interests of the owners', the then Secretary of the NLTB replied that the board did (Nayacakalou, 1971:225). Taken to its logical conclusion, this interpretation gives the NLTB almost absolute power over any native land outside the reserved areas. Even within the reserves, the board's power could be wielded very strongly in issuing Class J leases to non-owning Fijians. Thus the question of who 'owns' native land today can be raised, and in relation to certain rights over the land there is little doubt that the NLTB is in a

244 LAND, CUSTOM AND PRACTICE IN THE SOUTH PACIFIC

stronger legal position than the 'native owners'. Matahau goes as far as arguing that the Native Land Trust Act stripped the native owners of 'their proprietary rights' (unpub. [1986]:4).

Court decisions in the 1980s have tended to reinforce the literal interpretation of the powers of the NLTB and to raise questions about the rights of landowning groups vis-à-vis the board. In particular 'the Court expressed dicta to the effect that, any recognition of customary institutions such as the Mataqali or the Itokatoka amounts to nothing, for customary institutions are not recognised by the common law or any statute' (Fa, 1989:149). Furthermore, individual members of a *mataqali* have no capacity to bring an action objecting to a lease or licence issued by the NLTB as 'the owner of the land is the *mataqali* and not its individual members' (Rooney, J. unreported decision, Supreme Court of Fiji, 801/1984, quoted in Fa, 1989:150). If such decisions stand and become a firm part of the legal basis for future decisions on land tenure matters, then the NLTB could be regarded as the 'owner' of native land in Fiji in many respects. Where there is ample land available to Fijian communities or little demand for the leasing of native land, 'ownership' by the NLTB would not impinge significantly on the occupiers. But that is not the case in urban and peri-urban areas where an increasing proportion of Fijians now live. Matahau argues that because of the board's willingness to lease land without prior consultation with, or appropriate concern for, the longer term interests of the land owners, 'it is now becoming a nightmare for all the native owners . . . [who] own land bordering on to urban areas. Where would the members of the owning Mataqali go if the Board continued to develop their land? Where would they live? How would they be guaranteed that the continuity of their culture would be preserved?' (unpub.[1986]:48).

The wide use of *vakavanua* in land dealings between Fijians and non-Fijians, even on reserve land, calls into question the role of the NLTB and the orthodox legal model of land tenure. Dissatisfaction with the board is widespread and of long standing (Nayacakalou, 1971:209; Ravuvu, 1983b:31). Little if anything has been done to address these issues at a political level. Perhaps the reason lies in the way 'the control of the NLTB [over land] became the material base for a modern chiefly elite' through the distribution of rents so that chiefs 'became part of invented tradition, [and] thereby became landlords' (Rutz, 1987:540) dependent upon the NLTB. Any legal freeing up of a lease market which allowed direct lease negotiations would probably result in a marked drop in income for many chiefs. Meanwhile other people throughout the country ignore the laws when dealing in land and thereby seek to maximise the benefits they can gain from the extra-legal land market.

FIJI

245

Conclusion

For 120 years many of the land tenure arrangements which have been practised on native land in Fiji have been markedly divergent both from those accepted officially as being 'customary' and from the legal position as codified in acts and ordinances. The orthodox model of 'communal ownership by a *mataqali* was, to all intents and purposes, imposed on the Fijian people, with their acquiescence . . . [and] many Fijians believe that this concept, enshrined in both the Native Lands Act, and the Native Land Trust Act, is in fact a reflection of some universally recognised traditional system of land tenure as narrated by their forefathers to the early colonial administrators' (Kamikamica and Davey, 1988:284–5). Practice now diverges from both the 'custom' of the orthodox model set down by the Native Lands Commission, which is often described as the core of the Fijian way of life, and from the actual practices of earlier times. Old practices are used to meet old needs despite being outlawed in the codification of the orthodox model; old practices are adapted for new goals; and new practices are introduced and are accepted as being in some way 'customary' in the current age.

In the first decades after Cession in 1874, village people continued to allocate and use land in much the same way as before, although warfare was no longer an acceptable way for land to change hands and alienation to non-Fijians was generally banned. Later, the social groupings for everyday life in many villages diverged from those recorded by the NLC. The recorded land holdings and the official *mataqali* in whose name the lands were registered came to be less and less related to the actual patterns of land use, garden ownership and land control. Because people could ignore the formally registered land holdings in areas where there was little commercial pressure on the land, the inflexibility built into the orthodox model did not immediately create serious problems for most Fijians.

In later decades, as commercial agriculture became more important and the commodification of land increased, the discrepancies between practice and garden ownership on the one hand, and 'custom' and registered land ownership on the other, became sources of possible difficulties. Land owners became less willing to allow others to use their land without payment, especially when commercial or long-term crops were involved. The inflexibility of the orthodox model became a constraint in some areas as it had no means to adjust land holdings to new needs. In the same period more and more farmers saw that they and their families might be better off, economically at least, if they concentrated their efforts on commercial agriculture and gave less commitment to participation in communal activities when these conflicted with the commercial imperatives of cash cropping or commercial cattle grazing.

246 LAND, CUSTOM AND PRACTICE IN THE SOUTH PACIFIC

Technical innovations, roads, education, and off-farm employment all facilitated this trend. Individuals in growing numbers sought to gain long-term personal control of tracts of their *mataqali* lands by using the customary practices of converting *veikau* into *qele* and then retaining control through long-term cultivation, grazing, or the custom of *veimada*. Land which was communal according to the orthodox model, began to be privatised de facto if not de jure. The push by government for economic development, especially in rural areas, emphasised the trend because most development projects were premised on the model of individual farmers working outside the communal village system. A new discrepancy was thus set up between the communal ideals of orthodoxy and the more individualistic realities of the rural economy.

At the same time as more Fijians were seeking longer term and individual control over segments of their *mataqali* land, the government wanted greater involvement by the Fijian community in the monetary sector and established corporate bodies which were seen as representative of the whole Fijian community and thus able, it was assumed, to bring benefits to all. This policy was a strong symbol of communalism from which only some, usually the elite, were to benefit as individuals. Within the NLTB and its offshoot, the NLDC, a stronger development orientation was in accord with this policy. Projects for rural and urban development were fostered which were based on the powers of control over native land vested in the NLTB under the 1940 act and with the board acting for the Fijian community as a whole rather than for the specific owners. The result of these trends is that 'ultimately virtually all land-users in Fiji [Fijians and non-Fijians alike], apart from those on freehold land and those in Fijian villages, will occupy their land on individual, leasehold titles (some on crown land, but the majority on native land)' (Kamikamica and Davey, 1988:298).

The first major attempt by Gordon and later governors to protect Fijians from the possible loss of their control over land resulted in the formal control of native land being moved from the level of individual, family or *tokatoka* to that of the *mataqali*. The second, under the Native Land Trust Act 1940, took the further step of moving formal control from *mataqali* to a government agency. As the implications of the orthodox model were ignored for some decades, so too were the implications of the 1940 act largely ignored by many villagers. The fact that the formal power to control native land is no longer necessarily held by the owners themselves only began to become apparent through court decisions in the 1980s, and it is doubtful whether this is appreciated by most Fijians. Control of land by corporate bodies such as the NLTB is counter to the trend towards individual holdings which has taken place under modern versions of *vakavanua* practice. It is also counter to both the 1870s proposals of the chiefs to subdivide the land into individual holdings, and the 1970s views of senior Fijian high school students as revealed in a survey of attitudes towards land. This survey showed that 75 per cent thought *mataqali* land should be divided to give individual titles (Farrell and Murphy, 1978). Opinion has either come full circle or, more likely, the idea of individual land holdings has remained strong throughout the century.

Where there was strong demand for land from non-Fijians and Fijian migrants from other regions, individuals or small groups of land owners often recognised that their personal interests were best served by ignoring the legal requirement to lease or otherwise deal in land only through the NLTB. Through sharecropping or extra-legal or illegal *vakavanua* practices people sought a better financial return from the land than if it were leased through the NLTB. Those seeking land also find some advantages in going outside the legal system to obtain land of a quality which would be unobtainable legally in the location or at the time needed.

The various attempts which have been made to revise land tenure laws have all recognised that the contemporary socio-economic context was different from that of the past. In most cases the proposals to change the law lagged well behind practice. Im Thurn's attempt in 1905 may be an exception but it did reflect some trends then current, even though the reactions of chiefs, Gordon and others were able to quash the proposed changes. The discrepancies between practice, custom and law, and the lack of action by law makers to reconcile them, raise obvious questions. Why, despite being honoured as much in the breach as in the observance, has the orthodox model of land tenure survived so long? Why is it still held up as the basis of land use and of Fijian society and identity?

There are a number of answers, none complete in itself. First, there is little doubt that the codification of the orthodox model of land tenure combined with the colonial system of indirect rule and administration of Fijian affairs by appointed chiefs to strengthen the power of chiefs. Registration of land by *mataqali* and the recording of lineages confirmed the status of chiefs. Law recognised it. Second, the NLTB system of rent distribution made many chiefs relatively wealthy and gave them a further vested interest in maintaining the orthodoxy. Third, for most of the time since independence, political power has rested with people drawn from much the same group.

The elite group has benefited from the colonial strengthening of chiefly roles and wealth gained from those roles is used to participate in the commercial arena. Thus this group has had much to gain from the promotion of both the communal ideal and economic development. That the two may be antipathetic can be ignored if the discourse is kept

248 LAND, CUSTOM AND PRACTICE IN THE SOUTH PACIFIC

on separate levels, and if the elite continue to control both the discourse and the political stage. Hence there has been little public recognition of the discrepancies which exist between practice in the villages and the orthodox model. Some would say that there is also a communication gap between those who live in the villages and work the land, and those who live mainly in town and only participate in village life in a ceremonial way. Perhaps the extent of individualism in practice is not known to some of the urban elite. Nevertheless, despite lack of public recognition, dissatisfaction is sometimes voiced with the present situation and the lack of accord between practice, custom and law. Nayacakalou reported that in the 1960s some Fijians considered 'that the Board should be abolished because it administers Fijian land not in the interests of the owners but as an instrument to satisfy the demands of the Fiji Indians' (1971:209). In October 1987 the Minister of Lands in the military government proposed that all forms of land title other than 'the pre-1874 traditional system' should be abolished (pers. comm. B. Lal, December 1993). The proposal was not acted upon after the military government was replaced. More recently Simione Duratalo suggested in a public lecture that a new Native Lands Commission be set up to recommend land use policies and revisions to the land laws (unpub. 1993).

The retention of an unreal ideal of native land tenure is now a basic component of the creation and maintenance of Fijian identity as set against that of Fiji Indians, other Pacific Islanders and the people of other nations. One frequently stressed component of Fijian public identity is the sense of community, communal responsibilities, and the respect for chiefs and their role in the social structure. Land is an integral part of this complex, both because the codified model of land tenure is based on that structure and because nominal authority over a group's land is one of the foundations of chiefly status. The inalienable control of land has become an icon of ethnic distinctiveness. It is what Fijians have and other ethnic groups do not.

Key questions for the future include whether or not the current extra-customary and extra-legal practices which have enabled people to avoid the constraints of law and 'custom' and meet their changing needs will continue to be effective. Will the trends toward individual holdings on native land, and the long-term occupation of tracts by a minority, result in other Fijians becoming landless? Are the wide range of vested interests which find advantage in ignoring the discrepancies between 'custom', law and practice likely to find that this is their best long-term strategy? If they do not, then the question of land reform in relation to the allocation of native land amongst Fijians could become a major and divisive issue. If the discrepancies are kept beneath the surface of public discussion and politics, then the country may find that the communal

FIJI 249

lands have been privatised de facto in response to the attractions of commercialism and individual interest, just as has happened in many other parts of the world in response to similar opportunities. The irony may be that a new attempt to record and register the new patterns of de facto land holdings might bring into being something akin to the proposals put forward by the chiefs in 1876 under which 'each individual would have his own allotment'.

Notes

1. The terminology for the various ethnic groups in Fiji can be confusing. In this chapter the term 'Fiji citizens' is used to refer to all ethnic groups who are citizens of the country; 'Fijians' refers to those citizens who are ethnic Fijians; 'Indians' to Fiji citizens of Indian ethnicity; and 'non-Fijians' to those who are not ethnic Fijians, regardless of citizenship.
2. In this chapter '*veimada*' is used as a general term although in other parts of Fiji different names may be used for the concept and practice.
3. The *Notes of the Proceedings of a Native Council* for the 1877 meeting are remarkable for giving a very brief summary of two days discussion on land tenure in one paragraph. There is no near-verbatim reporting as there is on other less important matters, or on the same land issues at the meeting of 1878. The discussion in 1878 shows clearly that many chiefs did not agree with the summary given in 1877. The 1877 statement may represent words put into the mouths of the meeting by the rapporteur in order to get a resolution which would fit the government's wishes, rather than a true record of what was said.
4. The wording of the regulations which set out the shares of rent going to the different recipients has confused a number of commentators. These shares are described as proportions of the balance remaining after the NLTB 25 per cent has been taken. A common but incorrect assumption is that the three named chiefs get 30 per cent and the rest of the *mataqali* share 45 per cent of the total rents (e.g. Eaton, 1988:24; Nayacakalou, 1971:216; Overton, 1987:140; Rutz, 1987:540; Spate, 1959:17), whereas the correct proportions are 22.5 and 52.5 per cent respectively of total rents, or 30 and 70 per cent of that part of the rent which the NLTB does not retain. Kamikamica and Davey (1988:289) give the correct proportions.
5. All three surveys were conducted on the scale of 1:50,000, the first by Ward (1965), the second by the Directorate of Overseas Surveys, London, and the last by the Land Use Section, [Fiji] Ministry of Agriculture and Fisheries. A fuller discussion is given in Ward, 1985.

CHAPTER 7

Beyond the Breathing Space

Antony Hooper and R. Gerard Ward

For the past generation, and while they have been endorsing the ideology of development, the leaders of most Pacific Island countries have also emphasised the importance of 'culture' and 'tradition' as the bases of national identity and the integrity of national institutions. The crucial role of culture is proclaimed in many national constitutions and the need for its maintenance is taken as a basic article of faith by many politicians (Henry, 1991; Somare, 1991), at least in their public utterances. Almost everywhere, native (or customary) land tenure is regarded as one of the cornerstones of national culture, in spite of the fact that what is now proclaimed as traditional may be different from what was customary in the nineteenth and, presumably, earlier centuries.

The case studies presented above show that many current land tenure practices run counter to what is said to be customary in appeals to 'immemorial' and unchanging tradition or to the law where land tenure has been codified. The discrepancies arise in part as consequences of growing population pressures, increased participation in wage labour, greater urbanisation, and the demands of cash cropping and commercial grazing. All create changes in the relative demand for and value of different pieces of land according to location and quality attributes related to the needs of new crops or animals or new types of land use. Land tenure practices have changed as a result, although there is often little public or political acknowledgement of the changes. New forms of socio-economic organisation have allowed or required some individuals to opt out of the older communally oriented forms of organisation. Through off-farm employment, usually within government bureaucracies, or through commercial agriculture, people find alternative ways of meeting current living requirements and new forms of long-term social security to replace that formerly offered by the communal group

250

BEYOND THE BREATHING SPACE

in customary life. As some people have come to favour nuclear family or individual interests over those of the extended family or community, so their attitudes to land have changed.

Although strategies for more individualised control and use of land have become widespread in practice in Pacific countries (and not infrequently involve extra-legal cash payments of some sort) there is little suggestion that any country in the region might formally abolish its traditional form of tenure in favour of a more 'modern' and economically rational system involving a free market for land. What is condoned in practice appears to be denied at the level of legal codes and national political ideologies.

The ways in which these apparent contradictions are manifest and played out differ from country to country. The key to understanding the apparent contradictions between what is said to be customary and what is actually practised under the guise of 'customary' land tenure lies in the difference between custom as unselfconscious, generally understood and accepted practice, and custom as objectified, codified and proclaimed as part of the essential character of one body of people as against others. 'Tradition' may also, in certain contexts, partake of similar dualities of usage. In Melanesia, the term *kastom* is widely applied to objectified and idealised representations of custom and the importance of this concept of *kastom* for land has been demonstrated in Chapter 3. In Polynesia and Fiji, the terms 'traditional custom' or the 'Pacific way', or nationally specific terms such, as *fa'aSamoa* or *vakavanua*, are more widely used.

The Principal Changes in Land Tenure Practices

In addition to country-specific features of land tenure, the four country studies presented above, and other studies referred to in Chapter 2, show trends in land tenure practices which recur through the region. They also demonstrate parallels with changes which have occurred in other parts of the world, some of which have been outlined in Chapter 1. However, as Chapters 3 to 6 show, the changes in land tenure in the island countries have neither followed a uniform path, nor reached the same point. Such uniformity is not to be expected given differences in land tenure prior to western contact, and in the cultural, historical, environmental and political developments since then. Nevertheless, some common tendencies can be discerned.

From usufruct to ownership: from communal to individual tenure

In the pre-commercial era most people held rights to use land by reason of their membership of a kinship or residential community. The

252 LAND, CUSTOM AND PRACTICE IN THE SOUTH PACIFIC

character of land rights in most places was captured by Thomson's comment in relation to Fiji, that 'the owner' of garden land had 'a little less than *dominium* and a little more than *usufruct*' (1908:359). Although ultimate ownership might lie with the community as a whole, and the authority for land allocation might be held by a chief, big man, kin group leader or the consensus decision of the relevant group, the user's rights were usually secure as long as use was maintained. Warfare and consequent transfer of territory was probably the main cause of disruption of the security of usufruct. Otherwise only out-migration or serious offence against the community would result in loss of usufruct rights.

Over the last century or more, new concepts of property rights have been adopted for a widening range of goods and land is no exception. Some Pacific Islanders began to apply concepts closer to outright ownership to their land. Chatterton has described the change in part of central Papua in words which could be applied very widely.

> In the part of Papua I know best, where land tenure has always been by descent groups, there is a growing tendency for nuclear families and even individuals to claim absolute ownership and right of disposal over those parts of their descent group's land of which they had traditionally had rights of usage. And the young men stoutly maintain this was the custom 'from time immemorial'. (Chatterton, 1974:15)

Where chiefs or big men held control over communal land by right of office they too sometimes began to personalise that authority. The power of some chiefs was also increased, or extended to new fields as a result of the application of indirect rule by a colonial power. The establishment of indigenous governments in Hawaii, Tahiti and parts of Fiji before they became colonies, and in Tonga when Tupou I came to power over the whole island group, had similar effects. In some cases the nature of the individual authority of chiefs over land was both changed and greatly strengthened.

Other forces had parallel effects. The expansion of the area under tree crops, especially coconuts in countries like Vanuatu, Fiji or Western Samoa, meant that usufruct remained in the same hands for much longer periods than under swidden cultivation of root crops for own consumption. The opportunity arose for the common concept of absolute ownership of the crop to be transferred to the land itself so that, to modify the Chinese proverb quoted in Chapter 1, long use could become property. The adoption of commercial farming and increasing commodification of land has reinforced the process, particularly in the last three decades, as farmers sought to secure the flow of cash benefits and possible returns from capital appreciation for themselves for as long as possible. Although much cash crop production was, and sometimes still is, carried out with the intention of applying the proceeds to customary ends, money, being fungible and storable, has increased the scope and incentive for using farming products and land for non-customary ends.

Development policies also contributed to the change from usufruct and temporary and shared use of territory to longer term and exclusive use by individuals. Communalistic principles of tenure are seen as barriers to development by many outsiders and some islanders, particularly those concerned in one way or another with the planning of economic development. Given the relative security of usufruct offered by customary tenure, these barriers may be more imagined than real. Nevertheless, in the planning of most agricultural development projects the assumption has been made that individual farm holdings on land for which the farmer has secure personal title would give the most efficient results. The single family farm has been the planners' ideal, and leasehold or other secure and transferable tenure has often been required by banks or other lending agencies as the security against which loans might be made. Thus planning and financial imperatives have added to the movement towards longer term exclusive forms of tenure, encouraging the establishment of consolidated holdings on land which has been taken out of customary communal tenure and placed under individual leasehold.

The case studies of Western Samoa, Fiji and Vanuatu presented in this volume give evidence of individuals obtaining use of much larger blocks of customary land through customary channels than was formerly necessary and retaining them in their own hands for lengthy periods without any formal removal of the land from the category of customary land. In Tonga, the constitutionally established land tenure system allows inheritance of tax allotments of 3.3 hectares in the male line, but there is also evidence that for many years individuals, often from the former chiefly class, held larger holdings essentially as private land under older customary forms of tenure. In Western Samoa and Vanuatu the wish to pass land directly to children is common and this is done quite frequently without any wider community intervention. In effect, rights of usufruct have tended to be replaced by claims closer to outright ownership, with the assertion of the right to give or bequeath land directly to one's heirs. In its initial phases this change from usufruct to ownership tends to occur through the use of certain conventions of customary practice in new ways and for new ends. Later, the authority of custom may be called upon to validate the new individualistic practices and purpose.

Some justification for the appeal to custom for validation can usually be found because 'in all tenure systems some rights in most lands are held by individuals . . . [while] some rights are held by groups (lineages, county councils or communes) and others by the community as a whole'

254 LAND, CUSTOM AND PRACTICE IN THE SOUTH PACIFIC

(Crocombe, 1972:220). What is now occurring in the Pacific Islands is not a simple transfer from communal to individual forms of tenure, but a complex, varied and often locality-specific widening of the range of situations in which individual rights are pragmatically accepted as pre-eminent, while there is a corresponding shrinkage of those in which communal rights dominate. There is also a decrease in the size of groups claiming rights, as nuclear families and households replace extended families as the normal units of production and consumption. As Hobsbawm notes, custom, unlike tradition, must change because life is not static (1983:2). The essential pragmatism of changing practice can be validated relatively easily by appeal to the authority of custom (often couched in the stronger term of 'tradition') because of the prior exis-tence of some individual elements in land tenure. For example, the old and common tendency for inheritance of usufruct may be used as a jus-tification of inheritance of ownership. It becomes a matter of extending the application of such principles, not the introduction of entirely new concepts.

As Chapter 1 has shown, the change in land tenure from most people holding usufruct rights over the land they use to ownership by individu-als being the norm has occurred in many places. The speed of change has varied greatly, but the reasons for it are often similar. In Japan, China and Europe the expansion of commerce gave landlords the opportunity to move into more profitable or, for them, more interesting or influen-tial spheres in the towns. The tendency in the Pacific Islands for chiefs and big men to become involved in politics, business and the bureau-cracy has a similar effect. For some, their interest in the land over which they hold rights and responsibilities becomes less one of direct personal and regular involvement in farming, land allocation or management and more a matter of maintaining social or political status by calling on tradition and the conventions of custom. Once the functional links between leaders and the people and the land have weakened, an author-ity vacuum can arise in rural areas in which others, commoners or other-wise, can more readily follow their own wishes in land matters.

The adoption of new technology and crops in the agricultural revolu-tion of western Europe and in eighteenth-century Japan, and the con-sequent tendency for manorial or common land to come under the control of individual farmers, also has its Pacific Islands parallels. The opportunities to specialise in cash crops, to enclose communal land for livestock grazing or other types of farming, to opt out of some com-munal obligations, to favour residence on individual farms rather than village residence, are having similar effects to some of the consequences of the English enclosure movement. These include both the commonly perceived benefits in a commercial context of individual and exclusive

BEYOND THE BREATHING SPACE 255

land holdings, and the costs of loss of access to the products of common or communal land which has been privatised.

Spate saw the tendency, the parallels and the changes in community settlement patterns and functioning as long ago as 1959 when he envisaged a:

> Fijian countryside . . . [which would] be a community of independent farmers, living or working on holdings heritable, and alienable at least between Fijians, but retaining in each village or Old Tikina [district] a common centre – church, school, guesthouse, parish hall, chiefly residence – where the old dignity which the *koro* [village] is so rapidly losing might be recaptured, and relying for essential joint services on some equivalent of a Rural District Council; a community less the old frustrations (though doubtless with its own), but not less rich in real satisfactions. (Spate, 1959:9)

The tenurial and related changes in Europe, Japan and China did not take place in a colonial situation, but somewhat similar trends in Africa were induced or accelerated in the colonial era. Recency and colonial influence are common features of tenurial change in both the Pacific Islands and the selected African contexts outlined in Chapter 1. Thus the parallels may appear closer than with the northern hemisphere examples, but this should not lead to the assumption that colonialism is the basic cause of the changes in either region. It is but one of a number of factors, of which the most important group consists of the variety of changes, social, political and economic, which flow from the move from predominantly subsistence to increasingly commercial agricultural systems. The African examples are also important in the present context because they emphasise the fact that local variation must be expected in the forms and speed of any general trend for usufruct and communalism to give way to ownership and individualism. They also show that attempts to replace introduced Western forms of tenure by a re-introduction of customary forms are not unique to the Pacific Islands, and may create another set of inconsistencies between custom and practice.

Codification and the loss of flexibility

An important consequence of the tendencies for land to be held in the hands of the same people for long periods and for usufruct to become ownership is loss of the flexibility to transfer land which was common in older customary arrangements. Arrangements under which land, after a period of cultivation, was returned to communal status for later redistribution are now being bypassed by very long-term use by the same individual or family. Furthermore, codification, the fixing of ownership of surveyed and registered land in the hands of a named group, may formally remove the opportunity to redistribute land by customary means.

256 LAND, CUSTOM AND PRACTICE IN THE SOUTH PACIFIC

As is shown in earlier chapters, there were many ways in which land could be transferred from one holder or owning group to another. The cessation of warfare obviously removed the ultimate method, but the legal acceptance of inalienability has had wide effects. Practices under which land could be given, lent or, in some instances, sold to others in return for a wide range of services are not condoned under most of the legal codes. For many decades people avoided the consequences of this by ignoring the 'letter of the law' of the codified native land tenure (see Chapters 5 and 6). But with greater pressure on land resulting from population growth and increased commercial farming, land owners have become less willing to permit land which is formally registered in the name of their kin group to be used under customary practice by non-members. In the case of Tonga, the system of tax allotments has also created what can become a more rigid system than the older customary arrangements that preceded it. In the latter, it was the responsibility of chiefs to ensure that their people had access to sufficient land for food production and land could be re-assigned if necessary to achieve this. In contrast, the tax allotment system ideally gives perpetual usufruct rights on an exclusive basis, and it may be more difficult for allotments to be recalled for subdivision and re-allocation to ensure that all eligible people have at least some land for basic needs. A consequence of these rigidities, which is not entirely removed by the introduction of provisions for leasing, is the growing inequality in access to land, even for food crop production, which is evident in parts of several countries. That the need for transfer mechanisms is strong is demonstrated by older practices continuing despite the law and by the existence in several countries of illegal 'markets' in land.

As noted in Chapter 2, another result of codification may be that people who move away from a community where they have held rights to land may be able to claim retention of those rights to a much greater degree than in the era before codification, registration and the maintenance of written lists of members of owning groups. Whereas in former times retention of rights depended upon continued meeting of communal obligations, the written record and the doctrine of 'once a member always a member to the nth generation' can give absentees the opportunity to assert rights which formerly would have 'grown cold' and disappeared. In some cases land codes assume and record bilateral inheritance when in former times the de facto practice would have been either patrilineal or matrilineal but not both. Thus the number of people with an interest in a plot can expand exponentially. Today, if a long-term absentee were to return and claim land rights, a version of custom might still be invoked by the home community requiring the returnee to contribute to the community in cash or other ways to reinstate his or her position in the group before having the land claim recognised. But in countries like Fiji and the Cook Islands, returnees now have a legal basis for their claim which did not exist to the same extent before codification. The legal retention of the rights of absentees can make management of land by the resident community more difficult. If, as is sometimes required by law, a high proportion of the legal co-owners must be consulted before land can be allocated to new users or for new uses, the impracticality of doing so can be a major inhibition on effective land use.

Land, State and Nation

A crucial watershed in the emergence of new forms of customary land tenure in the Pacific Islands was the establishment of centralised state authority. In Fiji, Western Samoa and Vanuatu the state was a colonial creation; in Tonga it emerged from indigenous internal struggles with the establishment of the present monarchy. Despite these differences of origin of the state, the principles of customary land tenure, like 'custom' itself, were subject to a new and overriding constraint in each country. Henceforth, only the state could claim to legitimate and enforce the alienation of customary land, either to itself, to foreign settlers, or to other citizens. In several countries, including Fiji and the Cook Islands, the state went further, codifying and regulating transactions in land, including customary ones – a process which set up a further duality between common practices and the explicitly formulated and codified 'custom' which was given the support of law. In Western Samoa, German and New Zealand administrations did not codify custom in written law, although regulations under which customary land could be leased were established. The Land and Titles Commission (now Court) was set up to resolve disputes over land and chiefly titles. By requiring the court to base its decisions on 'the customs and usages of the Samoan people', legal weight was given to what the court determined was 'custom'.

The intervention of the state in matters of customary land tenure inevitably changed the nature of that tenure. An almost invariable result was that what came to be viewed as the 'traditional' system was a simplified model. This frequently assumed a set of conventions which would not change with time, ignored the variety of local practice, and took the practices of one particular part of the country (often that of the leaders who had most contact with the colonial power at the time of the establishment of the colonial state) and applied them to the whole territory. These steps removed one of the key features of non-codified customary land tenure. This was the ability of people managing such systems to be pragmatic and to adjust to new circumstances including, in particular,

258 LAND, CUSTOM AND PRACTICE IN THE SOUTH PACIFIC

new technological and economic needs and the changing power structures within and around the community. However, in all four countries studied in detail in this volume, it is evident that for many years the 'ordinary customary practices' (unselfconsciously adapted by the participants to changing circumstances and new opportunities) continued to govern most transactions of land in the rural areas. This has allowed communities to adjust to new conditions at their own speed. But today problems of conflicting interests have emerged because some want to follow the accepted practices of their evolving custom unimpaired by government decree, while others see personal advantage in adhering to principles of older 'custom' or to the government-sponsored centralised and usually rigid models.

In each country the establishment of the state had somewhat different consequences for customary land practices. In those parts of Fiji where land was plentiful and the economy was dominantly subsistence-oriented, people simply ignored the newly surveyed boundaries of *mataqali* holdings and the exclusivity of ownership and use which the codified orthodoxy implied. Whether this implication was in fact realised by the majority is an open question. In any case, patterns of land use drifted away from those of registered land ownership in many parts of the country without causing complications which could not be dealt with through community channels. Later, when opportunities arose for earning money from commercial agriculture or leasing land, fewer members of the owning *mataqali* were willing to allow outsiders to use their land under the older practices. This more recent trend brought into focus the fact that inherent differences exist between codified 'custom' and common practice in both pre- and post-codification periods. The Fijian land tenure system of the colonial orthodoxy fits neither particularly closely.

In Western Samoa land tenure has not been codified, although a set of general principles has been partially reified through the operation of the Land and Titles Court and also the writings of some authorities. Most of the court's decisions have tended to ignore the de facto trend towards individualism in land management, and in some utterances to deny that it has occurred. In its interpretation of 'customs and usages' the court seems to have assumed that these are relatively unchanging criteria whereas, on the ground, the present usages do demonstrate considerable adaptive capacities. Thus an institution which had the power to foster adaptation became an agent of conservatism and day-to-day practice grew more distant from the court's model. Nevertheless, there are cases in which the court has dressed up new practices in the phraseology of old custom, thereby avoiding explicit confrontation with the divergences between custom and practice.

BEYOND THE BREATHING SPACE 259

In Tonga the constitution proclaimed by the newly established Tongan monarchy sought to extinguish completely the old customary tenure by creating a system of noble estates and individual leasehold rights. The new system was ignored for long periods by many people. In the Tongan case many people already felt secure in the use of land they held from their chief, and initially the new tax allotment scheme offered little advantage. It might even have been threatening for some as the relationships between chiefs, people and land were strong and multi-faceted. A commoner breaking the land link with the noble might fear loss of other ties, while nobles who freely approved the registration of tax allotments obviously stood to lose income from gifts in what was certainly an asymmetrical relationship. In the absence of positive advantages, such as those which later emerged as components of the trend towards commercial activities, it was safer for most people not to seek immediate allocation and registration of allotments under the new tenure. In more recent times the balance of advantage has changed and the security of holding a registered 'api has increased. So have opportunities for earning money from commercial farming or land transfers. As a result, a land market and informal methods of renting land for short-term use have emerged, both of which are extra-legal in some respects. These features of current land tenure tend to be officially ignored.

The decree of 1882 which gave every Tongan man the right to individual title to a piece of land is universally valued. Like the monarchy itself, this right is seen as a cornerstone of Tongan national identity, even though population increases alone have meant that, for the past generation or so, the system has not been able to work as it was originally conceived. Paradoxically, despite its egalitarian intent, it is the right of each man to a piece of land with secure tenure which has made it possible for some to lease or lend their land to others, and for entrepreneurial borrowers and lessees to accumulate much more land than others. This has exacerbated the land shortages and led to increasing numbers of landless people. Tonga, like other South Pacific societies, has come to be more socio-economically differentiated and the extra-legal and extra-customary land tenure practices of government elites (including some nobles) in conjunction with the rising middle class have played a leading role in the process.

In Vanuatu, where the chaotic joint French and British administration of the group was concerned primarily with the alienation of land to foreigners, customary land transactions were left very much in the hands of customary owners. As a result, customary tenure in Vanuatu may be less modified than in the other countries, but divergence does occur between the custom of earlier periods and new practices which people have accepted as 'customary'. The arrangements now used for direct

260 LAND, CUSTOM AND PRACTICE IN THE SOUTH PACIFIC

inheritance of land and the creation of unusually large holdings by some big men are examples. By keeping the idea but changing the terms of concepts like equity,[1] it has been possible for some to use 'customary' practices to establish claims to land newly cleared from forest, or to take over the land of others, in order to assemble relatively large personal holdings which are then used for non-customary purposes and non-customary forms of wealth and status accumulation. These practices, generally condoned by fellow villagers, are on the edge of acceptance as current custom because the changes have continued to be closely attuned to culture as lived experience.

When independence finally came after some years of struggle in 1980, there was no codified national system of customary land. As in Fiji, Papua New Guinea and Western Samoa, custom was called upon as a legitimating and founding principle for the new state. Since in Vanuatu *kastom* emphasised diversity and true local control, all land, including that which had been previously alienated, was returned to local control. But the constitution, in decreeing that all land belongs to the customary owners did not specify which owners or which custom or customs apply. By implication it is the custom and the occupiers of the era immediately before colonisation and the alienation of land to foreigners. That is now a past which is impossible to recreate, and certainly one in which land tenure differed from much current practice. Furthermore, in the urban areas where the most obvious new requirements are placed on land tenure, it has been necessary for the government to take steps which are inconsistent with the constitution in order to meet current practical needs. Once again, new needs and practices are not matched by existing laws, or by the rhetoric of *kastom.* Thus far the problems seem to have been circumvented by simple inaction. The new elites, while they may have been able to manipulate other aspects of *kastom* to their own advantage, as Philibert (1986) and Babadzan (1988) assert, have thus far been able to exert little influence on land tenure. That, however, may come.

As long as the indigenous populations remained largely rural and traditionalist in orientation, and as long as there was more than sufficient land and governments remained benignly paternalistic and remote, the differences between local practice and the official legally sanctioned principles of customary tenure were probably of little account. For the most part, change was slow and incremental. The churches became an integral part of neo-traditional life; formal education became more widespread and governments only gradually expanded their scope and influence with new services. The Pacific war, however, dramatically changed this situation, even in those countries which were remote from the actual battlefields. The changes were rapidly consolidated and given new impetus in the post-war years by increased flows of foreign aid, the new emphasis on development and commerce to include the indigenous population, and moves toward decolonisation.

It was a period of rapid and far-reaching social change. Government services expanded, providing employment opportunities which absorbed virtually all the most highly educated local people. Other developments called for an expanded and more permanent wage labour force. Urbanisation increased and from both Western Samoa and Tonga there was emigration for wage labour in New Zealand. Local populations became divided along new lines, with a marked differentiation between those who gained their livelihoods from wage and salaried employment, mostly in the towns, and those in the rural areas whose lives remained set within more traditional social milieux. This differentiation became more marked with independence, when local people inherited the power and prestige which had formerly accrued to expatriate colonials. These new elites also became the guardians of the new states, concerned not only to provide administrative services but with formulating the very principles of nationhood. In Fiji, Western Samoa, Vanuatu and several other countries the new constitutions asserted, explicitly or implicitly, some of their legitimacy in terms of culture and traditions – which meant, basically, a continuing place for traditional forms of leadership and communalist forms of land tenure. Ironically, the 'customary' or 'traditional' systems of land tenure carried forward into the new regimes of the Cook Islands, Fiji, Niue, Kiribati and some other countries were those that had been set up during the colonial period, and emphasised forms of communalism under the oversight of centralised state authority. Although it was now only Pacific Islanders who were involved, new differentiations along class lines made for conflicting interests and interpretations of what might be 'really Tongan' or 'really Fijian' principles of land tenure. Many members of the new elites of politics and government were either of high chiefly rank or else, because of their education and basically urban upbringing, had little experience of traditional rural life much less of anything involving direct contact with the land. For them, the 'customary land tenure' of official statements and rhetoric was the system legally sanctioned by courts or governments. They had effective control over it; they planned on the basis of it and, as many cases attest, they could use it to their own advantage.

What has clearly happened, then, in Fiji, Western Samoa and Tonga, as well as in other Pacific Island countries, is that land tenure has for years been caught up in other widespread and complex social changes. Indeed, land tenure changes have played an important part in bringing about many of the social changes. It can be genuinely useful for many national purposes to maintain an ideology of unchanging traditional

262 LAND, CUSTOM AND PRACTICE IN THE SOUTH PACIFIC

and customary land tenure systems. But most genuinely old practices were in fact radically modified even before they were proclaimed as national 'systems'. What 'system' now exists is a shifting arena peopled by conflicting interests, manoeuvres and both legal and extra-legal practices, driven increasingly by commercial and individual interests. As might be expected, it is those with power who have the advantage. At the same time, however, the communalistic and genuinely traditional aspects do act as a brake on power, providing security for those who might otherwise be swept away, particularly if all land were to be made freehold and subject to market forces.

The lack of action

Given the extent and variety of ways in which current land tenure practices differ both from custom as commonly proclaimed and from codified law, the question arises, why have post-colonial governments not taken steps to bring land law into closer accord with practice, or vice versa? A related question, and one which gives part of the answer to the first, is why does land tenure figure so importantly when leaders appeal to tradition and custom to assert national identity?

Establishing national identity requires differentiation from other peoples, and different histories, geographies, languages, life styles, cultural practices and beliefs can all be grist for the mill. In many Pacific Islands, competition for land between the indigenous people and Westerners has been one of the most important strands in the history of the last century. Contrasting concepts of ownership and methods of managing land have been prominent markers of difference. For decades entirely different systems of agriculture were practised on alienated land from those on customary land, with commercial, expatriate-owned plantation agriculture, often large-scale and employing wage labour, on the former, and small-scale, subsistence-oriented swidden cultivation on the latter. These symbolised entirely different economic and social life styles, and the land tenure difference was basic to the contrast. Where, as in Fiji, a large immigrant population existed which did not have access to native land, but which was competitive in many other fields, the fact of land ownership by the indigenous group has been a major and well-guarded differentiating feature. To be a Fijian is to be a land owner; to be a Fiji-Indian is to have restricted access to land.

Furthermore, when distinctive forms of social organisation, including kinship and descent systems, are called upon as markers of national identity, they in turn have a land component. Indeed, Leach argues that 'concepts of descent and of affinity are expressions of property relations which endure through time' (1971:11) and that 'kinship systems have no

BEYOND THE BREATHING SPACE 263

"reality" at all except in relation to land and property' (1971:305). In the Pacific Islands the land tenure system was always integral to the workings of social organisation and calling on custom as either long-term accepted practice, or objectified and idealised *kastom* as identity markers inevitably brings in the land and the methods of succession to its ownership or use.

The fact that governments and others have promoted this link to ethnic or national identity is one factor making it difficult for them to attempt any sweeping changes to customary land tenure. To do so risks being charged with undermining the way of life. But there are other reasons for the lack of action in some countries, and conflict of interest is one. As noted above, considerable overlap frequently exists between the political leaders and the economic and social elites. The status of members of these elites often stems from their ascribed position in chiefly hierarchies, or their wealth based on commercial agriculture or land rents. In the latter case, ability to manipulate customary or codified tenure practices for personal gain has sometimes been the basis of their success and any significant change in customary tenure could be detrimental to either, or both, their economic interests or their social status.

Whereas most members of the community once shared a common self-interest in maintaining the broad status quo in land tenure matters, this is no longer true. Pacific Island societies are now much more complex, and as in any nation state divergent interests and contested agendas are found. But without any clearly and publicly expressed alternative norms on which most people would agree, there is little momentum for change at the rhetorical or political level. People tend to select and follow those customary practices which suit them, and to ignore those which do not. While they can continue to do this, it is a sound personal strategy, and one which does not create too many explicit social tensions.

Movements for land reform in other regions have often arisen when landlessness has been at a high level, or exploitative landlordism has been common. Despite some signs of the former in some places, neither condition is serious in the Pacific Islands. The continuing strength of communal and kin-based social systems, and the fact that the subsistence component of the rural economy is still important, have limited the extent of class formation. Where people's land requirements have changed, it is still possible for the majority who remain in rural areas to obtain access to some land, for subsistence purposes at least, through practices which are either customary in terms of being 'traditional', or the equivalent of the Samoan *aganu'u*, or *kastom*, or follow practices which although new are generally condoned. There is little sign, therefore, of grassroots movements for formal land tenure reform.

264 LAND, CUSTOM AND PRACTICE IN THE SOUTH PACIFIC

The End of the Breathing Space?

In coming decades further changes will occur in the values to which Pacific Island peoples adhere (or ignore) when they organise their societies, arrange their settlement patterns, choose their political leaders, and decide how they use land. In all these issues, the manner in which land tenure is handled will be a factor. Until now Pacific Islanders have had a breathing space in which to ignore the contradictions between practice, custom and law in land tenure, and between the rhetoric of 'tradition' and what actually happens in villages, towns, squatter settlements and farms. In an increasingly commercial world these contradictions will doubtless become more evident. Each of the countries studied faces specific problems and risks when attempting to resolve the discrepancies within their 'customary' land tenure. Eventually all will need to come to terms with increasing individualism in land management. This will require political and formal recognition that current land tenure practice is neither 'traditional' nor in accord with the rhetorical models of the 'Pacific way' or *kastom*. It will be necessary to make legal some currently extra-legal practices which are now too common and functional to stop or ignore. It will also be necessary to acknowledge that current 'customs and usages' have changed and are now a better match with the socio-economic requirements of late twentieth-century Pacific Island life than either the codified land tenure inherited from colonial times, or the various idealised forms of 'traditional land tenure'.

To acknowledge and act in this situation is likely to be one of the major challenges for the region. It is a complex task, particularly for leaders whose own status may be bound up with their continuing roles in traditional groups which also control land rights. Naturally they have to balance these necessary roles with those of leadership in democratic states. But the examples of tenure change in nineteenth-century Tonga, the creation and acceptance of new land tenure orthodoxies under colonial rule in other countries, the changes made in other regions under the pressure of similar forces, and the incorporation of Christianity into 'custom' all suggest that the task can be performed within the pragmatic flexibility which Pacific Island custom and leadership have often displayed. It will take sensitive leadership, but the 'breathing space' which has allowed adjustment without confronting the inconsistencies of recent decades cannot be, in Howlett's phrase (1973:273), an 'infinite pause'.

Notes
1. For example, by giving weight to equality of opportunity rather than equality of outcomes.

Bibliography

(This bibliography includes only works which have been referred to in the text.)

Acquaye, B. and Crocombe, R. (eds) 1984. *Land Tenure and Rural Productivity in the Pacific Islands*, FAO, SPREP and Institute of Pacific Studies, Suva, pp. 102–13.

Adsett, N.J. 1989. *Laws of Tonga: comprising all laws, acts and ordinances and subsidiary legislation in force on the 31st day of December, 1988*, Rev. ed. 1988, prepared under the authority of the Laws Consolidation Act, Government of Tonga, Nuku'alofa.

Aiavao, U. 1993. 'Death in the village', *Pacific Islands Business*, November, pp. 20–6.

Alatoa, H. et al. (eds) 1984. *Land Tenure in Vanuatu*, University of the South Pacific, Suva.

Allen, M. (C. Leaney ed.) 1969. *Report on Aoba*, British Residency, Port Vila.

Allen, M. (ed.) 1981. *Vanuatu: Politics, Economics and Ritual in Island Melanesia*, Academic Press, Sydney.

Anderson, A.G. 1974. *Indo-Fijian Smallfarming: Profiles of a Peasantry*, University of Auckland Press, Auckland.

Arutangai, S. 1987. 'Vanuatu', in Crocombe (ed.), 1987a:261–302.

Ault, D.E. and Rutman, G.L. 1979. 'The development of individual rights to property in tribal Africa', *Journal of Law and Economics* 22:163–82.

Babadzan, A. 1988. '*Kastom* and nation-building in the South Pacific', in Guidieri et al. (eds):199–228.

Baker, A.R.H. 1973. 'Changes in the Later Middle Ages', in Darby (ed.), 1973:186–247.

Bakker, M.L. 1979. *A Demographic Analysis of the Population of Tonga 1777–1975*, South Pacific Commission Occasional Paper No.14, Noumea.

Ballard, B.C. 1976. 'Australian land interests in the New Hebrides; their acquisition and disposal: a note', *The Australian Journal of Politics and History* 22(2):283–7.

Barrau, J. 1958. *Subsistence Agriculture in Melanesia*, Bernice P. Bishop Museum Bulletin 219, Honolulu.

Beasant, J. 1984. *The Santo Rebellion: An Imperial Reckoning*, University of Hawaii Press, Honolulu.

266 BIBLIOGRAPHY

Bedford, R.D. 1973. *New Hebridean Mobility: A Study of Circular Migration*, Australian National University Press, Canberra.

Bedford, R.D. 1988. 'Population movement in post-colonial Fiji: review and speculation', *GeoJournal* 16(2):179–92.

Belshaw, C. 1964. *Under the Ivi Tree: Society and Economic Growth in Rural Fiji*, Routledge and Kegan Paul, London.

Bennett, J.A., 1987. *Wealth of the Solomons: A History of a Pacific Archipelago, 1800–1978*, Pacific Islands Monograph Series, No. 3, University of Hawaii Press, Honolulu.

Bequele, A. 1983. 'Stagnation and inequality in Ghana', in Ghai and Radwan (eds), 1983:219–47.

Betero, T. 1987. 'Boundaries', in Crocombe (ed.), 1987b:40–9.

Biebuyck, D. 1963. 'English summary', in Biebuyck (ed.), 1963:52–64.

Biebuyck, D. (ed.) 1963. *African Agrarian Systems*, Oxford University Press, London.

Bohannan, P. 1963. ' "Land", "tenure", and land-tenure', in Biebuyck (ed.), 1963:101–15.

Bollard, A.E. 1974. The Impact of Monetisation in Tonga, MA thesis, University of Auckland.

Bonnemaison, J. 1974. *Espaces et Paysages Agraires dans le Nord des Nouvelles-Hébrides*, Société des Océanistes, Paris.

Bonnemaison, J. 1984. 'The tree and the canoe: roots and mobility in Vanuatu societies', *Pacific Viewpoint* 25(2):117–51.

Bonnemaison, J. 1986. *La Dernière Isle*, Arlea/ORSTOM, Paris.

Bonnemaison, J. and Tryon, D. (eds) In press. *Arts de Vanuatu*, Réunion des Museés Nationaux, Paris.

Bott, E. with the assistance of Tavi. 1982. *Tongan Society at the Time of Captain Cook's Visits: Discussions with Her Majesty Queen Salote Tupou*, The Polynesian Society Memoir No.44, Wellington.

Brewster, A.B. 1922. *The Hill Tribes of Fiji*, Seeley, Service and Co., London.

British National Service 1976. *Report on the New Hebrides*, Ref. 973–4–5, Port Vila.

Brobby, K.W. unpub. [1984–5]. An Overview of the Native Land Trust Board (Analysis, Comparison and Critique), unpublished paper, Suva.

Brookfield, H.C. 1972a. *Colonialism, Development and Independence*, Cambridge University Press, Cambridge.

Brookfield, H.C. 1972b. 'Intensification and disintensification in Pacific agriculture: a theoretical approach', *Pacific Viewpoint* 13(1):30–48.

Brookfield, H.C. (ed.) 1973. *The Pacific in Transition: Geographical Perspectives on Adaption and Change*, Australian National University Press, Canberra.

Brookfield, H.C. (ed.) 1979. *Lakeba: Environmental Change, Population Dynamics and Resource Use*, Island Reports No. 5, UNESCO, Canberra.

Brookfield, H.C., Ellis, F.E., and Ward, R.G. 1985. *Land, Cane and Coconuts: Papers on the Rural Economy of Fiji*, Department of Human Geography Publication HG/17, Research School of Pacific Studies, Australian National University, Canberra.

Brookfield, M. 1979. 'Resource use, economy and society: island at the crossroads', in Brookfield (ed.), 1979:127–98.

Brunton, R. 1979. 'Kava and the daily dissolution of society on Tanna, New Hebrides', *Mankind* 12(2):93–103.

Brunton, R. 1981. 'The origin of the John Frum movement', in Allen (ed.), 1981:357–77.

Buck, J.L. 1964. *Land Utilization in China*, Paragon Book Reprint, New York.

BIBLIOGRAPHY 267

Burns, A. et al. 1960. *Report of the Commission of Enquiry into the Natural Resources and Population Trends of the Colony of Fiji 1959*, Council Paper No. 1 of 1960, Government of Fiji, Suva.

Burton, J. unpub. [1986] From Stone to Steel in the Papua New Guinea Highlands: a Case of Mis-representation?, unpublished paper, University of Papua New Guinea, Port Moresby.

[C3584]. 1983. *Correspondence Relative to Land Claims in Fiji, 1883*, British Parliamentary Papers, Vol. XLVI.

Campbell, I.C. 1992. *Island Kingdom: Tonga Ancient and Modern*, Canterbury University Press, Christchurch.

Caroe, O. 1954. 'Land tenure and franchise. A basis for partnership in African plural societies', *Journal of African Administration* 6:152–60.

Chapelle, T. 1978. 'Customary land tenure in Fiji: old truths and middle-aged myths', *Journal of the Polynesian Society* 87(2):71–88.

Chapman, M. (ed.) 1985. *Mobility and Identity in the Island Pacific*, Special issue of *Pacific Viewpoint* 26(1).

Chatterton, P. 1974. 'The historical dimension', in Sack (ed.), 1974:8–15.

Chung, M. 1988. 'The impact of a road', in Overton (ed.), 1988:97–122.

Codrington, R.H. 1969. *The Melanesians* (first published 1891), Clarendon Press, Oxford.

Colson, E. 1974. *Tradition and Contract: The Problem of Order*, Aldine Publishing, Chicago.

Connell, J. and Lea, J.P. 1993. *Planning the Future: Melanesian Cities in 2010.* Pacific Policy Paper 11. National Centre for Development Studies. Research School of Pacific Studies, Australian National University, Canberra.

Coulter, J.W. 1942. *Fiji: Little India of the Pacific*, University of Chicago Press, Chicago.

Crocombe, R.G. 1964. *Land Tenure in the Cook Islands*, Oxford University Press, Melbourne.

Crocombe, R.[G.] 1971. 'Trends in Pacific Tenure Systems', *Conference Papers, Fifth (1971) Lands and Surveys Conference*, Saipan, pp.20–31.

Crocombe, R.G. 1972. 'Land tenure in the South Pacific', in Ward, R.G. (ed.), 1972:219–51.

Crocombe, R. (ed.) 1971. *Land Tenure in the Pacific*, Oxford University Press, Melbourne.

Crocombe, R. (ed.) 1987a. *Land Tenure in the Pacific*, third edn. University of the South Pacific, Suva.

Crocombe, R. (ed.) 1987b. *Land Tenure in the Atolls*, Institute of Pacific Studies, Suva.

Crocombe, R. and Marsters, W.F.E. 1987. 'Land tenure in a test tube: the case of Palmerston Atoll', in Crocombe (ed.), 1987b:202–33.

Crocombe, R. and Meleisea, M. (eds) 1994. *Land Issues in the Pacific*, University of Canterbury and University of the South Pacific, Christchurch and Suva.

Darby, H.C. 1964. 'Historical geography from the coming of the Anglo-Saxons to the industrial revolution', in Watson with Sissons (eds), 1964:198–220.

Darby, H.C. 1973. 'The age of the improver', in Darby (ed.), 1973:302–88.

Darby, H.C. (ed.) 1973. *A New Historical Geography of England*, Cambridge University Press, Cambridge.

Davidson, J.W. 1967. *Samoa mo Samoa: The Emergence of the Independent State of Western Samoa*, Oxford University Press, Melbourne.

Davison, J. 1988. *Agriculture, Women and Land: The Agrarian Experience*, Westview Press, Boulder.

268 BIBLIOGRAPHY

Denoon, D. and Snowden, C. n.d. [1981]. *A Time to Plant and a Time to Uproot*, Institute of Papua New Guinea Studies, [Port Moresby].

Derrick, R.A. 1957. *A History of Fiji*, Government Press, Suva.

Dore, R.P. 1984 *Land Reform in Japan*, Athlone Press, London.

Douglas, B. 1972. A History of Culture Contact in North-Eastern New Caledonia 1774–1870, PhD thesis, Australian National University, Canberra.

Duratalo, S. unpub. Indigenous Fijian Land Ownership and Rights. Fiji Centre, University of the South Pacific Public Lecture, Suva, 11 November 1993.

Eagleston, J.H. n.d. Ups and Downs. Unpublished journal, typescript in Peabody Museum, Salem, Mass.

Eaton, C. 1988. '*Vakavanua* land tenure and tobacco farming', in Overton (ed.), 1988:19–30.

Elvin, J.M. 1970. 'The last thousand years of Chinese history: changing patterns in land tenure', *Modern Asian Studies* 4(2):97–114.

Emery, F.V. 1973. 'England circa 1600', in Darby (ed.), 1973:248–301.

Epstein, A.L. 1969. *Matupit: Land, Politics and Change among the Tolai of New Britain*, University of California Press, Berkeley.

Fa, I.T. 1989. Customary Land Rights over Native Land in Fiji, LlM thesis, University of Auckland.

Fairbairn, T. (ed.) 1988. *Island Entrepreneurs: Problems and Performance in the Pacific*, Pacific Islands Development Project, East-West Center, Honolulu.

Fairhurst, H. 1967. 'The rural settlement pattern of Scotland, with special reference to the north and west', in Steel and Lawton (eds), 1967:193–209.

Farrell, B.H. and Murphy, P.E. 1978. *Ethnic Attitudes toward Land in Fiji*, Center for South Pacific Studies, University of California, Santa Cruz.

Farrell, B.H. and Ward, R.G. 1962. 'The village and its agriculture', in Fox and Cumberland (eds), 1962:177–238.

Feldman, R. 1974. 'Custom and capitalism: changes in the basis of land tenure in Ismani, Tanzania', *Journal of Development Studies* 10(3–4):305–20.

Fifita, S.L. 1975. 'Problems of the land – people's view', in Fonua (ed.), 1975:31–42.

Fingleton, J. 1982. 'Pacific values and economic development? How Melanesian constitutions deal with land', in Sack (ed.), 1982:323–43.

Finney, B.R. 1973. *Polynesian Peasants and Proletarians*, Schenkman Publishing Company, Cambridge, Mass.

Finney, B.R. n.d. [1973]. *Big-Men and Business: Entrepreneurship and Economic Growth in the New Guinea Highlands*, University Press of Hawaii, Honolulu.

Fison, L. 1880–1. 'Land tenure in Fiji', *Royal Anthropological Institute Journal* 10:332–52.

Fonua, P. 1991. 'Land shortage worsens', *Matangi Tonga*, March–April 1991:16–18.

Fonua, P. 1993. 'Akilisi wants to be the opposition', *Matangi Tonga*, July–September 1993:16–20.

Fonua, S. (ed.) 1975. *Land and Migration*, Tonga Council of Churches, Nuku'alofa.

Fox, J.W. and Cumberland, K.B. (eds) 1962. *Western Samoa: Land, Life and Agriculture in Tropical Polynesia*, Whitcombe and Tombs, Christchurch.

France, P. 1969. *The Charter of the Land: Custom and Colonization in Fiji*, Oxford University Press, Melbourne.

Frazer, R.M. 1964. 'Changing Fijian agriculture', *The Australian Geographer* 9(3):148–55.

Frazer, R.[M.] 1973. 'The Fijian village and the independent farmer', in Brookfield (ed.), 1973:75–96.

BIBLIOGRAPHY 269

Freeman, J.D. and Geddes, W.R. (eds) 1959. *Anthropology in the South Seas*, Thomas Avery and Sons, New Plymouth.

Furushima, T. 1991. 'The village and agriculture during the Edo period', in Hall (ed.), 1991:478–518.

Galumalemana, N. Schmidt. 1994. 'The Land and Titles Court and customary tenure in Western Samoa', in Crocombe and Meleisea (eds), 1994:169–81.

Geddes, W.R. 1959. 'Fijian social structure in a period of transition', in Freeman and Geddes (eds), 1959:201–20.

Gerth, H.H. and Mills, C.M. (eds) 1947. *From Max Weber: Essays in Sociology*, Kegan Paul, London.

Ghai, Y. 1985. 'Land regimes and paradigms of development: reflections on Melanesian constitutions', *International Journal of the Sociology of Law* 13:393–405.

Ghai, Y. (ed.) 1988. *Land, Government and Politics in the Pacific Island States*, Institute of Pacific Studies, Suva.

Ghai, D. and Radwan, S. 1983a. 'Agrarian change, differentiation and rural poverty in Africa: a general survey', in Ghai and Radwan (eds), 1983:1–29.

Ghai, D. and Radwan, S. 1983b. 'Growth and inequality: rural development in Malawi, 1964–78', in Ghai and Radwan (eds), 1983:71–97.

Ghai, D. and Radwan, S. (eds) 1983. *Agrarian Policies and Rural Poverty in Africa*, International Labour Office, Geneva.

Gifford, E.W. 1929. *Tongan Society*, Bernice P. Bishop Museum Bulletin No.61, Honolulu.

Gilson, R.P. 1970. *Samoa 1830 to 1900: The Politics of a Multi-Cultural Community*, Oxford University Press, Melbourne.

Goldman, I. 1970. *Ancient Polynesian Society*, University of Chicago Press, Chicago.

Golson, J. n.d. [1981] 'Agricultural technology in New Guinea', in Denoon and Snowden (eds), n.d. [1981]:43–53.

Golson, J. 1989. 'The origins and development of New Guinea agriculture', in Harris and Hillman (eds), 1989:678–87.

Gordon, A. 1880. Memorandum, in [C3584] *Correspondence Relative to Land Claims in Fiji*, 1883, XLVI:367.

Gordon, A. 1897. *Fiji, Records of Private and of Public Life, 1875–1880*, Vols. I–IV, privately printed, Edinburgh.

Government of Western Samoa [GWS]. 1975. *Report on Matai Titles, Customary Land and the Land and Titles Court*, Department of Justice, Apia.

Government of Western Samoa [GWS]. 1991. *Annual Report for 1989 and 1990*, Department of Land and Titles Court, Apia.

Grange, L.I. and Fox, J.P. 1953. *Soils of the Lower Cook Group*, Soil Bureau Bulletin (n.s.) 8, Department of Scientific and Industrial Research, Wellington.

Grossman, L.S. 1984. *Peasants, Subsistence Ecology, and Development in the Highlands of Papua New Guinea*, Princeton University Press, Princeton.

Groube, L., Chappell, J., Muke, J. and Price, D. 1986. 'A 40,000 year-old human occupation site at Huon Peninsula, Papua New Guinea', *Nature* 324:453–5.

Guiart, J. 1956. *Un siècle et demi de contacts culturels à Tanna, Nouvelles-Hébrides*, Publication de la Société des Océanistes 5, Musée de l'Homme, Paris.

Guidieri, R., Pellizzi, F. and Tambiah, S.J. (eds) 1988. *Ethnicities and Nations: Processes of Interethnic Relations in Latin America, Southeast Asia, and the Pacific*, Rothko Chapel and University of Texas Press, Houston.

GWS, see Government of Western Samoa.

Hailey, Lord. 1957. *An African Survey: A Study of Problems Arising in Africa South of the Sahara*, Oxford University Press, London.

270 BIBLIOGRAPHY

Hall, J.W. (ed.) 1991. *The Cambridge History of Japan*, Vol. 4, Cambridge University Press, Cambridge.

Halliburton, T.W. 1992. *Urban Policy in Vanuatu: A Review*, United Nations Economic and Social Council for Asia and the Pacific, Port Vila.

Handler, R. and Linnekin, J. (eds) 1984. 'Tradition, genuine or spurious', *Journal of American Folklore* 97:273–90.

Hanley, S.B. and Yamamura, K. 1977. *Economic and Demographic Change in Preindustrial Japan, 1600–1868*, Princeton University Press, Princeton.

Hardin, G. 1968. 'The tragedy of the commons', *Science* 162:1243–48.

Harding, T.G. 1972. 'Land tenure', in Ryan (ed.), 1972:604–10.

Harris, D.R. and Hillman, G.C. (eds) 1989. *Foraging and Farming: The Evolution of Plant Exploitation*, Unwin Hyman, London.

Hellen, J.A. 1969. 'Colonial administrative policies and agricultural patterns in tropical Africa', in Thomas and Whittington, 1969:321–52.

Henningham, S. 1992. *France and the South Pacific: A Contemporary History*, University of Hawaii, Honolulu.

Hennings, R.O. 1952. 'Some trends and problems of African land tenure in Kenya', *Journal of African Administration* 4:122–34.

Henry, G. 1991. 'The challenge of change', in Lewis (ed.), 1991:77–80.

Hirst, J. et al. (eds) 1988. *Small Scale Agriculture*, Commonwealth Geographical Bureau and Department of Human Geography, Canberra.

Hobsbawm, E. 1983. 'Introduction: inventing traditions', in Hobsbawm and Ranger (eds), 1983:1–14.

Hobsbawm, E. and Ranger, T. (eds) 1983. *The Invention of Tradition*, Cambridge University Press, Cambridge.

Holmes, L. 1971. 'Samoa: custom versus productivity', in Crocombe (ed.), 1971:91–105.

Hooper, A. and Huntsman, J. 1987. 'Tenure, society and economy', in Crocombe (ed.), 1987b:117–40.

House, W.J. and Killick, T. 1983. 'Social justice and development policy in Kenya's rural economy', in Ghai and Radwan (eds), 1983:31–69.

Howlett, D.R. 1973. 'Terminal development: from tribalism to peasantry', in Brookfield (ed.), 1973:249–73.

Huggett, F.E. 1975. *The Land Question and European Society*, Thames and Hudson, London.

Hunter, D. 1963. *Tongan Law Reports*, Government Printer, Nuku'alofa.

James, K.E. 1991. 'Migration and remittances: a Tongan village perspective', *Pacific Viewpoint* 32(1):1–23.

James, K.E. 1993. 'Cutting the ground from under them? Commercialization, cultivation, and conservation in Tonga', *The Contemporary Pacific* 5(2):215–42.

James, K.E. 1994. 'The Pro-Democracy Movement in Tonga', *Pacific Affairs* 67(2), to appear August, 1994.

James, K.E. (ed.) 1993. *Pacific Village Economies: Opportunity and Livelihood in Small Communities*, Special Issue, *Pacific Viewpoint*, 34(2).

Jolly, M. 1982. 'Birds and banyans of south Pentecost: *kastom* in anti-colonial struggle', in Keesing and Tonkinson (eds), 1982:338–56.

Jolly, M. 1991. 'Soaring hawks and grounded persons: the politics of rank and gender in north Vanuatu', in Strathern and Godelier (eds), 1991:48–80.

Jolly, M. 1992. 'Custom and the way of the land: past and present in Vanuatu and Fiji', *Oceania* 62:330–54.

Jones, H.M. 1865. 'Report on the social conditions of Fiji and Tonga, 1866', in *Commercial Reports Received at the Foreign Office from Her Majesty's Consuls,*

BIBLIOGRAPHY 271

British Parliamentary Papers [3582], *Accounts and Papers*, 1866, LXIX, pp.603ff.

Jones, H.M. 1866. Report by Mr Consul Henry M. Jones on the Trade of the Fiji and Tonga Islands during the Year 1866, reprinted in *Correspondence and Documents relating to the Fiji Islands*, House of Lords Sessional Paper No. 47 of 1872, pp.62–4.

Joralemon, V.L. 1983. 'Collective land tenure and agricultural development: a Polynesian case', *Human Organization* 42(2):95–105.

Jupp, K.M. 1956. *Report on the Population Census 1956*, Census Commission, Territory of Western Samoa, Apia.

Kamikamica, J. and Davey, T. 1988. 'Trust on trial – the development of the customary land trust concept in Fiji', in Ghai (ed.), 1988:284–303.

Kandawire, J.A. 1980. 'Village segmentation and class formation in southern Malawi', *Africa* 50(2):125–45.

Keesing, F.M. 1934. *Modern Samoa: Its Government and Changing Life*, Allen and Unwin, London.

Keesing, R.M. 1989. 'Creating the past: custom and identity in the contemporary Pacific', *The Contemporary Pacific* 1(1–2):19–42.

Keesing, R.M. 1993. 'Kastom re-examined', *Anthropological Forum* 6(4):587–96.

Keesing, R.M. and Tonkinson, R. (eds) 1982. *Reinventing Traditional Culture: The Politics of Kastom in Island Melanesia*, Special Issue, *Mankind* 13(4).

Kirch, P.V. and Sahlins, M. 1992. *Anahulu: The Anthropology of History in the Kingdom of Hawaii*, University of Chicago Press, Chicago and London.

Kramer, A. 1902. *The Samoa Islands*, E. Schweizerbartsche, Stuttgart. Typescript translated by D. H. and M. de Beer, Dunedin, 1930.

Lambert, B. 1987. 'The Gilbert Islands: micro-individualism', in Crocombe (ed.), 1987a:146–71.

Lane, R. 1971. 'The New Hebrides: land tenure without land policy', in Crocombe (ed.), 1971:248–72.

Larcom, J. 1990. 'Custom by Decree: legitimation crisis in Vanuatu', in Linnekin and Poyer (eds), 1990:175–90.

Larmour, P. 1984. 'Alienated land and independence in Melanesia', *Pacific Studies* 8(1):1–47.

Larmour, P. 1990. 'Public choice in Melanesia: community, bureaucracy and the market in land management', *Public Administration and Development* 10:53–68.

Lasaqa, I. 1963. Dawasamu-Bure, North East Viti Levu, Fiji, MA thesis, University of Auckland.

Lasaqa, I. 1984. *The Fijian People Before and After Independence*, Australian National University Press, Canberra.

Lātūkefu, S. 1974. *Church and State in Tonga*, Australian National University Press, Canberra.

Lātūkefu, S. 1975. *The Tongan Constitution*, Tongan Traditions Committee, Nuku'alofa.

Lawson, S. 1993. 'The politics of tradition: problems for political legitimacy and democracy in the South Pacific', *Pacific Studies* 16(2):1–29.

Layard, J.W. 1942. *Stone Men of Malekula*, Chatto and Windus, London.

Leach, E.R. 1971. *Pul Eliya: A Village in Ceylon*, Cambridge University Press, Cambridge.

Legge, J.D. 1958. *Britain in Fiji, 1858–1880*, Macmillan, London.

Lewis, N.D. (ed.) 1991. *Proceedings of the XVII Pacific Science Congress*, Pacific Science Association, Honolulu.

272 BIBLIOGRAPHY

Lewthwaite, G.R. 1962. 'Land, life and agriculture to mid-century', in Fox and Cumberland (eds), 1962:130–76.

Lieber, M. (ed.) 1977. *Exiles and Migrants in Oceania*, University of Hawaii Press, Honolulu.

Lindstrom, L. 1990. *Knowledge and Power in a South Pacific Society*, Smithsonian Institution Press, Washington, DC.

Lindstrom, L. 1993. 'Cargo cult culture: toward a genealogy of Melanesian kastom', *Anthropological Forum* 6(4):495–513.

Linnekin, J. and Poyer, L. (eds). 1990. *Cultural Identity and Ethnicity in the Pacific*, University of Hawaii Press, Honolulu.

Lloyd, D.T. 1982. *Land Policy in Fiji*, Occasional Paper No. 14, Department of Land Economy, University of Cambridge, Cambridge.

Lockwood, V.S., Harding, T.G. and Wallace, B.J. 1993. *Contemporary Pacific Societies: Studies in Development and Change*, Prentice Hall, New Jersey.

Lovell, P.R. 1981. Children of Blood, Children of Shame: Creation and Procreation in Longana, East Aoba, New Hebrides, PhD thesis, McMaster University, Hamilton, Canada.

Loy, T.H., Spriggs, M. and Wickler, S. 1992. 'Direct evidence for human use of plants 28,000 years ago: starch residues on stone artefacts from the northern Solomon Islands', *Antiquity* 66:898–912.

LTC [Land and Titles Court], Various dates. Unpublished case records, Western Samoa Land and Titles Court, Mulinu'u, Apia.

Ma'afu, Hon. 1975. 'Land from the landlord's view', in Fonua (ed.), 1975:1–3.

McArthur, N. 1958. *Report on the Census of the Population, 1956*, Council Paper No. 1 of 1958, Government Press, Suva.

McArthur, N. 1967. *Island Populations of the Pacific*, Australian National University Press, Canberra.

MacClancy, J. 1980. *To Kill a Bird with Two Stones: A Short History of Vanuatu*, Vanuatu Cultural Centre Publications No. 1, Port Vila.

MacWilliam, S. 1988. 'Smallholdings, land law and the politics of land tenure in Papua New Guinea', *Journal of Peasant Studies* 16(10):77–109.

Mantoux, P. 1928. *The Industrial Revolution in the Eighteenth Century*, Jonathan Cape, London.

Marcus, G.E. 1977. 'Succession disputes and the position of the nobility in modern Tonga', *Oceania* XLVII (3):220–41.

Marcus, G.E. 1978. 'Land tenure and elite formation in the neotraditional monarchies of Tonga and Buganda', *American Ethnologist* 5:509–34.

Marsack, C.C. 1961. *Notes on the Practice of the Court and the Principles Adopted in the Hearing of Cases Affecting (1) Samoan Matai Titles; and (2) Land Held According to Customs and Usages of Western Samoa*, revised edn., Land and Titles Court, Western Samoa.

Martin, J. 1817. *An Account of the Natives of the Tonga Islands in the South Pacific Ocean. Compiled and Arranged from the Extensive Communications of Mr William Mariner, Several Years Resident in those Islands*. 2 vols, London; reprinted 1981, Vava'u Press, Tonga.

Mason, L. 1987. 'Tenures from subsistence to Star Wars', in Crocombe (ed.), 1987b:3–27.

Matahau, A.V. unpub. [1986]. The Native Land Trust Board – Powers and Duties: the Handling of the Land at Delainavesi, unpublished paper, Suva.

Matheson, T. 1987. 'The absent majority: the case of Rakahanga', in Crocombe (ed.), 1987b:169–87.

BIBLIOGRAPHY   273

Maude, A. 1965. Population, Land and Livelihood in Tonga, PhD thesis, Australian National University, Canberra.

Maude, A. and Sevele, F. 1987. 'Tonga: equality overtaking privilege', in Crocombe (ed.), 1987:114–42.

Maude, H.E. 1959. 'The Tahitian pork trade 1800–1830', *Journal de la Société des Océanistes* 15:55–95.

Maxwell, G.V. 1913a. [Report] to Colonial Secretary, 6 June 1913, in *Native Lands Commission*, Council Paper 27 of 1914, Government Printer, Suva, pp. 1–4.

Maxwell, G.V. 1913b. [Report] to Colonial Secretary, 11 August 1913, in *Native Lands Commission*, Council Paper 27 of 1914, Government Printer, Suva, pp. 7–12.

May, R.J. and Nelson, H. (eds) 1982. *Melanesia: Beyond Diversity*. Vol. 1, Research School of Pacific Studies, Australian National University, Canberra.

Mead, M. 1930. *Social Organization of Manu'a*, Bulletin 76, Bernice P. Bishop Museum, Honolulu.

Meek, C.K. 1949. *Land Law and Custom in the Colonies*, Oxford University Press, London.

Meek, C.K. 1957. *Land Tenure and Land Administration in Nigeria and the Cameroons*, H.M.S.O., London.

Meleisea, M. 1987. *The Making of Modern Samoa: Traditional Authority and Colonial Administration in the Modern History of Western Samoa*, Institute of Pacific Studies, University of the South Pacific, Suva.

Mifsud, F.M. 1967. *Customary Land Law in Africa*, F.A.O., Rome.

Milner, G.B. 1966. *Samoan Dictionary: Samoan–English, English–Samoan*. Oxford University Press, Oxford.

Minister of the Navy and Colonies, 1854. Minister of the Navy and Colonies to Foreign Minister, 22 February 1854, Paris, in Douglas, 1972:369.

Morgan, R.C. 1985. Competing Circuits in the Vava'u Social Economy, PhD thesis, Research School of Pacific Studies, Australian National University, Canberra.

Morrell, W.P. 1960. *Britain in the Pacific Islands*, Oxford University Press, London.

N.I.D. [Naval Intelligence Division], 1945. *Pacific Islands: Vol. 1: General Survey*, Naval Intelligence Division, [London].

Nayacakalou, R.R 1955. Tradition, Choice and Change in the Fijian Economy, MA thesis, University of Auckland.

Nayacakalou, R.R. unpub. Some Problems of Social and Economic Development in Fiji, unpublished paper, Royal Anthropological Institute, London, March 1959.

Nayacakalou, R.R. 1960. 'Land tenure and social organisation in Western Samoa', *Journal of the Polynesian Society* 69:104–22.

Nayacakalou, R.R 1965. 'The bifurcation and amalgamation of Fijian lineages over a period of fifty years', *Transactions and Proceedings of the Fiji Society for the Years 1960–61*, 8(1–2):122–33.

Nayacakalou, R.R. 1971. 'Fiji; manipulating the system', in Crocombe, R. (ed.), 1971:206–26.

Nayacakalou, R.R. 1972. 'The leasing of native land for tourist plant development in Fiji', in Ward, M.W. (ed.), 1972:151–8.

Nayacakalou, R.R. 1975. *Leadership in Fiji*, Oxford University Press, Melbourne.

Nayacakalou, R.R. 1978. *Tradition and Change in the Fijian Village*, South Pacific Social Sciences Association and Institute of Pacific Studies, University of the South Pacific, Suva.

274 BIBLIOGRAPHY

Needs, A.P. 1988. *New Zealand Aid and the Development of Class in Tonga*, Sociology Department, Massey University, Palmerston North.

Newbury, C. 1972. 'The Makatea Phosphate Concession', in Ward, R.G. (ed.), 1972:167–88.

Notes. 1876. *Notes of the Proceedings of a Native Council*, Waikava, Vanua Levu, November 1876, Government Printer, Suva.

Notes. 1877. *Notes of the Proceedings of a Native Council*, Rewa, December 1877, Government Printer, Suva.

Notes. 1878. *Notes of the Proceedings of a Native Council*, Bua, November–December 1878, Government Printer, Suva.

Ogan, E. 1972. *Business and Cargo*, New Guinea Research Bulletin, No. 44, Australian National University, Port Moresby and Canberra.

Oliver, D. L. 1974. *Ancient Tahitian Society*, 3 vols, University Press of Hawaii, Honolulu.

O'Meara, J.T. 1986. Why Is Village Agriculture Stagnating: A Social and Economic Analysis of Western Samoa, PhD thesis, University Microfilms, Ann Arbor.

O'Meara, J.T. 1987. 'Samoa: customary individualism', in Crocombe (ed.), 1987a:74–113.

O'Meara, J.T. 1990. *Samoan Planters: Tradition and Economic Development in Polynesia*, Holt, Rinehart and Winston, New York.

Orange, J. (ed.) 1840. *Life of the Late George Vason, of Nottingham, One of the Troop of Missionaries First Sent to the South Sea Islands by the London Missionary Society in the Ship Duff, Captain Wilson, 1796*, John Snow, London.

Ottino, P. 1972. *Rangiroa*, Editions Cujas, Paris.

Overton, J. 1987. 'Fijian land: pressing problems, possible tenure solutions', *Singapore Journal of Tropical Geography* 8(2):139–51.

Overton, J. 1988a. 'A Fijian peasantry: *galala* and villagers', *Oceania* 58:193–211.

Overton, J. 1988b. 'Resettlement re-examined: accumulation and differentiation in Waibau and Lomaivuna, Fiji', in Hirst et al. (eds), 1988:67–81.

Overton, J. 1989. *Land and Differentiation in Rural Fiji*, Pacific Research Monograph 19, National Centre for Development Studies, Australian National University, Canberra.

Overton, J. 1992. 'The limits to accumulation: changing land tenure in Fiji', *Journal of Peasant Studies* 19(2):326–42.

Overton, J. (ed.) 1988. *Rural Fiji*, Institute of Pacific Studies, University of the South Pacific, Suva.

Panoff, M. 1971. 'The Society Islands: confusion from compulsive logic', in Crocombe (ed.), 1971:43–59.

Perminow, A.A. 1993. 'Between the forest and the big lagoon: the microeconomy of Kotu Island in the Kingdom of Tonga', in K. James (ed.), 1993.

Philibert, J-M. 1986. 'The politics of tradition: toward a generic culture in Vanuatu', *Mankind* 16(1):1–12.

Philibert, J-M. 1992. 'Social change in Vanuatu', in Robillard (ed.), 1992:98–133.

Philibert, J-M. and Rodman, M. In press. 'From Condominium to Republic: a hundred years of history in black and white', in J. Bonnemaison and D. Tryon (eds), in press.

Pirie, P.N.D. 1964. The Geography of Population in Western Samoa, PhD thesis, Australian National University, Canberra.

Pitt, D. 1970. *Tradition and Economic Progress in Samoa*, Clarendon Press, Oxford.

Ponter, B.A. n.d. 'Land, economy, custom and conflict in Atchin, North East Malekula', unpublished manuscript.

BIBLIOGRAPHY

Powles, C.G. 1979. The Persistence of Chiefly Power and Its Implications for Law and Political Organisation in Western Polynesia, PhD thesis, Australian National University, Canberra.

Powles, C.G. 1986. 'Legal systems and political cultures: competition for dominance in Western Samoa', in Sack and Minchin (eds), 1986:191–214.

Prasad, P.C. 1984. 'Fiji: sugar cane production and land tenure', in Acquaye and Crocombe (eds), 1984:102–13.

Pratt, G. 1893. *Grammar and Dictionary of the Samoan Language*, London Missionary Society, London.

Quain, B. 1948. *Fijian Village*, University of Chicago Press, Chicago.

Ranger, T. 1983. 'The invention of tradition in colonial Africa', in Hobsbawm and Ranger (eds), 1983:211–62.

Ravuvu, A. 1983a. *Vaka i Taukei: The Fijian Way of Life*, Institute of Pacific Studies, University of the South Pacific, Suva.

Ravuvu, A. 1983b. 'The Fijian village in transition', working paper prepared for the Fiji Employment and Development Mission, 1982–3, Suva.

Ravuvu, A. 1987. *The Fijian Ethos*, Institute of Pacific Studies, University of the South Pacific, Suva.

Ravuvu, A. 1988. *Development or Dependence: The Pattern of Change in a Fijian Village*, Institute of Pacific Studies, Suva.

Report. 1896. *Report of the Commission Appointed to Inquire into the Decrease of the Native Population*, Government Printer, Suva.

Republic of Vanuatu. 1991. *National Population Census May 1989. Main Report*, Statistics Office, Port Vila.

Republic of Vanuatu. 1993. *Third National Development Plan 1992–1996*, Port Vila.

Republic of Vanuatu. n.d. *Second National Development Plan 1987–1991*, Vol. 1. Port Vila.

Ritterbush, S.D. 1988. 'Entrepreneurship in Tonga', in Fairbairn (ed.), 1988: 137–64.

Robillard, A.B. (ed.) 1992. *Social Change in the Pacific Islands*, Kegan Paul, London.

Rodman, M. 1984. 'Masters of tradition: customary land tenure and new forms of social inequality in a Vanuatu peasantry', *American Ethnologist* 11(1):61–80.

Rodman, M. 1985a. 'Contemporary custom: redefining domestic space in Longana, Vanuatu', *Ethnology* 24(4):269–79.

Rodman, M. 1985b. 'Moving houses: residential mobility and the mobility of residences in Longana, Vanuatu', *American Anthropologist* 87(1):56–72.

Rodman, M. 1987. *Masters of Tradition: Consequences of Customary Land Tenure in Longana, Vanuatu*, University of British Columbia Press, Vancouver.

Rodman, M. 1993. 'Empowering place: multilocality and multivocality', *American Anthropologist* 94(3):640–56.

Rodman, M. and Rodman, W. n.d. 'The eye of the storm: cyclones and the social construction of place in Vanuatu', manuscript under review.

Rodman, W. 1985. 'A law unto themselves: legal innovation in Ambae, Vanuatu', *American Ethnologist* 12(4):603–24.

Rodman, W. 1993. 'The law of the state and the state of the law in Vanuatu', in Lockwood et al., 1993:56–66.

Rodman, W. and Rodman, M. 1985. 'Rethinking kastom: on the politics of place naming in Vanuatu', *Oceania* 56(2):242.

Rogers, G. 1977. ' "The father's sister is black": a consideration of female rank and powers in Tonga', *Journal of the Polynesian Society* 86(2):157–82.

Roth, G.K. 1953. *The Fijian Way of Life*, Oxford University Press, Melbourne.

BIBLIOGRAPHY

Rubinstein, R. 1978. Placing the Self on Malo: An Account of the Culture of Malo Island, PhD thesis, Anthropology, Bryn Mawr College, Bryn Mawr, Pa.

Russell, B.J.F. 1982. 'Adjudication of disputes over ownership of customary land', Vanuatu Government Discussion Paper.

Rutz, H.J. 1978. 'Fijian land tenure and agricultural growth', *Oceania* 49(1):20–34.

Rutz, H.J. 1987. 'Capitalizing on culture: moral ironies in urban Fiji', *Comparative Studies in Society and History* 29(3):533–57.

Ryan P. (ed.) 1972. *Encyclopaedia of Papua and New Guinea*, Melbourne University Press, Melbourne.

Sack, P. (ed.) 1974. *Problem of Choice: Land in Papua New Guinea's Future*, Australian National University Press, Canberra.

Sack, P. (ed.) 1982. *Pacific Constitutions*, Research School of Social Sciences, Australian National University, Canberra.

Sack, P.G. and Minchin, E. (eds) 1986. *Legal Pluralism: Proceedings of the Canberra Law Workshop 7*, Law Department, Research School of Social Sciences, Australian National University, Canberra.

Sahlins, M.D. 1957. 'Land use and the extended family in Moala, Fiji', *American Anthropologist* 59(3):449–62.

Sahlins, M.D. 1962. *Moala: Culture and Nature on a Fijian Island*, University of Michigan Press, Ann Arbor.

Sahlins, M.[D.] 1992. *Anahulu: Historical Ethnography*, Vol. 1 of P.V. Kirch and M. Sahlins, *Anahulu: The Anthropology of History in the Kingdom of Hawaii*, University of Chicago Press, Chicago and London.

Salisbury, R.F. 1962. *From Stone to Steel: Economic Consequences of a Technological Change in New Guinea*, Melbourne University Press, Melbourne.

Saussol, A. 1979. *L'Héritage: Essai sur le problème foncier mélanésien en Nouvelle-Calédonie*, Société des Océanistes, Paris.

Sayes, S.A. 1982. *Cakaudrove: Ideology and Reality in a Fijian Confederation*, PhD thesis, Australian National University, Canberra.

Scarr, D. 1967. *Fragments of Empire: A History of the Western Pacific High Commission 1877–1914*, Australian National University Press, Canberra.

Scarr, D. (ed.) n.d. [1982]. *Fiji: the Three-legged Stool: Selected Writings of Ratu Sir Lala Sukuna*, Macmillan Education for the Ratu Sir Lala Sukuna Biography Committee, Suva.

Scholefield, G.H. 1919. *The Pacific: Its Past and Future*, John Murray, London.

Schultz, E. 1911. 'The most important principles of Samoan family law, and the laws of inheritance', *Journal of the Polynesian Society* 20:43–53.

Serpenti, L.M. 1965. *Cultivators in the Swamps*, Van Gorcum N.V., Assen.

Sheldon, C.D. 1958. *The Rise of the Merchant Class in Tokugawa Japan: 1600–1868*, Monograph V, Association for Asian Studies, J.J. Augustin, Locust Valley.

Shiba, Y. (trans. M. Elvin) 1970. *Commerce and Society in Sung China*, Michigan Abstracts of Chinese and Japanese Works on Chinese History, No. 2, Center for Chinese Studies, Ann Arbor.

Shineberg, D. 1967. *They Came for Sandalwood*, Melbourne University Press, Melbourne.

Silverman, M.G. 1969. 'Maximize your options: a study in values, symbols, and social structure', in Spencer (ed.), 1969:97–115.

Simpson, S.R. 1954. 'Land tenure; some explanations and definitions', *Journal of African Administration* 6:50–64.

Smith, T.C. 1959. *The Agrarian Origins of Modern Japan*, Stanford University Press, Stanford.

Somare, M. 1991. 'Melanesian leadership', in Lewis (ed.), 1991:104–8.

BIBLIOGRAPHY 277

Sope, B. 1974. *Land and Politics in the New Hebrides*, South Pacific Social Sciences Association, Suva.

Spate, O.H.K. 1959. *The Fijian People: Economic Problems and Prospects*, Council Paper 13 of 1959, Government Press, Suva.

Spence, J.D. 1990. *The Search for Modern China*, W.W. Norton, New York.

Spencer, R.F. (ed.) 1969. *Forms of Symbolic Action*, American Ethnological Society, Seattle and London.

Spriggs, M. 1990. 'Dating Lapita: another view', in Spriggs (ed.), 1990:6–17.

Spriggs, M. and Anderson, A. 1993. 'Late colonization of East Polynesia', *Antiquity* 67:200–17.

Spriggs, M. (ed.) 1990. *Lapita Design, Form and Composition: Proceedings of the Lapita Design Workshop, Canberra, Australia – December 1988*, Occasional Papers in Prehistory 19, Canberra.

Stair, J.B. 1897. *Old Samoa: Or Flotsam and Jetsam from the Pacific Ocean*, R. McMillan, London, 1983 printing, Papakura, New Zealand.

Steel, R.W. and Lawton, R. (eds) 1967. *Liverpool Essays in Geography*, Longman, London.

Steubel, C. (trans. Bro. Herman) 1987. *The Myths, Legends, and Customs of Old Samoa*, Polynesian Press, Auckland.

Stober, W. 1984. 'The Land Trust Board', in Alatoa, 1984:34–46.

Strathern, M. and Godelier M. (eds) 1991. *Big Men and Great Men: Personification of Power in Melanesia*, Cambridge University Press, Cambridge.

Sukuna, J.L.V. 1932. 'Notes on custom regarding land for F.R. Charlton, Native Lands Commission, 20 May 1932', in Scarr (ed.), n.d:116–20.

Sukuna, J.L.V. 1936. 'Contemporary translation, with his help, of Ratu Sukuna's speech in the Council of Chiefs, 1936, on Native Land', in Scarr (ed.), n.d.:212–9.

Sutter, F.K. 1971. *Agriculture Development: Western Samoa Land Tenure, Technical Report 1*, UNDP/FAO, Rome.

Taliai, S. 1975. 'Theology of land', in Fonua (ed.), 1975:18–30.

Taylor, M. (ed.) 1987. *Fiji, Future Imperfect?*, Allen and Unwin, Sydney.

Thomas, M.F. and Whittington, G.W. 1969. *Environment and Land Use in Africa*, Methuen, London.

Thomas, N. 1990. 'Sanitation and seeing: the creation of state power in early colonial Fiji', *Comparative Studies in Society and History* 32(1): 149–70.

Thomas, P. 1981. 'Food for the gods or malnutrition for man?', *Journal of Pacific Studies* 7:37–80.

Thompson, V. and Adloff, R. 1971. *The French Pacific Islands: French Polynesia and New Caledonia*, University of California Press, Berkeley and Los Angeles.

Thomson, B. 1908. *The Fijians: A Study in the Decay of Customs*, William Heinemann, London.

Thurston, J.B. 1886. *Upon the National Ownership of Land in Fiji*, Government Printer, Suva.

Tiffany, S.W. 1974. 'The Land and Titles Court and the regulation of customary title successions and removals in Western Samoa', *Journal of the Polynesian Society* 83(1):35–57.

Tiffany, S.W. 1975. 'Entrepreneurship and political participation in Western Samoa: a case study', *Oceania* 56(2):85–106.

Tiffany, S.W. 1980. 'Politics of land disputes in Western Samoa', *Oceania* 50(3): 176–208.

Tiffany, W. 1975. 'High Court adjudication of chiefly title succession disputes in American Samoa', *Journal of the Polynesian Society* 84:67–92.

278 BIBLIOGRAPHY

Tonga. 1948. *The Government Gazette* 12, Nuku'alofa, p.128.
Tonga. 1976. *Census 1976*, Statistics Department, Government of Tonga, Nuku'alofa.
Tonga. 1988. *Statistical Abstract 1987*, Statistics Department, Government of Tonga, Nuku'alofa.
Tonga. 1989. *Statistical Abstract 1988*, Statistics Department, Government of Tonga, Nuku'alofa.
Tonga. 1990. *Master Plan for Popua Peninsula and Islands* (Riedel and Byrne), Ministry of Lands, Survey and Natural Resources, Kingdom of Tonga.
Tongilava, S.L. 1993. 'Land-holding before outside influences', *The Tonga Chronicle*, 29 Dec., p.3.
Tonkinson, R. 1977. 'The exploitation of ambiguity: a New Hebrides case', in Lieber (ed.), 1977:269–95.
Tonkinson, R. 1982. 'Vanuatu values: a changing symbiosis', in May and Nelson (eds.), 1982:73–90.
Tonkinson, R. 1985. 'Forever Ambrymese? Identity in a relocated community, Vanuatu', in Chapman (ed.), 1985:116–38.
Trevelyan, G.M. 1959. *A Shortened History of England*, Pelican Books, Harmondsworth.
Tuiatua Tupua Tamasese E. 1992a. 'Conflicts and continuities – New Zealand/ Samoa relations', unpublished paper, Macmillan Brown Centre for Pacific Studies, Christchurch, New Zealand.
Tuiatua Tupua Tamasese E. 1992b. 'Who is the son of a bitch who drew this map!', unpublished paper, Macmillan Brown Centre for Pacific Studies, Christchurch, New Zealand.
Turner, G. 1884. *Samoa a Hundred Years Ago and Long Before*, reprinted, Institute of Pacific Studies, University of the South Pacific, Suva, 1984.
Turner, M. 1980. *English Parliamentary Enclosure*, Dawson, Folkestone.
Urbanowicz, C.F. 1973. 'Tongan adoption before the constitution of 1875', *Ethnohistory* 20(2):109–23.
Va'ai, S. 1993. 'The legislative history of the Land and Titles Court', unpublished manuscript, Australian National University, Canberra.
Van der Grijp, P. 1993a. *Islanders of the South: Production, Kinship, and Ideology in the Polynesian Kingdom of Tonga*, 154, Koninklijk Instituut voor Taal-, Landen Volkenkunde, Leiden.
Van der Grijp, P. 1993b. 'After the vanilla harvest: strains in the Tongan land tenure system', *Journal of the Polynesian Society* 102(3):233–54.
Van Trease, H. 1984. The History of Land and Property Rights in Vanuatu, PhD thesis, University of the South Pacific, Suva, Fiji.
Vanuatu Cultural Centre Publications No. 1, Port Vila.
Walsh, A.C. 1964. Nuku'alofa, Tonga: A Preliminary Study of Urbanisation and In-migration, MA thesis, Victoria University, Wellington.
Walter, M.A.H.B. 1978a. 'The conflict of the traditional and the traditionalised: an analysis of Fijian land tenure', *Journal of the Polynesian Society* 87(2):89–108.
Walter, M.A.H.B. 1978b. 'Analysis of Fijian traditional social organisation: the confusion of local descent grouping', *Ethnology* (17)3:351–66.
Ward, A. 1982. *Land and Politics in New Caledonia*, Political and Social Change Monograph, Australian National University, Canberra.
Ward, J.M. 1948. *British Policy in the South Pacific*, Australian Publishing Co., Sydney.
Ward, M.W. (ed.) 1972. *Change and Development in Rural Melanesia*, University of Papua and New Guinea, Port Moresby, and Research School of Pacific Studies, Australian National University, Canberra.

BIBLIOGRAPHY

Ward, R.G. 1960. 'Village agriculture in Viti Levu, Fiji', *New Zealand Geographer* 16(1):33–56.

Ward, R.G. 1962. 'Agriculture outside the village and commercial systems', in Fox and Cumberland (eds), 1962:266–89.

Ward, R.G. 1964. 'Cash cropping in the Fijian village', *Geographical Journal* 130(4):484–506.

Ward, R.G. 1965. *Land Use and Population in Fiji*, Her Majesty's Stationery Office, London.

Ward, R.G. 1969. 'Land use and land alienation in Fiji to 1885', *Journal of Pacific History* 4:3–25.

Ward, R.G. 1972. 'The Pacific bêche-de-mer trade with special reference to Fiji', in Ward, R.G. (ed.) 1972:91–123.

Ward, R.G. (ed.) 1972. *Man in the Pacific Islands*, Clarendon Press, Oxford.

Ward, R.G. 1985. 'Land, land use and land availability in Fiji', in Brookfield et al., 1985:15–64.

Ward, R.G. 1987. 'Native Fijian villages: a questionable future?', in Taylor (ed.), 1987:33–45.

Ward, R.G. 1993. 'South Pacific island futures: paradise, prosperity, or pauperism?', *The Contemporary Pacific* 5(1):1–21.

Ward, R.G. and Proctor, A. (eds) 1980. *South Pacific Agriculture: Choices and Constraints*, Asian Development Bank and Australian National University Press, Canberra.

Waswo, A. 1977. *Japanese Landlords: The Decline of a Rural Elite*, University of California Press, Berkeley and Los Angeles.

Watson, J.W. with Sissons, J.B. (eds) 1964. *The British Isles: A Systematic Geography*, Nelson, London.

Watters, R.F. 1958a. 'Settlement in Old Samoa', *New Zealand Geographer* 14(1):1–18.

Watters, R.F. 1958b. 'Cultivation in Old Samoa', *Economic Geography* 34(4):338–51.

Watters, R.F. 1969. *Koro: Economic Development and Social Change in Fiji*, Clarendon Press, Oxford.

Webb, A.S. 1922. *Diary*, Pacific Manuscripts Bureau Microfilm No. 8. Canberra.

Weber, M. 1947a. 'Politics as a vocation', in Gerth and Mills (eds), 1947:77–128.

Weber, M. 1947b. 'The social psychology of the world religions', in Gerth and Mills (eds), 1947:267–301.

Weisbrot, D. 1989. 'Custom, pluralism, and realism in Vanuatu: legal development and the role of customary law', *Pacific Studies* 13(1):65–97.

Whyte, J. (ed.) 1990. *Vanuatu: Ten Years of Independence*, Other People Publications, Rozelle, Sydney.

Wilkinson, D. n.d. unpub. Land Claims Commission Report No. 546, Report No. 3 on Nakama, Fiji Archives.

Williamson, R.W. 1924. *The Social and Political Systems of Central Polynesia*, Vol. III, Cambridge University Press, Cambridge.

Wood Ellem, E.O. 1981. Queen Salote Tupou III and Tungi Mailefihi, PhD thesis, University of Melbourne.

Yen, D.E. 1974. *The Sweet Potato and Oceania*, Bernice P. Bishop Museum Bulletin 236, Honolulu.

Yen, D.E. 1980. 'Pacific production systems', in Ward and Proctor (eds), 1980:73–106.

Index

Note: In order to indicate which country is referred to under the headings and subheadings in this index, code letters are given in brackets. When all the references under a heading refer to one country, eg. "*aiga* (WS)", the code is placed directly after the title entry. When the heading includes reference to several countries, the code is placed before the relevant page number(s), (eg. 'banks' and 'boundaries'), with country sequences separated by a semi-colon. Page numbers for general entries are placed before the country-specific sequences. Headings with few page entries, or entries each of which refers to a number of countries, do not carry the codes.

The code letters are: A – Africa; B – Britain; CI – Cook Islands; Ch – China; F – Fiji; FP – French Polynesia; J – Japan; M – Melanesia; NC – New Caledonia; PNG – Papua New Guinea; SI – Solomon Islands; T – Tonga; V – Vanuatu; WS – Western Samoa.

absentee, land holder, 256; (J) 20; (Ch) 21; (CI) 52; (FP) 62; (T) 172–3, 178, 185, 187, 188: land rights lost, 52–3: land rights preserved, (T) 52–3; 187, 188; (F, CI) 256–7

Africa, 12, 14, 16, 21, 27–33, 34, 141, 255

agricultural land, 45; (WS) 89, 110, 115, 123–35, 142, 144, 148; (T) 183; (F) 210, 226, 243: lease, (T) 187; (F) 222, 233: survey of, (J) 18; (WS) 123: value of, (T) 11, 190

agricultural revolution, 24–5, 26, 33, 254

agriculture, 1, 9, 21, 30, 58, 223: commercial, 2, 4, 23, 33, 54, 57–8, 60, 255, 262, 263; (B) 26; (A) 29, 30, 33; (T) 180, 185–6, 191, 196; (F) 245, 250: credit for, 61; (T) 191: development projects, (F) 224, 253: individualism in, 62: labour, (T) 185, 190, 191; (F) 222–33: new crops in, 47, 53: production, 32, 62; (T) 164: subsistence, 11, 12, 16, 39, 40, 55–8, 255, 262–3; (B) 21–2, 26; (J) 19; (Ch) 20; (A) 28, 30, 32; (M) 51, 56, 57; (WS) 109; (T) 161, 163–4, 171, 179, 180, 184–5; (F) 204, 211, 213, 219, 220, 225,

227, 230, 232–3, 236–8, 258: technology in, 7, 27; (J) 19; (A) 26, 29; (F) 237

aid, foreign, 3, 4, 59, 261; (T) 185; (F) 222, 236

'*aiga* (WS), cooperation within, 110, 113, 132, 134, 142: and individualism, 4, 113, 118, 122, 124, 129–40, 143, 150, 153: land allocation within, 4, 118, 124, 131, 134: land ownership by, 110, 112, 120, 122, 123–8, 131, 132, 134, 135–40, 149, 150, 153, 154: land use by, 56, 132, 142, membership of, 110, 140: and titles, 110–11, 112, 123, 129, 132, 135, 138, 140, 149

alliances, 112, 113, 120, 211

Ambae (V), 67, 69, 72, 85, 91, 97, 105

America, Americans, 47, 48, 50, 53, 78, 79

Aoba (V), 56, 77, 85

Apia (WS), 58, 117, 128, 131, 140, 150, 151, 152, 153, 154

arable land, (B) 23, 25, 26; (T) 159, 172, 173, 181, 183; (F) 200, 220

Asia, 11, 16, 17–21, 33, 35, 141

Australia, 6, 75, 80, 178

authority, 71, 75: chiefly, 38, 252; (WS) 110–13, 114, 117, 119, 121, 134–5,

280

INDEX 281

143, 149, 152; (T) 160, 161, 164; (F) 248: of courts, (V) 105–6: of custom, 253–4: over gardens, (WS) 123, 132; (T) 161; (F) 209: of individuals, (WS) 133–5; (F) 237, 239: of king, (T) 157, 162: over labour, 20–1: over land, 7, 9, 28, 44–6, 252; (V) 68–9; (WS) 110, 113–14, 117, 121, 123–4, 129, 133, 142, 149–50; (T) 165; (F) 237, 248: legitimation of, 7, 13, 211: of *matai, see* chiefs: of nobles, *see* chiefs: of state, 120, 257, 261: over people, (T) 160; (F) 211. *See also* power, *pule.*

Ba (F), 215, 230, 240
bananas, 42, 56, 86; (F) 224, 232: export of, (T) 164, 183, 184; (F) 219, 222, 226
banks, 253; (PNG) 61, 62; (V) 103; (T) 187, 191; (F) 199, 222, 223, 233
big men (M), 12, 44, 62, 68, 252, 254, 260
bongi (V), 89, 90, 96, 103
boundaries, 40; (WS) 125, 131; (F) 204, 232: contested, 217, 218; (V) 82–3, 90; (F) 210: defined, (F) 51–2; (V) 82; (T) 167, 168: not defined, 9, 10; (V) 84, 87; (F) 209: forest (F), 209–10: garden (F), 209–10: of freehold land (F), 213: ignored (F), 258: shifting, (V) 84; (T) 165; (F) 206, 210: of states, 47
Britain, British, 25–6, 30, 33, 50, 74, 75, 80, 115; (V) 74, 75, 76, 77, 78, 79, 80, 81, 82, 92, 259; (T) 163; (F) 206, 208, 236: government, (V) 81, 82: law, (WS) 152
Burns Philp and Company, 75, 80
bush land (V), 79, 80, 87

capital, 223, 236, 252: accumulation of, (V) 102; (T) 185: investment, 11, 39, 43, 59; (T) 185: land as (V), 93: loans, 19; (F) 233
capital towns, 190, 193; (T) 179, 181, 186. *See also* town names.
capitalism, 103, 104, 197
cargo cults (V), 78, 79, 106
cash cropping, (A) 29–32; (J) 19; and communal activities, (F) 245: expansion of, (V) 74, 92; (WS) 118; (T) 183–4, 191; (F) 219, 222: income from, 55; (WS) 128, 144, 152; (T) 163, 167, 180, 190: and individualism, 31, 57, 58, 61–2; (WS) 131, 144; (T) 180; (F) 238, 245: land for, 39; (A) 29–30; (T) 171; (F) 236: and land prices (T) 190: and land tenure, 31, 250, 252–5; (V) 77, 92–3; (WS) 131, 144; (T) 173, 183; (F) 226, 232: work in, 57; (T) 180
cassava, 47, 58; (V) 86

cattle farming, 10, 57, 250; (V) 79, 102–3; (F) 223, 240, 245: on commons, (B) 22, 23, 25, 26; (A) 30: and individualism, (F) 224, 245: and land tenure, 48, 254; (B) 23; (A) 28; (PNG) 56, 62–3; (F) 59, 232, 233, 246: projects, 59–60; (F) 224, 232, 233, 237, 243
CCNH, *see* SFNH
chiefs, advocating individual holdings, (F) 215–6, 247, 249: in Africa, 28, 30, 31: authority of, (WS) 113, 114, 117, 120, 141, 146, 147; (T) 161; (F) 200: authority over land, 9, 13, 17, 28, 30, 38, 44, 46–7, 62, 248, 252, 256, 259: (WS) 114, 117, 118, 123, 133–4, 142, 147, 149; (T) 157, 160, 162–3, 164, 165–7, 180; (F) 199, 207, 209, 211, 215–6, 247: changing roles, 34, 48, 252, 254; (V) 104; (WS) 122, 134, 147; (T) 157, 159, 162–3, 165–7; (F) 200, 221–2, 247: Council of, (F) 207, 215–6, 243: and invented tradition, 244: as landlords, 17; (V) 102: relations with people, 13, 16, 44, 46–7, 252, 256, 259; (WS) 111, 143, 144, 145; (T) 157, 160–2, 165; (F) 200, 211, 248: rents to, (F) 211, 221–2, 244, 247: role in disputes, (WS) 112; (T) 160: selling land, 49; (F) 207, 212: tribute to, 44, 196, 211; (T) 160, 179; (F) 221: views on tenure, (F) 215–6: warrior, (V) 97, 102. *See also matai,* nobles.
China, 20, 21, 27, 34, 254, 255
Christianity, *see* churches, missions.
churches, 24, 260; (B) 22; (T) 179, 185; (F) 255: Anglican, (V) 73, 80, 86: and land, 49; (V) 75, 97; (WS) 124, 131, 133; (T) 162, 182, 184, 185–6, 191, 196; (F) 199, 212, 233: Methodist, (F) 199, 233: Presbyterian, (V) 73, 75: Wesleyan, (T) 163
cocoa, 55, 56; (A) 29; (V) 74, 102; (WS) 128, 144; (F) 232
coconuts, commercial, 54, 55, 63; (V) 67, 74, 77, 92, 95, 104; (WS) 163, 183; (F) 226, 232: expansion of planting, 54, 56, 63, 252; (V) 67, 74, 92–3, 95; (F) 224: income from, (V) 102: labour needs, (WS) 128: land for, 40–2, 56, 63; (V) 89, 93, 95: ownership of, 43, 55, 61, 63; (V) 93, 102, 103; (WS) 144; (F) 236: plantations, 55; (V) 67, 89, 104, (T) 186: value of, (V) 77. *See also* copra.
codification, and chiefly power, (F) 247: of custom, 106, 251
codification of land law, tenure, 3, 4, 6, 15, 36–7, 38, 50–3, 256, 257, 258, 260, 262,

282 INDEX

codification, *cont.*
264; (V) 106; (WS) 148: and European
theory, (F) 208: in Fiji, 198, 208, 245,
248, 257: in future, 64
coffee, 55; (A) 30; (PNG) 56; (V) 74
colonialism, colonial era, 7, 15, 29, 31, 37,
53, 66, 77, 85, 106, 120, 225, 255, 261:
government, 4; (T) 154; (F) 198, 216,
243: law, (V) 106; (WS) 56, 115, 117,
122, 257
commercial agriculture, *see* commercial
farming
commercial crops, *see* under crop names
commercial era, 47–64
commercial farming, change to, 11, 26, 29,
30, 54, 57, 250; (T) 164; (F) 224: and
commodification of land, 252; (F) 232,
245: effects of, 55–64; (T) 184:
expansion of (F) 223, 245: government
and, (T) 186: and land market, 259;
(T) 191: and land requirements, 58,
256; (T) 180; (F) 232: and land tenure,
20, 29, 60–2, 250, 258; (F) 245: and
prestige, 263; (T) 185
commercialisation, 4; (T) 163, 180–6, 196:
and land tenure, 21; (F) 178: of rural
areas, 17, 34
commercialism, 17, 61; (J) 19–20; (Ch) 21;
(T) 163–5: and individualism, (T) 180;
(F) 222–57: and land tenure, 7, 33–5,
62; (T) 159; (F) 227, 249
commodification of land, 34, 37, 49, 252;
(V) 55, 62, 84; (WS) 142;(T) 178;
(F) 230, 232, 245
common land, 1, 8, 10, 12, 16, 24, 26, 42,
51, 54, 62, 245–5; (F) 227: enclosing of,
(B) 24–5: grazing on, (B) 22–5;
(A) 30–1; (PNG) 62–3; (F) 220:
privatising of, (B) 25–7; (A) 33: 'tragedy
of the commons', 30–1
communal, group, 250; (WS) 118:
obligations, 52, 55, 254, 256; (B) 25;
(F) 224, 248: organisation, 60, 250, 261,
263; (F) 223: reciprocity, 11, 45: work,
11, 57, 61; (B) 22, 25; (F) 222, 237,
245–6
communal land, 19: tenure of, 6, 8, 11, 12,
33, 44, 60–1, 62, 251–5, 261; (J) 20;
(Ch) 21; (B) 22, 25, 28; (A) 32; (V) 85,
87; (WS) 128, 144; (T) 157, 160;
(F) 207, 215, 223, 225, 230–9, 245–6,
248: use of, 8, 12, 255; (B) 22; (F) 223
communalism, 7, 17, 45, 47, 255, 261;
(Ch) 21; (B) 23; (WS) 144; (T) 159;
(F) 213, 223, 224, 230–9
communities, and commercialism, 55;
(F) 223, 232, 246: and custom,
(WS) 147–8; (F) 255: and government,

(A) 29; (V) 84–5: and land tenure,
7–16, 33–4, 36, 39, 42, 43–7, 48, 55, 59,
60, 62, 64, 251–2, 253, 256, 257–8, 263;
(J) 17–20; (Ch) 20–1; (B) 22–3;
(A) 27–31; (V) 71, 84–5, 97, 253; (WS)
253; (T) 169, 171; (F) 198, 207, 209,
218–9, 220, 232, 244, 246: membership
of and obligations to, 45, 46, 52–3, 55,
57, 251, 256, 263; (T) 171; (F) 204–6,
211, 218–19, 221, 223–4, 225, 232, 248:
and resources, 39, 40, 42; (F) 204–6,
220, 244: self-sufficient, 7, 39, 54; (J) 17;
(Ch) 20; (A) 28; (F) 204, 220:
subsistence, *see* agriculture, subsistence:
and work, 45, 47–8, 55; (F) 223–4
compensation, (V) 91: in land matters,
(V) 68, 82, 83, 86, 90, 96–7; (T) 188
Condominium, Anglo-French, (V) 66, 73,
74, 78, 79, 80, 81, 82, 92, 106, 107
constitutions, 2, 4, 47, 250, 261: and land,
(F) 261; (T) 36, 46, 49, 157, 159, 162–3,
165, 167, 168, 174, 179, 189, 196, 253,
259; (V) 34, 47, 65, 81–5, 91, 106, 107,
260, 261; (WS) 120, 121, 150, 261:
dispossession by, (T) 165, 167:
prohibition of land sales under,
(T) 159: right to land under, 34, 107,
159
Cook Islands, 40, 41, 50, 51, 52, 140, 257,
261
copra, 49, 54; (V) 68, 74, 77, 92, 102, 103,
107; (WS) 128; (T) 163, 184, 196;
(F) 219, 222: prices, 68, 77, 92, 103, 107,
164
cotton, 49, 74, 213: plantations (F) 212
court(s), and land, 261; (A) 31, 33;
(FP) 53; (V) 68, 104–7; (T) 173, 192;
(F) 242, 244, 246; Joint Court of New
Hebrides, (V) 75–9, 81–2: Land and
Titles Court, (WS) 113, 115, 120–4,
129–31, 134, 135, 140, 145–54, 257, 258
crops, *see* individual crops, cash cropping,
food crops, tree crops
Crown, colony, (F) 199: grants, 22;
(F) 208, 213: land, 30; (T) 157;
(F) 199–200, 208, 215, 218, 219, 220,
246; *see also* state land leasing from,
(T) 187: power of, 13; (T) 162, 182;
(F) 207, 208: Prince, (T) 166, 184
culture, 36, 250, 260, 261; (V) 80: and
land, 37, 250; (V) 66; (WS) 151–2;
(F), 218, 244
custom, 13–15, 22, 23, 59, 64, 251, 253,
257, 264; (A) 28; (WS) 141, 147, 154;
(T) 169–80; (F) 207: and government,
34, 63, 257, 258, 261; (A) 29; (T) 36;
(V) 84; (F) 215, 218: and identity, 63,
260, 262, 263; (F) 46: and land, 13, 39,

INDEX

283

44, 57, 255; (A) 28, 29; (V) 47;
(WS) 117, 118, 121, 123; (F) 216:
reimposition of, 255; (A) 32–3; (V) 47,
65, 80–2, 91. *See also kastom*, practice.
custom and law, 3, 4, 15; (V) 105, 107;
(WS) 120, 257; (F) 207, 239–44, 257:
divergence, 8, 37, 64, 67, 260, 262, 264;
(V) 91, 260; (WS) 146, 150; (T) 169,
173–4, 177, 185, 259; (F) 198, 233, 236,
239–44, 245, 247, 248
custom and practice, (A) 29; (T) 169–80;
(F) 215: divergence, 3, 4–5, 6, 8, 12–13,
13–15, 36, 43, 57, 63, 64, 67, 251, 253–5,
258, 262–4; (A) 31; (V) 55, 65, 66, 85,
97, 103, 108; (WS) 117, 118–9, 120, 121,
129, 143, 145, 146–8, 149, 150–1, 259–60;
(T) 169–80, 197; (F) 198, 230, 237–8,
241, 245, 246, 247, 248; (PNG) 252
custom and tradition, 13–15, 57, 254,
261–3; (A) 31; (F) 46; (V) 66–8, 85, 104;
(WS) 120: divergence, 2, 3, 6, 15–16, 36,
37, 57, 59, 63, 254, 264; (V) 67–8, 85,
104, 106, 108; (F) 203, 245, 250. *See also
kastom*, tradition.
cyclones, 74, 97, 193

decolonisation, *see* independence
Deed of Cession (F), 199, 213, 215
demography, *see* population
development, projects, 34, 59, 60, 61, 63,
253; (V) 84; (F) 224, 232, 237, 246:
tenure as constraint on, 60–3, 253;
(V) 84, 105, 107; (WS) 131, 152, 153;
(F) 221, 222–5, 243, 246: urban, (V) 83;
(T) 196; (F) 246. *See also* banks.
disease, 74, 86, 161
disputes, 52; (V) 67–8, 92, 95, 105;
(T) 141, 144; (F) 204, 206, 210. *See also*
gardens, land.
dowry, land given as, (WS) 114; (F) 211

education, 18, 260, 261; (T) 180, 184, 185;
(F) 246
Efate, (V) 74, 76, 78
elites, 8, 63, 259, 260, 261, 263; (T) 197;
(F) 244, 246, 247, 248
enclosure, (B) 21–6, 34, 254; (J) 33;
(PNG) 56, 63: of commons, (B) 24, 25;
(A) 30–1: for livestock, 24, 56, 63, 254:
movement, 24, 33, 254
England, 13, 21–4, 26, 31, 34, 208
estates, (J) 18; (Ch) 20–1; (B) 22; (T) 33,
157, 159, 161–6, 168, 169, 172, 181, 182,
186, 187, 190, 191, 193, 197, 259;
(PNG) 59; (WS) 117, 153: division of,
(B) 12; (T) 164–5, 166, 168, 173, 181,
182, 186: holders or owners of, (B) 13,
208; (J) 18; (Ch) 21; (T) 159, 162–5,

169, 172, 174, 178, 182, 186–90. *See also*
plantations.
Europe, 11, 13, 16, 17, 21–7, 33, 34–5, 47,
141, 212, 254, 255
Europeans, 12, 15, 47, 53; (V) 65, 73, 86,
89; (WS) 110, 114, 118, 129, 141, 144,
151, 154; (T) 157, 161, 162, 163, 164;
(F) 199, 206–8, 212–3, 215, 216, 239,
243: demand for land, 48–9, 50-1, 55;
(V) 73–85; (F) 208, 212, 219, 243: land
claims, 30, 50; (V) 79; (F) 207, 212–14:
land conflicts with, (V) 66, 80: law,
(V) 106; (WS) 154: settlers, 51; (V) 66,
75, 80; (F) 199, 212, 239: traders,
(V) 92; (T) 163: views on land, 30, 48–9,
(V) 66, 79; (WS) 115, 151; (F) 208, 215,
217, 219
exchange, of goods, 39, 40, 47; (V) 74, 90:
of land, (A) 31; (V) 80; (T) 167, 187,
189, 190; (F) 218, 241–2: obligations,
42; (V) 87: of women, (V) 72
export crops, 31, 51, 54, 56; (T) 56, 164,
183, 185, 190, 191; (F) 56, 212, 213,
226, 227; (V) 77; (WS) 134

fa'aSamoa (WS), 15, 118, 119, 120, 144,
146, 152, 154, 251
fallow, 10, 11, 42, 43, 55; (V) 86, 87;
(T) 183, 190; (F) 204, 206, 209, 227.
See also forest, gardens.
families, extended, 55, 57, 254; (WS) 122,
133, 141, 143, 144, 145; (T) 160, 163,
168, 171, 175, 179, 186, 197; (F) 200,
209, 211, 251: nuclear, 2, 4, 42, 54, 57,
61, 122, 135, 143, 144, 180, 251, 252,
254. *See also* '*aiga*.
farmers, independent 16, 61; (J) 18–19,
33; (WS) 118, 129, 132, 143; (T) 159;
(F) 224, 255
farming, 11, 12, 17, 22, 23, 25, 26, 58, 253,
254; (T) 56, 167; (F) 213, 219, 223, 224:
commercial, *see* commercial farming:
labour, 17, 19, 45; (A) 30; (WS) 141;
(T) 197; (F) 222, 237: and land tenure,
9, 10–11, 17–18, 27, 33, 34, 58–9, 60, 61;
(A) 28, 32; (F) 230, 232, 236–7, 238,
241: share, 11; (T) 192; (F) 240. *See also*
agriculture.
fee-simple, *see* freehold land
Fiji, 15, 33, 34, 36, 40, 43, 47, 49, 50, 51,
54, 56, 58, 59, 60, 62, 63, 66, 68, 73, 85,
107, 153, 162, 198–249, 251, 252, 253,
257, 258, 260, 261, 262: government of,
54–5, 198, 200, 207, 208, 213, 215, 216,
218, 220, 222–5, 237, 243, 246, 248:
non-Fijians and land, 198, 200, 207, 208,
213, 217, 218, 220, 221, 222, 223,
230–42, 244, 245, 246, 247

284 INDEX

fishing, 9, 39; (WS) 141; (T) 171, 172, 195
fono (WS), 112, 117, 123, 138, 152
food crops, 30, 42, 56, 58, 256; (V) 92, 95, 103; (WS) 131, 142; (F) 227, 232. *See also* under crop names.
forest, fallow, 46, 55; (F) 237: land cleared from, 18, 45, 260; (WS) 119, 128, 131, 134; (F) 237: plantations, (F) 237: products of, 39, 42: tenure of, 10, 42, 55, 62; (V) 87; (WS) 117, 118, 128, 138; (T) 184; (F) 209, 210, 211: terraces under, (F) 218
France, (V) 66, 74–75, 76, 79, 80, 81, 92: administration, (V) 259: government, 77, 81, 82: law, (FP) 53; (V) 66: naval commanders (V) 74: settlers, (V) 74, 75, 77, 78, 81. *See also* French Polynesia
freehold land, 4, 8, 10, 12, 16, 17, 48: (J) 18; (Ch) 20; (B) 22, 25, 26; (A) 27, 30, 31; (V) 12, 83, 91, 107; (WS) 117, 128, 138, 151; (T) 157; (F) 200, 208, 213, 246: abolition of, (V) 65, 82: claims to, (V) 75; (F) 208, 213: market for, 262; (WS) 152–4; (F) 221
French Polynesia, 51, 52, 61, 62. *See also* island names, Polynesia.
funerals (V), 86, 89, 90, 91, 96, 103

gaindumu (V), 88–9, 92, 93, 96, 102, 106
gardens, 44; (B) 22; (V) 92–3, 103; (WS) 112, 133; (T) 157, 160, 161, 164, 171; (F) 209: area of, 12; (T) 172, 173: disputes over, (V) 87; (WS) 143: fallowing of, 42–3, 55; (V) 86: food, 42, 55; (V) 93; (T) 164, 171, 180; (F) 225, 230: land for, 95, 102, 103; (T) 157, 186, 190: location of, 42; (V) 54–5, 58; (V) 79, 86, 93, 95; (WS) 133; (F) 209–10, 226, 227–30: 232, 236, 237; ownership of, *see* land use, rights to, 43, 44; (WS) 123–4, 132; (T) 169; (F) 208, 209–10, 226–30: 232, 236–7, 245, 252: subsistence, *see* food crops: work in, 45; (PNG) 53–4; (WS) 143; (T) 175–9, 180, 223
gathering, *see* hunting and gathering
gifts, (V) 90, 96; (T) 164, 182, 184, 185, 186, 189, 197, 259; (F) 225: of land, 43; (V) 90, 96; (WS) 113, 114; (F) 210, 211, 219
gods, 38; (T) 160; (F) 211
government, agencies, 20, 34; (F) 246: colonial, 36–7, 47, 49, 50–1, 53, 54; (WS) 117, 154; (F) 198, 200, 218, 224, 243: and development, 59, 61; (V) 84, 107; (F) 223, 246: estates (land), (WS) 117; (T) 162, 172, 181, 182, 184, 187, 191, 193, 195; (F) 198: indigenous, 36, 252; (T) 49: and individual tenure,

31, 59–62; (WS) 151–2; (T) 157; (F) 215, 222–5: and land tenure, 31, 32, 34, 37, 49, 51, 55, 59, 64, 258, 259, 260, 261, 262, 263; (V) 79, 81, 83, 84, 107; (WS) 130, 150, 152–3, 159, 186, 195; (F) 207, 208, 213, 215–16, 220: and law, 29, 31; (F) 198: local, 9, (WS) 119: officials, 57; (T) 195; (F) 218

Ha'apai, (T) 166, 168, 171, 177, 180, 181, 189, 190, 193
Hawaii, 6, 12, 44, 162, 252
heirs, 9, 61, 253; (WS) 140, 147, 148; (T) 173, 174; (F) 199, 209; (V) 103–4; (F) 236: absentee, (WS) 124; (T) 178: division of land between, (V) 89–90, 93, 103; (WS) 124, 128–9, 131, 133–4, 140, 144: not succeeding, (WS) 118, 150; (T) 174. *See also* inheritance.
hierarchies, of alliances (WS) 113: of authority, 13, 46; (WS) 143; (T) 165: of places (V), 72: of rights, 13: of titles, 263; (V) 71; (WS) 112; (F) 221: urban, 21
holding(s), 2, 12, 20, 23, 26, 27, 29, 31, 40, 56, 57, 255, 259; (V) 72, 85, 88, 92–4, 97, 102; (WS) 115, 142, 143; (T) 160–3, 178, 180, 185; (F) 203, 204, 211, 223, 232, 236, 237, 241: consolidated, 33, 34, 58, 59, 253; (B) 25–6, 31: customary, (V) 83, 85, 95, 108; (T) 165–9; (F) 227: enclosure of, (B) 24–5: extra-legal, (F) 236: fragmented, 21, 59: group, 62; (V) 69, 83: individual, 59, 253, 254–5, 260; (J) 19; (A) 30, 33; (J) 19; (Ch) 21; (A) 30, 31; (V) 69; (T) 157, 192, 196; (F) 207, 210, 215, 216, 255, 233, 236, 237, 246–8: large, 12, 34, 54, 55, 56, 58, 65, 253, 260; (V) 65, 67–8, 74, 90, 93–4, 102; (T) 187; (F) 233, 236: lease (F) 220–1, 238: of nobles, (T) 18, 33, 163, 260: recording/registration of, 51, 53, 258; (V) 77; (T) 182–4; (F) 204, 216–18, 225, 226, 230–1, 233, 245, 249: small, 18, 20; (V) 74; (T) 159, 192; (F) 224
houses, 54; (B) 22, 25; (V) 97, 104; (WS) 110, 122, 144; (T) 179, 192, 195; (F) 210
hunting and gathering, 8, 9, 30, 39, 42, 51; (V) 71, 79, 86; (F) 209

identity, and custom, 12: and kinship, (T) 171: and land, 37–8, 46–7, 63, 262–3; (F) 248; (T) 259: national, 3, 7, 14, 66, 250, 257–63; (V) 104; (F) 224; (T) 259: and place, (V) 88
ideology, 8, 15, 29, 250, 251; (V) 66; (WS) 142; (T) 189, 197; (F) 218: and land tenure, 11–13, 261–2; (T) 189; (F) 218

INDEX

income, (A) 30; (WS) 144, 152; (T) 184; (F) 241, 244: from farming, 23, 58; (FP) 61; (V) 102; (WS)143–4; (T) 167, 180, 184: from gifts, (T) 259: from government employment, 58; (T) 179–80, 185: and migration, 30; (T) 179: monetary, (V) 102; (WS) 144, 152; (T) 180, 184–5: from rent, (T) 185; (F) 221–2, 241, 244: replacing reciprocity, (F) 211. *See also* wages.

independence, 4, 7, 14, 260–1; (A) 32; (V) 65, 81, 103, 106, 260; (WS) 109; (T) 157, 162; (F) 224, 243: and land tenure, (V) 34, 65, 68, 76, 79, 81–5, 91, 107, 108; (WS) 109, 119–20; (T) 162; (F) 224

individualism, 3, 59, 264; (B) 25; (FP) 62; (WS) 109–10, 118, 121, 122, 258; (T) 169, 192, 196; (F) 213, 222–225, 248, 255: and government policy, 222–5

inequality, increasing, 56; (V) 108; (WS) 154; (F) 218: in land, 17, 56, 256; (V) 67, 97, 108; (WS) 154; (F) 218, 233: rural/urban, (V) 108

inheritance of land, 8, 12, 21, 23, 256; (V) 82, 83, 89–91, 259–60; (WS) 110, 113, 119, 123, 129–30, 138, 140, 148; (T) 162, 169, 174, 177, 179, 180, 192, 253; (F) 210, 227: by individuals, (WS) 113, 124, 131, 140, 150–1, 153; (T) 159; (F) 237: matrilineal, 256; (V) 69, 85, 87, 88, 90; (F) 202: patrilineal, 256; (V) 69, 71, 85

inheritance of usufruct, 254; (A) 28; (F) 209

irrigation, 10, 43, 218

Japan, 17–20, 21, 27, 33, 50, 254, 255; (T) 183: government of, 17, 34

kastom (V), 15, 66, 67, 68, 73, 79, 85, 104, 106, 107, 108, 251, 260, 263, 264

kava, 42; (V) 71, 91, 92, 93, 97, 111; (T) 164, 180, 189; (F) 226, 232

kinship group, and access to land, 42, 43, 251–2, 256, 262–3; (T) 167, 179, 185; (F) 242: as land holder, 42, 43, 49, 56, 57, 59, 262–3; (A) 27; (FP) 62; (V) 69, 71, 87, 88, 90, 96; (WS) 131, 142, 154; (T) 168–9, 171, 172–4, 179, 185; (F) 204, 207: links with, 52; (T) 171, 184–5: security of, 55: working as, 17, 40, 45, 54, 57; (A) 30; (V) 102; (WS) 141–2; (T) 160, 196; (F) 223, 237. *See also 'aiga, mataqali.*

knowledge, 16, 45; (V) 68, 71, 72, 74, 88, 89, 103, 106, 107; (T) 184, 191; (F) 200. *See also gaindumu.*

labour, 11, 17, 23, 48, 53, 57; (V) 73, 77, 85, 92; (WS) 128, 141, 142; (T) 161, 190–1; (F) 198, 211: family or individual, 47; (J) 19; (A)29: plantation, 47, 58; (V) 73, 74, 92, 100: and reciprocity, 1, 11, 17, 45, 55, 57, 61, 63; (V) 100; (T) 160; (F) 222: requirements, 17, 47–8, 54, 56, 58; (J) 19; (Ch) 20; (V) 77; (WS) 128, 143; (T) 180: supply of, 17; (V) 77: and tenure, 39, 43; (F) 209, 210: tied, (B) 3, 26: timing of, 11, 17, 45; (Ch) 20–1: wage, 1, 11, 17, 55, 57, 58, 250, 261, 262; (J) 19; (A) 29, 30; (V) 92, 100, 103; (T) 163, 171, 180, 185, 196; (F) 222, 237

land, access to, 7, 9, 12, 13, 22, 28, 45, 58, 69, 71, 87–89, 95, 108, 144, 179, 186, 188, 198, 233, 240, 256, 262, 263: authority over, 69, 71, 87–9, 95–6, 180: common, 24, 255: exclusive, 237: through women, 95–6

land, alienable right to, 8 9, 12, 114, 157. *See also* land rights.

land, alienated, 262; (A) 29; (V) 65, 76, 79–80, 82, 85; (WS) 114; (T) 157; (F) 199, 206–8, 218: returned to local control, (V) 65, 79–80, 260

land, alienation of, 2, 19, 50, 257, 259, 260; (V) 65, 66, 67, 73–85, 91; (F) 203, 206–8, 213, 218, 245: (WS) 120

land, allocation of, 20, 37, 47, 252, 254; (J) 17; (V) 71, 87; (WS) 118, 123; (T) 183, 196, 259; (F) 203, 236, 238, 248: changes in methods, (B) 25; (A) 32; (WS) 118; (F) 218: by chiefs, 252; (A) 28, 32; (WS) 143; (T) 165, 167: flexible, (F) 198, 211: to individuals, (WS) 117–18, 138; (F) 215, 216–17: reallocation, 10, 24, 26, 28, 256; (T) 169, 174, 183; (F) 216–17, 237

land claims by foreigners, 30, 50; (V) 74–6, 79–80; (WS) 115; (F) 206-8, 212–14

land, customary, 1, 6, 14, 15, 34, 57, 62, 253, 257, 262, 263; (A) 30; (PNG) 34; (V) 65–6, 68, 80–3, 84, 85–92, 95, 104; (WS) 56, 109, 110, 115, 118, 119, 120, 123, 148, 151, 153, 257; (T) 165, 166–80, 233: disputes, (V) 66, 77, 79, 104–7; (WS) 147: markets in, 62: registration of, (V) 83, 107, 108; (WS) 130; (T) 168, 172; (F) 230, 245, 256, 257, *see also* codification, land, native.

land, exclusive control of, 9, 10; (V) 104, 108; (WS) 142; (T) 180; (F) 230–9

land, exclusive ownership of, 8, 9, 10, 12, 42, 48–9, 253–4; (V) 84, 93; (WS) 142, 150, 163; (T) 180, 192; (F) 212, 230–9, 258

286 INDEX

land, exclusive use of, 8, 9, 48, 59, 253–4; (V) 93; (T) 180, 192, 197, 256; (F) 212, 230–9, 258

land disputes, 30; (V) 66, 68, 74, 75, 78, 79, 80, 92, 93, 105, 106–08; (F) 216

land market, 11, 60, 62, 65, 251, 259; (A) 29, 31, 32, 34; (V) 80, 84; (WS) 140, 152–4; (T) 159; (F) 242: extra-legal, (T) 196; (F) 244: illegal, 256; (T) 159: informal (T) 188–92. *See also* leases.

land, native 6, 15, 250; (V) 65, 76, 77; (WS) 117–18; (T) 157; (F) 199, 220, 236, 238, 248, 262: acts or ordinances, (WS) 119; (F) 207, 208, 216, 219, 220, 239, 240, 243, 244–5, 246: alienability of, 49–50, 55; (F) 200, 207, 218, 220: control or ownership of, (F) 242–4, 246: disputes over, (F) 216: leasing of, (F) 216, 220–2, 225, 243–4: practice not customary or legal, 15, 36, 250, 256; (F) 198, 233, 236, 239–40, 245, 248: registration of, 50–3; (V) 77; (F) 213–19, 220. *See also* land customary.

land, private 253; (J) 18–19; (Ch) 20; (A) 31, 32; (FP) 62; (WS) 113; (T) 182

land, public, (J) 18; (V) 81, 82, 117

land reform, 8, 12, 56, 64, 263; (J) 17, 18, 19; (V) 47, 82, 85; (T) 157, 159, 160–80, 181, 186–8, 192

land rights, transfer of, 2, 10, 11, 23, 32, 34, 37, 39, 43, 44, 49, 50, 51, 52, 61, 62, 177, 253, 254; (B) 22; (A) 32; (T) 49, 165, 169; (V) 92, 107; (WS) 114; (F) 203, 211: colonial era ban on (WS) 120: and commodification, 62, 259; (V) 107: conditions guiding, 252; (T) 168; (F) 206–7, 210, 212, 219, 238: loss of flexibility in, 255–7. *See also* inheritance, land, alienable rights, leasehold, registration.

land, sale of, 9, 48–50; (A) 32; (B) 34; (V) 91; (WS) 152, 153-4; (F) 212: ban on, (J) 18, 34; (A) 28; (WS) 115; (T) 159; (F) 55: by chiefs, (F) 207: extra-legal, 259; (A) 34; (T) 188–90; (F) 239–42, 244: involving Europeans, 74; (WS) 114; (F) 207: and Land Claims Commission (F), 212–19. *See also* leases, land market.

land and the state, 257–62

land title to, (A) 30; (V) 68, 75, 83; (WS) 117–8; (T) 157, 179: abolition of, (NC) 37; (V) 84; (F) 248: individual, 61, 253; (A) 31; (V) 68; (WS) 118, 150; (T) 259; (F) 220, 223, 224, 246, 247: registration of, 61; (A) 31; (V) 75, 76–7, 82, 107–8; (F) 230: uncertainty of, (A)

31; (V) 74, 79, 82, 84. *See also* freehold, land rights, transfer of.

land, uninhabited (T) 93, 180, 182, 184

land use, 8; (V) 85–92: changes in, 54, 55, 250, 251, 253, 258; (B) 21–2, 24; (A) 29; (V) 95; (T) 159, 183; (F) 198, 215, 218, 225–39, 245: commercial, (T) 191–2: constraints on, 9, 39, 256, 257; (V) 74; (F) 220, 238, 245: control over, 7, 251; (J) 19; (A) 28; (V) 84; (WS) 110, 140, 142, 149; (T) 164, 165, 180; (F) 223, 225, 232, 238, 239: in exchange for gifts, (T) 184, 189: exclusive right to, 8, 9, 59, 258; (T) 180, 192, 197; (F) 212, 230–239: long-term, 43, 252, 255; (T) 173, 189; (F) 204, 212, 236: and ownership, (A) 27–8; (V) 81; (WS) 123–35, 138; (F) 198, 207, 219: rights to, 16, 42, 251, 252; (J) 17; (A) 30; (F) 61–2, 207, 209, 211; (PNG) 62–3; (V) 69, 84, 89, 93; (WS) 123–35, 140; (T) 165, 181, 192: sale of rights to, 259; (T) 184, 190; (F) 245: security of, 39: transfer of right to, 34, 43, 44, 252; (T) 168, 178–9, 190; (F) 198, 207, 219: urban, (F) 240–2. *See also* usufruct.

land, waste and vacant, 51; (B) 22, 25, 26; (F) 243: governments claim control over, 37, 50

landlessness, 17, 34, 56, 58; (B) 25; (A) 32; (V) 87, 88, 97; (T) 174, 179, 181, 183, 185, 193; (F) 248

landlords, changing role, 16, 34, 254; (J) 18, 20; (Ch) 21: exploitative, (F) 242, 263: gifts and rents to, (T) 182; (F) 244

Lau, (F) 202, 204, 215, 216, 217, 238, 242

law, 8, 34, 250, 256, 257; (J) 19; (A) 28; (V) 66, 75, 93, 106; (WS) 112, 120, 147, 148, 152; (T) 159, 167, 169, 173, 174, 175; (F) 198, 209, 225–44: codified, 15, 51, 67–8, 256, 257, 262; (WS) 148; (F) 207, 208, 216, 218: customary, (A) 29, 31, 32; (V) 105; (WS) 147; (F) 208, 210: ineffective, (FP) 53, 62: land, (V) 76, 82, 85, 106, 107, 108; (WS) 117, 151; (T) 159, 162, 165, 189, 192, 196–7; (F) 225–44, 247, 248. *See also* custom and law.

leaders, 11, 44, 47, 57, 250, 257, 263, 264; (Ch) 21; (V) 72, 79, 86–7, 92, 97, 105; (WS) 119, 143; (F) 204, 206, 221, 222: and land, 6, 12, 44, 46, 254, 262, 263, 264; (V) 65, 68, 80, 81, 88, 91–2, 100, 103, 104, 106; (WS) 117: accumulating land, 63; (V) 56, 67, 91–2, 93, 100: and sale of land, 49. *See also* chiefs, *matai*, nobles.

INDEX

287

leases, 11, 25, 34, 49–50, 63, 257; (B) 23; (A) 29; (V) 82; (WS) 117, 118, 120, 134, 144, 152, 153, 154; (T) 159, 162, 182, 184, 185, 187–9, 191, 192, 196, 259; (F) 199, 211, 219–22, 224–5, 230, 232, 233–8, 239–44, 246, 247: conversion from freehold, (V) 82–3: conversion to freehold, (WS) 152–3: in development projects, 59–61, 253; (F) 59–60, 219: longer, 26; (T) 187, 190: market, (A) 32; (F) 244; *see also* practices, extra-legal

land: rent from, (T) 185–6, 189, 190, 193–5; (F) 211, 221, 239, 247

lineages, 10, 40, 42, 43, 51, 53, 61; (Ch) 20; (F) 204, 211, 232, 242

livestock, 16, 42, 53, 250; (B) 23–5; (A) 27; (V) 87, 95

Longana, (V) 56, 67, 68, 72, 80, 85–104, 105, 106, 108

Malakula, (V) 69, 79, 91, 92

Malie, (WS) 114, 122, 128–31, 135

manorial system, 17, 254; (J) 18; (Ch) 21; (B) 22–3, 25, 26

marine resources, 40, 41; (WS) 142; (T) 172. *See also* fishing.

matai, (WS) 109–30, 133, 134, 135, 140, 142, 143, 144, 148, 149, 150, 151, 152, 153

mataqali, (F) 200, 202–5, 210, 215, 223, 224, 247, 258: and extra-legal arrangements, 238–42, 246: inequality between, 232–3: and leases, 59, 220–2, 224, 232, 236–7, 244: as registration unit, 51, 215–9, 227, 245, 247: using land of other, 225–33, 258

matrilines, *see* inheritance of land

mats, (WS) 113, 114, 122

Melanesia, 15, 46, 47, 51, 56, 57, 73, 74, 86, 88, 90, 104: equalitarianism, 12, 68: land matters, 38, 44, 50, 65, 84, 251

migration, international, (WS) 140, 261; (T) 159, 178, 180, 181, 183, 184, 188, 261; (F) 219: and land, 6, 52, 53; (A) 29, 30, 32; (V) 71, 97; (WS) 131, 151–2, 153; (T) 171, 178, 181, 183, 186, 188; (F) 211, 238, 242, 247, 252, 262: to towns, 58; (WS) 140, 153; (T) 179, 186, 192, 193

missions and missionaries, 16, 47, 51: and land, 48, 54; (V) 76, 86, 88; (T) 161; (F) 207, 212: and social change, 57; (V) 73–4, 77, 78, 87, 92; (WS) 109; (T) 109, 162

mobility, and land, (V) 71–2, 85; (F) 203–6, 218: residential, (V) 97

money, and farming, 1–2, 45, 55–64; (J) 19: and labour, 45, 55, 61; (V) 77;

(F) 222, 223: and land, 52; (Ch) 21; (WS) 113, 114; (T) 159, 164, 188–91, 259; (F) 242: remittances of, (T) 171, 185, 188: and society, 11, 16, 17, 47, 57, 253; (V) 78, 102; (T) 164, 184; (F) 222, 246, 258

mortgages, 9, 61; (J) 19; (V) 83; (T) 187, 191–2

myth, and land, 6, 7, 46; (F) 211–12: as symbols, 7, 14: and tradition, 14; (V) 66

Native Land Trust Board, (F) 153, 220–2, 244–5, 230, 232, 233–6, 238, 239–44, 246–7: avoiding leasing through, 238–42: ownership of native land, 242–4

Native Lands Commission, (F) 202–3, 204–6, 209–10, 216, 218, 220, 226, 230–31, 233, 241, 245, 248

Native Reserve land, (NC) 51; (V) 76, 77; (F) 199, 220–2, 233, 240, 241, 243, 244

Neiafu, (T) 114, 122, 124, 128, 130, 131, 144, 171, 193, 195

New Caledonia, 6, 50, 51; (V) 73, 81: government of, 37

New Hebrides, 49, 50, 65, 66, 69, 71, 73, 74, 75, 76, 78, 79, 80–82. *See also* Vanuatu.

New Zealand, 6, 257, 261; (WS) 109, 118, 119; (T) 164, 191: government of, 117: land wars, 200

nobles, (T) 162, 169, 189, 196: estates, (T) 157, 159, 162–3, 164, 165–74, 182, 189, 190, 193, 259: and land, 13; (J) 18, 33; (T) 33, 56, 159, 164, 165, 171–4, 180, 184, 186, 187, 196: relations with people, 11, 16, 17; (T) 164, 167, 169–71, 174, 178, 185, 259. *See also* chiefs, *matai*.

Nuku'alofa, (T) 166, 175, 181, 186, 190, 191, 192, 193, 195, 196

'orthodox model' of Fijian land tenure, 2, 202, 203, 215, 216, 218, 223, 225, 230, 244, 246, 248: codification of, 247: as constraint, 232: inflexibility of, 245

ownership, individual, 21, 251–5; (A) 31–2; (WS) 109, 113, 117, 119, 121, 123–9, 135, 138, 140–5, 147, 148, 150–2, 154, 192, 196; (F) 210, 227, 246: advocacy of, (F) 224: increasing, 6; (V) 93; (WS) 110, 118–19, 129–31, 133, 140–5, 149, 152. *See also* tenure.

pacification, *see* peace

Papua New Guinea, 6, 34, 38, 43, 47, 53, 59, 61, 62, 81, 85, 104, 252, 260

pasture, 55, 59, 62; (B) 22, 23, 24; (F) 236, 237

288 INDEX

peace, 4, 47, 54, 56; (V) 72, 86, 87, 88, 92, 102; (WS) 112, 117, 122, 145; (T) 161; (F) 210, 218

Pentecost, (V) 69, 72, 79, 87, 102

permissive occupancy, 49; (V) 86; (T) 173, 179, 191; (F) 212, 239

pigs, 12, 73; (V) 86, 87, 90, 91, 93, 95, 102, 104; (WS) 113, 118; (T) 195

plantations, 55; (A) 29–30; (WS) 117: alienation of land for, 48–50; (A) 29; (V) 79; (F) 212–4: demand for land for, 49; (V) 79, 93: 'European' owned, 262; (PNG) 56; (V) 74, 79; (T) 186; (F) 212–3, 219: indigenous owned, (PNG) 56; (V) 93, 95–6, 102, 103–4; (WS) 109; (F) 210, 237: labour on, 47, 58; (V) 73, 74, 77, 102, 103; (F) 219

politicians, statements on land by, 3, 36, 47, 59, 63, 250

Polynesia, 12, 13, 38, 46, 51, 52, 61, 62, 251

population, 7, 10, 23, 30, 51; (V) 69, 71, 80, 97, 102; (WS) 129; (T) 161, 171, 181; (F) 223, 241: decline, 16–7, 23, 51; (F) 202: growth, 7, 30, 191, 192, 196; (WS) 131, 132, 141, 145; (T) 159, 180–3, 191, 192, 196, 259; (F) 206, 219, 236: and land requirements, 10, 37, 51–2, 260; (J) 18; (V) 102; (WS) 112, 132, 152; (T) 180–5, 196; (F) 204, 206, 211, 218, 233, 236: pressures of growth, 6, 7, 17, 37, 250, 256; (A) 30; (WS) 131; (T) 159, 170, 181–3; (F) 206, 233, 262: urban, (T) 191; (F) 241–2. See also migration, mobility.

Port Vila, 75, 80–3, 103

power, changes in, 11, 27, 48, 252, 258, 261; (B) 24; (V) 73, 102, 106; (WS) 120, 141, 146; (T) 159, 162, 196, 252; (F) 200, 247: colonial, 27, 49, 252, 257, 261; (NC) 37; (V) 75, 81; (WS) 115, 117; (T) 157, 162, 163; (F) 200, 247: over labour, 17; (F) 211: over land, 7, 13, 38, 44–6, 262; (J) 18; (B) 24; (NC) 37; (M) 44; (V) 71, 72–3, 88; (WS) 113, 114, 145, 147, 149; (T) 161, 168, 169, 174, 197; (F) 212, 233, 241, 242–6; over people, (WS) 111; (T) 157, 164; (F) 211: supernatural basis of, 13, 44; (M) 74; (V) 92: of tradition, 14; (V) 104: in warfare, 44; (V) 72; (F) 206. See also authority.

practice, changed, 51–3, 55, 58, 62, 64, 250, 251–7, 258, 260, 262, 263; (V) 95, 108; (WS) 115, 118, 122, 135, 145, 147, 154; (T) 174; (F) 198, 203, 222, 225–44: disparity with law, 251, 259; (T) 159, 169, 174, 179, 186, 196–7; (F) 198, 202–3, 207, 225–44, 258, 260, 262, 264:

and dispute resolution, 105: uniform, (WS) 114, 251, 259: variety of, (F) 215–6. See also custom and practice.

practices, extra-legal land, 3, 11, 34, 251, 259, 262, 264; (V) 83; (T) 159, 165, 169, 174, 189, 191, 192; (F) 233, 236, 196, 238, 241, 244, 247, 248

privatisation of land, 62, 255; (F) 246, 249

pule, (WS) 112–13, 122, 123: over land, 110, 114, 118, 121, 123–4, 130–1, 133–4, 135, 144, 149, 150–1

rank, see status

reciprocity, 11, 12, 45, 197; (J) 18, 20, 21; (B) 22; (P) 44: and chiefly system, (T) 160; and labour, 17, 61, 63: replaced by money, 55; (F) 222, 225, 237, 241

redistribution of land, (J) 17–18; (T) 188; (V) 68; (F) 232: bongi, (V) 89–90: extra-legal mechanisms, (F) 233: traditional mechanisms, 12, 25–35, 45, 57. See also gifts.

registration (land), 50–53; (J) 19; (V) 75–7, 82; (A) 31; (FP) 62: of customary land, (V) 68, 83, 107–8; (WS) 130–1; (T) 164–70, 198: native land, (F) 198, 215: in name of mataqali, (F) 59, 200, 204, 216, 217, 218, 219, 221, 225, 230, 242, 245, 247: leasehold, (V) 82, 118; (WS) 153; (T) 189–91: to individuals, 61, 63, 75–80; (WS) 115, 118, 149–50; (T) 172, 183; (F) 217, 220: delays in, (V) 82, 107: of hereditary allotments, (T) 164–70, 182, 186: by NLC (F) 204, 216, 218, 230, 233: hindrance to sharing, 255–6, 258; (F) 227–30: older methods of redistribution become extra-legal, (F) 233

remittances, (WS) 140, 143, 144; (T) 185, 188: in growth of land market, (T) 159

rent, 263; (J) 18; (B) 26; (A) 29–30, 32; (V) 80, 82, 83; (WS) 134, 153; (T) 159, 188, 190, 191, 259; (F) 210, 236: as disincentive, (F) 221–2: from urban leases, (V) 83: from government leases, (T) 185: replacing share-cropping, (F) 241: through NLTB leases, (F) 221, 230, 238–9, 241, 244, 247

reserve land, (NC) 51; (V) 76, 77; (WS) 184; (F) 199, 241, 243: and NLTB, (F) 220–2: Class J leases, (F) 222, 233, 243: and non-Fijians, (F) 239, 240, 244

residence sites, 49; (WS) 110, 115, 118, 123, 132, 134, 152; (T) 193; (F) 222, 224: and inheritance of land rights, (FP) 52; (V) 69, 71: and movement, 58: and resources, 58; (WS) 142, 144: and title, (WS) 124–30: away from village, 59; (F) 224, 254

INDEX

289

Rewa River, (F) 58, 210, 212, 226
rhetoric, and land tenure, 37, 59, 261, 264;
(V) 90: and national identity, 63;
(V) 106, 260; (F) 224
rights, individual, (WS) 121, 145, 147;
(T) 162: land, 8, 12, 26, 43, 254; (A) 32;
(V) 69; (WS) 119, 121; (T) 157, 162,
196; (F) 210. *See also* land rights.
root crops, 39, 42, 56, 232, 252
rule, indirect, 27, 29, 252; (F) 200, 247

Saliadrau, (F) 226, 227, 229, 230, 232, 237
sandalwood, 48, 73, 212
Santo, (V) 69, 78, 79, 81, 83, 103
Sasa, (F) 148, 210, 226, 227, 103
Satupaitea, (WS) 122, 131, 148
Savaii, (WS) 112, 122, 129, 153
Scotland, 21, 25, 26, 216
Second World War, 78, 159, 222
security, of usufruct, 8, 20, 22, 25, 39, 58,
61, 252–3; (F) 211: for credit, 61, 253;
(F) 222-3, 233: social, 23, 155, 250, 262;
(V) 104; (WS) 143–4: of tenure, 259,
(WS) 120, 130–1, 153; (T) 173, 187;
(F) 238
settlement patterns, 1, 2, 17, 21, 264;
(B) 25; (T) 168; (F) 203–5, 219, 220,
230, 255: dispersed, 33, 40, 61; (B) 26:
(A) 29; (V) 95: fluid, (F) 206: hamlets,
92, 97; (F) 225, 237: nucleated village,
22, 25, 26, 27, 58; (F) 237: for security,
(V) 86, 92; (F) 217: squatter, urban,
264; (V) 83; (T) 195; (F) 241. *See also*
urbanisation, villages.
SFNH, Société Française des Nouvelles-
Hébrides, (V) 50, 65, 74, 75, 76, 77
share cropping, 11, 29; (T) 192; (F) 230,
240, 247
shifting cultivation, 9, 10, 11, 12, 42, 252;
(A) 28, 30; (B) 26; (F) 204, 226, 238
Sigatoka, (F) 217, 226, 233, 239
Solomon Islands, 6, 37, 47, 49, 50, 53, 63,
78, 85, 104
Sote, (F) 60, 204, 205, 226, 227, 231, 232,
237
squash, (T) 56, 180, 283, 285, 190–1, 192,
193
state land, 8, 12, 257–62; (J) 19; (M) 37;
(V) 50–51, 76, 84, 85; (WS) 120;
(T) 190; (F) 199, 220. *See also* Crown
land, government estates.
status and land, 3, 7, 12, 55, 57, 63, 254,
260, 263, 264; (P) 38, 44; (SI) 49; (T)
56; (V) 93, 95, 102; (WS) 111, 118, 141,
142, 143, 145, 151; (T) 160, 163, 164,
178; (F) 211–12, 224, 247, 248. *See also*
authority, big men, chiefs, hierarchies,
power.

sugar cane, 59; (F) 219, 224, 230, 233, 239,
240
supernatural and land, 13, 44, 45, 46;
(A) 28; (V) 71, 72, 90; (T) 160: sorcery
and poison, (V) 87, 88, 92, 93, 102, 104;
(WS) 141, 143, 146
surveying, (J) 19; (V) 53, 76, 80; (WS) 118,
128, 129, 152; (T) 163, 165, 167–8, 172,
180–2, 184, 186, 189, 195–6; (F) 210,
219, 230, 247, 255, 258
Suva, (F) 60, 75, 232, 241, 242
sweet potato, 47, 86
swidden, *see* shifting cultivation

Tahiti, (FP) 12, 40, 44, 48, 49, 53, 54, 57,
58, 62, 140, 162, 252
Tanna, (V) 48, 71, 72, 78
taro, 42, 43, 47–8, 56, 58; (V) 86;
(WS) 133, 134; (F) 210, 217, 218
tax, food as, (J) 20; (F) 54: on land,
(B) 17–18; (V) 78, 82; (T) 157–9, 195
tax allotments, (T) 157–97, 253, 256, 259.
See also town allotments.
technology, and land tenure, 6, 7, 9, 16,
34, 45, 48, 53, 254, 258; (B) 19, 21, 27;
(A) 29; (M) 47; (WS) 143; (F) 222–3,
237, 246
tenancy, 11; (Ch) 21; (A) 29–30, 32;
(T) 192; (F) 211, 220, 230, 238–9: rents
from, (A) 29, 31; (T) 185
tenants, 16, 17, 34; (J) 18; (Ch) 20–1;
(B) 24, 26; (A) 31–2; (T) 160, 162, 164,
166, 167, 182, 185, 187; (F) 219, 238:
tribute from, (T) 160, 164, 185, 186
tenure, customary, 1, 2, 14, 15, 21, 43, 60,
64, 250, 251, 253, 255, 257, 258, 261,
263; (A) 29, 32; (V) 12, 47, 55, 65–108,
259; (PNG) 38, 108; (WS) 109, 110,
114–5, 117, 119, 121, 123, 124, 128–9,
135, 140, 142, 145, 149–50, 151, 154,
258; (T) 157, 165–80, 259; (F) 198, 207,
210, 215, 225, 227, 236, 241. *See also*
codification.
titles, (V) 69, 77; (T) 159, 160, 162, 163,
165, 166, 187; (WS) 257. *See also matai,*
nobles.
tobacco, 239, 240
tokatoka, (F) as land owning unit, 200, 202,
215, 216, 217, 221, 225, 227, 232, 246
Tonga, 12, 33, 34, 36, 44, 46, 47, 48, 49, 52,
56, 62, 64, 68, 117, 140, 157–197, 204,
216, 217, 252, 253, 256, 257, 259, 261,
264
Tongatapu, (T) 161, 162, 166, 168, 171,
180, 181, 183, 184, 185, 186, 188, 190,
191, 192–6
tools, *see* technology

290 INDEX

town allotments, (T) 157, 162, 166, 167, 171, 172, 173, 179, 182, 184, 187, 189, 192, 193, 195

towns, 17, 19, 21, 34, 37, 48, 50, 52, 58, 254, 261, 264; (V) 103; (F) 222, 224, 226. *See also* town names.

traders, 48, 53, 54; (V) 73, 77, 85, 90, 92; (T) 163

tradition, 6, 13, 14, 15, 36, 37, 57, 63, 250, 251, 254, 262, 264; (V) 66, 67, 68, 71, 88, 92–104, 108; (WS) 115, 120, 151, 154; (T) 164; (F) 203, 204, 206, 211–12, 218: invented, 13–16, 37, 66, 85, 108; (F) 36, 218, 244. *See also* codification, custom and tradition, *kastom.*

transport, businesses, (F) 56, 58: of food, (WS) 142; (T) 164, 190; (F) 219, 226. *See also* mobility.

tree crops, 9, 10, 39, 40, 42, 43, 55, 56, 57, 59, 62, 63, 252: and ownership, (V) 93; (WS) 128; (F) 219: rights to, 28, 39; (T) 161; (F) 210, 236: as symbol, (V) 71, 72, 73, 87, 90; (T) 160, 167. *See also* crop names.

tribute, (A) 28–30; (T) 160, 161, 163, 164, 165, 179, 185, 196; (F) 211. *See also* reciprocity.

Tupou I, (T) 33, 49, 157, 159, 162, 183, 252

Upolu, (WS) 112, 117, 122, 126, 130, 153

urban areas, development of, (V) 83; (T) 162, 192–6; (F) 243, 246: land, (F) 240–3, 244: leasing of, (V) 83: markets, (F) 222: planning, (WS) 152: population, (T) 191; (F) 241–2: remittances to, (WS) 143: views about, 261; (WS) 150–2, 154; (F) 230, 248: as threat to way of life, (F) 223. *See also* town names.

urbanisation, 37, 250, 260, 261

usage, *see* custom

usufruct, 2, 10, 251–6; (F) 213, 225, 236; gaining of, (V) 89; (F) 236: through inheritance, 28; (WS) 131, 157; (T) 187, 188, 191, 192: limitations on, 8, 9, 12; (V) 89: transfer of rights to, 39, 43. *See also* land use.

Vaega, (WS) 113, 114, 122, 123–4, 125, 128, 130, 131–40, 144, 148

vakavanua, (F) 15, 66, 225, 238, 23940, 241, 242, 244, 246, 247, 251

vanilla, (T) 56, 179, 180, 183, 185, 190, 191

Vanua Levu, (F) 43, 200, 202, 219, 224, 232

Vanuatu, 6, 12, 15, 33, 34, 43, 46, 47, 48, 53, 56, 63, 65–108, 197, 252, 253, 257, 259–60, 261

Vava'u, (T) 169, 171, 172, 179, 181, 190, 191, 192

veikau, (F) 209, 211, 218, 225, 227, 230, 236, 237, 246

veimada, (F) 209, 211, 227, 230, 232, 236, 238, 241, 246

Vila, (V) *see* Port Vila.

village, community, (J) 18; (A) 28; (WS) 112–3; (F) 202, 222, 224, 225, 245, 255: deserted, (F) 204, 206: and garden location, 58; (V) 95; (F) 228–9, 232, 234–5, 236: land, 54; (J) 19; (B) 22–3, 25; (A) 30; (WS) 40, 112–3, 114, 115, 117–9, 123–35, 138–9, 140, 142, 150, 152; (T) 171, 192–3; (F) 209–10, 225–30, 232, 237, 245, 248: meetings and land, 9; (V) 68, 105; (WS) 111, 112–3, 117–8, 120, 123, 138, 152: organisation, (J) 20; (F) 202–3. *See also* settlement patterns.

Viti Levu, (F) 59, 200, 204, 206, 219, 222, 224, 227, 233, 237, 238, 240

wages, (B) 23, 25; (V) 92, 102; (WS) 144, 152; (T) 179; (F) 241: labour, 11, 55, 57, 58, 250, 261, 262; (J) 18, 19; (A) 30; (V) 103; (WS) 131, 140; (T) 163, 171; (F) 222, 237. *See also* income, labour.

Waibau, (F) 224, 233, 238, 240

warfare, 6, 44, 47, 54, 252; (V) 86, 87, 91, 92, 93; (WS) 112, 141: cessation of, 256: and chiefs, (WS) 143; (T) 160; (F) 204, 206, 245

wealth, accumulation of, 17, 57, 263; (J) 19; (V) 102, 103; (F) 221, 247: disparities in, (A) 32; (V) 108; (F) 233–4: through land sales, 49. *See also* big men, cash cropping.

Western influence, 14, 15, 255, 262; (A) 27–8; (T) 197; (WS) 118, 140–1, 146, 152; (F) 64

Western Samoa, 33, 50, 51, 52, 53, 56, 58, 63, 64, 85, 109–56, 252, 253, 257, 258, 260, 261: government of, 54–5, 120, 130, 144, 151, 152, 153, 154

women, (A) 10, 30; (M) 57, 86; (V) 72, 73, 87; (WS) 122; (T) 187: and inheritance, (T) 173, 174–8: and land, (V) 88, 95; (WS) 113, 123, 124, 130, 131; (T) 162, 164, 179, 187

yams, 47, 58, 86; (F) 48, 210

yaqona, see kava

yavusa, (F) 200, 202, 203, 204, 209, 210, 217, 225, 227, 242

For EU product safety concerns, contact us at Calle de José Abascal, 56–1°,
28003 Madrid, Spain or eugpsr@cambridge.org.

www.ingramcontent.com/pod-product-compliance
Ingram Content Group UK Ltd.
Pitfield, Milton Keynes, MK11 3LW, UK
UKHW011655080825
461487UK00024B/264